Family-Centered Social Work Practice

Ann Hartman
Joan Laird

THE FREE PRESS
A Division of Macmillan, Inc.
NEW YORK

Maxwell Macmillan Canada
TORONTO

Maxwell Macmillan International
NEW YORK OXFORD SINGAPORE SYDNEY

The Free Press
A Division of Macmillan, Inc.
866 Third Avenue, New York, N.Y. 10022

Maxwell Macmillan Canada, Inc.
1200 Eglinton Avenue East
Suite 200
Don Mills, Ontario M3C 3N1

Macmillan, Inc. is part of the Maxwell Communication Group of Companies.

Printed in the United States of America

printing number

9 10 11 12 13 14 15 16 17 18 19 20

Library of Congress Cataloging in Publication Data

Hartman, Ann.
    Family-centered social work practice.

    Bibliography: p.
    Includes index.
    1. Family social work—United States. I. Laird, Joan.
II. Title.
HV699.H35   1983   362.8′2   83–47656
ISBN 0–02–914100–1

The following illustrations have been reproduced by permission of the copyright holder from Ann Hartman's article "Diagrammatic Assessment of Family Relationships" in *Social Casework* (Oct. 1978); copyright © 1978 by the publisher, Family Service Association of America (New York): Fig. 8–1 (Eco-Map), p. 160; Fig. 8–4 (Eco-Map), p. 163; and Fig. 10–3 (Genogram), p. 218.

The epigraph on page vii is from "Little Gidding" in *Four Quartets*, copyright 1943 by T. S. Eliot; renewed 1971 by Esme Valerie Eliot. Reprinted by permission of Harcourt Brace Jovanovich, Inc., and by Faber and Faber Ltd.

TO DUNCAN

Contents

Preface and Acknowledgments   *vii*

**Part I   The Context Of Family–Centered
          Practice**   *1*

Chapter 1   A Family Focus in Social Work Practice   *3*

Chapter 2   The Family Today   *23*

Chapter 3   The Family Policy Context   *41*

Chapter 4   An Epistemological Framework   *59*

Chapter 5   Family Theory for Family-Centered Practice   *75*

Part II   Beginnings   *109*

Chapter 6   Getting Started: Agency and Case
             Management Issues   *111*

Chapter 7   Getting Started: Contracting and Interviewing   *133*

Part III   Assessment And Intervention   155

    Chapter 8   The Family in Space: Ecological Assessment   157

    Chapter 9   Family–Environment Transactions as Target
                 and Resource for Change   187

    Chapter 10   Assessment in Time: The
                 Intergenerational Perspective   211

    Chapter 11   The Intergenerational Family System as
                 a Resource for Change   231

    Chapter 12   Inside the Family: Inner System Assessment   269

    Chapter 13   The Family Unit as Resource and Target
                 for Change   305

    Chapter 14   Persistence, Coherence, and Paradox   326

    Chapter 15   Family-Centered Practice in the Fields of
                 Aging and Health   354

    Notes   381

    Bibliography   388

    Name Index   409

    Subject Index   413

Preface and Acknowledgments

We shall not cease from exploration
And the end of all our exploring
Will be to arrive where we started
And know the place for the first time.

T.S. Eliot, "Little Gidding"

THE SOCIAL WORK PROFESSION and the family have traveled a long distance together, sometimes in close companionship and sometimes on divergent paths, only to meet once again on the same road. Our profession began in the company of the family and has returned to it once again. Perhaps now we shall know it for the first time.

The decade of the seventies and the beginning of the eighties have witnessed a growing national dialogue about the family, an activity marked by both concern and controversy. There are those who predict the eventual demise of what is viewed as a weak and fragile human system. Others claim that the family, although undergoing radical change, is not only persisting, but thriving. Whether optimist or pessimist prevails, one thing is certain: the family is currently in the spotlight and of considerable interest to politicians, social scientists, artists, the professions, and the public at large.

In the political arena, mounting pressure for the development of a more comprehensive family policy and for a fresh, thorough look at the relationship between the State and the family led in 1980 to the perhaps disappointing but long-needed White House Conference on the Family, an event which left the hopes of many family advocates unfulfilled. In the university, social scientists from a variety of academic disciplines, who had to some extent ignored the family in the past, have turned in large numbers to the study of this human system. In the field of mental health, the family therapy movement has proliferated as increasing numbers of practitioners are defining the family rather than the isolated individual as the target and the resource for change. Among the general public, a growing interest in the family can be seen in the enthusiastic response to Alex Haley's *Roots* (1976), in the expanding interest in family history, genealogical study, and reunions, and in the growing popularity of family sagas in literature, television, and the theater, to cite just a few examples.

Some social workers have taken leadership in shifting the family to the center of concern; all of us have been affected by this fascinating movement. Although social work, perhaps more than any other profession, can point to a rich history of volunteer and professional work with and on behalf of families, its practitioners now find themselves assuming new roles and experimenting with new approaches. In policy and planning positions, social workers are concerned with the potential impact on family life of proposed policies and programs. In a variety of fields of practice, a focus on the family is increasingly evident. Workers in health-care delivery systems, for example, now commonly consider the family of the patient as central in both the assessment and treatment process. Many child welfare programs are questioning their tradition of child-centered practice and shifting emphasis to the support of family systems. Social workers are attending training programs and developing in-service education in a range of settings; and they are highly visible in both leadership and participant roles at family institutes and workshops, attempting to translate their learning experiences into new approaches to practice. Schools of social work are offering courses and even concentrations in "the family" in an effort to integrate the burgeoning array of interdisciplinary theory into practice approaches.

It is in the context of this widening interest in the family that this book on family-centered practice is presented. In the following chapters we will describe a model of practice which has been developed from many sources, influenced by thinkers and practitioners from several fields, and, of course, shaped by our own convictions, observations, philosophical biases, and teaching and practice experiences. Predominant among these many influences is a deep commitment to and identification with the social work profession.

Social work has a long tradition of borrowing knowledge from a variety of sources and translating, reworking, and applying this knowledge in ways that enhance practice in the wide range of settings where social workers work, in the varied roles they perform and with the diverse client populations they serve. Further, social work, with its emphasis on person-in-situation, has tended to be holistic in its world view and eclectic in its practice. This book lies firmly and comfortably in that tradition. It is a "social work" book, not a book on family therapy. However, it is also a book that explores the riches of family theory and therapy in pursuit of the

development of a family-centered practice model—useful for social
workers wherever they practice, teachable and portable from one setting
to another.

Certain biases and choices will soon become clear. We have, for example, drawn unevenly on the range of developments in clinical work
with families. We have emphasized family systems, ecological, and intergenerational family theories and practice techniques, with an eye fixed on
the total family system in context. One of the most notable omissions is
the exploration of a behavior modification approach to practice with
families. Perhaps in the near future representatives of both the family systems and behavior modification traditions will be able to clarify their symmetrical and complementary aspects. At this stage, however, while we
find ourselves using some techniques originating in behavior modification,
the two traditions remain quite distinct in terms of their theoretical foundations and their approaches to change.[1]

The same point may be made concerning family approaches
grounded in or at least more sympathetic to psychodynamic and psychoanalytic theory, which have also received scant attention in this volume.
Framo argues against what he calls a "purist" view of family therapy—one
which polarizes the intrapsychic and interactional dimensions of human
functioning—concluding that "what goes on inside people's heads is just as
important as what goes on between them" (1981:132). While we agree a
meaningful merger might advance work with families, it is extremely difficult to understand human behavior in the context of two seemingly different "world views" and even two different languages at one and the same
time. No contemporary model of family therapy seems to have achieved an
adequate integration between the two.

Another striking omission, and one which leaves us vulnerable to
legitimate criticism, is that we have not located family-centered practice
in the context of research and research-based practice. It is clear that
neither our integrative model nor any of the approaches on which we draw
has been adequately "tested" according to prevailing paradigms of social
science and practice research. The omission of a meaningful consideration
of the research issues in no way reflects a lack of conviction concerning the
importance of researching practice in general and family-centered practice in particular. The decision to omit a chapter dedicated to research
questions was made for several reasons. First, several excellent, critical
summaries of the state of research in the family practice field exist and our
work at best would summarize the summaries and, like them, raise far
more problems than solutions.[2] Second, although we recognize that research and practice should go hand in hand, we did not believe we could
do justice to both research and practice in the same book. Research in the
field of family therapy lags far behind practice, the methodological problems are enormous, and most observers seem to agree that very little of the

existing body of research meets commonly accepted criteria for reliability and validity. Our own conviction is that the continuing call for more research in the same tradition is not particularly useful. There is a far greater need for reexamination of the research paradigms themselves, for questioning the methodologies and the criteria on which most studies depend. Most contemporary researchers of family-centered practice have yet to find ways to capture the complexities of families in interaction. These issues, we believe, deserve their own forum.

Although any practitioner in one of the helping professions might find our presentation of use, it is primarily intended for practicing social workers and students who are interested in working with families and marital pairs, or who wish to ground their work with individuals in a family systems theoretical context.

At this point, if we wish to be true to the ecological systems perspective which frames our approach, it seems appropriate to describe the context which has given this book its particular shape and character. First, the professional practice of the authors has nurtured and influenced the direction the book would take. We both began our careers in public child welfare, Joan in protective services and Ann in foster care. We have both worked in family agencies which encouraged new learning and new approaches to helping. Ann was executive director of a community mental health clinic during the early years of the community mental health movement. Although always working with and interested in families, Ann's formal exposure to and excitement about the family therapy movement came through her participation in staff training conducted by Sanford Sherman in the early 1960s. Both authors became inveterate followers of the movement, traveling all over the country to hear what Bowen, Fogarty, Whitaker, Satir, La Perriere, Paul, the Duhls and other early leaders had to say about the theory and practice of work with family systems.

Since 1976 we have both been staff members of Ann Arbor Center for the Family, a multidisciplinary family institute that combines family-centered practice, training, and research. Our experience continues to develop through a constant "doing" and "reflecting on the doing" process, lively interchanges with our colleagues at the center, following the exponentially growing mass of family therapy literature, bringing leaders in the family therapy field to Ann Arbor for training and consultation, and continuing to attend seminars and institutes whenever possible. A particularly important turning point for us was the two days Lynn Hoffman spent in Ann Arbor a few years ago, and our subsequent attendance at the Toronto workshop presided over by Mara Selvini Palazzoli and her associates.

Both our practice with families and its expression in this book have been shaped too by our teaching of social work students and others in conferences, workshops, in-service training programs, and consultations. The requirements of teaching and the incisive and challenging questions of both our clients and our students have forced us to try to make our practice more intelligible and transmittable.

This work, then, five years in the making, is a product of the circular processes of learning, practicing, teaching, and writing. Each process has been affected by and has affected all of the others and the formulations in this book, if not subjected to formal research efforts, have been "tested" in practice, in the classroom, and with practitioners in workshops and other presentations. This circular process has been difficult to interrupt, as our editors ruefully know. At some point the presses must freeze and reproduce in a moment in time what is a constantly changing and ongoing process. We do not feel finished with either the process or the book. We have, however, been forced to call a temporary halt, fortuitous for us and for the reader, since this adventure was becoming, in Hoffman's words, a "too richly cross-joined system."

As with any co-authored book, the question inevitably rises concerning who wrote what. We both wrote it all. Although one or the other of us usually sketched the first draft of a particular chapter or portion, the pages have all been passed back and forth many times and have now achieved such a fusion that in some instances we can't remember who wrote the original drafts.

Turning briefly to some of the finer editorial issues, a few words are in order. First, the book is infused with case examples, almost all of which come from our own practice. The few which do not are gifts from colleagues, trainees, or students. All of the identifying information has been disguised or omitted to protect client confidentiality.

Second, like all authors today, we wracked our brains for a comfortable solution to the lack of gender neutral pronouns in our language. She and he, she/he, s/he and all those other awkward compromises were discarded. We finally elected to use one or the other randomly throughout, and have no idea if "he" or "she" has been favored.

We now turn to the decidedly pleasurable task of thanking the people who helped us "arrive where we started." Our collegial family at Ann Arbor Center for the Family has contributed to this work in many significant ways, some of which are clearly identifiable and others which are not. These wonderfully encouraging folk not only gave us many valuable suggestions which led to major reorganizations and other improvements in the final product, but they shared freely their own creative thoughts, energy, and time, helping to build a context which was and is stimulating and supportive. We thank Eric Bermann, Douglas Ensor, Sue Golden, Robert Pasick, Kenneth Silk, Mary Whiteside, and especially Jo Ann Allen, who has spent many hours behind the one-way mirror helping us learn new ways of helping families. Sharon Keyes is the glue that holds things together so that all of the staff can be more productive, and has often joined the typing brigade. Fernando Colon's strength and patience helped carry the Center through its formative years and his own "intergenerational" enthusiasm has been contagious. Glenn Kagan and Glenn Whitelaw allowed us to use their work with families and we are most grateful for their generosity. We also appreciate Betty Turner's comments on the manuscript and Alfreda Iglehart's help in updating some of the research reported in the early chapters. We are grateful to all of those who helped with the typing and retyping: Diane Katz, Stevie Anderson, Roxanne Loy, Ann Page, Pam Downie, WANG the Word Processor, and several others who were just as helpful if less visible.

There are many others, friends and colleagues from the University of Michigan and Eastern Michigan University, our students, and many other fellow workers whose ideas have enriched our own. Special thanks go to two special friends, Carel Germain and Carol Meyer, who have encouraged and inspired us just as they have many, many others in social work.

The Free Press, as personified by the three editors who have nudged this project along, has also been a good friend. Gladys Topkis convinced us we could and should write this book. It was her enthusiasm that started the marathon. She passed the baton to Joyce Seltzer, whose burst of energy encouraged several fast miles, and we finished with Laura Wolff, whose endurance and tenacity cheered and towed us toward the finish line.

Finally, we need to recognize the contributions of our own families who are here on more pages and in more ways than they might imagine.

PART I

The Context of Family-Centered Practice

IN WRITING THIS BOOK we have been guided by two overarching objectives. First, we present a model of practice which we hope will be useful for social workers, students, and other mental health professionals with a variety of educational backgrounds. Second, we describe a model which keeps the family in focus but which can be used in many different settings—wherever, in fact, practitioner and client meet.

To be consistent with the ecological systems orientation described in chapter 4, we cannot describe our model without expanding our unit of attention in space and through time and without sketching, at least in broad strokes, the contexts within which practice with families takes place and the forces and reciprocal transactions which shape professional action and client change.

In chapter 1, family-centered practice is defined and the professional context illuminated through an examination of the relationship between social work and the family, the historical roots of that relationship, and the role of the family-centered social work practitioner in the family therapy movement.

In chapter 2, our attention is turned to our client, the family. We examine the difficulties involved in defining the family, and we offer two definitions that take such difficulties into consideration. We also enumer-

1

ate changing circumstances and emerging problems in contemporary family life.

In chapter 3, the contours of the family policy arena are traced. Special attention is given to the policy and programmatic context within which the direct service practitioner works, with suggestions concerning how the worker might assess the policy and program aspects directly influencing the practice.

In chapter 4, we shift our attention to the intellectual environment which has fashioned and continues to shape and support family-centered practice. We present a few of the most salient concepts from general systems theory and from theory about open living systems, and we consider the science of ecology as a metaphor for practice.

Finally, in chapter 5, we review and synthesize concepts from those prevailing theories of family therapy which have provided the greatest relevance for family-centered practice.

Chapter 1————————————————————

A Family Focus in
Social Work Practice

A REVOLUTION HAS BEEN BREWING for some time now, in the social sciences, in the helping professions, and in social work. Since the late 1950s and 1960s, social workers have been exploring the potential of general systems, cybernetic, and ecological theories for principles and concepts that might help to better understand people in their contexts. A scientific revolution has been in the making, one which, in Kuhn's sense, is ushering in a new paradigm, threatening to topple the more linear epistemologies in which our understandings of human and social functioning have been grounded.

During this same period, and perhaps not just coincidentally, we have also witnessed a heightened concern about the family and its future as a workable social institution. As social workers have once again been shifting their primary unit of attention from the individual to the family (as we shall soon see, an historical pattern) they have been arming themselves with new theories and new techniques being generated from models of helping based on systems principles and concepts.

It has been a heady experience to be participants in a profession undergoing major paradigmatic change, a time perhaps akin to the early years of the introduction of psychoanalytic theory in the helping professions. In spite of the voluminous body of literature being spawned in sociology and in the field of family therapy, the social work literature until recently has been quite sterile in terms of its contributions in this field.

3

Perhaps one reason for this curious phenomenon is the fact that those creative social workers who have been pioneers in their work with families have tended to identify themselves as family therapists, have joined new professional organizations, and contribute to a new tradition of professional literature. The riches of this movement have not been fully utilized and adapted for social work itself and the multitude of settings where social workers work. This book is an effort to help fill that gap.

In this introductory chapter, we will define family-centered practice and examine its relationship with social work practice in general. Further, in an effort to place the model in its historical context, we will look at how the family has fared as an object of professional concern in the historical development of social work.

WHAT IS FAMILY-CENTERED SOCIAL WORK PRACTICE?

Family-centered practice is a model of social work practice which locates the family in the center of the unit of attention or the field of action (Germain, 1968), or, as Meyer (1976) phrases it, "the 'what' to which social work pays attention. . . ." Based on a systems framework, the approach to helping described in this study grows out of the basic premise that human beings can be understood and helped only in the context of the intimate and powerful human systems of which they are a part. One of those powerful systems is the family of origin which has developed through the generations over time and which has deep and far-reaching effects on all of its members. Another is the current family system or network of intimate relationships as it exists in the present and which plays such a vital role in the lives of most people.

Consistent with our systems perspective, the family system itself has an environment and must be seen in that context. In other words, the model of practice defined later in this chapter is concerned with transactions among person, family, and environment and with a wide range of strategies for assessment and intervention which may strengthen or change those transactions.

We have broadly defined the phrase "family-centered" and the idea of the family as the "unit of attention." However, another part of the definition requires expansion and explication. We have defined our approach as a model of social work practice, and in order to clarify and even justify this claim, it is important to define what we mean by social work practice and what we mean by model.

Defining social work is not as simple a task as it might seem. Several generations of social workers have struggled to define and describe their wide-ranging, perhaps amorphous profession and to clarify for themselves and others the characteristics and domain of their practice.

Social work practice is generally described as being concerned with the relationship between people and their social environments. Mary Richmond's famous definition of casework as "those processes which develop personality through adjustments consciously effected, individual by individual, between men and their social environment" appeared in 1922 (1922:98). Bertha Reynolds clarified this focus in 1933 when she wrote, "The essential point seems to be that the function of social casework is not to treat the individual alone nor his environment alone, but the process of adaptation which is a dynamic interaction between the two" (1933:337). This theme reappears in more current definitions developed by, among others, Bartlett (1964), Gordon (1969), and Pincus and Minahan (1973). The domain of family-centered practice is consistent with this theme; it is restricted neither to families and their members nor to those larger environmental systems which affect the nature of family life. Its concern, its focus, its turf, are those transactions among person, family, and environment which affect individuals, families, and, though less well understood, even the larger social forces and systems in which families are enmeshed.

The family-centered practitioner may wear many hats, may perform several different roles and may work with different-sized client systems. The social policy analyst, the program developer, the agency administrator, the mental-health worker may each place the family at the center of his concern. The family-centered practitioner may, at various times, meet with extended family or network members, research a particular family theme, advocate for badly needed resources, mediate between a family and a community institution, find a substitute for an absent family function, or intervene in a faulty or dysfunctional family communication network. In short, the family can be in the center of attention whether one is working with individuals, groups, neighborhoods, or larger systems.

The model of practice presented in this and the following chapters, however, is intended primarily for the use of the direct-service practitioner. The emphasis will be on the knowledge and skills relevant to helping individuals and families. This does not mean that individuals and families are necessarily the sole or even primary targets for change. The family-centered practitioner, whose goal is to enhance and enrich the quality of life for individuals and families, must understand not only complex family systems, but the equally complex interactions between the family and their ecological milieu. Such a conceptualization stretches still further the needed repertoire of knowledge and skills.

The family-centered worker also needs to consider the importance of the powerful network of influences and systems in which he or she practices. Thus, it is essential that attention be paid to those social policies and organizational arrangements which underpin—and occasionally undermine—family-centered practice.

In defining the domain of family-centered practice, it is clear, as is the case with many other models of social work, that the boundaries of concern are so wide that they surely overlap with those of other professions providing similar if not identical services. But it has never been the possession of an exclusive domain that identifies social work. Indeed, it may well be a breadth of vision and a readiness to pursue a variety of options which typifies the creative, responsible social worker. That breadth of vision is a basic requirement of the family-centered social worker.

THE "MISSION" OF SOCIAL WORK

A second way in which social work practice is defined is through the specification of its purpose or "mission." In fact, some believe it is the mission rather than the domain that accounts for the uniqueness of the profession. But when we turn to describe the mission of social work we are again faced with many divergent definitions. In fact, Scott Briar (1977), in his summary of the first National Association of Social Workers' symposium on conceptual frameworks, reported that the task of defining such a mission proved to be extremely difficult. As each definition was presented it was found to be insufficiently broad or inclusive. The only thing which could be agreed upon seemed to be that the mission of social work was multifaceted.

As one surveys these definitions, however, some consistent themes do appear. The majority consider the mission of social work to be in some way related to the enhancement of social functioning and/or the solution of social problems. Throughout the profession's history, there has been a continuing debate concerning how much emphasis should be placed on changing larger systems. Along which path should social workers tread? What stops should be made along the way?

It is our conviction that the dual focus, on people and on larger systems—described in 1969 by William Schwartz as a focus on "private troubles and public issues"—is fundamental to our professional identity.

In our conception of family-centered practice, we rely on the metaphor of ecology, which helps us focus on the interface between families and the larger environment. Thus we say that the primary mission of the family-centered practitioner, then, is the enhancement of the quality of life, of that delicate, adaptive balance between human beings and their ecological environments. This enhancement may well come about through change in individual or family functioning, in the larger systems on which the family depends for nurturance and growth, or in the transactions among these systems.

Definitions of the mission of social work also differ in terms of how, where, and for whom services should be developed and located. Should the primary investment be directed toward institutional or residual services? Should services be woven into the fabric of society and located for all people, using Bertha Reynolds' famous metaphor, at the "crossroads of life"?[1] Or, given a variety of social, economic, and political contingencies, should services be developed primarily for those who may need them most, those who demonstrate need, and those whose social functioning has in some way broken down?[2] While one cannot escape the need for setting priorities, it is our conviction that social work must continue to emphasize both institutional and residual services. Both directions are fraught with pitfalls and challenges, yet one cannot be ignored at the expense of the other.

The direct service family-centered practitioner, as an "explorer" in the life space of human beings, may work for the enhancement of the quality of life in a variety of ways. He may participate in the establishment of developmental and preventive services located in the community at crucial junctures and available to all or most of its people. Examples include the organization of an educational community project on issues of family violence, the establishment of a cooperative drop-in center where parents can find relief from constant child-care responsibility, or the calling of a meeting of all of the high school's black families to work for a more positive relationship between the school and the district's black population. Such services, frequently aimed at preventing problems and crises, strengthening family coping skills, and developing accessible resource networks, may better prepare individuals and families for meeting a spectrum of developmental life tasks.

Family-centered workers may provide a variety of social services designed to strengthen or supplement family life where particular needs have been identified. Homemaker and home health aide services, family day care, meals on wheels, child placement, and counseling are just a few examples of services which may be offered.

Finally, a family-centered focus is appropriate in rehabilitative situations, in instances where the individual's or family's adaptive capacities are weakened or lacking. Examples here include families with mentally ill members, families in which there is physical or sexual abuse of children, or families struggling with alcohol or drug abuse.

In the real world, individual and family problems do not fall into these seemingly neat categories of prevention, provision, or rehabilitation. It is unlikely that any problem has a single cause. It is equally unlikely that any single intervention is the only legitimate or correct route to helping. In the case of wife abuse, for example, imagine just a few of the interventions in which family-centered practitioners might participate. Located in a family agency, they might find themselves counseling husbands or wives alone, married couples together, or couples with their children and/or their parents (the children's grandparents). They might seek to include others who are closely involved, such as other professionals or close friends. They might, after several such experiences, determine that the formation of a group of couples would greatly enhance the possibilities for mutual aid and conserve agency resources, and suggest such a group to the staff. Frustrated at the lack of public awareness or resources in the community, they might seek community support for the development of an educational project and the creation of an emergency housing facility for victims of family violence. They might be concerned about the way local police approach family violence, and initiate dialogue between the police and social work communities, leading perhaps to an exchange of inservice presentations or joint case handling. Many other interventions are conceivable. Which are selected depends not only on a full ecological assessment but on such diverse criteria as personal style, agency and community sanction, and resource availability and potential, issues to be discussed in more detail in later chapters.

We agree with Briar that the purposes of social work are certainly broad, and it is our intention that the family-centered practice model presented here share in the profession's multifaceted mission. Throughout this volume, we will describe ways in which the family-centered practitioner may move in different directions along the preventive/rehabilitative, institutional/residual, people-changing/environment-changing continuums.

Thus social work practice may be defined by its domain and its mission but these definitions are shaped and expressed by the values or preferences held by social workers. According to Compton and Galaway, "values can be thought of as beliefs which a profession holds about people and about appropriate ways of dealing with people" (1975:103). Various efforts have been made to reduce a myriad of ethical considerations to a few basic value premises said to be essential to the very identity of the social work professional. Compton and Galaway, for example, identify two which they see as essential: "(1) belief in the uniqueness and inherent dignity of the individual and (2) belief in client self-determination" (104). Yet even these broadly stated principles are riddled with dilemmas and are only rarely applied with complete clarity or certainty.[3] For, like all human beings, social workers are profoundly affected by the social, economic, cultural, political, and psychological contexts in which they carry out their professional roles. The family-centered practitioner does not escape these forces. Conscientious social workers, whatever the method, model or role, must constantly reexamine their own beliefs and biases as well as those of their professional milieu.

In family-centered practice, the worker must be aware of and sensitive to not only wider professional value issues, but some particular dilemmas generated by the family focus itself. For example, one cannot even begin to define "the family" without confronting issues which immediately send people to their philosophical battle stations. Thus, while we view family-centered practice as sharing the same value base (and its inherent difficulties) as the larger profession, in this study we will also highlight those value issues and choices which seem particularly germane to a family focus.

In defining family-centered social work practice, we have described what is meant by "family-centered" and have attempted to portray some of the ways in which this model of practice shares the domain, the mission, and the values of the larger social work profession.

Family-Centered Practice as a "Model"

As indicated earlier, the notion of family-centered practice as a "model" needs to be justified. The word "model" has become popular among social work theoreticians. Its wide use has led to considerable confusion, as the word has many meanings,[4] and there are many different kinds and levels of models. There are, for example, conceptual or theoretical models, cognitive maps which serve to organize our perceptions of reality. There are also, on the most concrete level, models which prescribe specific plans of action through which one may achieve specific objectives. Examples of such "blueprints" might include dress patterns or house plans.

A social work practice model incorporates these levels of abstraction. It includes an identifiable and clearly explicated conceptual framework, as well as specific patterns and plans which can guide daily action. The relationship between these two levels is that of a continuous feedback loop, in which the conceptual framework is fashioned out of continuous empirical experience and the concrete plans of action grow out of the conceptual framework.

These levels of abstraction can be exemplified in the development of family-centered practice as a model. On the most abstract level, the practice model rests on general systems theory as an epistemological platform. This perspective is concretized through the use of an ecological metaphor which focuses on the transactional relationships between living systems and their environments in the present and over time. The ecological metaphor specifies the unit of attention and also defines the knowledge base that supports the practice model. Such knowledge particularly includes those aspects of the social and biological sciences that add to our understanding of systems transactions.

On the most concrete level, family-centered practice will be translated into specific patterns for action. These include patterns for assessment such as the Eco-Map, a blueprint for understanding the family in its life space and for the development of specific patterns of intervention.

As we present our practice model in the following chapters, it will soon become clear that some aspects are more fully developed than others. In some areas, relatively precise and testable practice prescriptions have been developed. In other areas only a beginning has been made. We may claim that family-centered practice is a model; but we must caution the reader that it is a model under construction.

THE GENERALIST–SPECIALIST ISSUE

Our position on one final issue should be clarified, and that is the long-standing argument in social work over the "generalist–specialist" issue, a dichotomy which was debated during the Milford Conference of the late 1920s, which has surfaced periodically since that time, and which has emerged again in the last few years with renewed vigor. The initial question concerns the very basic challenge of defining the so-called core of social work practice, that array of knowledge, skill and values which the generalist practitioner should possess, and the reciprocal question asks what specializations are appropriate and how they should be characterized. This issue currently is being readdressed at great length, particularly by social work educators, as undergraduate and graduate curricula have been experimenting with new ways of dividing up the educational pie. While we do not wish to digress unnecessarily by jumping into the fray here, it is important to locate the position of family-centered practice in relation to traditional ways of conceptualizing social work practice.

Historically, specialization developed according to field of practice. Early social workers identified themselves as, among others, medical social workers, school social workers, or child welfare workers. This way of conceptualizing specialization is once again being adopted as some schools of social work are developing concentrations according to fields of practice. Another closely related conceptualization defines specialization by social problem area, such as substance abuse, juvenile delinquency, or teenage pregnancy. Family-centered practice, as conceived here, is a model useful in *any* field of social work practice, such as health care, school, child welfare, and corrections. Further, we cannot conceive of a social problem in which a family focus would not be relevant for the direct service practitioner.

The second major way practice has been conceptualized has been according to "method," social workers typically specializing in and identifying themselves as caseworkers, group workers, or community organizers, depending on the size of client system being helped. A family-centered direct service approach does not, in our view, hinge on the size of client system served. A family focus may be utilized in work with an individual, a couple, a family, a group, or an entire community. To give an example, an individual may be helped to cope with marital and parenting relationships through utilization of his own family of origin as an instrument for change. To give another example, a group consisting of parents of children with leukemia and the children themselves might be established to help families cope with the crisis of serious illness. The issue is not how many people are being directly seen by the worker, but whether the persons involved are understood in relation to their current networks of intimate relationships and their family of origin. In this way, the family-centered model is similar to the task-centered or crisis model, for the size of client system does not alter the basic conception.

As family-centered practice becomes linked with specialized methods, fields of practice, or social problem areas, the practitioner needs to incorporate the knowledge and special skills particular to that method or field. In family-centered group work, for example, the worker makes use of the knowledge and skills that have developed in group work practice such as understanding of group formation, group composition, group dynamics, and group process, as well as the family focus. In the delivery of health care services, the practitioner will need to integrate, for example, special information about health and illness and about health care delivery systems. Family-centered practice with the aging combines the growing body of knowledge from gerontology with a family focus.

In short, family-centered practice as presented here is seen as a "generalist" model of direct practice. Based on an ecological systems perspective, the model may be utilized in a wide range of practice settings and social problem areas, and with any size client system. Family-centered practice may be a vehicle for developmental, preventive, or rehabilitative services. It may include a wide range of worker roles from family advocate to family therapist.

Social Work and the Family: A Historical Perspective

Just as an individual is best understood in the context of his or her intergenerational family history, so can we enhance our understanding of the current relationship between social work and the family by turning to a brief review of the long association between the family and the social work practitioner.

The social work profession's history of concern for and association with the family is a complex and confusing tale. Although social workers have always thought of themselves and have been seen by others as professionals who "work with families," a study of their involvement with the family reveals considerable inconsistency and ambivalence in attending to a family focus. For example, the first professional direct practice journal was called *The Family* (now *Social Casework*). Social casework was born and nurtured in a nationwide network of agencies called "family service" agencies and the first social work practitioners who were employed to work in the hospitals and the early mental hygiene programs were expected to ameliorate the noxious elements in the patient's social environment, an environment which included the family.

Faced with a history of many strong links between social work and the family, one cannot help but wonder why it is that progress was so slow in integrating the family into the heart of our practice theory. Why is it that social workers are having to relearn a family focus, to return, almost as strangers, to that notion so central in early social work thinking, of the family as the unit of attention? Why is it that social services continue to be structured and delivered in large segments of our social welfare network without involving or sometimes even recognizing the existence of the family?

A review of the history of social work practice and particularly of the relationship of casework practice to the family suggests several hypotheses that may, at least in part, explain the fluctuating liaison between social work and the family. These hypotheses are as follows. First, the impact of both the mental hygiene movement and psychoanalytic psychology tended to shift attention to the individual. Second, the family focus was lost when social work became split between an "inner" and an "outer" focus. Third, limitations in the knowledge and theory base that supported social casework practice made the integration of a family focus with the new psychological emphasis difficult, if not impossible; and fourth, the organizational arrangements of practice by method and field meant that a family focus was difficult to categorize appropriately. An exploration of these hypotheses follows.

The mental hygiene movement as it developed through the twenties and the impact of psychoanalytic psychology in the thirties changed the face of casework practice in terms of method, of function, and of its view of human beings. These influences also wrought a major change in the way social workers defined the recipient of service and the "boundaries" of the case for assessment and intervention. In other words, the unit of attention for the casework practitioner shifted from the family to the individual.

Testimony to the change in direction emerges when we compare our professional beginnings and the work of Mary Richmond, who is generally considered to be the founder and early architect of casework as a professional practice, with subsequent developments.

Mary Richmond was convinced that "the family itself continues to be the pivotal institution around which our human destinies revolve" (1930:262). As she developed a professional model of casework and devised the now familiar practice steps of social study, social diagnosis, and social treatment, the unit of study, diagnosis and treatment was the family. This emphasis was based on her philosophy of the "theory of the wider self" which characterized people as being deeply immersed in and affected by their social environments. "A man really *is* the company he keeps plus the company that his ancestors kept," Mary Richmond wrote in *Social Diagnosis* (1917), her monumental formulation of practice. Addressing the

National Conference of Charities and Corrections in 1908, she emphasized the salience of the family to all people.

> To all here present . . . the great formative influences, the processes that have made us what we are, have gone on within our own homes quite unconsciously, for the most part. The way in which each one of you has entered and will leave this church, your feelings about this place and its associations, the greater or lesser degree of tolerance with which you are listening to what I am saying this moment, what you will think about it afterward, if you ever think about it at all, and what you will do about it. These things have been determined far more by the family into which you were born and in which you grew up than any single one of you has any conception. . . . [1930: 262–3]

Richmond translated her conviction about the importance of the family into her conception of practice. Throughout, she defined the "case" as a family, and warned that good results of "individual treatment would crumble away" if caseworkers failed to take account of the family (Richmond, 1917:134).

Social Diagnosis, which reflected and prescribed work done in the Charity Organization Societies in the first fifteen years of the century, was published on the eve of the beginning of the mental hygiene movement. The twenties saw a heightened interest in psychology, psychiatry, and the beginning shift to the individual as the object of study and of treatment. This trend was foreshadowed or perhaps announced by E. E. Southard's (1918) attack on *Social Diagnosis*, the year after its publication, at the 1918 National Conference. Southard, the director of Boston Psychopathic Hospital, employed the first social worker in a psychiatric setting. He and Mary Jarrett, the first psychiatric social worker, together founded the Smith School for Social Work, whose main purpose was to train social workers to move into the field of mental hygiene. Southard began his address with an analysis of the cases presented by Richmond in *Social Diagnosis*, concluding that "fully half of the cases in the book had the most important psychopathic factors at work, whether out-and-out psychosis, mild psychopathia, alcoholism, or attitudes of mind toward diseases and other maladaptations which were not exactly wholesome" (1918:336).

Southard went on to present what he termed a "psychiatric model" of individual analysis and to "demolish what seems to be an erroneous pet view of social workers. That is to say, I want to replace the family as the unit of social inquiry with the individual as the unit of social inquiry" (1918:337).

The following year Mary Jarrett reinforced Southard's view in her prophetic speech entitled "The Psychiatric Thread Running Through All Social Case Work" (1919). Criticizing her own title, she said that the psychiatric emphasis should not represent merely a "thread" in casework but the entire warp of the fabric. Emphasizing a psychological, individualistic view, Jarrett announced that "the adaptation of an individual to the environment, in the last analysis, depends upon mental makeup" (1919:587).

At the 1919 Conference, Porter Lee, Director of the New York School of Social Work, rose to oppose Southard's position and to support Richmond's family focus. The major portion of his paper deals with value issues, emphasizing the importance of the family in a democratic society. He then turns to address Southard directly on more specific issues related to methods of practice. He agrees that

> the family cannot be successfully treated by any methods known to social casework without treating its individual members. Whether these critics would concede to us that the individual members of a family cannot be successfully treated without treating the family as a whole, I do not know, and without waiting to find out I am ready to assert that they cannot. No individual is wholly an individual. [1919:325]

Although the language may have changed, the substance of this dialogue which occurred over sixty years ago is sufficiently current to give one pause! The discussion was an early expression of fundamental issues that were to shape the future of social casework practice and the approach of social workers to the family. First and most momentous was the evidence of the growing influence of psychological variables in the understanding of human beings and their behavior. The mental hygiene movement of the 1920s prepared the way for a stronger psychological emphasis in social work and for the introduction, a decade later, of psychoanalytic concepts into the mainstream of practice. Virginia Robinson's *A Changing Psychology of Social Case Work*, published in 1930, was the first major presentation of this new way of thinking and, as Bertha Reynolds commented in her review, "Miss Robinson has published her book, and we will never be the same again" (1932:109).

What was to be the fate of the family focus in the growing shift to a psychological orientation? Robinson made this clear when she wrote that she defined "social casework as individual therapy through a treatment relationship" (1930:187). Robinson described the change from an emphasis on sociological fact to psychological fact, and from environmental circumstances per se to their value and meaning as individual experiences. "The unit of study," she wrote, "has shifted to the individual" (95).

Even the family agencies, which had originally defined the family as the case, shifted to an individual focus in practice. In part, family agency workers were moved to repudiate their preprofessional pasts, wishing to separate themselves from their direct ancestors, the friendly visitors, who made home visits and counseled total families. In 1938 Herbert Aptekar, reviewing the function of a family agency, scorned the old approach in which the total family was conceptualized as the unit of attention and the worker usually became involved with all of the family members. He thought that the worker was doing all that was humanly possible in working with one member of the family at a time, adding that often changes in an individual could change the family (Aptekar, 1938).

The psychoanalytic influence pushed social workers toward an individual orientation in terms of both problem assessment and methods of treatment. The sources of problems in functioning were located within the individual. The psychoanalytic treatment method with its emphasis on the use of the transference as the major instrument of change also had its impact. Many saw casework as a one-to-one relationship therapy; the management and protection of that relationship precluded multiple interviewing and discouraged the worker from moving into the milieu of the client.

The work of Florence Hollis, whose writings have been influential in the development of practice theory, reflects the psychoanalytic influence on approaching "family" problems. In her volume on marriage counseling published in 1949 and entitled, interestingly enough, *Women in Marital Conflict,* Hollis locates the primary cause of marital conflict in personality factors located within each of the marital partners. This study focused on the female partners, defining typical problems as excessively close parental ties, dependence, masochism, and rejection of femininity. In terms of method, she felt that it was good practice to have at least one interview with the marital partner early in the course of treatment, for diagnostic purposes. However, she felt it "feasible for one worker to see both clients only when the conflict is rather slight and when very extensive or intensive contact is not needed with the second person" (183). She recommended that if insight development were to be undertaken, each member of the marital pair should have his or her own worker. The practice of drawing careful protective boundaries around the treatment situation consisting of one worker and one client became entrenched. Even in the sixties, a committee studying practice in family agencies across the country refers to joint client interviewing as an "experimental treatment approach" (Family Service Association of America, 1963).

Besides family agencies, the other major area in which social workers were specifically identified as working with families was the child guidance movement. There, too, a similar evolution of practice occurred. Lee and Kenworthy, in their volume *Mental Hygiene and Social Work,* described the social worker's role as follows:

> The direct treatment of the child was undertaken as a general practice by the psychiatrist. The direct work with parents, teachers, and others was usually done by the social worker under the direction of the psychiatrist. The general responsibility of the social worker for the adjustment toward which treatment was directed involved two types of activity: first, the provision of certain service opportunities or special kinds of experiences . . . and second,

a direct effort to change the attitudes of those persons most closely associated with the children. [1931:111]

In the early years, these efforts toward change of attitude in parents were primarily educational. This kind of change was seen as particularly difficult and sensitive, since attitudes had their roots in the unconscious and these parents might be resistant and defensive. As the influence of the psychoanalytic movement became more apparent, workers began to alter their approaches. In an early article, Madeline Moore illustrates the shift from a primarily environmental and educational approach. The mother's personality difficulties had become the target of change. In one case, the author writes, "The mother was led back through the current situation to her childhood attitudes and came to understand her present conflict in terms of childhood experiences" (1933:121).

As social work became increasingly interested in the individual treatment of personality difficulties, workers in child-guidance settings, generally "relegated" to working with parents, frequently experienced frustration and a sense of being "second-class" citizens. They adapted to this predicament either by beginning to treat parents as "patients" or by fighting for the right to "treat" the child. Social workers at that time were unaware that their assignment by default was really where the action was! In a historical review of family therapy, Murray Bowen commented, "The Child Guidance Movement passed close to some current family concepts without seeing them. The focus on pathology in the child prevented a view of the family" (1978:286).

The fifties saw a return to an interest in the family as the unit of attention. Frances Scherz, in her article entitled "What Is Family Centered Casework?," foreshadows the growing concern for the family. This paper, one of several on the family theme presented at the 1953 National Conference, describes and regrets the influence of psychiatry in leading social workers temporarily away from a major concern with the family as a unit. Scherz then turns to the developing knowledge about family dynamics in the social sciences and emphasizes the importance of understanding family interaction in case situations. She defines family-centered casework as practice which is "based on an understanding of the social, physical, and emotional needs of the family . . . . In family-centered casework, the improvement of the social functioning of the family unit is achieved by direct or indirect treatment of the individual family members, so planned, balanced, and controlled that benefits accrue to the total group" (1954:343). But how was one to make predictions concerning the impact of the treatment of individuals on the total family? How was one to assess the social, physical, and emotional needs of the family? Many of those interested in the family felt that the answers to such questions were to be found in the development of a theory of family diagnosis, and the literature began to report efforts in this direction. A review of these efforts to assess the family and to link that assessment with an understanding of the individual brings up another factor that hampered the development of a family focus. The efforts throughout the fifties to devise a typology of family diagnoses continually echoed the frustration experienced by those struggling with this task. This frustration resulted from the fact that the conceptual tools required for the integration of individual and family variables and for the development of such a family typology simply were not available.

Most social workers attempting to assess the family wished to preserve their learning from psychoanalysis and then, as Nathan Ackerman wrote, "to apply the dynamic insight of psychoanalysis to the mental health problem of marital relationships and family life" (1954:139). However, individually oriented psychoanalytic concepts seemed incompatible with a conceptualization of the larger social group.

In reviewing these efforts, Carol Meyer wrote:

> In our commitment to the concept of family diagnosis, we have done two things. We have attempted, first, to make either a cumulative or a parallel diagnosis of family members using the psychoanalytic concepts available . . . we then either total the individual diagnoses . . . or we relate the individual diagnoses to each other, and thus describe the balance or equilibrium achieved among members of the family. [1959:371]

Some attempted to use psychoanalytic concepts to assess the family as a whole. Such efforts tended toward reductionism, as exemplified in an early effort by Irene Josselyn entitled "The Family as a Psychological Unit." She wrote:

> The family can be analyzed by studying its individual parts but the findings must be synthesized before it can be understood as a unit. . . . If the family unit is anthropomorphized, perhaps we can better study its bisexual and asexual drives, its loves and its aggressions, the neuroses and psychoses of the unit. [1953:343]

Those interested in the family also turned to sociology in trying to incorporate a sociological dimension in family diagnosis. Viola Weiss and Russell Monroe (1959), for example, developed such an additive model for family assessment. The outline of their framework covered several pages and made obvious the problems faced by all those who were seeking to "diagnose" the family. First, the framework called for a staggering amount of information, more information than could be organized and mastered, to say nothing of leading one toward a plan of action. Second, concepts available from sociology were, for the most part, descriptive rather than dynamic. They added little to the understanding of the family, describing further aspects of the individual.

Toward the end of the decade, Robert Gomberg said:

> No diagnostic or conceptual system exists which describes, assesses, or classifies the family configuration, yet it is clearly needed if the diagnosis of the individual is not to be in a vacuum but rather within the context of the social and emotional environment in which he lives, adjusts, suffers, fails, or succeeds. [1958:73]

Not until the late 1960s do we begin to see concepts derived from general systems, cybernetics, and family systems trickling into social work. At the same time that social workers were attempting to return to a family focus and to develop the conceptual framework to enable them to do so, the roots of the family therapy movement were spreading, roots which had begun sprouting in the late 1940s and early 1950s. Family therapy pioneers such as Nathan Ackerman, Murray Bowen, John Elderkin Bell, Gregory Bateson, Jay Haley, Don Jackson, and Virginia Satir were researching and treating whole families. Searching for ways of understanding the enormously complex transactions which seemed to bear on individual and family dysfunction, they were faced with the same conceptual problems, problems which neither the individual-focused psychology or the social systems-focused sociology of the times could resolve. These psychiatrists, wrote sociologist Carlfred Broderick,

> initially knew little or no sociology, yet they found themselves dealing with the structure and function of groups. Out of necessity, they invented a sociology of family interaction without any roots in traditional sociological theory. Generally speaking, the constructs grew out of observing patterns in real families over time. [1971:150]

Bowen (1978), reminiscing about his team's early efforts in family research and theory building, describes how they attempted to free themselves from a psychoanalytic or psychiatric framework through refusing to rely on any of the customary terminology, thus forcing themselves to describe what they saw without reference to any existing theoretical framework or language.

The discovery of the linkages and cross-influences that existed between these parallel movements in psychiatry and social work would be a fascinating study in the sociology of knowledge. Descriptions of the development of the family therapy movement (see, e.g., Bowen, 1978; Guerin, 1976), make little mention of social work. The most obvious linkage in the fifties was between Nathan Ackerman, who very early pioneered in family diagnosis and treatment, and social workers at the Jewish Family Service in New York. Ackerman had a long association with that agency and social workers associated with Ackerman took major leadership in developing family unit treatment within the social work profession. A large portion of family-focused writing in the social work literature emanated from the J.F.S. staff: Sanford Sherman, Hope Leichter, Celia

Mitchell, Frances Beatman, and their associates. The central position held by that agency in the family field was demonstrated at the conference held in 1960 to honor the memory of the agency's executive, Robert Gomberg, who had contributed much to the development of family theory and case-work. The panel of participants included, in addition to Ackerman and the J.F.S. staff, Don Jackson, Virginia Satir, Lyman Wynne, and Gregory Bateson (Ackerman, Beatman, and Sherman, 1961).

Elsewhere social workers, with the exception of Virginia Satir, may not have fared so well in the developing family movement. For example, when Murray Bowen and his team (including a social worker) presented the findings of their National Institute of Mental Health research on schizophrenia and the family at the 1959 meeting of the American Orthopsychiatric Association, in his introduction Bowen writes of the social worker on the team:

> Her function in the clinical operation was well defined when she had individual relationships with various family members. After the change to the "family unit" orientation her clinical function was much less clear. In the course of the project, her main clinical function came to be that of assistant family psychotherapist. [1961:42]

In the wing of the movement that developed under medical auspices out of the study of schizophrenia and the family, the status differentials were in evidence. A decade later, however, the family therapy field was to move in the direction of being more truly interdisciplinary as social workers began to flock to family training institutes and as they themselves began to take leadership in theory and practice development. Unfortunately, many of those social workers who have made significant contributions to the burgeoning family therapy literature tend to be identified as family therapists rather than as social workers, and their writings rarely appear in the social work journals.

The struggles of the fifties to integrate psychological and social variables were not new to social work, a profession that had always defined itself as concerned with both the individual and the social environment. The history of social work can be described as a series of pendulum swings between emphasizing either the individual or the social order as the primary source of social problems and as the target for change. These pendulum swings, reflecting major political and social directions of the larger society, have at times challenged professional identity and threatened professional unity. This division in the profession has been reflective of the conceptual difficulties described above and the lack of a framework or integrative concepts which could link inner and outer variables. Psychological concepts concentrated on the innermost life of the individual while conceptualizations of the social environment tended to focus on the largest orders of social organization.[5]

This dichotomous view of person and situation may well have had implications for the place of the family in social work practice theory. Sometimes it almost seemed that the family, like a child in a "no-win" position between battling parents, got caught between social work's two competing, sometimes warring, approaches. To those concerned with social change, the family focus was "too psychological," whereas, as we have seen above, for those exploring the psychology of the individual, the family was lost as a result of the "inner" focus.

At no time in the history of social work practice were these lines between a psychological or a social change orientation so sharply drawn as in the sixties. Just when the family seemed to be moving to center stage as the new decade began, the War on Poverty, the civil rights revolution, the growing concern with the inequities and injustices of society shifted the interest and energy of social work to the solution of large-scale social problems. Casework was under fire as an ineffective method at best, and at worst as a manipulative instrument of social control.

At the height of this struggle, Sanford Sherman (1967) suggested that the family could perhaps be a unifying force to bridge the gap between what he termed an "anti-clinical sociological orientation" and the embattled psychologically oriented clinicians. The family could, he believed, as a truly psychosocial system and as the critical link between the individual and society at large, be a mediating force in unifying social work.

Although Sherman's recommendation may be found to be prophetic of the shape of social work in the late seventies and eighties, this rapprochement was not to occur in the sixties. In fact, it may be that the momentum toward a family focus within the field of social work was slowed by the attention to larger social concerns. Social workers who continued to be interested in the family as the unit of attention found their way into the family therapy field, while social work practice in most settings and fields remained relatively uninfluenced by the earlier flurry of activity and interest in the family as the unit of service.

This leads to the fourth area to be explored in the history of the relationship between the family and social work practice, namely, the development of social work according to either "field" or "method." One can hypothesize that the way social work was organized, both in terms of fields of practice and in terms of method, may have had a part in determining the fate of a family focus. The vast field of social work practice grew up organized around two main kinds of specialization. One centered on specific fields of practice; the other on "methods." Concerning "fields of practice" specializations, Roy Lubove, in his historical analysis entitled *The Professional Altruist*, wrote: "The emergence of specialists in medical, school, and psychiatric social work in addition to child care meant that no one had assumed responsibility for that most important institution of all—the family" (1965:40). Family agencies quite naturally moved into the gap, defining the strengthening of family life as their primary goal. But is the family a field of practice? Is not the family a unit which is served in all fields of practice? It may well be that the development of "family casework" within family agencies tended to define this approach as a specialty, rather than as generic to all social work in any field of practice. Perhaps most problematic was the structural division between the "field of child welfare" and the "family field," as if the destinies of children were not inexorably bound to those of their families.[6]

The place of the family as client was equally confusing when linked to method specialization, since methods were, in fact, organized around the size of the "client system." The casework method tended to involve services to individuals, while group work specialized in knowledge and skills relating to service to people in groups. Was conjoint family work, as a method of practice, casework or group work? Or both? Or neither? Most group workers, knowledgeable about group dynamics and skilled in group processes, did not seem to define the family as a group falling within their professional domain. In a paper delivered shortly before her death, Grace Coyle, who had taken major leadership in the development of professional group work, presented concepts on group dynamics which could be relevant to understanding and helping the family as a group. She saw the concepts as generic to any small group, but added that she believed that it was "the function of casework practitioners, rather than group workers, to determine the usefulness of such concepts and the precise ways they can be applied to the treatment of families" (1962:347). However, if social work methods were to be characterized by the size of the client system, the family unit was indeed a group.

In the sixties the usefulness of dividing social work practice into methods specialties in this manner was increasingly questioned. The conviction that social work practitioners should be equipped with generic skills enabling them to work with different-sized systems proliferated in the professional literature as attempts were made to develop generalist or integrated models of social work practice. The delineation of the family as the unit of attention appeared in a variety of ways in these models; in some models the family is included as one of the client systems to be served and in others it is considered an aspect of the client's environment.

In reviewing the relationship between social work practice and the family, it is clear that a family focus is far from new. Always an underlying theme in social work, the family has sometimes been in the spotlight and at other times in the shadows, eclipsed by other concerns or by new thrusts in knowledge and theory development. It has been suggested that the overall impact of both the mental hygiene movement and psychoanalysis, for example, was to move social workers away from a focus on the family.

Perhaps even more important, the dichotomization of social work between a psychological and a social orientation and the lack of an integrative conceptual framework limited social workers' ability to integrate the family as a psychosocial system into practice.

The development of systems theory and the integrative power of the general systems framework have given social workers the potential tools needed to fashion practice theory which can take into account the immensely complex reality of person/in family/in situation. As Warren Brodey said fifteen years ago when he spoke of the need for systems theory, "There is a profound need for a new kind of discourse with the environment. . . . Today, the root process of the dialogue among family systems, individual systems, social systems, and the changing environment is ready to be studied in terms of the family" (1967:10). It is in the spirit of Brodey's challenge that we will present in chapters 4 and 5 the conceptual framework upon which our work is based.

But before turning to the conceptual framework, the social context of family-centered practice should be sketched. In chapter 2, the current status of the family will be explored, and in chapter 3 the policy context in which social worker and family meet will be discussed.

Chapter 2

The Family Today

THE HISTORICAL RELATIONSHIP between social work and the family has been one of ambivalence. Perhaps this unstable alliance has been a reflection of wider shifting social attitudes toward that vital social system which has frequently found itself in the middle of our psychosocial disputes. There is little accord in the social sciences or popular literature about where the family has been, where it is now, and what will happen to it in the future. Beyond these issues, there is even less harmony when we search for answers to deceptively simple questions about what the family *is* and what it *ought to be*.

How social workers choose to address these questions, the norms for family behavior which are favored and sanctioned, indeed the very way in which social workers define "family" profoundly influence social work practice. In this chapter we will summarize current views on the state of the family. We will also describe difficulties in arriving at a useful definition of the family, and thereafter set down our own definition, which recognizes two kinds of family. Last, we will examine changes in contemporary family life, and point out several problems accompanying these changes.

Current Views of the Family

Dramatic, unsettling questions and warnings about the family are heard from many quarters. A prominent family sociologist asks, "It is an endangered species?" (Sussman, 1978). A well-known social scientist suggests it is becoming obsolete (Bronfenbrenner, 1974). Others decry it as an entrenchment of male chauvinism. Young people experimenting with communal family organization and a host of others seem to be selecting increasingly some model other than the traditional nuclear family consisting of a man and woman joined by marriage and their offspring for the performing of accepted family functions and the fulfillment of psychological and interpersonal needs for sharing and intimacy.

It has been popular for some time to talk of family breakdown and disintegration, and to portray the nuclear family as small, fragile, weakening if not dying—certainly no longer a viable social system. Such arguments are generally supported with studies which demonstrate that the basic family structure has shifted from extended to nuclear, that many traditional family functions such as education and protection of the young have been inherited by large, bureaucratic institutions, or that the family is not a strong enough unit to perform adequately its remaining accepted functions. Further, it has been largely assumed that industrialization and urbanization have stripped the family of its economic self-sufficiency and pushed many families into more transient, unstable patterns of living. And, of course, perhaps the greatest source of alarm is the continuously rising divorce rate. Although various interpretations are made concerning the escalation in divorce, and although the majority of those who divorce do indeed remarry, it has been increasingly questioned whether the modern nuclear family is meeting the goals of happiness and fulfillment for many adults.

Demos (1975) argues that family life since colonial times has become more isolated and disconnected from the life of the larger community, sex roles have become diffuse, and family relationships have become intensified and problematic. Others have described the family as at least anachronistic if not actually harmful in relation to its individual members. Birdwhistell (1970), for example, sees the traditional nuclear family as an impossibly overloaded and guilt-creating social unit, a short-lived, self-destructive, isolated system whose goals of meeting adult affectional and interpersonal needs are unattainable. He warns that "the self-centered husband-wife, parent-child unit, so idealized in Western European and American society today, may be not only a novel way of organizing familial functioning, but it may also be a temporary and ultimately nonviable social form" (1970:195).

A more positive view is offered by historian Carl Degler (1980). While he argues that the central values of the modern family collide head on with both those espoused by the women's movement and those central to the individualistic orientation of modern society, he also suggests that the family is, on the other hand, in its very denial of individualism, a source of strength and appeal which is "the best known alternative to the individualism, competitiveness, and egoism that infuse the modern industrial world" (1980). This view echoes Lasch's now-familiar concept of the family as a "haven in a heartless world" (1977).

Further, research has increasingly exposed myths, misconceptions, and stereotypes about the family of a century ago to which the family of today is contrasted. Goode (1963), who challenges prevailing nostalgic views of the way families used to be, suggests, for example, that the family in America has always been nuclear in its basic composition and was never either an important economic unit or economically self-sufficient. Nor did couples live harmoniously "till death do us part." Writing about the classical family down on grandma's farm, Goode says: "True enough, divorce was rare, but we have no evidence that families were generally happy. Indeed, we find, as in so many other pictures of the glowing past, that each past generation of people writes of a period *still* more remote, *their* grandparents' generation, when things were much better" (1963:6–7).

In fact, the authors of the recently published replication of the Lynds' famous study of Middletown (1929), fifty years after the original work was done, claim that the view that the family is declining is a sociological myth which serves a variety of purposes. On the contrary, they write:

> This volume has shown no appreciable decline in the Middletown family during the past 50 years. Insofar as changes in the institution can be measured, they seem to reflect a strengthening of the institutional form and increased satisfaction for participants. [Caplow et al., 1982:329]

Finally, it has been noted that much of the research and most of the pronouncements about the state and the future of "the family" have primarily focused on the white, middle-class family. The limitations of this view of the American family are being challenged in a growing body of literature that identifies the strengths of other family forms which also exist in our society and which have been instruments for adaptation and survival among oppressed minorities (Billingsley, 1968; Stack, 1974; Hill, 1971; McAdoo, 1981).

In reviewing these varied views of the family, it is difficult to know whether we should mourn the loss of a trusted, faithful friend, take comfort in discovering that our friend has been idealized and that perhaps some of its accepted virtues are suspect, reject the old friend altogether in favor of someone new and different, or recognize that despite troubles and trials, it is tough, adapting, and surviving.

Defining the Family

From the above sampler we can see there is wide divergence of opinion concerning the state and worth of the American family. There is even less consensus on what we mean or should mean when we talk about "the family." Yet how the family is defined and conceptualized is crucial to what practice models and social policies are stimulated and endorsed, and for what families social benefits are developed. Even more basically, our definitions influence who is considered "normal" and who is labeled deviant, and what goals or standards we exact or changes we seek for those families who come to the attention of the social welfare network.

Turning to the social sciences for assistance in defining and describing the family compounds the confusion rather than resolving it, as there is little unanimity among students of the family about what constitutes the family itself, that is, who is in it and what makes it different from other forms of human organization. It is tempting to beg the question here, to accept the confusion as a given, to conclude that an attempt to define the family would be presumptuous given the lack of agreement and the multitude of variables to consider. Yet such a stance leaves us uncomfortable.

How we understand and approach families who come for help with their inner-family or environmental relationships will be sharply influenced by our views of families. We all have notions about what we think families are and what we want them to become, as well as what we think they should want for themselves. Whether we acknowledge it or not, our perspectives and our goals for intervention are surely expressions of prevailing social norms, our own successful and painful family experiences, our ethnic and ethnocentric values, and our affectional experiences and sexual preferences. And while we need to understand that *all* families experience tension, problems, crises, and setbacks, and that family functioning should not be measured against some idealized image of how families ought to function, we need nevertheless some conceptual framework for defining families and for assessing family functioning.

PROBLEMS IN DELINEATING FAMILY BOUNDARIES

In exploring definitions any number of questions arise, only a few of which can be raised here. How do we decide what constitutes a family's boundaries? Are they determined by biological and legal relatedness? If so, who should be included? Those in the immediate household? Everyone perched on the family tree? Those, living or dead, whose psychological legacy is profoundly felt? If biological relatedness is crucial, how do we deal with foster and adoptive relationships, or other relationships of affiliation and affinity?

Is an unmarried and committed couple a family? A single parent and her or his children? Is a divorced father who doesn't support and rarely visits a part of the family?

If we look beyond biological and legal conceptions to consider other kinds of households whose members share physical space and a variety of functions, and may also share affectional and sexual relationships, still further questions emerge. What degree of continuity and what kind of commitment is necessary before a household should be considered a family? Is a childless married couple a family? Are the long-time members of a foster home for retarded adults a family? The members of a college fraternity?

While some family scholars challenge easy answers to such questions, others seem certain about what constitutes a family. In a widely used family sociology text, for example, the authors list certain characteristics which are common to the human family in all times and all places and differentiate the family from other social groups. The family is defined as "a group of persons united by ties of marriage, blood, or adoption; constituting a single household; interacting and communicating with each other in their respective social roles of husband and wife, mother and father, son and daughter, brother and sister; and creating and maintaining a common culture" (Burgess, Locke, and Thomas, 1971:6). The definition is further extended to include the families of orientation and procreation and may have different configurations such as conjugal, nuclear, and extended.

PROBLEMS IN EXISTING DEFINITIONS OF FAMILY

One can select from among several different approaches in defining the family, some less exclusive than others, though all probably failing to encompass adequately the rich pluralism of racial, cultural, and ethnic diversity and the wide variety of lifestyle choices which differentiate American families. More traditional social science definitions tend to be structural in nature and, like that of Burgess cited earlier, generally stipulate legal, conjugal, and consanguine relationships. One of the difficulties raised by structural definitions is how to draw the boundaries. In some families, for example, the identity of the biological father may not even be known or that of a deserting mother suppressed and secreted. Are these misty but psychologically significant figures part of the family? Many other couples have birthed and raised children in a common household without benefit of marriage, often because divorce from a previous partner has been too expensive or difficult to obtain.

Further, in defining the family structurally, are we considering the immediate nuclear family structure or does our family definition include kinship systems and extended families? If the latter, whose definitions of "kin" shall prevail? For example, do we include the long-house culture of certain American Indians or the fictive kin systems of migrating blacks? Rice (in press) points out that structural definitions tend to exclude various groupings of people who define themselves as families and who in fact organize and perform as families.

Watts and Skidmore (1978) argue that a distinction should be made between household and family, and that "household" should be used as the major criterion for classification. Mary Richmond (1930), in fact, took this position when she defined a family as "all who share a common table." Giele believes that "such a change in definition accords with the greater potential crossover and interpenetration of family and nonfamily boundaries that characterize modern society" (1979:280).

But the household view also has its contradictions. For example, the children of an employed single mother may be boarded by her sister on a fulltime basis, or a rejected and troubled teenage boy may be ensconced in a state training school. A father's work may take him abroad for months at a time. The father in a divorce situation may have custody of the oldest boy while the mother is raising the younger children. Or an aging parent may have recently left the household for nursing home placement. Are these persons part of the family and thus the legitimate concern of the family practitioner?

On the other hand, supposing that the household definition is utilized, what are its outer limits? When does sharing a common table cease to be a family matter? A fraternity house, or even a boarding house, comes to mind. Clearly, simply "sharing a table" is insufficiently inclusive in some cases and too inclusive in others.

In another definitional approach common in sociology, namely the "functional" approach, the family is conceptualized in terms of the functions it performs, for itself, for its individual members, and for the larger society. Most contemporary conceptions include such functions as rearing children, meeting affectional needs of adults, and transmitting the values of larger society. Functional definitions lead to yet another set of difficulties, however, since there is little social agreement concerning what functions families actually do, can, or ought to carry out. Debates in this area are heard over such issues as sex education, the discipline and care of children, and the care of the aged, sick, and handicapped. While most seem to agree that neither education nor economic needs can be met solely by families, unresolved questions surround the issue of responsibility as more and more functions formerly assigned to the family appear to be absorbed by social and governmental institutions, or people are afraid they will be, or government is afraid *it* will be depended on too much (Moroney, 1976).

Clearly the definitional issues are extraordinarily complex and the questions raised far outstrip our capacities for discovering answers. At one extreme, accepting more traditional definitions of the nuclear family, which generally combine the attributes of legally sanctioned marriage, progeny, and shared living space, we risk excluding from our focus and labeling as deviant or at least divergent a large number, if not the majority, of American families.

On the other hand, if we apply no restrictions in our definition, the concept of "familiness" becomes meaningless. What differentiates a family? Does it depend on the intensity of emotional commitment, the amount and quality of interaction and involvement, the legality of the relationship, the distribution of function and role, the degree of economic sharing, of sexual union? How do we measure these amorphous and elusive qualities? John Speigel, the noted psychiatrist, found in his search for a definition of the family that "families exhibited the most astonishing variety in their structure and function" (1971:144). On the basis of regional, ethnic, and social class differences he concluded, as have many other theorists from other disciplines, that it is impossible to study the family without referring to the surrounding social and cultural contexts.

IMPORTANCE OF AN ACCURATE DEFINITION

This definitional dilemma has emerged as one of the most troublesome conceptual tasks in thinking about families and in planning this book. How the family is defined affects every aspect of practice. First, how we define family membership determines whom we include within the parameters of the case. For example, consider the case of a middle-aged, single woman who is hospitalized for breast cancer. She has no living close biological family. She may be seen by the medical social worker, who has never been in the room during visiting hours, as an isolated person without family. It may happen, however, that this woman is deeply involved with an extended friendship family that has existed for twenty-five years. It is obviously only within the context of that "family" that this woman can be understood and appropriately helped.

Secondly, family definitions tend to establish practice norms and directions. If social work nurtures an ideal conception of the family, those who fail to fit its norms may be considered divergent or deviant, and consequently, encouraged, regardless of their own values, to achieve a more socially acceptable adaptation in family living.

It is our view that social work traditionally has sought to include rather than exclude, to reach out rather than to close in, and to extend our accessibility to all who might benefit. There has also been an increasing effort in recent times to value and respect a rich variety of "difference" in the ways people guide their lives, and indeed to respect the differences in our own personal and professional lives since we, too, exist in families.

Thus, while we recognize that social workers cannot do away with norms and standards and will need to construct some hypotheses or guidelines about what is functional and what is not in family life, we search for definitions of family which, like Mary Richmond's, encourage a pluralistic perspective.

What emerges are two major categories of families, one of which is clearly biologically rooted and the other of which may or may not be built on legal marriage or biological parenting.

DEFINITION OF THE FAMILY OF ORIGIN

The first kind of family is the family of origin, that blood family into which one is born. Included in this conception is not only that nuclear or extended family which is seen as the primary matrix in which most of us are shaped, but also the family of history. Powerful prescriptions which shape the identities and behaviors of individual family members, which may be functional or dysfunctional for physical health and psychological well-being, are handed down over the generations.

To explain further, by family of origin we mean that family of blood ties, both vertical (multigenerational) and horizontal (kinship), living or dead, geographically close or distant, known or unknown, accessible or inaccessible, but always in some way psychologically relevant. Also included in the family of origin are adopted members and fictive kin, people who, although not related by blood, are considered and have functioned as part of a family.

DEFINITION OF THE FAMILY AS THE INTIMATE ENVIRONMENT

To borrow Arlene Skolnik's graceful and vivid expression, the "intimate environment" describes a second kind of family, that current family constellation in which people have chosen to live. Such a family group in our context consists of two or more people who have made a commitment to share living space, have developed close emotional ties, and share a variety of family roles and functions. This family may consist of a middle-aged married couple whose children are reared; two elderly sisters, one a widow and the other a spinster, who share an apartment in a retirement community; a group of biologically related and unrelated adults and children who have formed a group or communal family in which a range of commitments exist and in which instrumental and expressive roles are shared.

We are adopting a phenomenological stance in saying that a family becomes a family when two or more individuals have decided they are a family, that in the intimate, here-and-now environment in which they gather, there is a sharing of emotional needs for closeness, of living space which is deemed "home," and of those roles and tasks necessary for meeting the biological, social, and psychological requirements of the individuals involved.

We do not limit our definition to those who would be given recognition by a court of law but rather, like Feldman (1979), would also include those without any legal sanction who have strong commitments to each other and who behave in a conjugal or consanguine fashion. We have found this functional definition useful in guiding our thinking and our practice.

Thus, all of us have at least one family and most of us have two families to understand and assimilate: the family of origin and the current intimate family network. Some of us have three or more. Consider, for example, the case of many adopted individuals who, now raising children of their own and affectionately and permanently psychologically linked with their adoptive parents and *their* families of origin, may be searching for their own biological families in an effort to complete and integrate their complex family identities.

In sum, while we risk a lack of clarity and scientific predictability about the nature of families, we opt for an open, flexible conception of the family out of concern that more narrow definitions tend to carry subtle and not-so-subtle implications about deviance and pathology. We do not believe there is sufficient knowledge to take stances which suggest that the traditional American nuclear family form is the only viable and morally supportable family form. Indeed, future generations may discover that many of the emerging family forms are highly functional adaptations, *solutions* to problems in our changing and complex environment rather than problems in and of themselves.

The Family and Society

The family is in the often unenviable position of middle management. On the one hand it must meet the demands of the larger society, carrying out its policies and transmitting its social and economic expectations, values, and norms for behavior; on the other hand it must tend to the needs, performance, and morale of its individual members. The requirements from above and below are not always easy to decipher, nor are they always congruent. From yet another perspective, the mediator itself has needs and aspirations, and ways of pursuing them, which may conflict with those between whom it seeks to mediate.

Whether or not the American family is fragile or unworkable, perhaps even in danger of extinction, most observers agree that both the family itself and the social, economic, and cultural contexts in which it is immersed are experiencing major changes. Sociologists, in studying family life and family change, have traditionally viewed the family as a dependent variable, vulnerable to powerful societal forces which impinge on the very shape and form of the family and which shift and erode family functions. In our somewhat different view, the exchanges among individuals, families, and their social environments are reciprocal and dynamic, and the three forces interact in such complex ways that the usual analytical tools at our disposal often prove inadequate in helping us gain a holistic view. The following pages summarize some of these changing patterns in society, in families, and in individual behavior, without attempting to determine what is cause and what is effect. Rather the effort is to sketch broadly what appear to be some of the major patterns in a constantly changing kaleidoscope.

CHANGING FAMILY FUNCTIONS

In their examination of the state of the American family, Kenneth Keniston and the Carnegie Council on Children begin with these words:

> American parents today are worried and uncertain about how to bring up their children. They feel unclear about the proper balance between permissiveness and firmness. They fear they are neglecting their children, yet sometimes resent the demands their children make. Americans wonder whether they are doing a good job as parents, yet are unable to seek expert advice. And many prospective parents wonder whether they ought to have children at all. [1977:3]

These worries and discomforts undoubtedly reflect deep changes in family life and society, but in large measure they also may be a reflection of the way we react to and assign responsibility for such changes, and, where changes are perceived as having negative impacts on families and children, how we propose to deal with the effects on family life. Keniston believes that our reactions (which usually take the path of "blaming the victim") are based on outmoded sets of views and myths about how families work.

Many family analysts have described the weakening, shrinking position of the family in performing a number of its traditionally ascribed functions. While some would argue that in economic matters or in a variety of parenting and social roles the family has never been as self-sufficient as we would like romantically to assume, certainly the family has become increasingly dependent on large, complex institutions for meeting many of its basic needs. Generally, the loss or diminution of what are viewed as traditional family functions is attributed to family response to industrialization and its by-products, urbanization and specialization. As work has taken people out of the home and away from the farm, the community and its formally organized institutions have assumed such functions as protection of its citizens, education of its children, and increasing responsibility for the care of the sick and aged. Moral and religious instruction has been largely relegated to external institutions and even recreation and entertainment have become more organized and formalized as family games and outings have been replaced to a large extent with a variety of spectator sports and team competitions. Television, of course, has assumed a new, and to many an alarming, role in family life, affecting the family's recreational activities, the transmission of culture, and the relationships between adults and between parents and children; this "handy but uncontrollable electronic baby sitter" plays an increasing role in how families spend their time and how children are raised (Keniston, 1977:7).

If the family no longer directly and solely performs many of these functions, it is at least expected to mediate between those often highly specialized systems which have emerged to meet human needs for socialization and survival, and its own members. As mediator, the family should at the very least have the power to advocate, bargain and negotiate for services and supplies on its own behalf, and have as well a working knowledge about how and where such supplies may be obtained. The family must be particularly wise and educated enough to sort out from a deluge of conflicting social and cultural expectations what it should teach its young: what values it should instill, what goals they are to seek, how they are to act, and who they should become. A family needs the expertise of a budget director and the skills of a certified public accountant to determine, from among the seductive exhortations to buy the beautifully displayed wares around them, what it needs, what can be postponed, and what can be afforded. Each parent must be developmentally sophisticated and astute at preventing emotional distress, diagnosing a variety of often masked and confusing "symptoms," and healing psychological wounds. And of course it must, in the face of these challenges, maintain the highest patience, understanding, and integrity at all times!

CHANGING ROLES OF WOMEN

Perhaps the most dramatic and frequently cited social metamorphosis concerns women. Women are altering the way they see themselves and the directions which they choose in life, alterations which may deeply affect the ways in which women participate in family life. Nowhere is this more clearly documented than in the world of work. Statistics demonstrate that participation of women in the labor force has increased dramatically—68 percent in the period from 1940 to 1973 (Price, 1977:22). By 1978, 50 percent of all women of working age were in the labor force (Dept. of Health and Human Services, 1980:129). Of the women who work, an increasing number are mothers, and of that group, the most rapid increase in recent years has been in the number of working mothers with children under the age of six (National Research Council, 1976:2). In 1976, 37 percent of all married women with children under six were in the labor force, a percentage three times higher than that in 1948 (15). Some 52 percent of married women with children within the ages of six and seventeen were working or looking for work in March, 1975, twice the percentage of thirty years ago. Moreover, this data applies only to women who had husbands in the home. The figures for those women who were single parents are much higher, "almost three-quarters (72%) for those with children ages six to seventeen and well over one-half (56%) for mothers of children under six" (19). We can anticipate that participation of women in the labor force will contine to expand.

Women of today leave the home to work, some to pursue psychologically and financially rewarding careers, some to obtain more of the material artifacts desired to complement and enrich the basic necessities of family living, and still others to meet minimum survival needs for themselves and their families. Other women leave the home, however, to pursue nonpaying interests and activities, in part because the traditional roles of mother and homemaker may not completely satisfy their needs for intellectual and social stimulation. Many universities, for example, are developing continuing education and advocacy programs for the older, so-called nontraditional female student, a student who appears to be increasingly visible among the college population. The proportion of women of college age attending college has steadily increased since the mid-sixties, while the population of men of college age attending college has decreased, a trend leading to the expectation that by the early 1980s the same proportion of women as men between the ages of twenty-five and twenty-nine will have a college degree (Rice, 1977:27). A number of factors seem to be converging to affect changing roles profoundly for both sexes and thus the family itself. These factors include the drive for egalitarianism in employment and education spurred by the feminist movement, technological advances which may free women from some housework demands, changing needs in the labor market, more effective birth control measures, and the increased demands on family income produced by spiraling inflation.

No one can be certain how the dust will settle after the resolution of what many see as a prolonged battle, if not a full-fledged war between the sexes. A couple can no longer be clear about whose career takes precedence, or how family expressive and instrumental tasks should be distributed. These and other dilemmas raise particularly difficult questions when we turn to the issue of who will care for and rear the children.

In this heavily value-laden and emotionally charged arena, how social workers understand and react to these issues is crucial to how they work with families. The most "laissez-faire" among us have our own ideas of what families ought to be and how they should fulfill their functions. In the past, as we have mentioned, social workers have tended to try to help individuals and couples better fulfill widely accepted socially and culturally prescribed sex roles. We can no longer be so certain about what those roles are.

MARRIAGE, DIVORCE, AND REMARRIAGE

Several social trends have converged to cause some commentators concern about the future of the institutions of marriage and the family. For example, marriage rates appear to be slowing. The age at first marriage is increasing for both men and women, and the number of men and women in the younger age ranges (twenty to twenty-four and twenty-five to thirty-four) who have never married has increased significantly (Rice 1977:23). It is not clear how these trends should be interpreted. It could indeed portend that marriage may be becoming less preferred to other lifestyles; or it could simply mean that young people, for a variety of reasons, may be delaying a commitment to marriage, since it is beginning to appear that most of these young people do eventually marry. Perhaps it is not the case that people are avoiding marriage but rather that they are more cautious in the process of mate selection.

At the same time that marriage rates are slowing, the divorce rate is booming. In the past hundred years, 1875 to 1975, there has been a sixteen-fold increase in the divorce rate, while the number of children of divorced families has increased some 700 percent since 1900 (Keniston, 1977:4). By 1971, the divorce rate in the U.S. was the highest among populous nations throughout the world (Rice, 1977:27).

About one out of every three marriages culminates in divorce these days. Furthermore, for the last thirty years, couples with children have been more likely to divorce than childless couples; and while divorced persons marry at rates even higher than single persons, the remarriage rates do not keep pace with those of divorce (National Research Council, 1976:19). For every ten persons in 1980 who were in an intact marriage, there was one person who was divorced and had not remarried (Bureau of the Census, 1981:2). It is now estimated that four out of every ten children born in the 1970s will spend part of their childhood in a one-parent family, usually with their mother as head of the household (Keniston, 1977:4).

These statistics allow us only a glimmer of insight in speculating about the ramifications of divorce and separation within family life. While divorce can have many positive outcomes for both adults and children who are caught in unhappy and stressful situations, and indeed may often be the best alternative available, the economic and role strains of single parenthood, the hurtful separations and emotional losses, the complex financial difficulties, and the often tense step-relationships encountered in blended families are problematic for many.

BIRTH CONTROL, FERTILITY, AND CHILDBIRTH

Concomitant with the slowing of marriage rates are trends which indicate that the rate of childbirth is decreasing. "In 1975 the number of births per

1,000 population was only 76 percent as high as ten years earlier (1965) and only 49 percent as high as the rate in 1910" (Beck and Jones, 1973:12). Several factors may be significant here. It is possible that, with the combination of an increase in knowledge about and availability of birth control procedures, and the liberalization of abortion laws, men and women now have more options in controlling their own fertility. Between 1970 and 1974 there were almost five times the number of legal abortions reported during the period before the liberalization of abortion laws. This trend may slow as recent Congressional action, prohibiting Medicaid funds being used for abortions by choice, constricts the availability of legal abortion for poor women.

We can anticipate that family size may decline even farther ("the average household has shrunk in size from five persons in 1910 to less than three persons in 1975. . . ." Beck and Jones, 1973:12) as both married and unmarried people have more freedom of choice concerning assumption of the parenting role.

While childbirth in general has been decreasing, "the proportion of first births to women who have no legal marriage partners has almost doubled—from 5 percent in the late 1950s to 11 percent in 1971—and almost one-million of these mothers are setting up their own households with their babies every year" (Keniston, 1977:5). Contrary to popular myth, teenage childbearing has also leveled off, but the illegitimacy ratio—the proportion of illegitimate to legitimate births—has increased substantially in general and among the teenage population in particular. At the beginning of 1960, 15 percent of the births among teenage women were out of wedlock. By 1970 the proportion of illegitimate births had nearly doubled, causing widespread concern in both government and social welfare circles and generating a number of intervention efforts directed at preventing adolescent illegitimacy (Furstenberg, 1976:10). In 1978, 44 percent of births to teenagers were illegitimate (U.S. National Center for Health Statistics, 1978).

EXPANDING ELDERLY POPULATION

Another change with tremendous implications for family life and family-centered practice concerns the current and anticipated rise in the proportion of elderly in the population. In 1900 the percentage of people over sixty-five was 4.1; by the year 2000 the indication is it will be 11.7 and by the year 2050, 16.0. From an economic perspective the prediction is that there will be an increasing proportion of persons economically dependent on the family or the State. With the current alarm over the faltering Social Security system, futurists are particularly concerned about the shrinking ratio of earner to nonearner.

From a social and familial perspective a second issue of concern becomes that of caregiving. Who will provide care for an increasing proportion of very old, frail people? Changes in women's roles become most salient here. Moroney points out that the dependency ratio is changing, that is, the number of persons under fifteen or over sixty-five per 100 persons aged fifteen to sixty-four. Also, the number of women who are defined as potential caregivers for the elderly, namely nonworking women between the ages of forty-five and fifty-four, increased by only 46 percent between 1900 and 1976, while during the same period the elderly population increased by 158 percent (1980). It seems clear that a greater proportion of women are becoming more educated and opting for lifelong careers. It is less clear how and if the family can continue to care for its aging, dependent members to the extent it still does today, at least without a major shift in available social resources.

THE EXTENDED–NUCLEAR DEBATE

It has become a cliché to describe white American families as nuclear. These nuclear families, the by-products of industrialization and urbanization, are variously depicted as isolated and overburdened, or necessary and adaptive in a highly mobile, technological society. But we have had little useful knowledge of the actual extent and nature of kinship relationships in contemporary society. Beginning with Sussman's (1965) and Litwak's (1965) research, this assumption of nuclearity has been increasingly challenged; current thinking suggests that the dominant form of family structure may be a "modified extended family." Sussman describes this family as follows:

> The theoretical position assumed . . . is that there exists in modern industrial societies . . . an extended kin family system, highly integrated within a network of social relationships and mutual assistance, that operates along bilateral kin lines and vertically over several generations. [1965:63]

According to Moroney, the evidence indicates that families of all social classes have functioned in extended kin networks, offering mutual support including physical care, financial help, and of course advice and counsel. Litwak's and Sussman's early findings have been confirmed by more recent study. An account of a survey completed by Cantor in New York (cited by Moroney, 1980) and based on the experiences of elderly from all social classes and ethnic groups concludes that the majority of parents "see half their children at least once-a-week and two-thirds at least monthly. Intergenerational support includes assistance in carrying out chores of daily living; giving advice; intervening in a crisis . . . and giving of gifts and money" (Moroney, 1980:31). A national survey of the elderly by Harris called the nuclear stereotype to question, discovering that 81 percent of their sample of elderly had had contact with their children and 73 percent with their grandchildren within the previous week. Further, they found that the elderly give concrete help to both children and grandchildren. Findings indicated that 68 percent of the grandparents help out when someone is ill and 45 percent with financial aid (Harris, 1975:73–74).

If we have tended to think of white families as nuclear, we have at the same time assumed that black families more often tend to be extended in structure. Again, this extendedness has been variously seen as either tremendously adaptive, or retarding the social and economic progress of the black population. Stack (1974), for example, suggested that the highly intertwined, mutually supportive extended networks in the black urban ghetto she studied, while making survival in a harsh and depriving environment possible, also tended to render it more difficult for particular nuclear families to get ahead. She concluded that those couples who left the ghetto because of the demands on them for sharing their resources would of necessity become cut off from their extended networks. McAdoo (1978) challenged this conclusion. In her study of a black, middle-income group, she concluded that the families studied "did not have to avoid the reciprocal obligations of their extended kin-help network in order to realize their own mobility goals" (775). McAdoo suggests that extended help patterns are culturally rather than solely economically based.

We must reexamine also the assumption that our ancestors lived as extended families. Bane (1976), entering the extended-nuclear controversy, disputes many nostalgic notions about the family of yesterday. Her research indicates, contrary to conventional wisdom, that the modern family is *more* likely than the eighteenth century family to have grandparents or other relatives in the home, and questions the notion that families have shifted from extended to nuclear in basic form. She believes that today's working mother probably spends at least as much time with her children as did the often overburdened homemaker of the past. She also questions the assumption that greater family transience and mobility today are destroying family and community continuity, since she has discovered that eighteenth and nineteenth century households showed a higher rate of mobility than households of the 1970s.

THE CHANGING AMERICAN HOUSEHOLD

What these and many other social indicators say about the changing quality of family life, if not the demise of marriage and family as we have known it in the past, is open to broad speculation and value-laden interpretations. What does seem apparent is that something is happening to the American household. Its growing diversity is demonstrated in table 2–1, compiled by sociologist James Ramey and based on statistics from the Bureau of Labor.

TABLE 2-1 Distribution of Adult Americans by Type of Household

Household Type	% of Households
Heading single-parent families	16
Other single, separated, divorced, or widowed	21
Living in child-free or post-childrearing marriages	23
Living in extended families	6
Living in experimental families or cohabiting	4
Living in dual-breadwinner nuclear families	16
Living in no-wage-earner nuclear families	1
Living in single-breadwinner nuclear families	13

SOURCE: James Ramey, *Marriage and Family Review* I:1 (Jan./Feb. 1978), p. 1. Copyright © by The Haworth Press, Inc., New York. All rights reserved.

It is startling to comprehend that the traditional nuclear family (consisting of husband as breadwinner, wife as homemaker, and offspring, and living in a residence apart from other relatives) accounts for only 13 percent of all American households! It begins to appear that the nuclear family itself might be labeled "divergent" or "alternate." Interestingly, child-free households account for the largest percentage, a statistic attributed to the "small-size family norm, zero population growth, values and persistence of the pattern that after children are launched into college, jobs or marriage they establish households independent of the family in which they were reared" (Sussman, 1978:34).

Single-parent families, most of them headed by women, account for 16 percent of all households, reflecting a dramatic rise. Between 1970 and 1975 there was a 45 percent increase in the number of children living with their single-parent mother (Rice, 1977:28-29). By 1980, 20 percent of all children under eighteen lived in one-parent families (Bureau of Census, 1981:3). Further, between 10 percent and 15 percent of all households in 1979 were stepfamilies (Dept. of Health and Human Services, 1980:55).

A growing understanding of these variations and of their particular strengths and potential stresses should inform our practice as we adapt our family focus to different kinds of families.

These dramatic changes in the form of the American family and the contemporary problems of family violence, delinquency, adolescent suicide, and alcohol and substance abuse provoke endless debates about the threatened survival of the family as a social system, its ability to perform, its traditionally accepted functions, and in fact what those functions are or should be. Questions emerge concerning what kinds of families are workable in today's complex world.

It has not been our purpose here to take a stand on the state of the family, although we are optimistic about its vitality, durability, and adaptability. Rather we have summarized some of the more salient trends and issues which affect the ways in which families are understood as well as the directions which need to be considered for family policy and family-centered practice. The picture is complex and confusing but it provides an important part of the context within which the family-centered practitioner functions.

Chapter 3

The Family Policy Context of Practice

THE PURPOSE OF THESE introductory chapters is to portray the overall context within which the social worker serves families. Now that we have described the historical context of family practice and presented a brief overview of the changing family today, we will sketch the social policy framework as it affects work with families.

Social policies and the programs that are expressions of these policies determine social work practice to a considerable extent, whether or not the social worker is aware of their pervasive effects. They establish the parameters of practice, announce the social goals of programs and activities, and draw the boundaries that may expand or curtail the worker's ability to develop and deliver services.

There will be no attempt in the following pages to present a comprehensive description of the content of social policy in the many different fields of practice where families are served. Rather, we will raise the issues and attempt to heighten the reader's sensitivity to the potential impact of policy and program in their daily work and in the lives of their clients. We will particularly focus on the very confusing and contentious area of family policy.

Parameters of Social and Family Policy

Family policy, which some would prefer not to define as a separate area, exists within the broader area of social policy, and social policy itself can hardly be separated from economic policy and from the political arena which gives birth to public policy.

For example, concerning the relationship between social and economic policy, Rein (1977) suggests that the traditional distinctions made between *social* policy, which he indicates is concerned with *re*distribution and increasing economic equality or at least relieving poverty, and *economic* policy, which is concerned with distribution and output, are unsatisfactory. In the view of this and other policy analysts, social and economic policies are so tightly interwoven, one cannot consider one without the other.

In fact, considering the complex relationship between economic forces and social or family policies, some analysts believe that policies which are developed ostensibly to promote the well-being of families have implicit economic or labor market purposes. For example, it has been suggested that AFDC and other income maintenance programs have the effect, if not the overt intention, of regulating and institutionalizing a permanent underclass of cheap labor (Piven and Cloward, 1971).

Neither can social policy or family policy be separated from the political contexts in which they are immersed. Many well-intentioned policies may be economically possible and socially desirable, but not politically feasible. For example, Nixon's Family Assistance Plan (FAP), which would have mandated national minimum welfare payments and doubled the existing number of welfare recipients, and which for the first time would have supplemented the income of intact families of underemployed adults, was widely hailed as a progressive beginning to resolving perplexing welfare issues. Its eventual scuttling has been attributed to many factors. Partly the blame may be laid at the door of Nixon's "ideological intransigence and political neglect"; but the fuller explanation, according to Hoffman and Marmor, is "rooted both in the peculiar political machinery by which this nation handles issues of poverty and welfare and in the strange character of the American public's concern for poor people and disdain for welfare recipients" (1976:12–13). These analysts suggest that FAP, which called for bigger, more expensive government involvement in families, was justifiable within the conservative position, in spite of Nixon's desire to minimize the government's "interference" with family autonomy, because its programs could be constructed and administered with fewer services and fewer social workers. However, despite support from both the right and the left, factors that helped spell FAP's downfall in 1971 included divisive Congressional rhetoric and policy disaggregation, that is, Congressional jurisdictional or turf disputes over both various parts and the whole of FAP, all of which led to increasing political warfare, confusion, and, in the end, defeat.

The fate of the famous, or more accurately, infamous Moynihan Report (1965), a proposal for national action on behalf of the black family, was sealed by similar political infighting. It was seen by many as a "bold synthesis" of remedies for economic, social, and family variables which were negatively affecting families and children and for which Moynihan proposed income maintenance policies to strengthen family structure; nevertheless, it evolved into a political disaster, torn apart by charges and countercharges of racism (Rainwater and Yancey, 1967). Again, the implication that the problems lay within the structure of the black family, as well as poor choices of political timing, unsuccessful tradeoffs, and failure of strategies for persuasion, are some of the political factors which are thought to have helped destroy the proposal.

Both FAP and the Moynihan Report illustrate dramatically the sensitivity of social policy to the political process, and the destruction (when political, economic, social, and value goals are in conflict) of seemingly useful efforts.

Values as Determining Factors in Public Policy

Social policies are, perhaps above all, concerned with choices among competing values (Rein, 1971). This maxim has come into bold relief recently, particularly in respect to the family. The diversity in this country of emotion-laden beliefs and values concerning all aspects of the family hinders political agreement on family policy, especially in an era of "issue" politics. Values—convictions concerning what is morally or culturally desirable—are of course implicit in both economics and politics, and must be taken into account in every level of analysis of policy-making.

Sometimes the use of a single catchword for conflicting values is confusing, as in the case of those groups of varying political persuasion who hold strikingly different value positions, yet have been proclaiming themselves uniformly "pro" family. On the more conservative end of the continuum, a variety of interest groups have typically attacked legislation on such issues as no-fault divorce, women's rights, and abortion. Divorce, for example, is viewed by some as adulterous, immoral, or at the least neurotic, and studies which purport to show that children are damaged in one-parent families are drawn upon to sustain the argument that such families should be discouraged as a viable form. Such proposals can be accomplished to some extent by withholding income or services to families who do not meet certain kinds of structurally defined norms. On the other end of the continuum, those who tend to define themselves as liberals, humanists, or feminists may see divorce and other family changes as healthy or necessary adaptations to the exigencies of post-industrial society and to rising expectations for personal fulfillment. Separation or divorce, for example, may be seen as an opportunity for betterment or as a strong, independent choice which may in the end lead to stronger families and better care for children. Consequently, legislation which supports a variety of family forms may be endorsed.

There is reason to believe that the "pro-family" value position of the 1960s, occupied by liberals such as Moynihan, Glazer, and others who were promoting national antipoverty action on behalf of families, has been co-opted by the New Right, the Right to Life groups, the Anita Bryants, and the Moral Majority of the 1970s and 1980s.

This current "pro-family" loose coalition of conservative interests in general takes the position that the best family policy is no policy at all, that government should stay out of family life. It is paradoxical, and damaging to the hopes of their liberal counterparts, that some well-intentioned legislative efforts on behalf of families have had effects opposite to those intended. Some analysts from among those identified as liberal, most notably Nathan Glazer (1971), have lately become concerned that some of our social policies have been eroding such traditional institutions as the family, and have reluctantly taken a more cautious position of the role of government vis-à-vis the family. These value conflicts over the family and family policy were dramatically enacted on the stage of the 1980 White House Conference on Families.

Finally, in our attempt to delineate the parameters and describe the context of social policy, we have discovered that the boundaries are not clear. Economic policies clearly have major social implications; labor policies may masquerade as social policies; political processes and value conflicts shape or paralyze policy goals. With these intricacies in mind, we turn to the definitions and goals of family policy.

DEFINITIONS AND GOALS OF FAMILY POLICY

In attempting to define family policy we are, of course, faced with the same intricacies. It is difficult to imagine a national policy position, at least in the domestic arena, which would not have some effect on the family. How broadly, then, do we draw the boundaries around family policy? There are two major ways. First, family policy may be described as consisting of that body of legislation, directives, and programs which are designed to achieve explicit, agreed-upon goals concerning the family. Even this narrow definition includes a wide range of public initiatives in such varied areas as family planning, income maintenance, divorce and custody, adoption records, day care, and maternal and child health.

The more inclusive definition of family policy, the "family impact" definition, identifies family policy as surfacing in almost every area of governmental activity and as being embodied in the effects, or impact, that governmental activities have on the family. These effects are generally implicit rather than explicit, and may be a result of policy or program in areas as diverse as trade regulation, taxation, immigration, land acquisition, highway building, or energy. The Family Impact Seminars (1977) were developed to make the consequences, intended or unintended, of this implicit family policy more explicit, to make clear the impact on the family of various legislative and programmatic developments. These are not necessarily competing definitions, but these distinctions do become important in providing clarification when debates over national family policy surface.

And what are the goals of family policy? This question is yet another major area of disagreement and discussion among legislators and others who influence policy development. The foremost issue is whether policies should be characterized by preventive, developmental, and structural approaches or, with more limited scope, by a rehabilitative approach, problem-focused in emphasis and objective, and targeted to those in greatest need.

Social workers have tended to support the former view. Schorr (1979), for example, insists that the real challenge is to address those structural forces which *create* social problems, particularly in terms of supporting family needs against "unbridled economic forces."

For the most part their emphasis, to use Cloward and Piven's (1966) term, has long translated into the call for a "strategy to end poverty": attention to massive problems of unemployment, underemployment, and poor distribution of labor; an end to racial and other kinds of discrimination; and in general, an amelioration of those social and economic conditions which are widely assumed to produce social pathology and generations of welfare dependence. Social workers have further been in the front lines of those calling for some kind of universal income redistribution, usually in the form of family or children's allowances, or a guaranteed annual income plan. They seek as well an improved delivery of programs and services to the neighborhoods where they are needed—in Bertha Reynolds' (1934) words, to the "crossroads of life where ordinary traffic passes by." Kahn (1976), for example, has long advocated for a rational, planned, coordinated, neighborhood-based service delivery system characterized by visibility and accessibility, and constructed to meet a range of developmental needs and problems. He has envisioned such services as "social utilities," similar to fire protection or public education.

Those who emphasize preventive approaches point to the tremendous costs involved in the rehabilitation, repairing, or custodial caring of those who are the "fallout" or victims of inadequate and inequitable economic and social opportunities, policies, and programs. It is argued that initiatives designed to enhance the human condition will, in the long run, prove more effective and less expensive than costly rehabilitative programs and institutions.

One of the most important questions in considering the goals of social policy is this: Who will or should benefit from it? The preventive, developmental view tends to align itself with the notion of universality, that is, the idea that resources and services should be available to anyone who wants or needs them. Such a perspective generally calls for the elimination of narrow definitions of eligibility or elaborate means tests. The opponents of this view argue for programs favorable to the middle class, claiming that such programs are more palatable to the voting public and may eventually benefit the poor through a filtering-down process. To this argument the developmentalists object that when eligibility is broadened, the possibility exists that the proportion of scarce resources will be "creamed off" by the higher-income applicants. Still other voices suggest that, given limited resources, policies and programs must be selectively targeted toward those in most dire need.

In these days of cutting social programs to the bone, of concern about economic recession, inflation, and unemployment, and of a prevailing "safety net" philosophy in government, discussions of universal and preventive programs tend to be somewhat academic. We will comment on the current directions of family and social policy toward the end of this chapter.

The Family and the State

No matter how family policy is defined or specified, no matter what its goals, it rests on and is an expression of the family's relationship with the State. In exploring this relationship, once again we run head on into political, social, economic, and value issues. These issues are all reflected in the key question in considering State-family relationships, that is: To what extent should the State intervene in family life?

Robert Moroney (1976; 1980), who has researched this issue in England and the United States, suggests the following questions as a useful test of defensibility in government intervention:

1. Under what conditions is intervention appropriate?
2. For what purposes?
3. In which areas of family life?
4. What tasks are appropriate for the family to carry out? What should they be required to do?
5. What responsibilities should be shared by both family and government?

Moroney's central assumption is that "the structure of the Welfare State has been shaped by a number of beliefs concerning the responsibilities which families are expected to carry for the care of the socially dependent and a set of conditions under which this responsibility is to be shared or taken over by society" (1980:1).

While value or philosophical issues predominate when we define families, rarely is there total repudiation by any of the competing interests of this basic assumption of shared responsibility. However, there have been major differences and shifts over time regarding whose responsibility should be increased, under what circumstances and for what purposes, and regarding what proportion of responsibility family or State should carry. Moroney has attempted to demonstrate what sharing has actually meant in terms of specific policies and programs, by analyzing a particular set of activities and populations, and by examining the interactions between families and social welfare agencies. Some of his findings are of great interest. Using the handicapped as an example, he concludes that the State is actually benefiting from the tremendous amount of social care being provided for these individuals and that, in fact, families provide more social care than do organized health and social services. If families were to pull out, to refuse to care for their handicapped members, their action would lead to incalculable, in fact, devastating costs to the State. Further, a relatively small number of people are receiving a relatively large share of the services. Finally, he discovered that families are actually penalized when they care for their dependent members and rewarded when they stop caring.

Another issue at the heart of the relationship between family and State is the concern that State interference via its policies may indeed *shape* families. It is probably fair to say that most family policies do, in fact, tend to support particular kinds of families, and thus intentionally or unintentionally to promote or discourage family composition patterns, and to violate people's rights to select their own lifestyles. Familiar to most of us is the contention that "workfare" requirements and "man in the house" rules used in income maintenance policies have, in the past, contributed to family breakdown, forcing unemployed, discouraged husbands to desert their families.

Some are concerned that too much assistance to intact families will make it possible for, or indeed encourage, women to leave stressful and unsatisfactory marriages. In the last few years there have been a number of research efforts which explore the impact of higher AFDC benefits on family composition. Ross and Sawhill (1975) concluded that higher benefits have not so much led to family breakdown but rather made it possible for women to delay remarriage, while a study by Duncan and Morgan (University of Michigan, 1974) found a higher divorce rate in states with higher AFDC benefits. Bradbury (1977) suggests that to date the available research is flawed, and Giele concludes "there is only weak evidence that AFDC levels affect either separation or remarriage rates" (1979:292).

Related and currently hotly contested issues concern the provision of Medicaid funds for abortion and government funding for sex education or birth control, matters which also influence family formation and composition.

Certainly labor and manpower policies, and federal sanction and support for child-care arrangements can also significantly affect the potential for labor force participation on the part of married women and mothers, again influencing the role structure of the family. All of these issues tend to be responses to, but also forces in shaping, our portraits of the socially acceptable and desirable family.

Yet another extremely sensitive and complex issue concerns the right of the State to directly and specifically regulate intergenerational, marital, and parent–child relationships. This delicate and shifting balance of family–State interests is central in divorce and child custody law, in policies and stances on spouse abuse, on the protection of aging and dependent relatives, and of course in the treatment of child abuse and neglect.

In sum, the family–State relationship is a complex one. By sharing with families the responsibility for meeting social needs, the State may subvert family functions, destroy delicate and sustaining family connections, or control the form and style of family life. This concern bears on the crucial question of whether a national family policy is something to be desired.

A National Family Policy: Pros and Cons

If one opts for a definition of family policy as a rational, deliberate, coherent, explicit set of national principles which guides legislative action in relation to families, then most observers would probably conclude that no such policy exists. In fact, while many social commentators and scholars have called for a coherent national family policy, others have questioned whether such a goal is either socially desirable or politically feasible. Moynihan, illustrative of the "pro" position, decrees that "a nation without a conscious family policy leaves to chance and mischance an area of social reality of the utmost importance, which in consequence will be exposed to the untrammeled and frequently thoroughly undesirable impact of policies arising in other areas" (1968). The family, seen as the major and primary social service system, should be supported in a variety of ways, a view strongly endorsed in several recent national studies and reviews of family policy (Keniston, 1977; National Research Council, 1976; Shyne and Schraeder, 1978).

Many families, according to the National Research Council, face difficulties as a result of social and economic forces beyond their control. No amount of advice, exhortation, education or treatment will provide solutions for what are seen as larger, structural problems. This study and others have also described the increasing isolation of families from a variety of resources which have traditionally played essential roles in family life, the church, kinship systems, the neighborhood, and the community.

While government activity in correcting social and economic conditions devastating to family life is essential in the view of many analysts, there is also "a decidedly personal aspect to support systems which help parents raise children. Once basic provisions have been made to avoid calamity, more still is needed" (Rice, 1977:109). In addition to rehabilitation efforts or programs defined as meeting "residual" needs, parents need respite from child-rearing stresses, opportunities for social exchange and stimulation, and access to a wide variety of expertise in meeting their social, health, economic and other needs. It is less clear what role government can or should come to play in enhancing the ecological balance of family life.

Although social workers since the 1960s have generally supported the notion of a coherent, explicit national family policy, recent political and social directions have tended to call to question this position. Barbaro, as early as 1979, warned that "the United States cannot deal with an issue so emotionally charged as family life in a comprehensive manner and could not attempt to do so without violating civil liberties or discriminating against nonconventional families" (1979:455). Any comprehensive family policy is potentially an anathema in a free society, according to him, and may violate family autonomy or civil liberties. It is Barbaro's view that the nature of our political process, the struggle between competing interest groups and the requirement that action be based on some sort of consensus would mean that any national family policy, if it could indeed be formulated, would "encourage prescribed behavior for families. Families that comply with existing norms will be rewarded; nontraditional families and unmarried individuals are likely to be discriminated against" (1979:457).

Schorr (1979) believes we are unlikely to see a national family policy. He concludes that three major traditions militate against an explicit family policy: a tradition of individualism, a pervasive suspicion of government, and the idea that the ethnically diverse structure of our society and the nature of our political process, with its wide variety of competing interests, does not lend itself to broad areas of agreement. Schorr also contends that as a nation, we have been unwilling to meet the cost of expensive family policies which usually imply some kind of fairer distribution of national income.

The positions of both Barbaro and Schorr seem to have been validated, both in the immobilizing struggle between interest groups that marked every step of the White House Conference on Families and in the effort on the part of members of the New Right to utilize national family policy to regulate personal behavior and to control and shape family life, as reflected, for example, in the proposed Family Protection Act (S–1808 and HR–6028).

The current political climate has led social workers and social analysts who give primary emphasis to individual and family self-determination to retreat, at least temporarily, from the pursuit of a national family policy goal.

Individualism versus Familism in Policy and Program

We have reviewed the complexities inherent in defining social and family policy, and in translating policy into program. We have suggested that social and family policies must be understood in their economic, political, and value contexts, and considered in relation to their potential for enhancing or undermining the quality of family life. The threats to civil liberties implied in such initiatives as the proposed Family Protection Act (S–1808 and HR–6028) increase concern over the advisability of adopting a family focus in policy and program. However, a return to an individualistic perspective is also fraught with difficulties, as illustrated by the history of child welfare.

The field of child welfare has focused on a population of individuals—in this case children—rather than on the family, even though the child's welfare in many ways is basically inseparable from the welfare of its family. The field is an example of government's reluctance to be involved in family life. The current structure of services to family and children still reflects a hundred years of tradition which has divided families into parents and children, with parallel and often competitive agency structures to meet the needs of each. The child-saving and child-rescue movements of the nineteenth century gradually crystallized into a system of services which emphasized placement of children as a solution to a family's problems. In this situation as in others, when families experienced difficulty in caring for their members, the State tended to move in and take over completely, in loco parentis, rather than to enhance the family's ability to take care of itself. While there is certainly merit to the argument that children, like certain other groups with little power of their own, have needs which may conflict with those of their families, and thus that they require their own advocacy, rescue efforts by the State have rarely lived up to their promises.

In the last twenty years, for example, numerous studies have documented the failure of the foster care–child placement movement to meet the needs of many neglected, abandoned, or abused children, or to strengthen and reunite families (Fanshel and Shinn, 1978; Jenkins and Sauber, 1966; Jenkins, 1967). Clearly some children in jeopardy need to be removed from their own homes; and some children and some families may not be very "helpable," given the present state of our knowledge, skill, and resources. However, child placement has been used not only as a solution to child abuse and neglect but too often as a substitute for financial and social assistance to needy families.

Yet this nation has been peculiarly reluctant to support in any widespread institutional way day care or homemaker–home health aide programs. Day care has periodically received support when buttressed by welfare–workfare philosophy, but has rarely been seen by those with political power as a necessary service or entitlement for families, as it is in some European countries. Nixon's veto of the Comprehensive Child Care Plan in the early 1970s was a tremendous setback for the day care movement, and was at least to some extent based on the State's reluctance to "interfere" in family life. Probably for similar reasons, the use of homemaker–home health aides for maintaining families in crisis and meeting a variety of other family needs has never achieved its original promise, even though most studies agree that placement of children is more costly financially and emotionally. More recently homemaker–health aide programs have been seen as a positive vehicle for maintaining the elderly in their own or relatives' homes, and have benefited from increased public sanction and funding. Moreover, from the 1970s onward the government and the social work profession have begun to focus on reuniting children and parents through child welfare programs. This trend was reflected in the "permanency planning" movement and in a number of important legislative actions (Pike, 1977). The Indian Child Welfare Act of 1978 (P.L. 95–608), which has a number of provisions which give Indians more direct control over the fate of their children, was in part designed to halt the wholesale removal of "neglected" Indian children from their homes and to promote the stability and security of Indian tribes and families. The Child Abuse and Prevention Act of 1974 emphasized prevention, reunification, and rehabilitation of families, and with passage of the 1975 Social Services Amendments, it looked for a while as if a major federal initiative toward the strengthening of families and unifying services to children and to families was underway.

The provisions of the Adoption Assistance and Child Welfare Act of 1980 (P.L. 96–272) mandate that the bulk of child welfare appropriations, which heretofore have been used for foster care or employment-related day care, must be spent on preventive and reunification services for biological families. This law also sets standards for child welfare practice in those states that wish to participate in federal funding, not only in terms of how appropriations should be spent, but what must be done to insure certain safeguards for children and families. For example, case review and tracking systems are mandated in an attempt to interrupt planless and endless foster care.

While the child welfare field has been used illustratively, one can probably examine almost any other field of practice and note similar trends. Moroney (1980) points out that policies and programs are generally developed for specific individuals. Family members, depending on the area of practice, are seen as responsible for failures, as in the case of children's education or school behavior difficulties, as "necessary nuisances," as in the case of health and rehabilitation programs, or as "broken," in the case of female headed families. Giele (1979) describes a similar phenomenon when she writes that in the fields of health and mental health there has been a great deal of attention paid to the etiology of physical and mental illness and to the contribution of family structure and dynamics to these problems, but "there is an amazing lack of emphasis on policies and programs to give positive support to the family in achievement of (mental) health" (1979:122). In any case, policies and programs are developed on behalf of individuals, and the effects on families, whose sanction, support, and participation may be essential to the success of program or treatment, are often unknown.

Further, individual policies may contradict or even wipe out one another, or may operate to undermine or destroy families. Conversely, the family may equally undermine or destroy the service structure's best efforts to help an individual, if that help threatens some basic adaptation or homeostasis the family has achieved.

The Family Policy Dilemma

The dangers inherent in a social policy that places lopsided emphasis on either family or individual have placed us in a paradoxical situation. If we do support the notion of family policy, that is, the planning, packaging, and delivering of services with the family as the central unit of service and with the intention of enhancing family functioning (an idea congruent with our family-oriented conception of practice), then we run the risk that such policies and programs will shape family forms and mold family roles to the extent of interfering in areas where cultural diversity, individual choice, and free self-expression must be protected (an idea congruent with our definition of family). However, if we take the opposite position and support an individualistic focus in the social services, it is possible that unchecked threats to the family system will ultimately undermine its function and threaten essential human ties.

In working with families who are immobilized in paradoxical situations, a solution is frequently found through the process of reframing, of countering the paradox. Perhaps the solution to the family dilemma is the solution as well to the family policy dilemma: to reframe the definition of the family. In chapter 2 we suggested that the family should be defined according to household composition, levels and types of commitment, and the fulfillment of those functions generally conceded to be in the domain of families in contemporary society. This circular definition, by reason of its flexibility and reliance on self-determination and self-definition, can resolve the paradoxical situation by focusing not on specific family forms but on the importance of human connectedness and commitment. If the family is thus reframed, it is possible to develop a coherent national family policy without violating people's rights to choose their own life-styles.

The crucial importance of the redefinition of the family was clear to those who organized the White House Conference on Families, and clear also to conservative lobbies which moved to block the effort to reframe, successfully keeping the definitional issues off the agenda. It is a truism that the success or even the possibility of resolving the family policy dilemma through the "gentle art of reframing" (Watzlawick, Weakland, and Fisch, 1974) depends on the larger context. At this point, in a politically, socially, and economically conservative environment, such a redefinition of the family is not feasible, at least officially. The move to a more flexible view of the family has been preempted by the countermoves embodied in the Family Protection Act and in the formation by Reagan, even before his election, of a "Family Policy Advisory Board" for the purpose of "promoting a national rededication to traditional American family values" (COFO, 1981).

It is thus our view that, because it is not possible in the current political atmosphere to resolve the family policy paradox, social workers must temporarily remain content with a more pragmatic strategy promoting a vigilant case-by-case and program-by-program "impact" stance which is continuously watchful of the effects of policy and program on human connectedness, but which in no way abandons the professional mandate to influence and promote government activities for the relief of human deprivation.

The Content of Family Policy

In order to become more acute observers of the role of public policy in family life, we should consider the particular ways in which such policies make their impact. Janet Giele (1979) has developed a useful typology of family policy based on the major functions of the family and its relationship with the world. She suggests that family policies affect four areas of family life: its nurturant function, economic activity, residence, and cultural function. Such a classification may help us organize and evaluate with more precision the myriad of policy and program prescriptions which confront us.

The nurturant function of the family includes all personal caretaking among family members. This notion encompasses not only the day-by-day nurturance of all members, but often also the care of a dependent member, such as a physically or developmentally disabled child, a physically ill member, or a frail, elderly member. As discussed earlier, public policies applicable to this area may range from those that support the intimate network in their caretaking functions to those that replace it. Also included are policies that pertain to family relations, sexuality, and childbearing. Specific programs in this area include, among others, health care, family planning, in-home services, substitute personal care, and family-life education.

In the second area, that of economic activity, may be found policies and programs related to income maintenance, categorical financial supports, and other income redistribution efforts, and also policies that shape the family's transactions with the world of work. Labor force participation may be markedly affected by policies, legislation, or programs related to child care, retirement, flexible working hours, job training, and fair employment practices.

Where a family lives and the character of its ecological environment are also affected by public policy. Policies affecting housing and the maintenance or destruction of neighborhoods, and policies on conservation, energy, public and private transportation, road building, zoning, segregation, and school busing are all examples of governmental activities which affect families as they are enveloped in their physical environments.

The cultural function of the family, in Giele's words its "legal and cultural identity," can also be shaped by public policy. Divorce, child custody, child support, termination of parental rights, adoption law, and adoption records are all matters of public policy. The effects of public action in the sphere of culture can influence the connections among family members and the balance of various statuses and rights within the family system. The recognition by the state of the family's role as a preserver and transmitter of culture is found in its willingness to help preserve diverse languages, customs, religious beliefs, and culturally determined norms for family structure and function, connectedness, and caretaking.

Current and Future Trends in Family Policy

We have explored a wide range of issues in our consideration of social and family policy, and we may now discuss the role of the practitioner. First, however, we will take a brief look at the current rapidly shifting scene and attempt some speculations about the directions policy and programs can be expected to take in the next few years.

Clearly the directions in family policy and program are to a large extent influenced by such larger factors as economic growth rates, inflation and employment trends and policies, population trends, and social unrest, indeed on the issue of survival itself. In addition to these long-range trends, the more immediate issues affecting family life have to do with the marked shifts in economic and social philosophy ushered in with the Reagan administration. Perhaps the most salient issue to be considered is the relationship between the family and State. Reagan's position has consistently been one of easing the federal government out of family life, a

position reinforced by economic policies which initiate massive cuts in domestic programs and shift more tax money and more responsibility from
federal government to state and local governments, partly through a block-
grant approach to funding education and social service programs. In Reagan's view, the taxing power of the federal government should not be used
either to regulate the economy or to bring about social change—a dramatic shift in thinking from federal policy of the last several decades (Coalition of Family Organizations, 1981).

Spokespersons for the New Right define themselves as family-centered, and as fostering policies and programs which, theoretically at least,
encourage government to take less and families to take more responsibility
for the well-being of their own members. This group sees tax credit, rather
than direct funding, as the acceptable device for encouraging social goals.
Some of their proposals call for tax credits in the area of child care—presumably to allow more freedom of choice for families. Other potential tax
credits include credits for building additions on houses or for purchasing
special equipment to aid in the care of elderly or handicapped family
members at home.

A social "safety net" philosophy, under which only the most needy
can expect assistance, characterizes the administration's emphasis on encouraging independence for individuals and families. "Independence" is
also encouraged through stricter eligibility requirements for recipients of
most social service programs, a renewed emphasis on work requirements
for most AFDC mothers (that is, for all but those with children under the
age of two and those lacking day care for children under the age of six)
and drastic budget cuts in—or even total elimination of—many social service programs.

It is likely that in the next few years we will see a return of power
and authority from federal to state and local governments. There are in
fact several possible advantages in such a reversion. Local governments
are, theoretically at least, far more responsive to their own demographic
characteristics. Ethnic diversity, urban and rural population divisions, occupational patterns, and historic community values can be more individually accounted for in developing programs tailored to local areas. But
there are disadvantages as well. Lack of federal regulation and control
may make it easier for some states and localities to continue or renew discriminatory practices which maintain tremendous inequities or which fail
to assist adequately the most discriminated against, neglected segments of
the population (Leik and Hill, 1979).

Clearly the current federal government claims to be reluctant to intervene in family relationships or to assume what many would see as its
basic responsibility to protect the rights and civil liberties of women, children, racial minorities, and others who lack economic clout. The proposed
Family Protection Act, for example, limits the federal government's role

in child abuse programs and in policy regarding domestic violence, and it prohibits federal funds for abortion. On the other hand, congruent with conservative ideology, a policy of intervention can be seen in current federal proposals to prohibit school busing for the achievement of racial integration and in a provision which supports the reintroduction of prayer in public schools. Thus we see that the administration's call for a federal-state balance of power is not consistent and that it probably means to play a more active role or an intentionally inactive role in selected areas.

Sudden, massive changes in social policy are not characteristic in democracies such as ours. They tend rather to occur largely through incremental adjustment. Perhaps, as some have suggested, it is idealistic to conceive of policymaking as a well-planned, orderly process; it may more realistically be viewed as a muddling, fragmented process of bargaining, coalition-building, and logrolling, full of ambiguity and contradiction in its purposes (Rein, 1971). The drift of policymaking in the future, however, will very likely be toward a separation between income and services, reinforced with reductions in income programs, and an even greater erosion in services for the poor or near-poor. Whether or not these predictions are accurate or the current trends give way before long to a new swing of the political pendulum, the social policymakers of the future, pragmatists and dreamers alike, will have to consider more carefully economic growth rates, inflation, the limitations of resources, changing population trends, and shifting ratios of worker to nonworker. While priorities change over time and many argue there is still plenty of room in this affluent nation for policies which encourage income redistribution and strengthen social services spending at the expense of defense spending and a variety of other interests, the recent crisis in Social Security has forced a new and hard look at economic and social policy relationships.

The Practitioner as Analyst of Public Policy

We began this chapter with the statement that social policies and the programs through which they find expression greatly influence the social worker's practice and the direction of service. What role, then, can the individual worker play in this complex situation?

The social worker can, and hopefully does, keep abreast of national, regional, and local policy developments through the media and through reports from national organizations, professional journals, and the various legislative and political "watch" bulletins available. All social workers need this information—not only in terms of its potential impact on their own lives, but also in understanding and working with families. Moreover, most social workers practice within the context of a social or human service agency, and therefore they act as instruments of public policy as they administer programs. In fact, even social workers in private practice, seemingly free from agency constraints, are not free from the influence of public policy; they must be sensitive not only to the currently crucial issues of vendorship, licensing, and third party payments, but also to the policy and program contingencies which affect the lives of their clients.

Agency-based practitioners should become watchful analysts of agency policies, which may be explicitly spelled out in such sources as manuals, bylaws, forms, or agency publicity. Policy is also more implicitly expressed in the agency's programmatic directions, its priorities, and its use of space and time in daily operation. Actions *do* speak louder than words. Perhaps the best way to understand agency policy is to study agency operation, since program may be viewed as policy in action. Frequently, as in any social system, there may be a discrepancy between announced policy (the agency "mythology") and actual practice. The practice and its intended or unintended consequences constitute the agency's most powerful and accurate communication. It is the workers' responsibility to note, to try to resolve, and if necessary to expose these incongruities between policy and practice.

Agency-based practitioners should also question the impact of every policy or program on human connectedness, on the family and on their own practice. Several questions concerning family impact emerge here as we return to Giele's conceptual analysis of family policy:

1. Does the policy/program support, interfere with, replace or exploit the family's effort to nurture its members?
2. Is the family conceptualized as an obstacle to helping one of its individual members, as a resource to be mobilized on the individual's behalf, as a partner in the process, or as a totality working for the benefit of all its members?
3. Does the policy support the family's economic functioning? Does it open up options so that family members can form effective relationships with the world of work?
4. Is the family's kinship and social network understood and valued, and its rootedness in community cherished? Is the agency sensitive to the requirements necessary to the maintenance of connectedness?
5. Does agency policy and program force constraints on the family, or is an effort made rather to support the family's self-definition concerning form and structure?

A few more questions can illustrate the potential impact of agency policy on the family. In a child welfare agency, do policies support or inhibit visits between biological families and children in care? In a purchase-of-service agency, is payment figured on numbers of children in placement or are in-home services reimbursable? In the schools, are parents involved as a matter of policy in solving child–school tensions? Are parents seen as part of the solution rather than the problem? In a health-care delivery system, is home-based care available? Are adult children included in decision-making processes? In a family-oriented guidance agency, is the wife or mother and child routinely seen with the father's participation, or even his knowledge? In chapter 6 we will examine in some detail the various policy and procedural arrangements which can support a family-centered approach.

Once these policies and procedures have been identified and assessed, the next task is to discover their source. For example, does the agency policy conform to federal, state, or local law? Examples of policies directed by public legislation include those relating to abuse or neglect, and to the rights of workers to divulge or not divulge information about birth records to adult adoptees. Such laws are, of course, subject to varying local interpretation. In general, the more fully the agency is sanctioned to fulfill a public mandate, the more likely is the source of program and policy to be found in public statute.

On the other hand, it may be discovered that the major influence on certain program directions comes from the agency's board of directors, or the agency executive. Sometimes a worker may discover that what has been presented or understood as agency policy is in actuality an expression of an opinion or bias on the part of a supervisor or middle-level administrator. The discovery of the source of policy is extremely important in evaluating the potential for change and in designing strategies for change. Sometimes the way agencies go about the business of delivering services is a result of entrenched custom or tradition and implicit policy directions which are neither written down nor a part of the agency's discourse, and such policies may not be functional in the current context. As with implicit rules and outdated myths in families, simply revealing dysfunctional agency policies may serve to weaken their effectiveness.

In describing the policy context of family-centered social work practice we have taken the position that family-centered practitioners must become expert in identifying the sources and evaluating the impact of those policies which shape their roles as helpers. We will return to these issues in chapter 8, where we will assess the ecological environment of which worker, agency, and policy are a part.

Chapter 4

An Epistemological Framework

THE APPROACH TO FAMILY-CENTERED PRACTICE developed in this study is informed by what may be termed an eclectic systems approach. In recent decades, both the physical and social sciences have been undergoing what amounts to a scientific revolution; specifically, it is a "systems" revolution. Ervin Laszlo describes it thus: "We witness today another shift in ways of thinking: the shift toward rigorous but holistic theories. This means thinking in terms of facts and events in the context of wholes, forming integrated sets with their own properties and relationships. Looking at the world in terms of such sets of integrated relations constitutes the systems view" (1972:19).

As social workers of the 1950s turned increasingly to sociology for knowledge and theory, the growing emphasis on social systems theories in sociology influenced our profession as well.[1] Social systems theory was congruent with social workers' growing interest in groups and organizations. The concepts of "social role"[2] and "role functioning,"[3] and the theory of the relationship between personality development and role added to the profession's repertory of means for understanding people. Helen Harris Perlman (1960; 1968), who in the 1950s had challenged the profession to put the "social" back into social work, took leadership in the integration of role theory into practice.

General systems theory began to trickle into the field in the early 1960s. Werner Lutz's paper, "Concepts and Principles Underlying Social

59

Work Practice," which critically examined the possibility of applying concepts from general systems theory to practice, was published in 1956. Another early systems discussion was found in Gordon Hearn's *Theory Building in Social Work* which appeared in 1958. It was not, however, until ten years later that the impact of general systems theory began to be felt in the social work literature. In 1969, Gordon Hearn edited a series of papers which had been presented at the Council on Social Work Education meetings on the application of general systems theory to social work education and practice. That same year, Sister Mary Paul Janchill (1969) examined some general systems concepts and their relevance for practice, and Carel Germain (1968) described how a systems perspective could enhance the social study process and provide a framework for the integration of social work's dual focus, the psychological and the social. Social work texts which made use of a range of systems concepts began to appear. Carol Meyer's *Social Work Practice: A Response to the Urban Crisis*, published in 1970, utilized general systems concepts primarily in the assessment process. Social work theorists, educators and practitioners saw the integrative power of the systems perspective as an aid in developing generic practice models which spanned the traditional methods of casework, group work, and community organization. Pincus and Minahan (1973), in a widely used text, adopted the Lippett, Watson, and Westley (1958) systemic analysis of planned change. Howard Goldstein utilized general systems theory to organize his model of practice in *Social Work Practice: A Unitary Approach*, which appeared in 1973.

The growing impact of systems thinking was not unlike the revolution experienced a generation ago by social workers when psychoanalytic psychology reached American shores. And as in any period of rapid change, the integration of systems concepts into social work practice has been uneven and has often led to considerable confusion. Irma Stein (1974), in a scholarly analysis, writes:

> The literature on the application of systems theory to social work indicates that different theories are often equated with or substituted for each other, that empirical experiences are often equated with scientific constructs, that conceptual models and notions are conveyed in, or interwoven with, the language of persons and the language and ideology of the profession. [30]

Social systems and general systems were next joined by an "ecological" or "transactional" systems perspective which was developing in social work and in the field of social psychiatry. Utilizing the science of ecology as a metaphor, the ecological systems perspective focuses primarily on the adaptive balance existing between living systems and their environments.[4] As Stein commented, ecological and transactional models have been "appealing to social work in that they are middle-range, operational, interdisciplinary frameworks that allow for considerable latitude in practice interventions and are compatible with social work's humanistic orientation" (1974:72).

At the same time that social work was testing out the usefulness of a range of what Stein calls "systems type" theories, psychiatry, particularly in the robust but still infant area of family assessment and treatment, was also being influenced by this intellectual revolution, and, as the boundaries between psychiatry and social work have always been very porous, these developments in psychiatry also had their impact on social workers. Social work benefited from other influences as well. The development of cybernetics by Norbert Wiener (1948) and the work on communication by Reusch and Bateson (1951) led to a growing understanding of communication patterns which revolutionized the view of the family. The work of Don Jackson (1957; 1965), Paul Watzlawick (1967; 1974), and Virginia Satir (1967) developed out of this tradition. Gregory Bateson, not as therapist but as anthropologist, is considered by many to be the intellectual father of family therapy. Certainly his influence has been widely felt and his creative thinking continues to nourish the ongoing exploration of and lively dialogues concerning the epistemological underpinnings and conceptual framework for family therapy.[5]

As interest in the family grew, other family therapists and theoreticians began to utilize systems models, some focusing on family structure, others on process, and still others on the development of the family relationship system through time.[6]

In the face of this rich and creative intellectual revolution, one experiences systems overload. The task of unifying this growing body of theory in order to develop a coherent framework is indeed challenging and perhaps not possible. However, it is our intention to make use of contributions from these many systems type theories and to operationalize them into ways of helping individuals and their families in an eclectic systems approach. In this effort, coherence may well be sacrificed to breadth and inclusiveness.

In constructing this approach, we will utilize the general systems framework as an epistemological platform. Further, we will make use of some of the propositions growing out of general systems research and theory building on the nature of living systems. Within this framework and this understanding of living systems, we use an ecological metaphor for conceptualizing the person–family constellation in its life space and for focusing on the transactions between the person or family and the social environment.

Clearly, these are not distinct bodies of theory but rather overlapping and complementary ways of understanding the family. In this chapter we will summarize the major concepts from systems theory and the ecological perspective which will guide our approach to family-centered practice. In chapter 5 we will focus on the family itself as a system and on that body of theory concerning family structure and process which informs our understanding of families and our efforts to bring about change. Throughout this study, however, we will return time and time again to the ideas of system and ecology for help in arriving at prescriptions for practice.

The General Systems Epistemological Perspective

General systems theory provides an epistemological stance, a way of thinking, and a means of organizing our perceptions, in what Alfred North Whitehead called this "radically untidy" world. The general systems theorist understands the world in terms of relatedness. A particular entity is examined in relation to the things it affects and is affected by rather than in relation to its essential characteristics. For the most part, Western thought has tended to be linear, atomistic, and analytical rather than transactional and synthetic. Our mode of thought may well reflect the limitations of human mentation—the facts that we think in a linear stream through time, that we can think of only one thing at a time, and that we are limited in the amount of data with which we can deal. Such limitations lead us to attempt to master knowledge by partializing it; but analysis and partializing distort the nature of the very reality we are attempting to understand. The inadequacy of analytical thought has led over the last two or three decades to the introduction of systems models of conceptualization in one field of science after another. Perhaps the most important contribution from general systems theory has been that its conceptual model enables us to expand our minds and deal with infinitely more data.

The common-sense definition of a system is that of a whole that is composed of interrelated and interdependent parts. To elucidate and expand this definition, we may specify certain characteristics. A system has boundaries. Data are either a part of the system or are not. A system has a structure made up of those parts of the system included in the boundaries and the more or less permanent patterns of their relationship. Function, in systems terms, is defined as the result, or the outcome, of the structure. Systems have emergent qualities. This means, stated in familiar axioms, that the whole is greater than the sum of its parts and that the interrelatedness of units in a system gives rise to new qualities that are a function of that interrelatedness. A poem, for instance, is more than a list of all the words that compose it. Any practitioner who has seen the husband and wife separately in helping with a marital conflict knows how the understanding of the situation is altered and enriched when the couple is seen together!

Each system exists in a specific frame of reference, and in using a systems approach as an analytical tool, it is essential to specify that frame of reference. The domains of traditional disciplines are circumscribed by their frames of reference: psychology, sociology, physics, astronomy, biology, and political science, for example, all deal with specific frames of reference. A human being can be considered variously as a psychological system, a chemical system, a biological system, or as a subsystem of many social systems. In this example, each frame of reference may consider different data but is concerned with the same empirical object. Interestingly, many of the newer disciplines are a result of joining two previously separate frames of reference; astrophysics, social psychology, biochemistry, and most recently sociobiology are examples of such junctions.

A change in one part of the system affects the system as a whole and all of its parts. This statement may appear to be substantive or predictive, but in truth it simply follows from the original definition. The implication of this principle will be explored later in this chapter.

How, then, does this epistemological platform contribute to our thinking about social work practice? First, a general systems approach enhances our ability to deal with an immense amount of data. The efforts in the 1950s and 1960s to develop new ways of assessing families, for example, broke down under the weight of the enormous amount of data to be collected because no means existed to integrate and understand it. Thinking about and observing the family as a system has made possible major breakthroughs in understanding this flood of information.

Second, general systems theory encourages the discovery and use of isomorphisms, that is, characteristics shared by all systems whatever their frames of reference. Isomorphisms enable one to understand events in a wide range of systems. For example, the notion of "boundary" is an isomorphism that can be used to characterize families, egos, organizations, theoretical structures and individuals; all have boundaries which distinguish that which is within the system from that which is outside, and a useful way to assess any system is to assess the nature of its boundary. To continue our example, we point out that the boundaries of living systems are maintained and protected; the maintenance of boundaries, then, may be studied in individuals, families, groups, and societies. (We will return throughout our presentation to the highly generative concept of boundary.) Such isomorphisms are portable from one frame of reference to another and give social workers conceptual handles for seizing hold of usable concepts existing in other sciences.

Third, because systems theory focuses on the relationships between entities, rather than on entities in isolation, it leads us to focus on transactions, on social interaction, and on person–environment exchanges and adaptations. This emphasis is congruent with and permits a more sophisticated conceptualization of the traditional unit of attention in social work, namely, "the person in situation." Examples will be given later in this chapter in the discussion of an ecological systems perspective.

Fourth, systems theory forces us beyond the limitations of linear thought and language and provokes the use of other modes through which complex relationships may be captured and communicated. Visual portrayal, for example, is highly useful for interpreting complexly transacting systems. A picture is truly worth a thousand words. Systems diagrams can not only organize complex data but, on visual examination, can yield new information and insights. In subsequent chapters several such diagrams will be demonstrated and their usefulness for assessment and intervention considered. The use of additional visual methods—the one-way mirror, observation, and video recording—will be described as well.

Thus systems theory, by demonstrating the existence of analogies among living systems, reveals complex relationships hitherto concealed from us. Von Bertalanffy, founder of general systems theory, has insisted that the use of analogy and of conceptual and material models is not "half-poetical play but a potential tool in science" (1962:20). This claim was certainly borne out through the use of model building in finding the solution to the puzzle of the structure of DNA (deoxyribonucleic acid). Poets and artists have long understood the use of these conceptual and communicative modes.

The foregoing epistemological perspective provides a skeleton for science, or, as Kenneth Boulding has written, "a framework or structure of systems on which to hang the flesh and blood of particular disciplines and particular subject matter" (1968:98). Not only have general systems theorists developed a framework for organizing information, but they have also moved to fill out this framework with propositions about the nature of living systems. These propositions state principles or rules which characterize all living systems and thus provide isomorphisms which draw science together.

The Nature of Living Systems

Living systems are open systems. Although they have boundaries, these boundaries must to some extent be permeable, as living systems must import matter-energy and information from their environments for maintenance and survival. Living systems in transaction with their environments have the capacity for growth and elaboration and for increasing differentiation and specialization. Now let us apply these principles to the family. The extent to which a family's boundaries are permeable, that is, the extent to which a family allows new information and experiences to enter the system, determines in part its potential for growth and change.

Further, systems theorists speculate that closed systems move toward entropy, or randomness, or lack of organization and differentiation. Energy and information are required from the environment for the maintenance of order and differentiation within the system. In the case of biological systems, this principle is obvious. A biological system must import fuel for the production of energy and for the maintenance and repair of its structure.

Aided by these principles, social scientists have become increasingly aware of the impact of isolation and the lack of stimulus on individuals, families, and even communities. Clearly, certain populations can be identified as being at risk because their age or their economic, social, or environmental status has led them to be increasingly isolated. The situation of the aged in our society is a classic example of such a population. Retirement, growing lack of mobility, loss of relationships through death, the breakdown of extended family ties, have all tended to isolate the aging and leave them vulnerable and thus potentially entropic.

The predicament of the inner city raises the same issue. As resources shrink and disorder develops, more and more people with resources abandon the inner city. Visitors, shoppers, and investors are increasingly reluctant to cross the inner-city boundaries. Thus, input of all kinds is increasingly diminished; depletion and disorder increase. This deviation amplification continues unless major new inputs reverse the process. How to keep the inner city open with resources and information flowing freely across its boundaries is often the major issue to be dealt with by city leadership.

In considering the input needs of living systems, it is important to consider, in addition to matter–energy exchanges across boundaries, the system's information exchange with its environment. A system may experience information stress in a variety of ways. There may be input lack; the system does not have sufficient information from the environment, either because information is unavailable or the system for some reason is unable to receive it. People with visual or hearing handicaps, for example, are threatened with the stress of insufficient information. On the other hand, a system may be taxed with an *excess* of information, an input exceeding the system's ability to process and integrate it. A basic task in assessment is not only to identify the extent to which a system's boundaries are open but also to identify the resources available in the environment for the system's survival and development.

Living systems also strive toward some sort of balance or inner integrity, a tendency which has been given various names. Walter B. Cannon (1932) called it "homeostasis." He was one of the first thinkers to describe the various control and communication subsystems that maintain the body's inner integrity in the face of inner and outer stress. Ludwig von Bertalanffy (1950) seems to have been the originator of the term "moving steady state." This term implies a moving balance, and avoids the somewhat static implications of homeostasis.

Miller (1975) has described homeostasis, or the moving steady state, as a range of stability within which the system moves. An input which forces variables in the system beyond the limits of the range of stability constitutes stress for the system and threatens homeostasis. The concept of homeostasis has been of key importance in the development of family theory. In the very beginnings of the family therapy movement, Don Jackson (1957), drawing from his research with families having a schizophrenic member, speculated that the family is a homeostatic system, that it maintains a kind of balance through the use of a variety of equilibrating mechanisms, and that dysfunction in a member of the family might well be such a balancing mechanism. That is, he affirmed that the symptoms or problematic behaviors of the identified patient in the family play an essential role in the maintenance of the family's equilibrium. This view of the family as a homeostatic system has been modified and further elaborated by other theorists, but the basic conception that families are self-regulating in relation to some kind of coherence, order, or inner integrity has remained central in the understanding of families. This idea will be examined in greater detail in chapters 12 and 13.

Also growing out of an understanding of the family as a homeostatic system is the notion of crisis and its importance in change and growth. A crisis in a system may be defined as a state in which inputs and forces for change have pushed so far beyond the range of stability that the integrity of the system is seriously threatened. The system's structure may be overwhelmed and the equilibrating mechanism unable to restore balance. Individuals and families frequently come to the attention of social workers when they are in crisis and at that time they are frequently most ready to develop new and more differentiated means of responding to the demanding events and changes.

The events precipitating these crises may be developmental, occasioned by rapid growth and change in members of the family. For example, in many families the onset of adolescence in a child is experienced as a crisis; in others, the departure of the first grown child from the home. Other potential precipitants include painful and disrupting events such as illness, accidents, personal losses, or economic reverses. We will return again and again to the concepts of stability and of crisis throughout this study as we seek to understand dysfunction, resistance, and change.

PROCESSES OF ADAPTATION

We next turn to the most complex but perhaps the most significant area of theory about living systems, namely processes of adaptation. The living system, in order to survive, must sustain some sort of adaptive balance with its environment. Key to the entire process of adaptation is the system's ability to receive, process, store, and make use of information. The more complex the system and the system-to-environment adaptation, the more differentiated are the information-processing mechanisms. To explain this process we will use a cornerstone in information theory, that is, the concept of feedback. Feedback is the process whereby a living system monitors or "feeds back" the consequences of its outputs in order to alter future outputs. Wiener, the father of cybernetics, defined feedback as the "property of being able to adjust future conduct by past performance. It may be as simple as the common reflex, or it may be a higher order feedback in which past experience is used not only to regulate specific movements, but also whole policies of behavior" (1954:33).

The operation of a thermostat in the maintenance of the temperature of a house provides a simple mechanical example of a homeostatic mechanism equipped with feedback. Let us say that the thermostat is set at seventy degrees. This means that the "range of stability," in Miller's (1975) term, is from sixty-eight to seventy-two degrees. The thermostat monitors the temperature in the house and feeds the reading into the mechanism. When the furnace is off on a cold day, the temperature will fall. When it reaches sixty-eight degrees, defined by the system as too cold, a message is sent to the furnace to start up. The house begins to warm up and the output of the heating system is "fed back" into the control mechanisms which, when the deviation from seventy degrees is plus two degrees, or seventy-two degrees, sends a message to the furnace to shut off.

In goal-directed systems, such as human beings and families, the ability to feed back information and to make continuous corrections in the deviation of the system from its path toward a goal enables goal attainment. The transmission and storing of information and the function of feedback are basic to the understanding of the family as a communication system. It is important to understand also that family goals can be frustrated by feedback loops that maintain dysfunctional behavior or progressively amplifying deviations.

The ability of the individual system to receive and store information from its environment, and to make use of that information, is central to the adaptive process. The system stores information about the environment; this information pool becomes a map of the environment and ultimately a part of the structure of the system. Miller (1975) has described the living system as a constantly changing cameo which matches or fits the environment. Such a concept is useful in considering the family system's relationship with its environment. Further, this kind of adaptive transaction also takes place within families as one shifts the analytical level and considers the person as the system and the family as the intimate environment. It is through this adaptive process which takes place over time that we may assume that not only is the person in the family but the family is in the person.

A child, growing up and developing within a family system through the process of learning and adaptation absorbs the family's "culture": its values, meanings, myths, role assignments, patterns of communication, and style of doing things. As the individual is immersed in the family system throughout his or her development, the family culture becomes ego syntonic and therefore often not readily accessible to new awareness. Later in this study we will discuss the family of origin as a resource for change, whereby clients can learn to objectify their family systems, step outside of them, become more differentiated, and finally able to make free choices.

Related to this developmental process is, of course, the fact that a system exists over a period of time and has a history. This history is a part of the structure of that system. "Structure changes momentarily with function," Miller writes, "but when change is so great that it is essentially irreversible, an historical process has occurred, giving rise to a new structure" (1975:358).

Walter P. Buckley (1968) states the same idea in a slightly different way. The internal mapping of these system–environment interchanges, he says,

> make possible the system's control of its behavior in ways relevant to or coordinate with the nature of its environment such that, in effect, system and environment become interacting components of a larger whole. Such a conceptualization provides a common principle for the otherwise diverse facts of phylogenetic evolution, ontogenetic development, psychological learning, or sociocultural elaboration. [121]

Living systems must also have a "decider." Some subsystem within the system must have at least some control over the other subsystems or it would be impossible for a system to survive and to maintain its adaptive balance. How could an eight-person scull move down the river, for example, if there were no coxswain? The function of such a "decider" indicates two more characteristics in living systems. One is power. The existence of a decider implies that the decider has the power to affect or control other parts of the system. The second is choice. The decider "makes decisions" in relation to some sort of goal and in the context of a hierarchy of values. In sum, the decider's power propels the system toward a goal which is selected on the basis of a hierarchy of values. The issue of power, which has been a point of contention among family theorists and clinicians, will be explored at some length in our discussion of the family as a system.

General systems theory then, provides an epistemological stance, a way of thinking about and organizing our perceptions. Systems theorists have also developed a series of propositions concerning the nature of living systems which can inform our thinking about individuals, families, organizations, and environments. However, in order for this series of propositions to give guidance in day-by-day practice, it must be applied more particularly to the social worker's world. It is through the utilization of the science of ecology as a metaphor for practice that these abstract conceptions will be concretely applied.

Ecology as a Metaphor for Practice

Some years ago, Warren Brodey (1967) wrote, "There is a profound need for a new kind of discourse with the environment . . . the root process of the dialogue among family systems, individual systems, social systems, and the changing environment is ready to be studied in terms of the family" (1967:19). The adoption of an ecological perspective in assessment and in formulating practice principles stimulates this kind of dialogue.

The science of ecology studies the sensitive balance which exists between living things and their environments, and the ways in which this balance can be maintained and enhanced. Edgar Auerswald, who has helped to develop an ecological perspective in mental health practice, defines it as "the study of life and death in time and space" (1971:68), while Carel Germain defines it as "the science concerned with the adaptive fit of organisms and their environments and with the means by which they achieve a dynamic equilibrium and mutuality" (1973:326). Ecology has, in recent years, occupied more and more of the nation's attention and concern. We have become increasingly aware of the complex and often fragile balance that exists in nature. We have learned that all living things are dependent for survival on nurturant and sustaining environments and that they are interdependent on each other. We have learned that the unforeseen consequences of "progress" have too often been the disruption of these important relationships and we now know that even the most well-intentioned intervention may lead to further destruction.

Ecology as an Enlarger of Context

If ecology is adopted as a metaphor for practice in social work, then the unit of attention is that complex ecological system which includes the individual, the family, the salient environment, and the transactional relationships among these systems. As Hall and Fagen have said, "a system together with its environment makes up the universe of all things of interest in a given context" (1968:84).

If we accept this concept of the unit of attention, however, we find that we must deal with an extremely complex ecological system. A consideration of the human environment takes into account not merely air, water, food, spatial arrangements, and other aspects of the physical environment; in addition to these, human beings have erected over the centuries elaborate social, economic, and political structures which they must sustain and through which their needs are met. Thus people must maintain an adaptive mutuality with the intricate human systems which they require for growth and self-realization and with their elaborate social environment. An ecological orientation dictates that the individual cannot be understood outside the context of the intimate environment, the family; and a family can be understood only in the context of the larger environment.

Adopting an ecological perspective, as Gordon (1969) conceptualized it, leads us to focus on adaptive (and maladaptive) transactions between persons and between the person and the environment—in other words, the *interface* between systems. Such a view leads us to examine the sources of nurturance and stimulation which must be available from both the intimate and the extended social environment. It helps us evaluate the skills that a person or family must have to make appropriate use of possibilities in the environment and to cope with its demands.

An ecological metaphor applied to the practice of social work requires an expansion of our knowledge about the nature of transactions between person and environment.

Germain (1979) has recently reviewed the extent of our general knowledge concerning transactional phenomena and our specific knowledge of issues such as space, time, and crowding, and she has examined contributions from the social sciences and also from biology, geography, and ethology. She points out that our knowledge of person–environment transactions is still in the beginning stages, particularly in the social-psychological arena. While we have made connections, for example, between such phenomena as substandard housing and disease,

> we know little about the optimal level, balance, and timing of nutritive environmental elements required for the expression of potential. Little is known about how such inputs interact with individual factors of age, sex, culture, and experience to support psychosocial development, or even whether reversibility of damaging effects exerted by nonnutritive or missing elements is possible. [1979:16]

The work of Robert White has been particularly helpful in our exploration of the person–environment interface. White (1959; 1976) postulates an inborn effectance drive or a desire on the part of human beings to experience themselves as a cause, as effective in relation to their environment. Successfully interacting with the environment leads to a sense of competence and enhances self-worth. A recent collection of studies edited by Maluccio (1981) expands this concept and exemplifies how the notion of competence and the creative use of the environment may give direction to practice in diverse settings and with varied client populations.

Erik Erikson (1968) has also shed light on the person–environment transaction through his development of the concept of "identity," and he and Lidz have both attempted to clarify the relationships among human needs, potential, and developmental tasks, on one hand, and the responses of the environment on the other. Maslow (1954), who believes that individuals are instinctually motivated toward self-actualization, has described a hierarchy of human needs which must be satisfied in relation to the environment, ranging from those which are basically physiological to psychological and interpersonal needs for love, belonging and self-esteem. Other concepts which focus on person–environment transactions include Piaget's notions of assimilation and accommodation (see Phillips, 1969), and Durkheim's concept of anomie (Merton, 1957; Cloward and Ohlin, 1960; and Hartman, 1969).

Our understanding of relationships has benefited from a growing interest on the part of mental health practitioners in ethology, genetics, and sociobiology. Applications of concepts from ethology, for example, appear in the family therapy literature. Bateson's work with dolphins (Watzlawick, Beavin, and Jackson, 1967) has contributed to the understanding of analogic communication. Minuchin (1974) introduces his volume *Families and Family Therapy* with the touching story of the ecologically-oriented psychiatrist who understands an elderly woman's acute decompensation as a response to having to move to a new territory; he likens her situation to that of a mollusk which has lost its shell. His treatment, growing out of an appreciation of the ethological concept, helps her track, map, and master her new territory and interrupt the feedback from a community which is defining her fears as "illness."

As our knowledge about family-environment transactions is enhanced, so is our ability to think in systems terms—to describe transactions or interfaces and to grasp the elusive meaning of "ecological balance." As Leichter and Mitchell (1978) emphasize, in thinking about this balance it is important to remember that neither the individual nor the family, considered as a system, is a passive recipient of surrounding forces. The family is rather more usefully conceived of as an "actor" which

> contends with, selects from, redefines, modifies and creates aspects of its environment. The family cannot most usefully be conceived as a system so open that it is nothing more than the passive recipient of external forces; rather [it is] an active creator in a network of external forces over which it exercises some influence. In short, it is even clearer today than it was a decade ago that "environmental diagnosis" of the family should employ a two-way, interactional perspective. [xii]

An ecological metaphor, with its expanded view of the unit of attention, also extends the arena of action for the helping person. The social worker, assuming the role of the "explorer" so meaningfully described by Auerswald (1968), follows the problem wherever it may lead, creatively developing with the client measures for help. The empirical data gained from such methods, in conjunction with the analytical framework borrowed from systems theory, are likely to produce new insights, new practice models, and most important, new ways of helping those in need.

Ecological Principles for Practice

The science of ecology as a metaphor for practice not only expands our unit of attention but also suggests certain principles of practice. It is not intended that these principles be viewed as rigid prescriptions; rather they are suggested as useful guidelines that grow naturally out of an ecological perspective.

First, problems or difficulties that come to the social worker's attention are better understood as lacks or deficits in the environment, as dysfunctional transactions between systems, as adaptive strategies, or as results of interrupted growth and development rather than as disease processes located within the individual. This conception of "problem" or "need" has considerable implications for the location of strategies for change. In general, efforts for change are directed to the interfaces between systems or subsystems, the goal being the enhancement of the relationship between those systems.

Second, problems are seen as outcomes of the transaction of many complex variables. Because of the complexity and over-determination of causation in multivariable systems, the effort to locate a single cause and cure is largely abandoned in practice. Rather, a feedback model of change is initiated in which interventions are made and tested through the continued monitoring of the system's response. Interventions that redefine and thus alter the family's relationship system are evaluated in terms of outcome.

Watzlawick, Beavin, and Jackson (1967) have related this feedback model to the "Black Box" concept used in telecommunications. This concept, they maintain, is

> generally applied to the fact that electronic hardware is by now so complex that it is sometimes more expedient to disregard the internal structure of a device and concentrate on the study of its specific input-output relations. While it is true that these relations may permit inferences into what "really" goes on inside the box, this knowledge is not essential for the study of *the function of the device in the greater system of which it is a part.* [43-44] (Italics in original)

Third, in applying an ecological metaphor to practice, life experience is seen as the model for and primary instrument of change. In other words, strategies are devised which, insofar as possible, make use of natural systems and life experience and take place within the life space of the client. Further, the family itself is a natural helping system and thus can be not just the arena but the instrument of change.

Throughout this study, we will stress the importance of the family as a resource for family members. In a sense, social work developed as a family surrogate; in preindustrial society, our services were performed by families or other natural helping networks. The unintended consequences of this shift of caregiving to other institutions and to the professions may well have been a weakening of family ties, an undermining of family strengths, and a depersonalizing of care for individual family members. There is now a growing effort to reverse this trend by sustaining and supporting those in the intimate network who can themselves be the major sources of help. Examples of this effort are seen in the community mental health movement and in the increasingly active participation of families in progressive health-care systems as well as in conjoint family treatment and work with the family of origin.

A fourth principle growing out of our ecological systems stance has far-reaching implications for practice. This principle, which is central to the very definition of systems, states that a change in one part of the system has an impact on all other parts of the system. Thus, for example, even a minor change in the family's environment or in one individual's behavior or communication may reverberate throughout the family system. It is often impossible to predict or to monitor the many outcomes from any one intervention. Unfortunately, in many individual approaches to helping, little or no attention is given to ramifications of individual change in the larger system. The ecological approach makes such errors less possible. It is a key concept in family-centered practice that the total family system in its ecological context is of central concern. This does not mean that the total family must necessarily be directly involved in the change process. On the contrary, because changes in one subsystem affect the total system, work with one individual may well bring about significant change in the total family, as the "helped" individual moves back into the family system as, in some ways, a different person. However, under such circumstances the emissary for change must have sufficient strength, power, and support to be able to resist the family system's pressure to "change back." If he or she is able to maintain the new position, the other members of the family will also change. These comments are of special significance for those who, involved in direct work with children, are unable to gain access to the child's environment. Social workers in both school settings and child guidance clinics know how little power children usually have and how difficult it is to help a child when neither the school nor the family system is ready to accept changes in the child.

The principle that every change has far-reaching effects also forces one to be alert to the iatrogenic effects of even the most well-intentioned intervention into natural systems. We are slowly and reluctantly learning from the ecologists about the unforeseen negative results in our ill-considered efforts to "improve" our environment, through, for example, the massive use of pesticides. In the family field, Auerswald (1968) and Hoffman and Long (1969) have presented full-length case studies demonstrating how individuals and families have been caught up and virtually destroyed in double-binding "helping" systems which have failed to attend to the effects of particular interventions on the total system.

But this principle has a positive application as well; even a relatively minor intervention can produce a major change, as it may halt or reverse a deviation-amplifying process within a system. If a rather small intervention is targeted at the vortex of the system, or at that point where the maximum number of essential functions converge, considerable change can take place. This principle will be illustrated in our discussion of strategic family therapy.

We offer several additional principles of action. Natural means are better than artificial means: The attempt to devise strategies which make use of natural systems is an effort to avoid the development of artificial helping actions which may have unknown but pervasive iatrogenic effects. Moreover, the least intervention which has potential for achieving the objectives is the best intervention. If this advice is heeded, not only is there less likelihood of iatrogenic effect, but often a simple intervention at a crucial interface may have an extended ripple effect, bringing about needed change more quickly, more economically, and less disruptively than a more elaborate strategy. (This approach is in contradiction to a rather familiar belief in American culture, namely that if a little bit of something is good, then more, of course, is better.) Our preference, then, is for the short-term model of help, and for the gently initiated process which can then move ahead on its own momentum. Finally, a single effect can be produced by a variety of means. This is the principle of equifinality, which means that a number of different interventions may, owing to the complexity of systems, produce similar effects or outcomes. This principle encourages flexibility and creativity in seeking alternative routes to change.

The general principles discussed above offer guidance for family-centered practice and grow out of the adoption of an ecological perspective. As we stated above, they are suggestive rather than definitive. They alert the practitioner to the potential impact of strategies for change and they propose an evaluative framework for the selection of strategies from among what is generally a wide array of options. In constructing them we have borrowed eclectically from general systems theory, from theory about open living systems, and from ecological theory. To complete this presentation of the theoretical base which supports our practice, we will now discuss family system theories.

Chapter 5

Family Theory for Family-Centered Practice

UNTIL RELATIVELY RECENTLY, the study of the family has occupied the position of poor relative in the social science network. With a few notable exceptions, most of the key figures in the social sciences of the 1950s and 1960s were interested in larger sociocultural systems or, in the case of psychology, in the individual. The family was seen by many as a scientifically uninteresting and passive recipient of larger forces, or, in the case of individual dysfunction, as rather irrelevant to the fortunes of the "sick" member. In the last decade or so, however, the family has gained increasing respect as a subject for social science research. Courses on the family are taught in a variety of disciplines in most college curricula, and a vast number of family-oriented journals have appeared in the social sciences and in the humanities. These resources offer fruitful areas for exploration in addition to the huge body of practice theory and clinical research literature generated in the family therapy field itself.[1]

The body of theory informing the present-day practice of family centered practice is enormous and full of apparently conflicting views. In drawing upon it for the theoretical presentation which follows, we rely on three criteria. First, we will utilize primarily theories which have developed within the field of family therapy. Second, we will also draw upon theories that, although in some cases originating in the social sciences, have been widely employed by clinicians and clinical researchers because of their usefulness for practice and their explanatory and heuristic value.

Third, we will present some notions that, although not now widely utilized by family practitioners, offer considerable promise for enhancing our
understanding of families and enlarging our interventive repertoires.

It is certainly clear that, at this time, there is no single integrated
body of knowledge or theory that informs the practice or work with families. Further, as Gurman points out, family practitioners "have generally
failed to deal with common themes running through each other's work"
(1975:36). As a result, many concepts which address the same family phenomena or processes are called by different names. In spite of this confusion of riches, in our view there are important common themes which
inform family theory and treatment; what differs is that perspective from
which each theorist views the family landscape, and that aspect of the
family which is considered most salient and is placed in the center of the
lens. Starting with the basic assumption that the family is an open, adapting, and self-directing system, we have borrowed from a range of theorists
and practitioners to present an organized view of the family which (although perhaps untidy and at times even inconsistent) is, we hope, useful.
We will begin with a discussion of the intergenerational family system,
and go on to an examination of structural and organizational issues and
concepts, including boundaries, separateness and connectedness, and roles.
This material will be followed by a discussion of processes which promote
both stability and change, and the chapter will end with a consideration
of some of the more recent contributions to theory for family practice,
including meaning systems, family paradigms, and rituals.

An Intergenerational Perspective

Most psychological theories have attested to the importance of the family
of origin in individual human growth and development. In fact, both popular and professional literature is replete with family sagas which portray
individuals living out family themes, attempting to resolve family trage-
dies and guilts, and fulfilling family destinies. Anthropologists, too, acknowledged experts in the art of collecting life histories and genealogical
information, have used intergenerational materials for analyzing personality, cultural transmission, and particularly kinship patterns.

Our discussion of an intergenerational perspective begins with the assumption that *all* of us are deeply immersed in our family systems. Who
we are, how we think and communicate, what we choose to do and to
be, whom we choose to be with, to love, and to marry is in some part a
function of that complex system that has developed over the generations.
Although families are, of course, imbedded in a larger culture, they also
develop their own styles or cultures over the generations, and these traditions profoundly affect the lives of their members. Schwartzman (1982)

suggests that family traditions may be studied much as an anthropologist might undertake an ethnography of a larger cultural system. Such a family ethnography might be constituted by studying the family's relationship with the larger cultural context as it is revealed in intrafamilial communication and behavior, the family's immediate social context, and the world view of individual family members.

Without underestimating the crucial influence of the larger social and economic factors in shaping the nature of human life, or the uniqueness each actor brings to his or her own experiences, we believe that the living are intricately bound to those who have come before, both to their wider, historicocultural forebears and, more specifically, to their own ancestors.

It is popular to say that American ideology has long emphasized individualism; but perhaps it would be more accurate to suggest that the individual and the family have long engaged in some sort of paradoxical contest over which of them should come first. In many cultures, the immense power of the family—parents, grandparents, ancestors, and extended kin—in shaping one's destiny is taken for granted and accepted as an implicit part of life. Summarizing the beliefs of most African societies, for example, Ndeti writes:

> Because of the organic and psychological relationships that exist between the living and the dead, the spirits of dead ancestors seem to take keen interest in the affairs of the living. They mysteriously regulate the general conduct of individuals in African societies. Those who deviate from the normal activities in the culture, such as refusing to offer sacrifice to ancestors, disobeying cultural ethics, doing injustice to others, refusing to cooperate with others for the general good or ignoring one's responsibilities to himself and others must pay the price individually. [Ndeti, 1976:18]

In these societies the living are viewed as a culmination of a long historical chain tracing back to the beginnings of things. Diseases, for example, are seen by native doctors as originating with mischievous and dangerous spirits; physiological malfunctions cannot be separated from the individual's psyche, which in turn is shaped by ancestral, cultural, and spiritual forces. It is fascinating that in our own highly differentiated and specialized culture we tolerate an artificial separation between psyche and soma.

Several leaders in the family therapy movement have made special contributions to this growing field of interest. Murray Bowen, Ivan Boszormenyi-Nagy, Geraldine Spark, James Framo, Philip Guerin, Elizabeth Carter, Thomas Fogarty, and Norman Paul all focus on the relationships between current individual and family development on one hand, and powerful intergenerational themes on the other.

Murray Bowen (1978) is the person perhaps most closely identified with the intergenerational perspective. In his pioneering work with schizophrenics and their families in the early 1950s, he turned to the natural sciences such as biology, ethology, and phylogenesis for both language and concepts to aid in his efforts to develop a new way of thinking about emotional disturbance. Eventually eschewing tthe psychoanalytic model of human behavior, Bowen hoped that the study of emotional problems could share both the language and the greater scientific credibility of the natural sciences. The central concept in Bowen's theory, the concept that links the intergenerational and here-and-now perspectives, is that of "differentiation," a term relating to intrapersonal, interpersonal, and intergenerational processes.

In intrapersonal terms, differentiation of self and its opposite, fusion, refer to the relationship between the intellect and goal-directed activity on the one hand, and the emotions or feeling-directed activity on the other. The well-differentiated person is provident, flexible, thoughtful, and autonomous in the face of considerable stress, while the less differentiated, more fused person is often trapped in a world of feeling, buffeted about by emotionality, disinclined to providence, inclined to rigidity, and susceptible to dysfunction when confronted with stress.

In the sphere of interpersonal activities, differentiation means the ability to maintain a solid, nonnegotiable self in relationships within and outside the family and to take comfortable "I" positions, not forsaking intellectual and emotional integrity to obtain approval, love, peace or togetherness. The differentiated person, interestingly, is the one who can risk genuine emotional closeness without undue anxiety, and who is capable of sustained intimate relationships; while for the more fused individual, intimacy and closeness may threaten what little sense of self may exist, leading to extreme stress and a variety of maneuvers to create distance. It should be noted that geographic or physical distancing is not to be equated with differentiation. The differentiated person can leave the family to build his or her own life without feeling disloyal and still remain emotionally close, or can stay geographically close without being trapped emotionally in intense family relationships. Such a person can choose to be "like" and to be "different" at different times, without in either case fearing loss of basic self.

In the sphere of family relationships, differentiation refers to the family's ability to accept change and difference on the parts of its members; such a family can allow its members to become autonomous. The fused family, seen in an extreme form in families of schizophrenics, resists new ideas from without and experiences change as a threat. Fusion and differentiation in family systems will be explored in more detail later in this chapter.

The concepts of differentiation and fusion not only apply to the existing family system but are also inextricably linked to the past through a process of multigenerational transmission. The level of differentiation in an individual, according to Bowen, is determined by the differentiation level of one's parents, and by sex, sibling position, quality of relationships, and environmental contingencies at developmental transition points; and a person's more or less stable level of differentiation is largely determined by the time she leaves the parental family.

Bowen proposes the concept of the "family projection process" to explain the transmission of undifferentiation—another word for fusion—from parents to children. The projection process is one in which parental emotionality helps to shape and define what the child becomes, even though these definitions have little to do with the original realities of the child (Kerr, 1981). The concept of the "multigenerational transmission process" describes the ebb and flow of the family's emotional process and the family's projections over the generations. Bowen suggests that a number of outcomes may occur as the degree of family fusion or undifferentiation increases or descreases over the generations. Further, the undifferentiation is not distributed equally among all of the branches of the family tree. Undifferentiation tends to be distributed unequally among the children, as particular children are selected to absorb marital tension and parental projection. Some children may go on to spawn increasingly differentiated lines, others more fused and increasingly symptomatic lines. In Bowen's view, a number of serious dysfunctions, such as severe alcoholism, chronic obesity, and schizophrenia, have their roots several generations back in the family.

Bowen postulates further that the family is largely unaware of these deep-rooted characteristics, not because the family's culture has been necessarily repressed or relegated to the unconscious but because it is as close to the family as the air it breathes. As Frederick Duhl has pointed out, "that which is constantly experienced as neutral to awareness, being so immersed in the identity, so 'ego syntonic,' is rarely open to observation or challenge" (1969:400).

All persons are, to some extent, undifferentiated from this powerful intergenerational system and their lives are in certain respects the receptors of the historical family's transmissions. Our task in assessment is to come to understand the family of origin and its impact on the present, and our goal is to help a person become more differentiated from its powerful forces.

Another concept central to the theory of the intergenerational as well as the nuclear family system is that of the *triangle* or three-person system, which Bowen considers the basic building block of all emotional systems. Bowen believes "a two-person system may be stable as long as it is calm, but when anxiety increases, it immediately involves the most vulnerable other person to become a triangle" (1976:76). These triangles may become fixed and thus permanent and influential elements of the intergenerational family system. They also tend to be repeated in successive generations. In Bowen's view, the identification of these key triangles is a central assess-

ment task in "detriangulating" key threesomes. The process of assessing
the intergenerational family system and the use of that system as a resource
for change will be presented in chapters 10 and 11.

INVISIBLE LOYALTIES

Boszormenyi-Nagy and Spark have contributed yet another perspective on
intergenerational family systems. They view their approach as "the extension of and meeting point between dynamic psychology, existential phe-
nomenology and systems theory" (1973:xiv). They emphasize the subjective
growth processes of individual family members and believe that mental
health is determined by a reciprocal interaction of individual psychological characteristics and the bonds of genetic relatedness. Families develop
a hierarchy of obligations, or a multigenerational balance sheet of merit
and indebtedness which has tremendous impact on individual members,
since any move toward differentiation may imply disloyalty. The task of
the family therapist is to assist the individual to come to terms with ancestral codes of justice and to understand their effects on contemporary
family relationships. For Nagy and Spark the study of power games, communication patterns, or rule processes is only marginally relevant and is
monothetical, since these concepts, in their view, fail to explain the complexities of human interactions or to encompass, in their words, the "real
essence of human relationships. A study of responses without a commitment of responsibility and accountability is socially self-defeating or at
least meaningless" (17). In the dialectical, paradoxical struggle of each
person between individuation and family loyalty, the individual may be
sacrificed in order to pay back multigenerational debts and unresolved
obligations from the past, as the result of an effort to balance what might
be called a "ledger of life."

Norman Paul (1965; Paul and Grosser, 1967) also emphasizes the important effects of unresolved past events, particularly the inadequate earlier resolution of significant losses, on present dysfunction in families. For
Paul a "fixed family equilibrium" combined with a pattern of inability to
cope with loss is common in families with symptomatic members
(1965:341). Since often these are losses parents have suffered in the past,
before the birth of the identified patient, the prevailing family sadness
seems unexplainable and difficult to treat if one looks only at the current
context.

Structure of the Current Family System

Having sketched in broad strokes some of the theories about the intergenerational family, we now turn to examine the here-and-now family sys-

tem. We will tease out certain characteristics of family systems and define them. Our methods will lead to some repetition, as every aspect of the system is interrelated with every other aspect. For example, the presentation begins with a discussion of boundaries as an aspect of family structure, but later, when we examine the dynamic processes of stability, maintenance, and change, we will return to a consideration of boundaries as essential to an understanding of change. This process of weaving back and forth in an attempt both to untangle the different threads and at the same time maintain the pattern of the fabric will continue throughout our presentation.

FAMILY BOUNDARIES

All systems have boundaries which demarcate what is inside from what is outside them. To reiterate what has been stated in earlier pages, in all living systems these boundaries must be permeable enough to permit active interchange between the system and its surroundings. In the case of a family, the boundary consists of an invisible set of loyalties, rules, and emotional connections.

The way in which the family deals with territorial issues and monitors the possible avenues of access to its space determines the kind of boundary it has. Kantor and Lehr (1975), using the idea of boundary as an organizing or characterizing aspect, describe three different types of families—"open," "closed," and "random." In the "open" family, the boundary is clear but very permeable. The family with open boundaries is likely to have "numerous guests, frequent visits with friends, unlocked doors, open windows, individual and group explorations of the community and its resources, and a freedom of informational exchange. . ." (127). In the "closed" family, the boundaries are relatively opaque or impermeable. Such families, according to Kantor and Lehr, may be identified by their locked doors, careful scrutiny of strangers in the neighborhood, parental control over the media, supervised excursions, and unlisted telephones. In the "random" family, there is little difference between family and non-family space. In other words, there is very little boundary at all around the group. The motto for such a family might be: "Do your own thing."

It is important to note that the quality of the family's boundaries is not in itself functional or dysfunctional; Kantor and Lehr believe that families of all three types can be functional. Boundary characteristics reflect the family's style and value system, and its comfortable equilibrium. In all probability, boundaries are historically and culturally influenced. Boundaries can also be an expression of the value the family places on loyalty, closeness, and tradition on the one hand, and individual creative exploration on the other.

Difficulties arise only when families exemplify the extremes. The extreme of a "closed" family, for example, is one that has erected a strong fortress in defense of its physical and conceptual space. An extremely "open" family may fall into schism and conflict as members become confused over matters of loyalty and allegiance. The "random" family, in the extreme case, dissolves into an unregulated aggregate of individuals, a situation in which the family as a system becomes weak and unable to offer cohesion or support to its members.

The existence of boundaries implies the existence of rules for family members. Included are unwritten codes for behavior which orchestrate what family members in good standing should be thinking, feeling, and doing. In closed family systems these rules are more rigid and less easily changed. If a family member dares to be different, even in a small way, the boundary is threatened and the family reacts with some kind of powerful response designed to maintain the existing boundary. In some families, any individual effort toward autonomy or differentness, however small, is perceived as disloyalty, attack, or even abandonment.

Boundaries imply membership as well. As stated in chapter 2, different families and different cultural groups have varied views on where the boundary separating family from nonfamily should be drawn. It is particularly important for social workers to be sensitive to cultural variations and to the fact that some American ethnic groups, such as Jews, Italians, and Afro-Americans, tend to be more inclusive in defining family than Americans of northern European and English origins. Family membership may also vary according to circumstance, growing larger or smaller according to the specific situation in which, or purpose for which, the family is being defined.

SEPARATENESS AND CONNECTEDNESS

Intimately connected with the idea of family boundaries, yet requiring a shift in perspective, is the notion of separateness and connectedness in family systems. This concept has been widely discussed in the family therapy literature, and is the one probably most valuable of all in understanding and helping families. The considerable scholarly and clinical interest in this concept has led to a proliferation of terms and further theories about separateness and connectedness, but also a good deal of confusion.

Eskimos are said to have many different words for snow; the fact demonstrates the great importance of snow in their culture. The English language has few words for snow, but some forty words which refer to the concept of cohesion (Olson, Sprenkle, and Russell, 1979). Explaining the importance of this concept, Minuchin (1974) says that the human experience of identity has two elements, a sense of belonging and a sense of separateness. Karpel (1976), in his discussion of the same issue, writes:

Individuation involves the subtle but crucial phenomenological shifts by which a person comes to see him/herself as separate and distinct with the relationship context in which she has been embedded. The process of individuation from fusion is a universal developmental and existential struggle and a fundamental organizing principle of human growth. [1976:67]

Several leading family theorists have placed the concept of separateness–connectedness in the center of their work. In the next few pages we will briefly review some of their ideas, and then present our own view of this crucial aspect in family-centered practice.

Lyman Wynne, Salvador Minuchin, Murray Bowen, and David Olson are among those who have particularly emphasized separateness and connectedness in their understanding of families, although each of their perspectives is somewhat different, both in terminology and conception. Wynne and his colleagues explored in the 1950s what they claim is a universal conflict: All human beings need to move into relation with other human beings, and yet every human being strives continually to develop a sense of personal identity in which the self is differentiated from others (Wynne et al., 1960). They describe three possible solutions to this conflict, namely, mutuality, pseudomutuality, and nonmutuality.

They describe mutuality thus: "Each person brings to relations of genuine mutuality a sense of his own meaningful, positively-valued identity, and, out of experience or participation together, mutual recognition of identity develops, including a growing recognition of each other's potentialities and capacities" (1960:575). Pseudomutuality, on the other hand, describes those relationships in which separateness is sacrificed to a primary absorption in fitting together. "In pseudo-mutuality the subjective tension aroused by divergence or independence of expectations, including the open affirmation of a sense of personal identity, is experienced as not merely disrupting that particular transaction but as possibly demolishing the entire relation" (575). In Wynne's view, nonmutuality describes temporary, nonintimate, narrowly defined role relationships like, for example, that of customer and salesclerk. Nonmutuality does not tend to occur in families because of the persistent and recurring need for family members to deal with their relatedness. Wynne takes the position that family members cannot leave the emotional field, an idea reiterated in the writings of other family theorists.

Minuchin approaches separateness and connectedness by postulating a continuum between enmeshment and disengagement in family systems. In the enmeshed family, "a heightened sense of belonging requires a yielding of autonomy" (Minuchin, 1974:55). At its extreme, there are inadequate boundaries between family members, who feel each others' feelings as if their own. Family members intrude into each others' space, possessions, thoughts, and relationships. As in pseudomutuality, an effort by a family member to erect any kind of boundary is seen as a severe rejection or hostile attack. Lynn Hoffman (1975) describes such systems as "too richly cross-joined." With such a wide-open and reactive relationship network, unimpeded by boundaries, any change, need, or affect which occurs in any subsystem quickly reverberates throughout the system. This rich cross-joining has important consequences for the possibilities for change.

On the other end of the continuum is the disengaged family, whose boundaries between its members are rigid and opaque. There is little empathy and little meaningful exchange of any kind; the ties between members are weak or nonexistent (Hoffman, 1975). In disengaged or "too poorly cross-joined" families, there is little response to the needs of family members. Such families will tend to ignore all but the most dramatic bids for attention or for help, and family members are relatively impervious to or invalidating of one another's communications. For example, Minuchin has said that in the enmeshed family the parents are upset if a child skips dessert; in the disengaged family they may fail to notice if he does not eat all day.

One contrast immediately comes to mind between Wynne's and Minuchin's conceptualizations. Wynne is more person-oriented, conceptualizing separateness-connectedness in terms of the individual's needs and relationships between individuals, whereas Minuchin characterizes family systems. Another difference lies in the endpoints of their continua. Minuchin describes a continuum between two dysfunctional extremes which leaves one with some question about how the mean would be characterized, beyond his implication that families in the middle maintain clear boundaries. Further, Minuchin states that functional families can occupy a wide segment of the continuum, expressing different preferences in family style. Wynne, on the other hand, describes a continuum between the ideal state of mutuality and the pathological state of pseudomutuality. Furthermore, although Wynne's concept of nonmutuality sounds very much like Minuchin's concept of disengagement, Wynne, unlike Minuchin, implies that such extremes of noncommunication are rare in family relations.

Olson, Sprenkle, and Russell (1970), in the development of their model of family assessment, select family cohesion as one of the major variables to be measured. Cohesion is defined as "an emotional, intellectual, and/ or physical oneness that family members feel toward one another" (Russell, 1979:31). Using a language similar to that of Minuchin, these theorists conceptualize cohesion on a continuum or scale which ranges from disengaged at one end, through separated, connected, and finally to enmeshed at the other end. In describing the points along this scale, Olson et al. analyze characteristics of individuals as well as of entire family systems. Their hypothesis is that the more functional families will be found within the two central categories, separateness and connectedness, whereas families moving toward either extreme will exhibit a higher degree of difficulty.

In our earlier analysis of intergenerational influences we described Murray Bowen's (1978) concepts of differentiation and fusion. These concepts form yet another continuum of separateness and connectedness. Bowen used the terms differentiation and fusion to characterize both intrapersonal functioning and interpersonal relationships. He originally presented his concept of differentiation of self as a scale which described the characteristics of those located at various points on it. This effort was intended to emphasize the notion of a continuum which included all people and which demonstrated that function and dysfunction were not a matter of qualitative difference but of degree.

Bowen makes clear that differentiation of self inevitably relates to interpersonal processes as well. A highly fused person is dependent upon the relationship system, wherein a large portion of the self is negotiable; that is, behavior is directed toward pleasing or manipulating others rather than being directed by the self. A poorly differentiated person tends to fuse in intimate relationships. This fusion, which threatens what little sense of self there is, creates extreme stress and calls forth a variety of actions in order to deal with the attendant anxiety. Klugman observes:

> the . . . greater the degree of fusion, the more energy is put into balancing the emotional system, since the emotional security of the fused person is dependent on the behavior of the person(s) with whom he feels fused. "I-positions" are avoided, thus deflecting any confrontative aspects of the relationship, blurring the separateness and uniqueness of the individuals involved. [1976:321]

The issue of separateness and togetherness is also central in Bowen's conception of the nuclear family emotional system. According to his theory, intrapersonal, interpersonal, and intrafamilial differentiation are linked; if a person is poorly differentiated from his family of origin it is likely that he is poorly differentiated as well in the nuclear family system and in all interpersonal relationships. Further, such a person is also poorly differentiated in the sense that the emotions dominate the intellect.

Of particular significance in understanding the inner family system is Bowen's description of the processes that the family sets in motion to deal with lack of differentiation in the marital pair. As we said above, lack of differentiation in such a relationship causes extreme anxiety, as the couple is chronically threatened by loss of the self through fusion. Couples have a number of options for dealing with the anxiety. Most couples, Bowen thinks, handle the potential threat that intimacy entails by distancing one another. Chronic marital conflict serves this function particularly well. In such a marriage, the couple may have some periods of intense closeness, but these are quickly ended by a fight between the pair;

marital conflict thus serves to monitor and control the drift toward fusion. A second way the couple may accommodate to their respective lacks of differentiation is to fuse, becoming a single self. This requires that one member give up his or her self to the other. The outward result is a pair composed of a dominant overfunctioning mate and a dysfunctional adaptive mate. A third mechanism which an undifferentiated couple may use in dealing with fusion is the triangulating of a child. This method is part of the "family projection process," in which parents project their anxieties and difficulties onto their children, and it is the means by which the parents' lack of differentiation can be duplicated in the impaired child.

Bowen identifies yet another strategy of the poorly differentiated person, namely, the emotional cutoff. When people are emotionally cut off, they have withdrawn from any genuine contact and erected an emotional wall between themselves and those from whom they are cut off. In Bowen's view, the emotional cutoff is a reaction to the threat of fusion; the connections between people in that state can actually be very intense and influential.

From comparing and contrasting these four theories of the separatness–connectedness continuum, several notions emerge. Enmeshment, fusion, and pseudomutuality all deal with connectedness; they seem to describe similar phenomena. The differences among the concepts lie in the fact that they primarly refer to different systems. Enmeshment, in Minuchin's conceptualization, refers specifically to the family system and the lack of appropriate boundaries between subsystems within it. Bowen's fusion, on the other hand, may refer to either intrapersonal functioning or interpersonal relationships, whereas Wynne's pseudomutuality refers exclusively to interpersonal relationships. All of these terms, however, imply an insufficient separateness or faulty boundaries between people, and a relationship system or family system that is, in Hoffman's (1975) terms, "too richly cross-joined." A further comparison may be made regarding family of origin. Bowen states that individuals who tend to fuse have grown up in situations where they were highly fused in their family's emotional system. Applying the language of Wynne and Minuchin, we might suggest that such people have experienced pseudomutual relationships with one or both parents or have grown up in enmeshed family systems. One distinction, however, must be made. It is Bowen's particular view that although one or more of the children in a family may be fused into the parental relationships, others may not be; therefore, the total family structure need not be without boundaries.

Thus the four theories run parallel in their understanding of connectedness; but they differ regarding separateness. Both Minuchin and Olson characterize separateness and connectedness as a bipolar continuum with the implication that dysfunctional families are located at either extreme. Bowen and Wynne, on the other hand, envision a continuum from a state of fusion or pseudomutuality, which implies the potential for serious dysfunction, to mutuality or differentiation, which is an ideal, healthy, or functional state. Although mutuality and differentiation indicate the person's ability to maintain a clear and separate identity or solid sense of self, these concepts also describe a capacity for intimacy and closeness. Neither notion implies disengagement or alienation.

Wynne's idea of nonmutuality does not fall within our continuum because it does not exist in the family; he believes that family members are too closely connected over time to be truly uninvolved with one another. Bowen seems to agree, taking the position that a seeming lack of involvement between family members is really a reactive stance to the threat of fusion and that an apparently cut-off person continues to be highly influenced by the family emotional system. The Separateness–Connectedness Concepts of these four theorists are depicted in Table 5-1.

TABLE 5-1   Separateness–Connectedness Concepts

Theorist	*Concepts*
Minuchin	Disengaged .... Enmeshed
Olson	Disengaged .... Separated...... Connected .... Enmeshed
Wynne	Mutual...Pseudomutual
	(Nonmutual does not exist in families)
Bowen	Differentiated .... Fused
	Emotional cutoff

LOVING AND CARING

There is yet another aspect of separateness and connectedness that does not seem to appear very prominently in the family theory reviewed above, namely, the rather old-fashioned notion of loving or caring. Since it is not specifically dealt with, one is left wondering if loving or caring is an aspect of cohesion. If so, according to the logic of continuum models, love would exist on the continuum from the extreme of too little to the extreme of too much, and too much caring would presumably be connected with other characteristics of enmeshment such as high dependence or blurred boundaries, while the disengaged family might be labeled "unloving." Hoffman (1981) suggests that the disengaged, or "too poorly cross-joined," family suffers from some kind of formlessness, some kind of chaos, and seemingly, a quality of not caring. On the other hand, she points out that even in families which may have few routines and ceremonies, "individuals can still show great caring toward one another" (791).

Among family members, "caring for" or "caring about" one another does not necessarily imply enmeshment or "becoming one." This notion is clearly stated in the common expression, "You have to love your children enough to be able to give them up," which links loving to the fostering of autonomy. Therefore, just as being differentiated allows people to connect intimately, so does loving allow people to differentiate.

FAMILY ORGANIZATION

We now turn to describe those aspects of family structure which are concerned with the organization of and relationships among the various subsystems in the family. As Minuchin writes, "The family system differentiates and carries out its functions through subsystems. Dyads such as husband–wife or mother–child can be subsystems. Subsystems can be formed by generation, by sex, by interest, or by function" (1974:52).

According to Minuchin, the key and most enduring subsystems in a family are the spouse subsystem, the parental subsystem, and the sibling subsystem. The spouse subsystem includes the man and woman who have joined to originate the family in a system founded in complementarity and mutuality. Minuchin emphasizes the importance of the functioning of this subsystem to the functioning of the total family system. He writes that, "adults must have a psychosocial territory of their own—a haven in which they can give each other emotional support" (1974:57). The nature of the boundary around that system is crucial to family functioning. It must be firm enough to protect the spouse subsystem against interference from in-laws, children, and others.

In these days of varied family forms, the definition of the spouse subsystem has become increasingly complex. Step-parents, lovers who may live in the home or out of it, group living arrangements, all make the reality of the spouse system more complex. For example, an unconventional or nonlegalized spouse subsystem may have more difficulty defining and enforcing the boundaries around their relationship. Whereas a legally married spouse might feel fully authorized to exclude from the marriage the partner's children from an earlier relationship, an unmarried lover in the same situation might hesitate; and, likewise, "outsider" stepparents might be either reluctant to intrude on, or jealous of, the "insider" relationship between the spouse and his or her biological children.

The parental subsystem defines the parents in their roles with their children; among its tasks are the care, nurture, and guidance of the young. Ideally, the boundary around the parental subsystem allows each child to have access to each parent without at any time intruding upon the spouse subsystem. The linkage of role and subsystem organization is illustrated in this rather enigmatic statement. What is implied here is that the child should be allowed access to the parents specifically as parents, but not allowed access to the parents in their roles as husband and wife.

The boundary around the parental subsystem must also be sufficiently clear to protect the parents from interference by others as they go about the tasks of parenting. However, this issue may become quite complicated when others besides the biological parents are a part of the parental subsystem. In a single-parent family, for example, another adult such as a grandparent or close adult friend may become part of the parental system; in some families, the parental subsystem may be strengthened by the help of one of the older children. This state of affairs is not necessarily dysfunctional. It is the clarity of function and of membership rather than who belongs to the parental subsystem that has such significance for the family's functioning and coherence.

Whatever the parental circumstances, the notion of boundary has significance. The parental boundary must be clear enough so that the family has some orderly sense of authority, of "who's boss?" How often a parent must say to an older son or daughter, reinforcing the parental boundary, "Never mind about your brother's behavior, I'll take care of that!" There are many variations possible in the organization of the parental subsystem, which may change periodically and over time in relation to family activities, critical episodes, or life cycle transitions. For example, frequently parents will put an older sibling in charge during the parents' absence. In that case, the older sibling temporarily becomes part of the parental subsystem. This is an illustration of the "parental child" role found so often in large and in single-parent families.

Families of remarriage face a particular challenge in defining the parental subsystem. Children who visit back and forth between the homes of divorced parents who have remarried may have to reckon with four or more adults who have some claim on membership in the parental subsystem. Much of the pain and conflict in separation and divorce can be attributed to confusion over who has the right to parent the children and to receive the greatest loyalty from them.

The sibling subsystem consists of the children in the family. As Minuchin points out, "this sibling subsystem is the first social laboratory in which the children can experiment with peer relationships. . . . In the sibling world, children learn how to negotiate, cooperate, and compete" (1974:59). It is important that children have the opportunity to experiment in this laboratory without undue adult interference. Children, if adults allow them, learn early and quickly how to involve a parent in a sibling struggle, to their personal advantage, of course! Parents who enter the sibling subsystem to settle fights and mediate conflict report with great frustration that the conflict and fights become increasingly frequent and seem to escalate in intensity, calling for ever more parental arbitration.

In large families, sibling subsystems themselves may be further divided into new subsystems, often according to distinctions of sex or age, as in the case of the boys and the girls or the younger set and the older set. Other structural arrangements may develop across parent–child but along gender lines, with strong alliances between the male subsystem and the female subsystem. Some family theorists, following the leadership of

Parsons (Parsons and Bales, 1955), have emphasized the importance of role clarity within, and boundaries between, the male and female subsystems, a stance increasingly challenged in the context of the changing American family. The following statement made by Theodore Lidz, an acknowledged authority on the family, illustrates the Parsonian position, a position widely influential for many years in all of the helping professions. Clearly this statement is descriptive of some "ideal" form of the white middle class family of the 1950s.

> The nuclear family is also composed of persons of two genders with complementary functions and role allocations as well as anatomical differences. The primary female role derives from woman's biological makeup and is related to the nurturing of children and the maintenance of the home needed for that purpose, which has led women to have a particular interest in interpersonal relationships and the emotional harmony of family members—an expressive–affectional role. The male role, also originally related to physique, traditionally is concerned with the support and protection of the family and with establishing its position within the larger society—an instrumental-adaptive role. . . . We may hazard that in order for the family to develop a structure that can properly direct the integration of its offspring, *the spouses must form a coalition as parents, maintain the boundaries between the generations, and adhere to their respective gender-linked roles.* [1963:51, 57] (Italics in original)

The position contained in the above quotation is clearly vulnerable to attack from many directions. Most importantly, it does not reflect the adaptive structures of varying family forms, or cultural, ethnic, or religious diversity. The stance taken by Lidz also stereotypes sex roles, linking them to mental health. Further, it suggests that families which do not conform to this structure may be dysfunctional or unable to integrate.

In contrast to the Lidz position, we hold that the family is an open sociocultural system in transformation. In this period of rapid social change and in a land rich with ethnic diversity, family structure is highly varied and continually changing.

STRUCTURE AND AUTHORITY

An important aspect of structure, according to Minuchin (1974), Haley (1976; 1980), and others, lies in the nature of the lines of authority and power in the family. Haley attaches great importance to the hierarchically arranged authority system and, more often than not, in his view the goal of intervention in the case of dysfunctional parent–child relationships is one of restoring appropriate lines of hierarchical authority.

There has been considerable disagreement among family theorists concerning the seat of power or authority in the family. Palazzoli and her colleagues (1978; 1980) argue that the power does not reside in any one individual in the family or even within a subsystem. The power, in their view, lies in the "family game" or in the rules. This issue is elaborated upon when we turn to a discussion of homeostatic or equilibrating processes in the family.

TRIANGLES

In our consideration of theory about family structure, one of the most important structural elements is the triangle, which exists throughout the family system. Minuchin refers particularly to the triangle which develops when a child is brought into the spouse subsystem. The triangle is key in Bowen's family theory and practice, and, in fact, Bowen considers the triangle, or three-person system, to be the basic building block of all emotional systems in and outside of the family. Very briefly, in Bowen's view the two-person system is basically unstable, and such a system deals with tension or with the drift toward uncomfortable fusion by bringing in a third person. In periods of calm, a triangle consists of a comfortable twosome and an outsider. The outsider, however, attempts to develop a twosome with one of the original pair, thus shifting an insider to the outside position.

Triangles become particularly dysfunctional when they are rigid and unmoving. An example of a dysfunctional triangle is scapegoating, whereby parents deal with their problematic relationship by sharing critical and negative feelings about a child, thus finding some togetherness in keeping the child "stuck" in the outside position. Triangulating can serve to minimize genuine intimacy and to avoid person-to-person relationships, since two people, rather than talking about intimate and potentially painful issues between them, can always talk about other people or things.

FAMILY STRUCTURE AND ROLE

Role theory and specific applications of role to an understanding of family structure have long been an important part of family theory. Role may be defined as "a person's organized pattern or mode of behaving, fashioned by the status or functions he or she carries in relation to one or more persons" (Perlman, 1962:167). This definition contains two key notions. First, role is a transactional concept. It grows out of and expresses a relationship and the expectations, obligations, and prescriptions that develop in that relationship. Secondly, the pattern of role behavior is fashioned by a status or function, that is, role behaviors are tied to and shaped by particular positions or functions in social groups.

Nathan Ackerman, in the early days of the family therapy movement and before systems theory had become influential, thought that the concept of role might provide the linking mechanism needed to view the functioning of individual personality in the context of family dynamics. In his words,

> the treatment of a mother of a disturbed child is the treatment of a role, a highly specialized family function. It is not identical with the theory of a whole woman, but rather of the personality of that woman integrated into a special social function, that of mothering. For a proper conceptual approach to this problem, it is necessary to recognize the interdependence and reciprocity of family roles, to devise criteria for accurate appraisal of the mental health functioning of family groups and dynamic formulae for interrelating individual personality and family role. [Ackerman, 1954; reprinted in Erickson and Hogan, 1976]

Other family therapy pioneers began to view schizophrenia and other pathological disorders as the result of an individual's assuming a deviant family role, the best know formulation being that of "the emotionally disturbed child as the family scapegoat" (Vogel and Bell, 1960).

During the same period of the 1950s, social role functioning was becoming a key focus in social work, especially in individual, marital, and family assessment. The family was seen as a network of reciprocal roles, husband–wife, mother–child, father–child, and to a lesser extent, brother–sister, and families were evaluated in terms of the extent to which the various members performed their prescribed functions or met the expectations of these roles.

Although the identification and clarification of formal role assignments and expectations continue to be an important part of understanding families, the growing awareness over the past thirty years of the extent to which these roles are culturally defined leads to increasing caution in dealing with role issues. The complexities involved in using formal role in the assessment process will be discussed at length when we turn to this area of practice.

Certain concepts from role theory, however, are particularly useful in understanding families. These concepts are not descriptions of specific role expectations but rather they are metaconcepts about the qualities of or relationships between roles. They include role congruity, role conflict, role complementarity, role continuity, role flexibility, role ambiguity, and role competence.

INFORMAL FAMILY ROLE ASSIGNMENTS

Beyond the formal role structure discussed above, families are also characterized by a structure of informal roles. These role assignments may have significant impact on individual functioning, and may also contribute to the development, coherence and sometimes even the survival of the family system. Certainly they are central in the planning of strategies for family system change. A few examples illustrate the concept.

Perhaps the most well known and studied formal role is that of the family scapegoat. Bell and Vogel (1960), who first identified and researched this family role, reported that the family scapegoat becomes the receptacle for spoken and unspoken family tensions and hostilities, particularly those existing between the marital pair. The function of the family scapegoat is to maintain family solidarity by masking or siphoning off conflicts which might conceivably otherwise destroy the family. In describing their research, Bell and Vogel write:

> By focusing on one particular child, the families were able to encapsulate problems and anxieties which could potentially disrupt various family processes. There seemed to be an added solidarity between the parents who stood united against the problem child. [1960:395]

Many other common, informal family roles have been identified in terms of their function in the family system. The "family switchboard," often the mother, transmits and monitors communication throughout the family. The "family caretaker" is the member called upon to nurture or care for other members in need or difficulty. The "family pioneer" exposes the family to new experiences by taking risks, moving into unknown territory, testing it out, and then bringing the family along. The "family distracter" helps the family avoid or ignore painful or difficult matters by exhibiting noisy and demanding behavior which gains everyone's attention, while the "family joker" deflects tension with humorous comments or antics. The "family organizer" or "camp counselor," whose purpose is often to combat family sadness or depression, is the enthusiastic planner of family outings and group activities; she sees that everyone is given various tasks in family projects and expeditions. Kantor and Lehr (1975) distinguish four major roles which characterize the nature of individual participation in family activity or change the processes of it: 1) the movers, or those who initiate action, 2) the followers, or those who validate the mover's actions, 3) the opposers, or those who obstruct the mover's actions, and 4) the bystanders, those who observe but remain uninvolved.

Family Forces for Stability and Change

We have described certain aspects of the family as if they were somehow static or unchanging. This, of course, is not the case. The family is a dynamic human system in which there is constant movement. We now turn to dynamic processes and transactions within the family which either maintain stability or promote adaptation and change. In early explorations of the family as a system, there was a strong emphasis on homeostatic processes in the family, that is, processes that maintain family stability. It may be that this emphasis evolved in part from the characteristics of the particular families studied by early clinical researchers. As Don Jackson, a major figure in the application of homeostatic theory to family therapy himself, wrote, "It is significant in the development of family theory that it was the observation of homeostatic mechanisms in the families of psychiatric patients that led to the hypothesis of the family as a homeostatic and eventually specifically as a rule governed system" (1965:3).

Speer (1970) was among the first to clarify the fact that the emphasis on homeostatic forces mistakenly characterized the family as static and unchanging. Homeostasis, he points out, is the basic principle of biologic and organismic systems which, though open and living, exist and survive within rather narrow restraints and through the operation of consistent and relatively unchanging adaptive patterns. Families, on the other hand, are sociocultural systems. Body temperature, a biological function, has frequently been used as a metaphor for the application of the concept of homeostasis in family therapy, and well illustrates the limitations in the use of such concepts in characterizing families. The normative body temperature, 98.6 degrees, is unchanging and the range of variation possible without endangering the life of the system is relatively narrow. The processes involved in the maintenance of normal temperature are error activated and deviation correcting; they consist of negative and reactive feedback loops. The adaptive mechanisms always come into play to return the body temperature to 98.6 degrees. Finally, the deviation-correcting processes are patterned, as exemplified in the cardiovascular adjustment processes which heat or cool the body. The individual biological system does not develop novel ways to regulate temperature any more than it alters the desired stasis of 98.6 degrees. It requires eons of evolutionary time for biological systems to develop novel adaptive mechanisms.

In contrast to this homeostatic system, a much wider range of options for adaptation and change are available to a family. For example, the desired goal or basic rule can itself be altered, as the following example illustrates:

In the Martin family, there was a strong rule that everyone must attend college. This rule, which had been a part of the family's self-regulatory system for three generations, began to be tested by Steve in his early high school years. He continually veered away from the college-bound path by showing little interest in academics, devoting his energy to sports, friends, and his consuming hobby, woodworking. The family activated a number of negative feedback responses, attempting to urge Steve back on the track. Initially, they utilized the habitual mechanisms, supervision of homework, rules against TV, and expressions of anger and disappointment. As each deviation-counteracting action failed, the family escalated their efforts and moved to novel means to control his rule-breaking behavior. Conferences with the teachers and private tutoring were to no avail. Eventually, Steve, his counselors and other school personnel began to give the family new information about Steve's outstanding talent at woodworking, about training programs, and about career opportunities that could be available to a person with this skill, from custom furniture and cabinetmaking to industrial model building. The family also began to remember that Steve, as a very little boy, had spent hours with his beloved grandfather in the shop where the old man pursued the hobby of woodworking. The family then moved to a basic change, that is, they changed the family rule about college, and pride about Steve's achievements in using his hands began to develop.

Still another kind of change grew out of this rather painful period for the family—increased self-knowledge. Families seem to have the ability to receive secondary messages in a kind of systemic self-awareness process, and are able at least on an analogic level to integrate information about the status of their own internal organization and processes. This internal feedback may promote change in the family's basic operation.

In the struggle with Steve, the Martins became aware that for a long time they had not listened to him and had not allowed discussion about the college rule. They had been impervious to information which might have led them to reconsider the rule sooner, thus saving the family considerable conflict and pain. Out of this experience the family not only modified a basic rule, but it developed new rules about rules and rule-changing processes, thereby innovating opportunities for the exchange of information about family rules. For example, they initiated regular family conferences to facilitate communication and to consider adaptation of the rules.

In the above example, we see the family's capacity to not only allow itself to undergo a change in a particular rule, but to admit novelty and variety in its basic regulatory or governing processes. While such changes can occur in sociocultural systems with comparative ease, comparable changes in biological systems can only occur over many, many generations. In the Martin family, novel strategies for maintaining the rule were developed first. Then, on the basis of new information, the rule was changed. Finally, a change took place on a higher order when the family altered a metarule, or a rule about the rules. This example illustrates at least three ways in which change may be initiated. First, change can occur as a result of new input or information from the world outside the family; second, change may emerge from the exchange of information among components within the system, and third, an autonomous or differentiated position taken by one member of the family system may become the spur to change. Clearly if change occurs in any one of these ways, it is likely to effect transformations in the others.

For adaptive and goal-directed change to take place—for the family system to be viable, to use Speer's words—the boundaries between the family and the world, and also among the family members themselves, must be open enough for information to be exchanged. Further, boundaries among family members must be firm enough to allow an individual to take a differentiated position. Both Speer (1970) and Eleanor Wertheim (1973; 1975), drawing on the work of general systems theorists Walter Buckley and James Miller, emphasize the potential for change, growth, and self-direction in family systems and describe family processes as being characterized by two transactional forces, described as morphostatic and morphogenic. Morphostatic properties are defined as self-correcting processes that account for the stability of the system. Morphostasis gives the system its continuity and coherence. Writes Wertheim, "Without some optimal degree of morphostasis, the family system could not survive as a cohesive, viable social group" (1973:365). Morphostatic properties include family rules, shared meanings, values, and expectations. Such properties bring order to the family and make it possible for family members to communicate and function coherently within the family system. On the other hand, morphogenesis is an essential quality as well in the well-functioning family. "Morphogenic properties," writes Wertheim, "refer to self-directing processes that allow for change, growth, innovation and enhancement of the viability of the system" (364). Morphogenesis implies a departure from systems rules. It implies the choice of a new direction or a new solution. The balance between morphostatic and morphogenic forces sheds light on how a given system attempts to maintain its integrity and the extent to which change is welcomed. Wertheim explains:

> Morphostasis contributes to autoregulation by enabling the system to function in accordance with its expectations and to predict events. Morphogenesis gives the system the freedom to want and to change accordingly. Morphostasis provides a safeguard against a prospect of disintegration. Morphogenesis offers a safeguard against maladaptive rigidity and against a monotonous, non-creative existence. [1975:306]

THE FAMILY RULE SYSTEM

All families have complex systems of rules that provide stability and continuity through time. Shared meanings, consistent patterns of behavior, organization, and communication are expressions of family rules. Rules define patterns in the use of language, of space, and of time. They dictate the assignment of formal and informal roles and prescribe the various behaviors attached to different roles. Some rules are more central and more tenaciously supported than others. Some may be less invested with emotion, and more peripheral to the family's self-definition.

Without such a set of rules, life in a family would be chaotic, as each situation would be novel, and would require new planning and decision making. As anthropologist Victor Turner has expressed it, "By verbal and non-verbal means of classification we impose upon ourselves innumerable constraints and boundaries to keep chaos at bay, but often at the cost of failing to make discoveries and inventions" (1969:vii).

The sources of family rules are many and are probably not fully understood. Certainly cultural and intergenerational themes have strong impact on the character of many of the family rules. Family loyalties, habit, serendipity, and human creativity provide some of the rules. And, although it is important to attempt to determine if a rule is serving a vital function in the maintenance of the family system, we do not take the position that all rules are performing a function in the current context.

Palazzoli and her colleagues take the view that family systems, through a trial-and-error method, develop in time a series of rules which maintain the system. Key rules in the family, taken together, comprise the "family game," and if the family includes a pathological member, the symptomatic behavior of that person is generally an essential part of that game. Thus it is that the family cannot afford to allow the "patient" to relinquish that behavior, as such a change could shake the foundations of the family.

Further, as therapists of the Mental Research Institute point out, although problematic or pathological behavior may have originated in response to past events or circumstances in the family situation, it may now be maintained by responses in the environment, particularly those very responses which have been mobilized to alter, interrupt, or deal with that behavior. Invalidism which develops in order to achieve the secondary gains attending an illness exemplifies this circular transaction.

Finally, an important aspect of the family rule system is the set of metarules or rules about rules. These metarules govern the kind of process which may take place in relation to rule setting and rule changing. For example, rigid families that are extremely threatened by any kind of change may have a metarule which contains the unspoken but powerful message that rules in the family may not be questioned or commented upon. Such a rule ensures that family rules are not available for examination or challenge.

Yet families, in order to adapt and change, must have rules about how to discuss and change rules. In rigid families caught in a dysfunctional network of largely unarticulated rules, there is no system of rule changing. Such a situation is reminiscent of E. M. Forster's short story, "The Machine Stops." In an earlier time an elaborate machine had been built which up to the present has met all the needs of the populace; now, however, it begins to fall into disrepair. Those who built it are long dead and had not planned a repair system. Interestingly enough, as the machine begins to fail and the air becomes putrid, the lights dim, and the food spoils, no one is allowed to comment on the changes. In fact, propaganda is dispersed to convince everyone that things are *better* than they used to be.

Power in Families

We now turn to the subject of power in family systems, a matter which has been discussed and argued at considerable length. Palazzoli (1978), following the opinion of Bateson, takes the position that power resides in the family game, the network of rules that governs the family's transactions and maintains family stability. These rules, which develop over time out of the transactions of all family members and out of their pooled and negotiated motives and desires, incorporate the real power in the family, and individual members are powerless to change them. This notion is well illustrated by a marital pair who sought help for their escalating struggle over the control and definition of their relationship, commenting, "It's bigger than both of us!"

Haley (1976), on the other hand, who differed theoretically with Bateson on the issue of power, describes the family as a hierarchy in which some subsystems have power over other subsystems. Often, according to Haley, a major goal of family therapy is to restore the family's appropriate hierarchical organization. He writes:

> Every family must deal with the issue of organizing in a hierarchy and rules must be worked out about who is primary in status and power and who is secondary. When an individual shows symptoms, the organization has a hierarchical arrangement that is confused. It may be confused by being ambiguous so that no one quite knows who is his peer and who is his superior. It may also be confused because a member at one level of the hierarchy consistently forms a coalition against a peer with a member at another level, thus violating the basic rules of organization. [1976:103]

Wertheim (1973) believes that in a well-functioning family power is shared through consensus rather than applied by force:

> Consensual morphostasis derives from appropriately balanced, intra-family distribution of power. The term refers to genuine stability of the family system, consensually validated by its members. Forced morphostasis is rooted in intra-family power imbalances . . . and refers to *apparent stability* of the family system maintained in the absence of genuine, consensual validation by its members. [1973:365]

According to Broderick (1975), power may be utilized by the family in several ways, including (1) zero-sum power confrontations; (2) family rules and rule enforcement; and (3) principled interaction. In zero-sum confrontations, there is an attempt by one person to impose his or her will unilaterally on another member or members of the family. (The term zero-sum comes from game theory and means that whatever one wins, the other loses, so that the sum of the players' wins and losses are always zero.) Speigel's (1957) study of conflict resolution in the family found that such unilateral attempts were very common in families. This concept may also relate to Bateson's description of complementary schismogenesis discussed later in this chapter. According to Broderick, families who employ the zero-sum power confrontation can survive if the opponents are relatively well matched or if the powerless member has no way to leave the system. Certainly this description of zero-sum confrontations has a familiar ring to those of us who have attempted to help marital pairs or parents and adolescents locked in a stalemated struggle in which each feels that if he or she gives an inch, the other will somehow be victorious. Not only honor but survival itself seems to hinge on the outcome of such confrontations and everyone, including the practitioner, can feel powerless.

Governance by family rules is the second model described by Broderick. He notes that these rules, which develop over time, allocate family resources and authority and determine how rules can be changed. Broderick's final model is governance by principle. In this situation, power is invested in a few overarching principles which are internalized by each family member, and family governance is actually self-governance according to these shared principles. These principles may reflect value stances and notions of how things "ought" to be done. More subtly, such principles may be deeply embedded in the family mythology and thus they provide, in Ferreira's words, "an animated album of family pictures that no one quite dares erase or throw away, essential as they are to the legitimization and consecration of the ongoing relationships" (1971:363).

In view of these differing analyses of power in the family, it is clear that further research is needed to clarify the role and nature of power in family systems. In the interim, it seems useful to draw upon concepts from several perspectives in understanding family governance and potential for change.

Considering the issue of location, that is, whether family power resides in the rules of the game or within particular family members, we speculate that both people and rules are sources or repositories of power. The family game or network of rules is indeed powerful in most if not all families, but it may be primarily in very rigid, morphostatic families that all the power is concentrated in the game. However, we would speculate that in the trial-and-error development of the family rules and the family game, some members, generally the adults, have more opportunity than others to step outside the game from time to time, and more power in the trial-and-error process itself. Such persons, because of their power, are least likely to be victimized; it is rarely if ever that the most powerful person in the family is scapegoated. The scapegoating process is generally directed toward a relatively powerless, dependent member, for example a child who becomes inducted into the role and then participates in its continuance.

The family member who brings home innovative ideas embodies a constructive form of power. Bowen contributes the notion that individuals, through drawing on a variety of resources and life experiences, may differentiate from the family system, become more autonomous and, in a reworking back upon the family, provide an impetus for growth and change. Of course, the more rigid the family game, the fewer opportunities will arise for such individual differentiation.

We have also found useful Wertheim's (1973; 1975) concept of consensual morphostasis, an idea similar to Broderick's (1975) second model of family governance. Both of these conceptualizations seem to unite the two notions of power as something located either within the individual or within the family game. The central assessment question here relates to the metarules, the rules about how rules are to be developed, maintained, and changed. When there is consensual morphostasis, there are special rules that family members may participate in the development, challenging, or changing of all other rules.

Finally, we find the concept of principled family governance to be a useful notion. Principles which direct families are the shared meanings valued and adhered to by family members. Some of these principles may represent rational, moral, or ethical positions. For example, a family may hold very strongly to the value of fairness, and thus the adage "What's fair is fair!" may well give direction to the family system. The prescriptions and meanings handed down from the family of origin may provide a major portion of a family's guiding principles. But whether embodied in announced rational statements or embedded in family myths which "go unchallenged by everyone involved in spite of the reality distortions" (Ferreira, 1971:358), the power of belief systems and systems of meanings becomes evident as one works with families. We will return toward the end of this chapter to a consideration of the power of family meaning systems.

Family Communication Processes

We have been describing the components of process within the family, the morphostatic and morphogenic forces, rules, and power. However, we have yet to describe the information exchange that constitutes the means of family process. Everything that goes on among people is communication and thus, obviously, it is only as we can become skilled and knowledgeable students and observers of communication that we may gain access to processes in family systems.

Theory about communication has been an essential part of understanding families since the pioneering days of family therapy. Our discussion would not be complete without presenting some of the major principles of communication, principles which can sharpen our observational skills and guide our work with families. This presentation relies primarily on the work of the members of the Mental Research Institute in Palo Alto (Bateson, 1958; 1972; Watzlawick, Beavin, and Jackson, 1967; Watzlawick, 1976; Jackson, 1967; 1968).

Watzlawick et al. delineate several basic principles which are helpful in understanding the pragmatics of communication. First, it is impossible *not* to communicate, as all behavior is communication. For example, settling into a seat on an airplane for a long trip, and hoping to work, read, or rest, we quickly and nonverbally communicate to the passenger who is sharing the seat that we do not want to communicate. Again: father, sitting in the corner behind the evening paper, is saying wordlessly, "Do not talk to me." Our gestures, our facial expressions, and even our lack of gestures and facial immobility, communicate silently but eloquently.

Secondly, a communication not only conveys information but also generally contains a command. This double aspect of communication is made plain in dealing with computers. When using a pocket calculator one must both enter the information, that is the numbers, and then also tell the calculator what to do with the numbers, whether to add or subtract, divide or multiply. This second or command message is termed metacommunication, since it is communication *about* communication.

In human communication, the command or meta aspect, which makes a statement about how the communication is to be interpreted, is generally also communicating something about the receiver, something about the sender, and even something about the relationship between them. One of our favorite examples of this is found in a Nichols and May theater sketch entitled "Mother and Son." The mother, a prototype of the intrusive, complaining, demanding parent, at one point says, disqualifying her words with laughter, "I'm just an old nag . . ." Then: "No, I'm kidding." Her metamessage is, "Do not believe me; this is not true." Of course, the humor lies in the fact that her original verbal message *was* true and in her maddening lack of both self-awareness and awareness of her relationship with her son.

A third principle of communication relates to what Bateson referred to as the "punctuations" of the communicational sequences. Communication is a cybernetic or transactional process and in the interchange, each response contains the preceding communication and, in fact, the preceding history of the relationship. The sequence will be organized by the punctuation or syntax and patterns will emerge in the interaction which express the relation between the participants. Often the participants' and the observers' ways of punctuating the interchange might differ. Bateson and Jackson (1964) give us a humorous example of this when they describe that in the "training" of laboratory rats, the sequence is punctuated by the human participants to appear that the experimenter provides the "stimuli" and "reinforcements" while the rat is the subject who responds. The rat, however, may punctuate the transaction differently, by thinking how well he has trained the experimenter: "Each time I press the lever, he gives me food!"

The struggle over punctuation of communication sequences and thus over the definition of the relationship is a common factor in marital disputes. The "distancing" husband and the "intrusive" wife often exemplify this. He punctuates the sequence of communication thus: "I have to maintain distance because she won't give me any space." She, on the other hand, defines the relationship differently: "I must pursue him because he is so cold and distant."

Such a relationship can easily lead to a runaway situation wherein the farther he distances himself from her the more she pursues, and the more she pursues, the farther he distances himself. Interrupting and even reversing these deviation-amplifying feedback loops becomes an important strategy in helping families and marital pairs.

Finally, for an understanding of the nature of communication it helps to recognize that there are two major types of communication, digital and analogic. Digital communication occurs through the use of words which are assigned meanings in accordance with semantic convention. There is nothing about such a word that connotes the meaning it has been assigned (except for onomatopoeic words). The three letters d, o, g mean a specific animal familiar to us all, but there is nothing doglike about them. Another example can be found in speech transmitted by computer, as in book readers for the blind, which use digital means of communication exclusively; the words are spoken without expression, gesture, or cadence.

The second kind of communication is analogic, in which the idea or thing being communicated is transmitted nonverbally in a representational manner. All nonverbal communication, including "posture, rhythm, and cadence of the words, or any other nonverbal manifestation of which the organism is capable" (Watzlawick, Beavin, and Jackson, 1967:62) is considered analogic. Thus, the communication taking place between two people who have no knowledge of each other's language is fully analogic. It is interesting how much can be transmitted in this way. And the analogic communication which is received and interpreted by pets is also truly remarkable, as they observe and "read" their owner's slightest nuances of movement, expression, or cadence.

Under most circumstances, human communication involves both analogic and digital components, which complement each other in the message. Digital communication is more precise, versatile, and capable of abstraction and logic. It admits of qualifiers, of dealing with time, and with the logical connections between ideas.

Analogic communication, on the other hand, although imprecise and often ambiguous, tends to be a more effective and powerful way to communicate about relationships. Often, although not always, the content of communication is transmitted digitally, through words, while the "command" component is communicated analogically. It is the tone of voice and the facial expression that provide the metacommunication telling us how we are to take the digital message.

An awareness of this duality enables us to analyze the nature and effectiveness of communication. It is essential, for example, to determine the extent to which there is congruence between the message and the way it is delivered. Incongruence may take the form of inappropriateness, invalidation, or paradox. Inappropriateness exists when the analogic communication does not match the content of the digital message. This leaves the receiver uncertain as to which communication he is to respond to, as, for example, when someone reports a sad event with a smile. Invalidation occurs when the analogic message is, "Don't pay attention, I don't necessarily mean what I say." This device leaves the receiver without information. Paradoxical communication occurs when both the digital and the analogic communication transmit a command and it is impossible to comply with both, as, for example, when a wife complains that her husband is never affectionate but stiffens as he puts his arm around her. The husband is faced with two mutually exclusive demands, namely, "Come here" and "Go away," which immobolize him in a no-win situation.

Bateson, Jackson, Haley, and Weakland (1956), in observing the communication patterns of families in which there was a very disturbed member, formulated the concept of the "double bind" and speculated that the consistent use of this kind of communication can create very disturbed responses in family members. Several conditions are necessary for a double bind to take place. First, as in the case of the paradox, two mutually exclusive command messages are communicated. By this is meant that if one is obeyed, the other is disobeyed. These messages may be conveyed in a dyadic relationship by one person to another or in a three-person double bind, in which case each of the two conflicting messages is communicated by a different person to a third. Further, the recipient of the commands is dependent on the perpetrators, as in the case of a child, or an adult who is (or believes he is) helpless and cannot leave the field. Finally, the conflicting messages may not be commented upon, or if they are, such a comment is totally discredited.

The double bind has received such extensive study and exploration in the literature that other troubled and troubling communication patterns may have been partially obscured, although they have been described. The crucial importance of communication patterns in significant relationships arises from the fact that human beings require close human ties and depend on feedback from others for reality testing and for consolidation of a sense of self.

For example, when people make a statement about themselves in the context of an important relationship, helpful and supportive responses from the other confirm or validate their messages. In troubled communication, invalidating, unsupportive, and even destructive responses from significant others may include a rejection or negation of the statement. This response says, "You are wrong about yourself." Even more troubling is the disconfirming response. Disconfirmation does not concern the truth or falsehood of the sender's message, but rather negates the sender himself as a source of information. Rather than, "You are wrong," the disconfirming response says, "You do not exist." An effective way to communicate disconfirmation is to be immune to communication from the sender.

A final contribution to communication theory which is useful in understanding family transactions comes from Bateson's (1936) classic work *Naven*, in which he developed the principle of schismogenesis. This principle states that cumulative interaction between individuals tends to result in progressive change. In other words, whatever the balance is in a relationship, it tends to become exaggerated over time. In the practice of social work this process is dramatically portrayed by a marital couple's complaints about their partners regarding exactly the same qualities that originally attracted them, but that have become intensified through time in the interaction. The woman who complains that her husband is too passive was once drawn to him because he was quiet and gentle. The husband who liked his wife because she was lively and vivacious now feels overwhelmed by her and wishes she wouldn't talk so much.

Bateson identified two major kinds of dyadic transactions in schismogenesis, namely, complementary and symmetrical. In complementary transactions, each partner takes an opposite position, for example, dominant and submissive or distancing and pursuing, and thus as the transaction continues these stances are driven to polar extremes. Symmetrical transactions are built on similarity, that is, the minimization of difference. As symmetrical relations progress, they may become highly competitive, or may rigidly disallow any difference at all.

Meaning Systems, Family Constructions of Reality, and Rituals

To complete our effort to synthesize those family theories which have informed family practice and our own conceptions, we turn to some of the newest developments in the field. In our view these developments, now in the beginning stages of integration and application, hold considerable promise for providing unifying frameworks for family study and research, and for practice as well.

Some of the family theories we have described in the foregoing pages concern rules, communication patterns, or structural and organizational aspects of the current, here-and-now family. Others describe concepts which relate to the present or nuclear family but also link the relationship of that family to the family of origin. Further, several theorists have created concepts which attempt to account for multigenerational, historical, or even mythical processes which exist in families. We have posited that families do in fact develop "cultures," persistent systems of rules, predominant themes and patterns of behavior, and particular styles of adaptation and change which may be observed in the present and handed down over the generations. However, little convincing research exists concerning *how* such a transmission process occurs, how such meaning and belief systems are formed, and how they retain their power. Practitioners are understandably more interested in restoring function to dysfunctional families than in theorizing how family systems develop, a matter which they leave to evolutionists, geneticists, historians, and anthropologists.

In the following pages we will discuss two concepts which may have considerable value for exploring these questions and also for developing integrated approaches to family assessment and intervention. The first is the concept of the "family paradigm" or the family's construction of reality, and the second is the notion of "ritual." These concepts, both of them complex and many faceted, connect with each other in ways which may shed light on how family themes develop and persist.

THE FAMILY PARADIGM

A family paradigm, as defined by psychiatrist David Reiss (1981), is the family's construction of reality, or its fundamental assumptions about the world in which it lives. It expresses the shared sets, expectations, and enduring views and fantasies the family holds about itself and the world. This shared construction is a repository of the family's experience and it persists over time, even from generation to generation.

The concept of paradigm has particular integrative power as it at once pertains to family structure, the family's regulatory system, intergenerational family themes, and the family's relationship with its environment. The family paradigm, according to Reiss, shapes and stabilizes the sequences of everyday life and is dramatized in what he terms the "ceremonials" of family life. Ceremonials or rituals can perhaps be understood as the family's paradigm in action and as such can provide us with both a key to the understanding of the family's shared meaning system and with an instrument for change.

THE DEFINITION AND FUNCTION OF RITUAL

Anthropologists, in their study of culture and systems of meaning, have long explored the nature and the function of rituals in religious and secular life and have identified the use made by priests and shamans of belief, meanings, and rituals in curing and healing. We too, perhaps, can draw on these sources of power and realize the promise they hold for help.

Ritual is an enormously complex notion including such diverse activities as customary greeting behaviors (Goffman, 1967), stereotyped behaviors such as compulsive handwashing, much of the activity surrounding a college football game, the North American Indian potlatch, and the Catholic Mass.

There continues to be considerable discussion concerning the definition of ritual and the constellation of features that necessarily are present in order to differentiate ritual from other clusters of human acts. Moore and Myerhoff (1977) list the necessary characteristics of ritual: (1) repetition; (2) acting (saying, thinking, and/or doing); (3) special behavior or stylization (using actions or symbols which are extraordinary or using ordinary ones in an unusual way); (4) order (organized according to beginnings, ends, and prescriptions for behavior, but capable of containing elements of chaos and spontaneity which may be expressed at particular times and places); (5) evocative presentational style; and (6) a collective dimension (that is, charged with a social meaning or message, even if it is self sending the message to self).

Ritual is thus a social process, a form or pattern of human interaction and communication. As Bossard and Boll (1950) suggest, it is a pattern of social interaction which is definitely prescribed; the longer it continues the more binding its precision and the more approved it becomes as a sense of rightness emerges from its past history. If rituals stand at the very core of culture, since families develop their own cultures and are among the most central of transmitters of larger cultural processes, it may be that rituals also stand at the core of family life.

Anthropologists have described the functions of ritual as being both preservative and transformative. They symbolically and metaphorically enact, express, and legitimize a group's social prescriptions, moral stances, and world views. In bringing about change, they may introduce new ways of ordering and conceptualizing reality. They may also function to preserve by perpetuating myths, reenforcing and rigidifying beliefs, and suppressing information which could produce change.

RITUALS AND THE FAMILY

Another topic for discourse among social scientists concerns the state of rituals in American society today. Some feel that American society is underritualized, that people are forced to accomplish their life transitions and to express meanings alone, without the support of shared enactments. Others say that although rituals continue, they have become hollow and devoid of meaning. Still others believe that a rich ritual life in America continues to exist but that rituals have been altered in both form and content.

Some or all of these views may be relevant to the consideration of ritual expression in the American family. It is likely that some families are underritualized, some are locked into rigid rituals that are devoid of meaning or that suppress information, while other families employ a rich and innovative pattern of rituals which have meaning and value.

The implications of ritual theory for understanding and working with families are complex. As family-centered practitioners, we need to learn how to recognize and understand family rituals, to interpret their meanings and functions in preserving family paradigms, and to employ the ritual form ourselves in helping families to express their traditions and their values, to achieve coherence, to adapt to transitions, unsettling life events, and catastrophes, and perhaps to dismantle rigid, dysfunctional patterns of behavior themselves perpetuated by family ritual.

Throughout this volume, we will return to family paradigms and particularly to their expression in ritual, and to an exploration of the use of ritual in the conscious restructuring of troubled areas in family life.

PART II _____

Beginnings

IN THE PRECEDING SECTION we presented a somewhat sweeping view of the context in which family-centered practice occurs. Now we will concentrate our attention on specific elements that the worker must consider in embarking on family-centered practice. In Chapter 6 we examine the direct encounter between the agency practitioner and the family or its emissary. In such situations the agency, the worker, and the family each bring different constructions of reality to the exchange, and these views greatly affect the shape and direction of the initial encounter and subsequent course of the work. Sometimes the agency view, as it is expressed in administrative arrangements and procedures, precludes the use of a family-centered approach. Sometimes worker, client, and agency conceptions of problems and of appropriate help differ to the extent that no working alliance may be developed.

In chapter 7 we focus on the initial meetings between client and worker, including engagement, contracting, and interviewing. We will briefly review some of the generic elements in these beginning transactions and then discuss ways of adapting and elaborating them in work with family groups. Throughout, our emphasis will be on the process rather than on the actual content of the exchanges; in later chapters we will examine content devoted to assessment and intervention.

Chapter 6————————————————————————

Getting Started: Agency and Case Management Issues

SOCIAL WORKERS AND CLIENTS come together in many different ways, in a wide range of settings, and for a variety of purposes. For example:

A foster care worker knocks on the door of the apartment of a mother whose neglected children have been placed in foster care.

A worker assigned to the waiting room of a large inner-city hospital sits down next to an elderly man who, she notices, seems extremely apprehensive and confused.

A sullen adolescent arrives at the worker's office, one half hour late, referred to the court counseling center as a condition of her probation.

A husband and wife, considering a separation, come to a family agency seeking help with intense marital conflict.

A nine-year-old-boy, disruptive and uncontrollable in the classroom, is sent by his teacher to the school social worker.

An apologetic and embarrassed woman, arrested for driving while intoxicated, is referred by the court to the county alcohol abuse program.

From the moment of the initial contact, a process begins to unfold and a case develops, shaped by many influences, including the client's need or problem, the community's definition and response, the characteristics of the service environment, and the worker's frame of reference.

111

In this chapter, we will explore the issues and tasks involved in "getting started" in family-centered practice. We will start by considering what it is that the worker brings to the beginning encounter. We will examine the organizational context which envelops the worker, enumerating the supports and structural arrangements which facilitate family practice and also the obstacles which may discourage or even prohibit a family focus. We will explore issues concerning both accessibility of services and motivation of clients. A range of examples of the processes involved in initial contacts will demonstrate the differential application of principles which guide beginnings in family-centered practice in different kinds of situations.

Starting Where the Worker Is

All social workers bring to the helping situation a frame of reference, a world view, notions about the nature of social work practice, and ideas about appropriate practice roles and actions. Although an old and trusted social work maxim states that we should "start where the client is," it is also true that how the worker selectively hears about where the client is, how the worker understands the client's position, and what direction service takes from the initial moment of contact is radically influenced by where the *worker* is. The assessment process itself, which begins at the moment of contact, is guided not only by the client's situation but by the very questions the worker chooses to ask.[1] For example, a worker whose theoretical frame of reference is psychodynamically based may gear questions toward an assessment of the client's ego-adaptive and coping mechanisms. A practitioner whose frame of reference is behavioral might study the antecedents and consequences of the current troubling behavior. A family-oriented practitioner influenced by the structural family theorists might question the client concerning current family structural arrangements. Our three workers will emerge with different collections of information and thus different assessments. These different assessments will in all likelihood lead to different interventions.

In the previous chapters, a conceptual frame of reference was presented which underpins and shapes the practice described in this book. How can this conceptual framework be operationalized into specific practice principles which the worker can carry to the initial contact with any client system?

First, an ecological systems frame of reference guides the family-centered practitioner in conceptualizing and defining the "unit of attention," the universe of data which provides the raw material for the assessment process. This unit of attention, when used in an ecological systems approach to social study, is defined by Germain as "a field of action in which the client—his biological and personality subsystems—is in transaction with a variety of biological, psychological, cultural, and social systems within a specific physical, cultural, and historical environment" (1968: 408).

The ecologically-oriented practitioner, then, draws the boundaries of concern in any particular case to include the wide range of data described above. Such a conception allows the worker to study a vast number of variables and to choose among many possible points of intervention.

What distinguishes the family-centered practitioner's approach to a case situation is both the manner in which the variables are organized and the emphasis placed on certain aspects of the unit of attention. As Germain (1968:404–405) has pointed out, each worker gives the greatest attention to those variables that to him appear most salient and relevant.

The family-centered practitioner, while including and attending to the total "person-in-situation" complex, tends to consider the family or intimate social network as particularly salient and relevant, and therefore at the center of the unit of attention. In other words, when a family-centered practitioner meets an individual client, that client is viewed as a part

FIGURE 6.1   The Unit of Attention

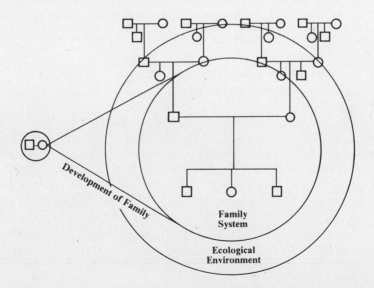

of a salient, intimate relationship system, usually the current family. Even the seemingly isolated individual, like the abandoned, institutionalized child, or the lonely resident of a single-room occupancy hotel, will be understood in the context of those painful but important family ties which have been severed. That relationship system itself, the family, is understood as being in constant transaction with the complex environment around it. Further, the individual is seen in the context of that family of origin which has developed over the generations; and this intergenerational family system is seen as particularly salient in understanding how individuals interpret, understand, and relate to current life situations. As Murray Bowen has said, "Whenever I see an individual, I see the generations of his family standing behind him."[2] This family-centered view of the unit of attention is pictured in figure 6.1.

In later chapters, this idea will be expanded by a discussion of tools useful in assessing the family as a system in space and through time.

Our family worker, then, greets the client armed with an ecological frame of reference and particular interest in the client's current intimate network as well as, where appropriate, his historical and developmental family roots. Our worker, as Auerswald (1968) conceptualizes it, is ready to assume the role of "explorer," to follow the problem wherever it should lead.[3]

A Supportive Environment for Family-Centered Practice

The philosophy of individualism runs deep in the world view of many Americans. It is expressed in the social, political, and economic contexts in which social workers practice. It shapes not only the kinds of services offered but to whom, how, and under what conditions services are made available. Individual clients are frequently viewed as if they were islands unto themselves and masters of their own destinies—a view which perhaps accounts for the continued emphasis in much of practice on inner, personal, psychological determinants of human functioning. Where this emphasis prevails, any attempts to define the unit of attention more broadly and to bring family-centered practice into a particular service delivery system will soon founder on organizational obstacles. This conflict may best be illustrated by considering typical and sometimes subtle roadblocks faced by workers attempting to move in this direction.

In a conventional mental health agency, all reporting forms are filled out on individuals. A family-centered worker regularly expands her definition of the client system to include several family members. However, the agency forms required for diagnostic, insurance, and statistical purposes must be completed on each individual, thus

multiplying the practitioner's paperwork and undermining all efforts to define the client system more broadly.

In a family agency, the receptionist in charge of telephone intakes
asks the applicant whether the problem is individual, marital, or
family. The client thus must make his own assessment and plan for
intervention before being seen by a worker. Thus, considerable socialization into a specific kind of client role has already taken place.

There are no funds to reimburse workers' travel expenses in the outpatient psychiatric clinic of a general hospital, although ostensibly
they are encouraged to develop contact with and understanding of
the client's immediate environment.

In an adolescent counseling center attached to a court, only in-person
contacts with the "identified patient," i.e., the adolescent, are
counted in determining and evaluating workloads. Contacts with
family members are considered "collaterals." These are supposedly
encouraged, yet are not considered when the worker's productivity
is assessed.

The physical environment of an agency consists of a series of small
offices, each of which contains a desk and two chairs. Where, we
might ask, will the seven-member family fit?

A child guidance clinic requires that the intake process include one
or two interviews with one or both parents by the social worker,
an interview with the child by the psychiatrist, and a testing of the
child by a psychologist. Following this workup, there is a diagnostic staffing, at which point the case conceivably could be viewed
as a "family" case. It is not surprising that this recommendation is
rarely made, or if made, not accepted by the family.

Although a certain community child placement agency encourages a
family focus, funding insecurity dictates that the workers average
at least twenty-five in-person client contacts per week. No matter
how many persons are seen in an interview nor how long the interview is, each contact counts as one.

A worker in a hospital setting, after attending a workshop on family
assessment, comes to the supervisory conference with great enthusiasm to show her mentor a genogram she has just done with an
elderly client suffering from a terminal illness. The supervisor says
impatiently, "What did you do all that stuff for?"

An agency is open five days and one evening per week. It is closed
Saturday and Sunday. How do we include working parents or family members with daytime commitments?

A graduate social work student with a specialization in family-centered practice has her second-year placement in a psychiatric hospital. Eager to do family work, she is told that the twenty-year-
old male patient assigned to her is "too sick" to participate in an

interview with his parents. Yet he has been living with these same people for twenty years and will continue to interact with them.

These are just a few illustrations of the deterrents and frustrations the social worker with a family orientation may encounter. Let us now turn to a consideration of the kinds of administrative and environmental supports which help make possible a family-centered focus.

FLEXIBILITY AND FREEDOM IN SPACE

The ecologically oriented family-centered practitioner needs the freedom to follow the needs of a situation wherever they might lead. This includes the freedom to move into the life space of the client and to search for the resources and linkages with other service delivery systems which might be required to meet the need or solve the problem. In the course of following the problem wherever it might lead, the worker requires agency support and sanction to go to school or hospital, to make home visits, to assist and accompany families in their struggles to negotiate on their behalf complicated, unresponsive bureaucratic service systems, and to help them overcome other obstacles as they appear. Such support may involve agency help in locating or providing concrete resources such as transportation or emergency funds, but more than that it requires an emotional and intellectual commitment from agency administration which endorses the belief that moving into the client's life space is an appropriate way of proceeding. The worker should be able to rely on agency backing if, in the course of pursuing the problem, he or she is forced to take certain risks on behalf of the family. For example, the worker may need to advocate vigorously for client rights or entitlements to a particular resource, or may need to take unpopular positions in the community.

The family-centered practitioner also requires flexible spatial arrangements within the agency or social work setting.[4] The enlarged unit of attention often results in multiple interviewing and thus the worker needs a physical place which can expand to include whole families and significant members of the family's network. What is required is an open, flexible space which can allow families to move around and arrange themselves in ways that are comfortable and expressive. Some agencies plan a "family therapy" room complete with heavy comfortable furniture and a "just like home" look, an arrangement which at first glance seems ideal but has some drawbacks. It tends to limit the flexible use of space and is far more expensive and elaborate than necessary. All that is actually required is adequate space, light but comfortable chairs which can be moved around easily, and some folding chairs which can be pressed into service as needed. Two or three large pillows on the floor expand the flexibility of how the space may be used. Further, a few simple toys in a corner can be useful when the family group includes some very young children. At the very least, if workers are to be encouraged to work with family groups, agencies must provide interviewing spaces large enough to accommodate families of varying sizes.

FLEXIBILITY AND FREEDOM IN TIME

Time constraints have also limited workers in their ability to respond to the needs of clients and families (Germain, 1976). Traditional nine-to-five working hours for agencies and staff have all but excluded some family members from participation. Many agencies have attempted to maintain evening hours, but these are often limited to a very few hours per week and thus available to only a limited number of clients. An increase of evening and weekend hours as well as the spread of flex-time to agencies, businesses, and factories would allow working family members to participate more readily in family sessions.

The traditional packaging of counseling services into a weekly "fifty-minute hour" also builds in a rigidity which tends to circumscribe and control the development of a case rather than to encourage workers and clients to collaborate in a way appropriate to the need or problem. The Milan family therapy group led by Mara Selvini-Palozzoli and the Brief Therapy Project at the Nathan Ackerman Institute are among those experimenting with team approaches. These therapists may spend an entire afternoon working with one family, interviewing and observing them during part of the time, and withdrawing for team consultation during the remainder. Families are usually seen only once a month since it is felt that a period of time is needed for the intervention to reverberate through the family and produce change. But adequate time allotments for interviews, at least, are essential to the success of such programs. Multiple interviewing, like practice with groups, tends to strain against the limit of the fifty-minute time slot, as a larger number of people compete for time to express their views and deal with their shared issues.

In addition to the fact that an hour-long session is often inadequate or inappropriate, agency methods for gauging worker activity can unobtrusively inhibit or even preclude a family focus. Whatever standards of accountability an agency may have for measuring worker activity, these must be responsive to the differential in time and energy needed for various kinds of cases. A caseload of fifteen families may require commitment of worker time quite different from a caseload of fifteen individuals. Thus, a reasonable system of accountability should evaluate rather than shape the worker's practice, and should credit a worker's time more fairly.

ADMINISTRATIVE SUPPORT FOR FAMILY-CENTERED PRACTICE

It is difficult if not impossible for an individual worker to carry on eco-logically oriented, family-centered practice in a setting which does not support this orientation. Constraints in the management of time and space, as described above, can undermine such an approach. There are a variety of other administrative provisions which can also thwart a family focus. For example, if the agency's application and intake procedures are in-fluenced by an individual orientation, then the problem is likely to be assessed as one existing primarily *within* the person. Once this judgment has been made, it is extremely difficult to shift the focus, to redefine the problem, or to expand the unit of attention. This difficulty is most dra-matically illustrated when family conflict is temporarily alleviated through the institutionalization of a family member. Workers frequently lament that although the family of the referred person or the so-called "identified patient" is central to rehabilitation, no means exist to get them involved.

Parents tend to bring their children for help, and often wives bring themselves to resolve marital conflict; but it can become an intensely dif-ficult contest when the worker attempts to involve a missing family mem-ber. Whitaker and Napier (1978), in their fascinating presentation of the course of a single family's treatment, vividly describe a therapist–client battle over who would attend the first session. In this case, the family attempted to test the therapists' mandate that all family members needed to attend the initial session by neglecting to bring in one of the children. The authors, not without some trepidation, held fast, refusing to do busi-ness until the entire family was present. The family members finally re-turned home promising to bring in the missing member and the initial session was rescheduled for the following day.

If an agency wishes to engage in family-centered practice, then, there are particular administrative procedures which must be developed to sup-port such a view. Most important of all, the majority of cases must be defined as family rather than as individual cases. Even in those situations where, for example, an adult individual is living geographically apart from any other family members, and is the only person who will be seen, the focus may be family-centered in that the client is understood in the context of extended family and may be helped to change through it. The very definition of a case as a family case expresses to all those involved the expectation that every matter discussed is of concern to the entire family.

The identification of a family case in terms of caseload management means that statistical case counts and recordings are done by family or by household rather than by individual, even if the applicant is an individual family member. This of course does not mean that every family member always must be directly involved in the problem-solving effort, but it does mean that if the case expands to include members of the intimate network, new cases need not be opened for them—a saving of new numbers, new files, and even new assessments and staffings. These may seem like minor points to belabor, but the administrative definition of the case has important influence in shaping practice, and particularly in determining how both worker and client view the problem.

The redefining of an individual concern as a family matter tends to push for an opening up of the case boundaries. For example, the components and direction of a residential program for the aged will differ significantly depending on whether or not the program is designed for the aged individual in isolation from his or her family. If the program is geared exclusively to the individual, efforts to involve family members will be seen as "extras" rather than as a core part of the service.

As a matter of fact, in individually oriented programs for the aged, family members tend to be treated as visitors or guests, and the staff communicates in many ways that the aged person belongs to the institution, not to the family. These subtleties of course reinforce the family's sense of helplessness and guilt, encouraging them to distance themselves even farther from the aging family member—a source of relief, perhaps, to family members struggling with painful feelings of loss. If, however, the total family were assumed to be a part of the case, then they would be involved throughout, not only as recipients of service but also as an essential part of the helping network. Clearly, then, an emphasis on the continued involvement of family members in the life of the aged person is to be considered a necessary and central part of the intervention, not a side issue to be dealt with on an ad hoc basis.

SUPERVISION AND LEARNING OPPORTUNITIES

Ecological family-centered practice is demanding, calling for skills and knowledge that are not always an integrated part of a worker's repertoire. The cognitive task of organizing and understanding the complexity of multiple systems in transaction can be overwhelming, and a frequent response to such information overload is the attempt to partialize, to zero in on one segment of the complex reality in order to make it more manageable. But partialization, while simplifying the cognitive task, tends to distort reality. It of necessity narrows the unit of attention and ignores the fact that every element in a system is in interaction with every other element and with the total system itself.

There are several better ways of mastering this difficult intellectual demand. One is expressed through the old adage, "Two heads are better than one." Case consultation and supervision, both in its traditional and newer forms, bring to the worker a valuable resource in problem solving. There has been a consistent tradition among those interested in family-centered practice to share cases, to think about families together in peer and supervision groups, to view one another's work through one-way mirrors, and to involve families themselves more actively in the assessment process.[5]

We may speculate about the source of this tradition. It may be that patterns of learning and supervision tend to follow patterns of practice. Intensive one-to-one work is often supported by intensive one-to-one supervision. Just as the boundaries around the one-to-one worker–client relationship are kept relatively closed, so is the exclusiveness of the worker–supervisor relationship often protected. Enlarging the client system to include the network of intimate relationships may be accompanied by parallel shifts in the model of learning and supervision favored. Peer supervision in groups, case sharing, observation of work through the one-way mirror, and bringing the consultant right into the session are some of the ways of opening up the boundaries in the learning–teaching situation, ways which seem more congruent with family-centered practice.

The mobilization of support from colleagues in family-centered treatment may also be an adaptive effort developed by family therapists to buttress the worker's strength in confronting that complicated and powerful emotional system, the human family. Such group support can help the worker maintain differentiation from the family system while continuing to be meaningfully connected with that system. Some models of such shared practice will be described in more detail in later chapters.

For the present, in a summary of learning–teaching requirements for family-centered practice the following appear to be essential. First, just as a family orientation enlarges the boundaries which define the treatment situation, so must the norms of learning and teaching be enlarged. The willingness to share one's thoughts, to expose one's work to peer and supervisor observation, to learn and practice in a complex network of ideas, to admit uncertainty, all become highly valued. These changing ways of working and learning together also require a reconsideration of some of social work's prevailing assumptions about the nature of confidentiality. We have sometimes assumed that clients might object to the introduction of other professionals into the helping situation. It appears, however, that this reluctance is a reflection of the worker's concern about professional self-exposure, for we have learned that clients tend to see the introduction of additional observers, advisors, or consultants as an expression of the worker's wish to bring a useful resource into the situation.

Secondly, the agency must make time for learning available despite demanding schedules. Staff training and development should be given high priority, with workers allowed opportunities not only for workshops, peer discussions, and ample supervision but also for working in teams as both observers and observees. Whenever possible and appropriate, agencies should enhance employees' familiarity with family assessment and intervention processes through the employment of consultants and the implementing of in-service training programs conducted by professionals skilled in family theory and practice.

Service Accessibility and Family Motivation

Social workers have long debated issues concerning accessibility of service and struggled with a range of obstacles that block their professional efforts. Tension has existed between norms which encourage workers to "reach out" and conflicting norms which place high values on the client's right to be left alone.[6] The process of intake too often becomes a screening out, as elaborate procedures which must be completed before service is offered can discourage all but the most determined clients. The locus of activity chosen by family-centered practitioners has important consequences in the resolution of these conflicts, as do the purpose and the sanction of the institution within which practitioners find themselves.

One solution to the dilemma has been to locate social workers where people travel in their everyday lives. The social work literature of the last decade reflects an increasing interest in the location of social workers in the life space of potential clients, where they will be readily available to help clients master tasks and handle the crises that are a part of family life. The location of social workers in those places where people go about the business of daily living automatically overcomes some of the obstacles that frequently prevent families from making use of services. Under these improved conditions clients and families do not need to go through a process which defines them as having a "problem," a labeling process that may inadvertently be demeaning and often deters people from seeking help. Likewise, people in need of help do not have to make formal application, but simply may make use of the social worker as an important resource in the environment. Almost fifty years ago, Bertha Reynolds discussed these vital issues of accessibility, motivation, and self-determination in her classic monograph, *Between Client and Community.* Consider the following charming analogy:

> I wonder if we, ourselves, do not get our best counseling help when it comes in the course of contacts for other things. It is hard to admit so much of failure in directing our own lives as to ask for formal appointment with a professional person for counsel. Do we not rather find ourselves talking to someone, just anywhere, who seems to have a gift for understanding? I am reminded of a woman who lays her state of spinsterhood to the fact that her mother would not allow her to have more than one date with any boy unless he would declare his intentions to be serious. But who wants to announce serious intentions the first time he meets a girl? And who would not prefer to avoid, if he can, making his problems seem of great moment when he is not at all sure that he will have the courage to do anything about them? How

shall clients and skilled counselors be sure of meeting, if not at the cross-roads of life where ordinary traffic passes by? [1934:12–13]

When social workers are employed in so-called host settings, that is, institutions such as schools or hospitals, which have been established primarily to offer other than social services, they can often move quite naturally into the client's life space provided that the structure of the setting and the philosophy of the practitioner allow for such flexibility. Meyer (1976) has conceptualized what practice at Reynold's "crossroads of life" should look like, giving us a rich variety of examples. Describing the location and role of the school social worker, she points out that the school is a social institution used by almost all families in a particular geographic area, and as such "is a likely place to pick up incipient family troubles that range from lack of solvency to marriage conflicts to parent–child problems. The PTA, for example, is a logical place for a social work service to be addressed to some kind of specific social action, and the halls and the lunchroom are ideal offices for the preventive social work practitioner" (1976:197–198).

Traditionally structured family counseling agencies can also increase their accessibility to those who might most benefit from available services, yet are least likely to take advantage of them. Reynold's conception of practice was clearly illustrated when one family agency created an outpost in a low-cost housing project in a Long Island community. The staff, in an effort to extend services to a population which included many disadvantaged, anomic, frightened, and suspicious families "previously characterized as unmotivated, untreatable, or unreachable" (Sunley, 1968) developed what they termed a "non-problem" approach: They encouraged ordinary conversation in a friendly, informal setting, and generally after a time the clients took the initiative in bringing up their personal problems.

In this life space approach, workers were accessible to people as they went about their daily lives. As residents and workers encountered each other in friendly, informal ways, clients gradually began to bring up issues of concern to them. Thus, as Sunley writes: "The client then talks when motivated; it is not the *agency's* motivation that produces the significant encounter between client and worker" (1968:66).

Such an approach gives clients the opportunity to test us out before deciding to engage us as their helpers. Lewis, in his examination of these issues, has enunciated the principle that "the recipient of service should have the opportunity to experience his role in its provision as a test of its fairness and not be expected to assume such fairness as a precondition for service" (1972:408). A violation of this principle is found in some agencies, for example, which require applicants to fill out an extensive social and personal history form before the scheduling of an initial interview. Such a procedure requires the client to take the trustworthiness of the agency and its staff on faith or on previous experience.

The unanticipated consequence of such preconditions for service is the development of a caseload that is culturally similar to the staff. Social distance between worker and client, including differences in race, sex, age, economic level, and social class, tends to promote feelings of strangeness and distrust; whereas a common social background enhances the likelihood that clients will trust agencies and workers sight unseen. And so it happens that if trust is a necessary precondition for service, the client population will, over time, tend more and more to resemble the staff!

When the worker is located in the potential client's life space, there is opportunity to bridge social distance and to build trust, making it easier for a person or family to consider asking for help. Further, the family-centered practitioner located in a natural setting is more readily available to families in dealing with crises and life tasks. However, although school and health-care settings are especially natural environments for this model of practice, it does not automatically develop. In many schools, for instance, the expectation continues to be that social workers should remain in their offices and conduct weekly play therapy sessions with children who have been identified by school authorities as "problems" and thus referred for "treatment." It is often the task of the ecologically-oriented family-centered school social worker to redefine the shape of practice, to alter administrative expectations, and to move into the mainstream of school and community life.[7]

THE FAMILY-CENTERED PRACTITIONER IN COUNSELING AND MENTAL HEALTH AGENCIES

A large proportion of family-centered practitioners are located in counseling and mental health agencies. Generally individuals and families approach such agencies voluntarily with a request for some kind of help for themselves or a member of their family. Sometimes these approaches to the agency are not truly voluntary, as the family has experienced a certain amount of coercion from authority, expressed in some form of the directive, "You get help for Johnny, or else . . ." Whether this approach ends in a useful episode of service is again related to issues of availability, accessibility, the motivation of clients, and a variety of obstacles which can separate worker and family.

Among other matters, the visibility of the agency, its location, the convenience of transportation, the responsiveness of the agency to the request for help, and the simplicity of the application process all have consequences for the developing relationship between family and agency. Furthermore, from the first telephone contact on, the case begins to take shape and direction. The importance of this initial contact is illustrated by the following description by Franklin and Prosky (1973) of the application procedure of the Nathan Ackerman Family Institute.

> Family therapy begins the first moment of the therapist's telephone contact with a family. . . . It is in this conversation that the therapist sets the ground rules for a family system approach. . . .Our practice is to answer all incoming telephone calls ourselves. If the occasion does not permit a telephone review of the problem and a canvas of family membership, we set aside another time for doing this." [31]

There has been considerable discussion in the family field concerning motivation and eligibility for services. Some family-centered practitioners working in counseling situations will not provide service unless the total family unit attends the sessions. Others will see part of the family unit initially, hoping later to involve missing family members after overcoming the family's resistance. While it is possible, of course, to bring about both individual and family change by seeing one person or subgroup in a family, still, as Haley points out, "it can be a slow and difficult procedure and often fails, as therapy outcome studies have shown. It is much more sensible to interview the natural group where the problem is expressed and so to proceed immediately toward the solution" (1978:10–11). Thus Haley and other leading family therapists usually expect everyone involved in the intimate network, including (if appropriate) the referring person, to attend at least the first meeting. A noted exception to this rule is Murray Bowen, who generally chooses to work with that individual family member who elects to work on his own behavior in the context of the extended family. Haley remarks that "Some family therapists, learning from Carl Whitaker, argue that the battle over who will be involved in the therapy can determine the outcome of the therapy" (1978:15). The family-centered practitioner should also consider carefully where the meeting should be held. It may make sense to meet where the referral originates, at the jail, hospital, or school, for example, or at the family residence.

There will be times when it is not possible to see the entire family. Some of its members may live too far away or may be physically incapacitated. In some cases a member may adamantly refuse to participate. The worker must carefully evaluate the family's presentation, distinguishing between an attempt to control who is allowed to participate and a genuine inability to attend. The following case illustrates this point:

The Dupree family, consisting of mother Betty, father Jim, and two sons, David, aged thirteen and Douglas, aged eleven, attended the first session. David, who was defined as the family's problem child, participated angrily and ambivalently, while Douglas (who had written on the waiting room blackboard prior to the session "I am the greatest: I am Douglas") read a book which he held high in front of his face. Two or three hours before the next session, Betty called to say the boys planned to go on an organized bike trip and she and Jim would be attending alone. The worker suggested making another appointment at a time when all could attend, offering the family alternative times. The whole family decided to come in that day after all. This time Douglas listed the names of all the family members on the waiting room blackboard, concluding with "We are a family," and opened the session by describing with considerable pride a new way the family had resolved a fight between the boys that very morning.

In this illustration, the worker was uncertain concerning the meaning of the family's efforts to leave the boys out of this session, but wanted to communicate to the boys that they were an essential part of the family's efforts to change.

Although clearly the rules over who must participate should represent the worker's careful assessment of the problem and the availability and accessibility of family members, few family-oriented workers will see a child initially without that child's parents. Such a commitment on the part of the agency or clinic so strongly confirms that family's definition of the problem and the use of the child as symptom bearer that it may totally undermine the potential for needed family change. The family may even be falsely reassured that the problem is going to be taken care of without the necessity of any further action on their parts, particularly action which might mean painfully examining other aspects of their family life.

The issues of resistance to change will be examined in more detail shortly. However, in considering obstacles to family-centered work, we must take care not to fall into the trap of refusing services to families who have views of the problem and of what might be helpful that differ from those of the professionals. The records of such families often end up in the closed case files with a final entry which reads . . . "Case closed—family not motivated" or "Case closed—family uncooperative." Such a conclusion may instead reflect the worker's lack of knowledge, skill, or sensitivity to what services are possible and appropriate for particular families.

A recent request for help from our practice illustrates a few of the challenges which may confront the worker:

Mrs. Bascomb calls, saying her husband attempted suicide two weeks ago by taking an overdose of pills. He was seen on an emergency basis at a local community mental health clinic and our agency has been recommended for ongoing treatment. She begins to talk of *his* problems in a hushed, secretive manner. I ask if her husband is home and if they have a telephone extension, suggesting it might be helpful to talk with both of them at the same time, in order to describe our services. She rejoins with, "Yes, we do have an extension, but I can tell him anything important. He can't come to the phone right now." She continues by saying that the children don't know (about the suicide attempt), and states emphatically,

"By the way, I don't want a social worker! My son was in the mental hospital for two years and I don't know what it's all about and they don't tell you nothing! All I want is someone who will help my husband."

In this instance the worker is faced with a situation in which the wife is defining the problem as the husband's emotional illness and is attempting to engage the worker in a secretive, dyadic discussion about him. She rebuffs the worker's attempt to include the husband at this stage of the contact. Further, she is saying that the children do not know what is going on and should not become involved. And finally, she insists she knows what kind of help is needed and who should (or should not) provide it. If, as in this case, the worker *is* a social worker, her ability to help is already challenged. How the worker deals with these dilemmas will influence whether the case assumes an individual or family focus, and indeed the potential for successful family intervention.

Case management at the point of entry is complex and difficult. We do not want to force our definitions and views on people nor do we want to take actions which may be in direct opposition to our best professional judgments about what will work. One of our colleagues offered a suggestion which we have found very helpful in resolving such dilemmas. When a family, for example, refuses to bring a key person to an initial or later session, or otherwise will not comply with the professional's requests, one can say, "OK, we'll do it your way, but I don't think it is going to work." This puts the family practitioner in a "no-lose" situation. If the family begins to do better, the worker can say, "I'm amazed; that's wonderful; I didn't think it would work!" If, which is more likely, the family does not make progress, the trouble persists, and the family complains about the lack of change, the professional can say, "I was afraid of this. I really didn't think it would work if we took this route." The family may, by now, be willing to try it the worker's way.

The following are a few suggestions which may guide the beginning encounter, usually over the telephone, in a typical voluntary situation:

1. Briefly explore the caller's presenting issue, need, or problem and his or her view of it.
2. Find out who is living in the household, including nonrelated members who may be intimately connected with the situation.
3. Ask who knows about the call. This question reveals important information about the family's typical ways of communicating and handling problems. If the call for help is being kept secret from one or more family members, you may want to help the caller discuss the referral with the rest of the family.
4. In arranging the first appointment, communicate to the caller the fact that you (and/or your agency) believe that situations which

involve one family member affect all of the others, that each "owns a piece of the action" and has a stake in the outcome, and that initially at least, you want to see the whole family together to understand everyone's point of view.

5. At this point, the caller may propose a variety of alternate courses, explaining why one or another person cannot or will not come in. Explore this response as fully as possible, since this is often a time at which valuable family data emerges. Based on your assessment of the reality, either reaffirm your original position and hold out for a time when *all* can come, or, if in your best judgement the family is not undermining your definition or you believe you should proceed anyway, agree to see certain family members the first time.

The following is one illustration from our own practice of how such a process might occur:

Thelma Ortiz calls the family agency for counseling for her seventeen-year-old son Frank. Frank has recently been hospitalized for his third serious bout with gastrointestinal symptoms. This time the doctors have suggested that his physical symptoms may have psychological components and have recommended counseling. We learn that Frank, a bright, ambitious student from an achievement-oriented, upwardly mobile Mexican-American family, has been unable to decide what college he wishes to attend. We speculate to ourselves that Frank may be under considerable pressure to succeed or is having difficulty "leaving home." When we attempt to arrange a family session, Mrs. Ortiz insists that her husband will not be able to attend any of the times we offer since he works at three different jobs, precluding a daytime or evening appointment. She suggests that she and the children come and he may be able to participate later "when he has more time." Taking the risk of "losing" the family, the worker reiterates her perspective and suggests the family discuss this and attempt to plan a time when all can attend. A first appointment for the whole family is finally scheduled; it is changed two more times when the father cannot attend, and finally the third appointment is kept.

Obviously this family had not yet accepted the worker's philosophy, but at least a beginning redefinition had occurred. Such a family may continue to maneuver to keep the child in the "identified patient" position. In this particular situation father, having planned to meet the family at the agency, was twenty minutes late, and the worker had to make the difficult decision whether to wait for his arrival or to begin on time. The risks in beginning without a family member are many, and the worker needs to be sensitive to such traps as being triangled or told "secrets" and then warned not to mention certain things when the missing member arrives. As this case developed, the son's physical symptoms were understood in the context of and in response to a number of family issues, including marital and sibling relationships, intergenerational patterns, and the family's transactions with the world around it.

The counseling or mental health agency needs to perform an educational role in sensitizing not only potential clients but also potential referral sources to its family perspective. If the referring source is familiar with your family-centered approach, a considerable amount of important groundwork can be done before the actual referral is made. For instance, a school social worker may help prepare the family of a student for family help; a court worker can help motivate the angry and discouraged parents of a delinquent youngster to explore family counseling; or a local minister, aware of marital and family–child conflict in a church family, might suggest a family-centered approach. Agencies doing such work need to acquaint the community with what family-centered work is like and what potential it offers for help to individuals and families in need of service, particularly in communities in which even other mental health professionals may be largely unfamiliar with this perspective.

ADOPTING A RELUCTANT POSITION OR "GOING WITH THE RESISTANCE"

We have discussed a variety of direct methods of enabling families to involve themselves in the helping process and to overcome the obstacles created by their lack of trust, hope, or information. We have cautioned against a too ready conclusion that the family is unreachably resistant or uncooperative, as this can lead to an implicit refusal of service.

Some families, however, even though they may call for an appointment on their own initiative or at the suggestion of another professional, are extremely resistant or, in Papp's (1980) words, "defiant." These are often families who have had a great deal of experience with mental health professionals, have one or more very dysfunctional members, and have been referred for family therapy as a "last resort." In their desperate need to preserve the rigid but fragile coherence of their family system, they may approach family therapy not in order to bring about change but to demonstrate to themselves, the referral source, and the family worker that the symptom bearer's problems are *not* family related and that a family approach will most assuredly fail. The referral for family treatment, although ostensibly accepted, has been experienced as so threatening that the family must undo it by agreeing to go but at the same time defeating the effort.

The use of direct, encouraging approaches to such families tends to threaten them even more, hardening their oppositional position. Even the giving of information about a family-centered approach can be experienced by the family as both a challenge to its definition of the problem and a criticism, and can quickly deteriorate into an argument, no matter how covert and polite, about the effectiveness of family-centered work.

With such families, it is often useful to adopt a reluctant stance and to express serious question as to whether they are ready at this point to become involved in family counseling. If they are critical of the family perspective, it may be well to agree that it certainly isn't an approach for everyone. Members of the Ackerman Brief Therapy Project, for example, in working with such families, sometimes put the family in the position of having to "earn" their way in by taking certain steps before an appointment will be set.

The process of "going with" rather than challenging the resistance can undermine the family's oppositional stance. Resistance requires something or someone to resist; it takes two to make a fight. Thus when the worker takes what the family perceives as a strong position for change, the worker offers a challenge that they feel forced to resist. On the other hand, if the worker cautions against change, the family's oppositional position may well force them to take a prochange stance.

The following two examples illustrate this approach to the threatened and resistant family. In the first case, the resistance was not immediately recognized in the initial telephone contacts.

Mrs. Day called to request help for her nine-year-old daughter who was exhibiting disruptive behavior at home and was reluctant to go to school. A few questions elicited the information that Mr. Day had recently been discharged from a five-week stay in a local mental hospital. He had been admitted because of increasing depression, which Mrs. Day attributed to the fact that he could no longer work following a serious automobile accident some months earlier.

An appointment was set for the family, but shortly before they were to arrive, a message was received that they were unable to come because the daughter had a cold. A telephone call confirmed the family's continuing interest in family treatment, and once again an appointment was arranged. Again the family canceled on the day of the appointment, for the same reason.

At this point the worker decided not to pursue the family, but sent instead the following letter:

Dear Mrs. and Mr. Day, Karen, and Peter,

We have received the message that you were unable to come in for the family meeting and hope everyone is well now. It is an important step to decide to be in family counseling and not one that all families are able or ready to take. Often even the consideration of such a step can create apprehension and concern on the parts of one or more family members. We have been wondering if perhaps your family is not quite ready at this time to begin to attend family meetings, and if this is the case, we would recommend against your making another appointment.

However, if you decide that you would like to start family work, please call, and we will do our best to find time to schedule a family session.

Sincerely,

Janet Levy, A.C.S.W.

Mrs. Day called the day the letter was received and with considerable firmness convinced the worker that the family was indeed ready to come in. In a second case, the resistance was much more obvious.

Mrs. Hansen, who was calling on the advice of a mental hospital social worker to make an appointment for the family, quickly established a rigidly defiant position. In the space of a few minutes, she told the worker that she was willing to participate in family sessions on behalf of her twenty-four-year-old son who had recently been discharged from a mental hospital, because, she said, "I would walk on the ceiling if it would help!" She advised the worker, however, not to get any ideas about "some big success story" because her son John was "schizophrenic" and a "very sick boy!" She also requested individual appointments for him along with the family sessions, questioned the worker regarding her expertise in schizophrenia, described a very limited time schedule when the family would be able to attend, and concluded with the caveat that her son wouldn't have anything to do with any kind of therapy anyway.

In the face of this defensive barrage the worker took a very reluctant stance, agreeing that family therapy probably wouldn't help and questioning whether it would be wise to start family sessions at this time. This telephone call was followed by several others devoted to scheduling difficulties and other negotiations regarding how, when, and with whom the sessions would occur. The worker continued to express doubt that they should come, at one point recommending against family counseling, all of which seemed to ignite the mother's persistence further.

Joining with the family's resistance, recommending against therapy, or advising against the risk of change are techniques closely related to therapeutic paradoxes which are often used by family therapists with oppositional families.

The adoption of such techniques may seem foreign to a traditional social work approach and some social workers object to such strategies on the grounds that they are manipulative or even dishonest. These issues will be discussed at greater length in future chapters. However, at this point we may suggest that rather than being critical of this method of engaging resistant families, one must remember that it may be the only way to get them involved; it may be an opportunity to help them alter a destructive and dysfunctional situation which is causing great pain and which more conventional helping approaches have failed to ameliorate.

THE FAMILY-CENTERED PRACTITIONER AND NONVOLUNTARY CLIENTS

We have discussed accessibility, motivation, and case management in situations in which the worker is available in the client's life space or in which the client has approached a counseling or mental health agency requesting some kind of help.

Workers and clients come together in yet another way, and that is when the client or family is required or coerced to meet with the worker. This may take place when a legally sanctioned authority has identified a problematic situation, such as occurs in child protection agencies or in circumstances when family counseling services are required to satisfy probation in the case of a delinquent. Coercion also exists in more pervasive forms in institutions where persons are required to remain and to receive treatment, as in mental hospitals and some prisons. In these situations, social workers may well be faced with clients who do not want help and who see the worker as an intruder in their lives, a violator of their privacy, or an interloper who must be tolerated or manipulated in order to "outwit the system."

It is a misnomer to call such persons or families "clients." They are at best "potential" clients (Pincus and Minahan, 1973:57) and the task of the worker is to attempt to overcome intervening obstacles so that such persons can at least freely choose whether or not they wish to engage the worker's services. There has been considerable discussion in recent years, not only about the right to treatment but also the right to refuse treatment. Henry Miller has questioned the right of social workers and other helpers to "deprive an individual of the one freedom that is primary to all others and that endows him with the core of his dignity—the freedom to make a shambles of his life" (Miller, 1968:30). However, a choice can be free only if it is an *informed* choice; and thus it is the worker's task to give the client as much opportunity as possible to learn about the options and their consequences. Further, if the client is driven to shut out others and to refuse help because of deeply rooted but in this case unfounded feelings of suspicion, fear, and hopelessness, can we say he has a free choice? The aim of the worker, then, is not to coerce people or families into the client role but to do everything possible to enable them to consider the options freely.

Although entry into the life of a family by way of the power of an external authority is a difficult way to start, often straining the worker's skills to the limit, it is not an impossible route. It does give the worker an opportunity to meet with a family who might otherwise not seek help, to demonstrate trustworthiness, and perhaps to dispel their fear of using outside resources. The authority gives the worker a foot in the door, but always with the understanding that the client does not have to let the worker in. For those who decide to open the door, the engagement process is similar to any other; but the obstacles are greater and perhaps more obvious, and the process may require more time, energy, patience, and commitment on the part of the worker.

In this chapter, we have outlined the contextual requirements necessary to begin family-centered practice. We have also discussed case management issues which arise both in the beginning contacts between workers and clients, and in setting up initial interviews. We now turn to an examiniation of the early phase of face-to-face contact between family and worker.

Chapter 7

Getting Started:
Contracting and
Interviewing

ENGAGEMENT IN FAMILY-CENTERED PRACTICE, as in any helping practice, is a mutual process. The worker must engage the client, that is, draw favorable attention to the proposed work; and the client must decide whether to engage—that is, take on—the worker. Discussion of the generic skills, techniques, and attitudes required in this process abound in the social work literature and will not be repeated here (cf. Biestek, 1957; Compton and Galaway, 1979; Maluccio, 1979; and Perlman, 1979). Later in this chapter, however, we will discuss some of the special approaches utilized in engaging family members in conjoint family interviewing.

The Preliminary Agreement

The first steps of the engagement process have been completed when worker and family have reached some kind of preliminary agreement to work together. Such a decision may be reached very quickly, sometimes early in a first meeting; or it may extend over two or three contacts and require considerable negotiation until finally worker and client either achieve a mutual understanding or mutually conclude that there is no common ground or shared purpose, and therefore no rationale for continued work together. In the latter case, if the worker is carrying out a mandated community or protective function, the contact may need to be continued even in the absence of any shared purpose or agreement.[1]

At a minimum, the preliminary agreement, usually verbal, must include the identification of a shared purpose, even if a very tenuous one, and an agreement to meet together for a specific number of sessions at a mutually satisfactory time and place. The goal during this phase is to determine whether client and worker can together agree on the central issues and concerns which need to be resolved, and formulate some beginning ideas concerning the means by which that resolution might occur. The preliminary agreement, without implying or mandating a long-term commitment on the part of either the family or the worker, proposes a testing and study period and defines some of the rules that will be observed; thus, such an agreement is particularly reassuring to the client unsure of her goals or of the amount of time and energy she is willing to commit.

This initial period should also include some beginning opportunity for the family to learn about the worker's point of view or approach to practice. Although long, intellectual explanations are seldom useful, the client should at least know enough about the worker's point of departure so that the nature of the exploration process makes sense to the family, and so that the questions pursued together are not perceived as inappropriate or intrusive. The following two vignettes illustrate the use of a preliminary agreement. In the first example, an agreement for ongoing family-centered work is reached.

The protective services worker has made an appointment for a home visit to the Martin family after a school nurse noticed several bruises and large, red welts on six-year-old Brenda Martin's legs. The nurse called Child Protective Services and the worker wrote to the Martins indicating when she would be visiting the home.[2] Mrs. Martin, highly nervous and tearful, quickly begins a disjointed explanation of how accident-prone Brenda is, assuring the worker she and her husband love their children and would never harm any of them. The worker, aware of Mrs. Martin's fear, defines her role simply and briefly, assuring her she wants to understand and help the family. She also responds to Mrs. Martin's anxiety and suggests that she seems to have her hands full with care of the house and her two preschool children, one an infant and the other a toddler. Mrs. Martin begins to share the fact that she *is* overwhelmed and that she and her husband have been having marital difficulties. She finally acknowledges that her husband, who is frustrated in his job and has begun to abuse alcohol, has on a few occasions, taken out his frustration on her and Brenda. She feels, however, that they can resolve their troubles and that her husband will be furious if he finds out she has talked with a social worker. The worker further explores these concerns, helping Mrs. Martin discover a way to share the worker's visit with her husband and to prepare him for a phone call from the worker. Both parents finally agree to meet together as a family with the worker for three or four sessions, not only to determine if there is any reason for further protective services involvement, but to explore if there are any ways the worker can help alleviate the stress the family is experiencing.

The Martins' preliminary agreement phase included three home visits. During this time several needs and problems were identified, a discussion began of how the family and worker could approach some resolution of these matters, and a mutual commitment was achieved to understanding the sources of these difficulties and developing plans for change.

In the second example, worker and clients are unable to negotiate a shared purpose and the case is closed.

Mrs. Bylinski contacted the family agency for "divorce therapy," indicating that she and her husband had been separated for several months, planned to be divorced, and needed help in coming to better agreement on issues of child support, visitation, and settlement of family property. During the initial meeting together, it quickly became apparent to the worker that, while Mr. and Mrs. Bylinski verbally agreed they were there to work on the above issues, each had markedly different views about what they hoped would happen during the counseling process. While Mr. Bylinski wanted to negotiate a settlement quickly and directly, Mrs. Bylinski hoped to reexamine the relationship and the entire question of whether or not the divorce should occur. In fact, she hinted she would fight a divorce action. Her reluctance to accept the divorce was further evidenced in her unwillingness to negotiate or compromise on any of the issues. Mr. Bylinski, on the other hand, refused to look back and continued to insist that he wanted a quick conclusion to these proceedings. The worker had yet another view. It was apparent that Mr. Bylinski, although expressly stating his wish to divorce, was still experiencing a tremendous amount of guilt and ambivalence which prevented him from maintaining his separated status. For example, he was "babysitting" several nights a week, had done nothing to establish a new social network, and although he had his own apartment, he was still puttering around the house and frequently wangling invitations to meals.

The worker felt, in view of his behavior and his wife's position, that the couple needed first of all to identify the conflicts which had led to their separation.

At the end of four sessions, the couple could not agree on a shared purpose or on a plan for work which would, in the worker's judgment, have potential for success. The worker stated her opinion that there was no basis for continued conjoint work at that time. The possibility for individual work on one or both their parts was explored, and Mrs. Bylinski subsequently began family-centered counseling on her own.[3]

During the initial phase and indeed throughout family-centered work, another very important task of the practitioner is to widen the unit of attention, that is, to redefine the locus of concern in terms of broader systems. This task can be facilitated by making simple statements such as, "I tend to think that families are terribly important—not only the ones we live in now, but the ones we grew up in, too." This point of view is further illustrated when, for example, the worker comments to a young couple in a marital conflict, "If we end up working together, we may eventually want to plan some joint sessions with your parents." Such a comment is sometimes greeted with strong surprise and resistance, but at least it has been said out loud, the family focus has been reinforced, and the couple has been forewarned of things to come. The worker then consistently communicates a sense of "familiness" by his own words and actions. This task is similar to that of the group worker who recognizes how essential it is to nurture a sense of "we-ness," "groupness," or "lending a vision" (Schwartz, 1961) by encouraging a mutual aid network in which all group members actively work on problem solving. It is in fact this very "we-ness," the fact that there are many helpers and shared responsibility, that gives both group and family intervention tremendous potential for rapid growth and change. The awareness of this potential enhances the family's sense of competence and hope.

Role Induction and Congruence of Expectations

The contracting process has provided a useful structure within which the initial engagement can take place. Seabury (1979), who has explored both the uses and abuses of the contracting process, describes the steps in reaching an initial or preliminary agreement in terms of the reciprocal process of role induction. Understanding this process requires charting its steps and objectives; thus informed we can begin to resolve the confusion and misunderstandings that so often exist between workers and clients, and which obviate the development of a working relationship. Investigators such as Meyer and Timms (1969) and Maluccio (1979), by studying and comparing worker and client views of service, have made us aware of how differently and thus incongruently workers and clients often view the helping process.

Seabury (1979) has analyzed in a very helpful way the negotiation process which can lead toward congruence, as figure 7.1 illustrates. This diagram shows clearly that in order for a working relationship to develop and for the helping situation to be actualized, both worker's and client's expectations of the worker's role (boxes A and D) must move toward con-

FIGURE 7.1

	Worker	Client
I	A Worker's expectations of own role	B Client's expectations of own role
T h o u	C Worker's expectations of client	D Client's expectations of worker

gruence. In other words, each must have similar expectations of the worker's goals and methods. Reciprocally, worker and client must also have reasonably matching ideas or expectations about the client's role in the process (boxes B and C). In the most workable situation, the client wants and needs the service the worker is prepared to give, and the worker believes in and is ready to deliver the service the client expects to receive. This process may best be illustrated through an extensively analyzed example. Let us begin with the basic details of the case:

Janet Sears, daughter of a terminally ill woman, meets the hospital social worker in order to make plans for Janet's mother, who need not remain in the hospital at this time but will need some nursing care. In the opening minutes of the interview, Janet is somewhat hostile and defensive. The worker is nonplused. He wants to help Janet with what he knows must be a difficult and painful situation, yet he feels attacked and frustrated. The worker and the daughter here are clearly at cross-purposes and are experiencing considerable incongruence in their conceptions of their respective roles and the purposes of their meeting.

WORKER'S EXPECTATIONS OF OWN ROLE (BOX A)

The worker sees his task as one of helping Janet, her mother, and other family members involved work out a plan which will meet the mother's needs for physical and medical care and emotional well-being and, at the same time, will accord with the wishes of the family. Thus he expects to explore the views of everyone concerned and to acquaint them with available resources, whether suitable nursing homes or a range of supportive services which might make in-home care manageable. Further, he knows from prior experiences that the family may be denying and avoiding some painful issues that must be examined before they can accept the illness and work through their feelings of loss and grief, and even before they may be able to maintain supportive contact with the ill woman. He sees his role as helping the family deal with the complex feelings generated in this crisis. He also plans to help the family negotiate the appropriate resources for meeting the extensive medical expenses.

CLIENT'S EXPECTATION OF OWN ROLE (BOX B)

Janet is not certain what her obligations are financially or morally, or how she should proceed. She is very worried and extremely sad about her mother and she wants to do what is best for her, but she is also overwhelmed with the prospect of assuming responsibility for her care because of a full-time job and other heavy responsibilities. She is afraid the worker will put pressure on her, making her feel even more torn and guilty.

WORKER'S EXPECTATIONS OF CLIENT (BOX C)

The worker hopes Janet will share her concerns, feelings, and views, and provide needed information about her own home situation. He does not feel that Janet and her husband should be expected to take her mother home, but he does believe the family should, or at least hopes the family will, maintain supportive contact with Janet's mother in whatever ways are possible. Finally, he hopes the client will accept his advice and assistance in figuring out how to deal with the hospital bill.

CLIENT'S EXPECTATIONS OF WORKER (BOX D)

Janet fears the worker will be critical and judgmental, expecting her to take her mother home. She assumes that the worker believes families should take care of their aging parents at home and that he will not be understanding of her complicated home situation. Further, the hospital bill has reached terrifying proportions, and Janet believes the worker will press for some immediate resolution. Janet is upset about the confusion between her mother's Medicare eligibility and the coverage her private health insurance will provide.

There are, at this stage of the engagement process, then, differing views and conceptions on the part of both worker and client in their expectations both of each other and of their own roles. This configuration is presented in figure 7.2. The dissonance in their respective views of the purpose of the service contact and the role of the worker must be resolved before any preliminary agreement to work together can be fashioned. Janet may initially want part of what the worker has to offer, especially concrete help in planning for appropriate care for her mother. However, she may not want to engage in any discussion of the illness itself or family relationships. The worker, on the other hand, aware of this avoidance is concerned about it, not only because the family seem to be removing themselves from the aged patient who is feeling frightened and abandoned, but because they may lose an opportunity to help prevent a dysfunctional adaptation to the present illness and eventual loss of their relative.

THE SOCIAL WORKER'S TASK IN THE INITIAL CONTACT

The social worker's tasks in moving toward clarity and congruence are as follows. First, the worker must explore the potential client's expectations of the service and of the worker. It is important to help clients express their views before presenting one's own notions. If the worker gives information about agency function and his own role first, it may short-cir-

	Worker	Client
I	**A** I will help family work out plan they want to pursue. I will help them maintain a supportive emotional network for mother. I will help them deal with medical expenses. I will help them with their feelings of loss and their avoidance.	**B** I'm not sure what is right or what I should do. I must defend myself against the impossible demands being placed on me by the hospital and worker. I feel so terrible about mother. I cannot stand to see her suffer. I should take mother home but I just can't.
T h o u	**C** You should share her concerns and provide any necessary information to determine and carry out plan. You should maintain supportive contact but should not be expected to take mother home unless you want to and have the necessary resources. You should begin to deal with loss and grief in a better way.	**D** He thinks I should take mother home. I want him to give me time to think. Can he tell me about nursing homes? He is going to ask me a lot of personal questions. I will bet he is supposed to check with me on the hospital bill. He probably wants mother discharged immediately.

FIGURE 7.2

cuit the client's expression of differing views. It may, in other words, drive the client's views underground.

Secondly, the worker should be interested in the client's views but should seek out any sources of confusion or distortion in the client's expectations. In some instances, the distortion may be based on the client's prior experience with other helpers. To return to the vignette above, in the process of clarifying expectations the worker discovered that one of the attending physicians, herself under administrative pressure, had made several comments to family members about discharge, thus increasing the family's anxiety. Janet then assumed that the worker would take the same position. The worker's discovery of this pressure and of how upset the family had been about it, and his reassuring comment ("I can certainly see why you thought I was here to put more pressure on you about discharge") defused the tensions and enabled the client to hear better what the worker had to say about his role.

Thirdly, the worker should clear up any ambiguities or confusion in his expectations of the client. Clients sometimes do not know how to occupy a productive role in order to facilitate change or resolution. They are uncertain about what information they will need to provide, how it will be used, and what actions are expected of them.

Finally, the worker should share information about his own role and the agency's function. In the process of expressing and examining the expectations of both worker and client, differences are identified and distortions or misconceptions corrected. Many differences are negotiable, requiring compromises by worker, client, agency, or all three. As congruence is reached at the end of this phase, the worker next outlines methods for collecting needed information and for obtaining needed help. This plan should prescribe mutual responsibilities and tasks during the study period, address the time and place of meetings or other contacts, and when necessary, should clarify financial arrangements. The issue of confidentiality should be dealt with so that clients know how any information they give will be used and how their privacy and rights will be protected. The nature of the setting and the services creates varying conditions regarding the obtaining and handling of information and, whatever these are, they should be openly discussed with the clients.

As stated earlier, the preliminary agreement may be reached in a few minutes, as might occur under the pressure of a crisis, or it may take two or more meetings. However long it takes, it lays the groundwork for the development of a relationship and for the study process which follows.

In working with multiple client systems, the task of negotiating a beginning agreement is difficult and complex, as each member of the potential client system may well have a separate agenda, often unshared or in conflict. This is very common in cases of marital conflict, as we saw in the case of Mr. and Mrs. Bylinski. In another case, a parent or parents may want the family worker to "straighten out" an adolescent daughter whom they perceive as belligerent and out of control, while the adolescent may hope the worker will side with her need for autonomy. Parents may believe their role is to talk about the children, while the worker may believe it would be more productive to learn more about the parents and their marriage. A marital pair may first express the shared purpose of "saving the marriage," but then incongruously expect the worker to listen to both sides and judge which one is right. If these differing expectations are not exposed and discussed there is likely to be little or no progress, since there is no shared purpose to guide the mutual endeavor.

Contracting in Conjoint Family Treatment

We have reviewed engagement and preliminary contracting with individual clients in family-centered practice. Although such principles are also relevant for conjoint family treatment, contracting with families sometimes requires special consideration.

In some models of family treatment, for example, special formats must be clarified as part of the contracting process. For example, family sessions are frequently videotaped; if taping is planned, it is essential that the family consent to it, know exactly how the tape is to be used, and have an opportunity to sign a release. Our experience is that after explaining its importance to our work, we have very rarely encountered a family who refused to be taped, although some families—or, more likely, one member of a family—may initially protest. We introduce the notion in the first minutes of the contact, before the video is turned on. The children often like to see how the equipment works and also enjoy seeing themselves on the monitor. Although families seem to experience a few initial moments of discomfort, the video is quickly forgotten as the session progresses. In fact, some families are later insulted if the video is not available for their session.

Other formats may include the use of consultant–observers, or a team behind the mirror. Again, the family should be informed about this process and the helping role of the consultant or team. Although therapists differ on the advisability of a meeting between the two, we always ask the family if they would like to meet the team early in the initial meeting. They usually say yes and the team is briefly introduced. Sometimes they say no; yet once, at the end of a session, a young man who had earlier declined said, "Now I'm ready to meet the team." If the worker is likely to be interrupted by the people behind the mirror for consultation or instruction, the family should be prepared for that occurrence and, if appropriate, for the way the session will end; for example, in the strategic model developed by Mara Selvini-Palazzoli and the Milan group (1978), the team regularly consults with the worker at the end of the session while the family waits, sometimes for a considerable period of time, and then a message or assignment resulting from the consultation is delivered to the family. Again, the family should understand at the outset that this will be the format.

The issue of confidentiality must also be clarified with the total family. We tend to tell the family that we cannot be counted on to keep secrets within the family system but will not share any information with persons outside the family (excepting our consultants) without the family's permission.[4] Further, we assure families that any written reports requested by other agencies will be approved by them before being transmitted.

Thus there is general agreement that straightforwardness is essential to successful contracting. But regarding straightforwardness in the application of strategies for change there is much debate. Strategic family therapists often rely on surprise, paradox, and the power of an unseen and unattainable team behind the mirror to bring about change in family systems; they state that "showing their hand" to the family will undermine their ability to bring about change. It certainly can be argued that some family systems are so powerful that such strategies are required to give the therapist a chance at shifting the system, particularly with very "stuck," resistant families. In fact Palazzoli, one of the authors of *Paradox and*

Counterparadox (1981), maintains that "anything predictable is therapeutically inefficient." Indeed, the Milan team discovered that families who had read their book had immunized themselves to the change strategies described therein, as the team no longer could command the power of the unexpected.

Critics of this approach accuse these strategists of playing games, using tricks, and being manipulative. Ultimately, all practitioners must resolve their own minds on this matter. Is it manipulative that Peggy Papp (1980) scratches her ankle to signal to the team that she wants them to summon her behind the mirror? Is it somehow a violation of professional ethics to keep the team members unavailable and mysterious like some Wizard of Oz behind the curtain? An interesting case in point is that of the young family therapist trained in strategic work who practiced alone in a small city where he had no colleagues with whom to share his professional work. During the course of family sessions he would excuse himself to talk with his consultant, although no one was there, and would return with a recommendation that carried the weight of the invisible outside expert.[5]

The use of such artifice is a moot issue which may be argued endlessly. Our own stance is that the basic purpose of helping the family should be clear and shared; that format and issues about confidentiality, dependability, and responsibility must be a part of the contractual relationship; and that long-term goals must be agreed upon and shared. However, in cases where the effectiveness of the strategy would be undermined by complete openness or where knowing the worker's mind might be used by the family to support their resistance, we believe the worker should keep his or her own counsel. Openness, after all, is a relative, not an absolute value.

Interviewing Families

No matter how experienced a person is in interviewing individuals, the leap to interviewing families requires new and different perspectives and skills. Frequently, in beginning family interviews even seasoned workers feel inundated by the enormous amount of information and confusing communication among family members, and they resort to doing what amounts to individual interviewing with a family member while the rest of the group observes. Occasionally this may be done as a planned strategy, but it is not the usual approach to family interviewing. Even worse, as conflict grows the anxious worker may decide to separate family members.

Although there is nothing that can replace experience in the development of skill and confidence in family interviewing, the following suggestions, drawn from various leaders in the family therapy field and from our own tortuous and halting experiences, may hasten the development of competence.

ENGAGING FAMILIES

In some respects, the engagement process for conjoint family treatment is similar to that for family-centered treatment of the individual client. However, the facts that there are several people in the room, and moreover that the family is an ongoing, persisting system, while the worker is the outsider, the stranger in the midst of a closely knit group which shares a long history, make the engagement process somewhat more complex. Before the family comes in, the room should be arranged in a way that is appropriate to the group and the setting. Chairs should be strategically placed and if young children are to be present, two or three toys should be in the room. The way members enter the room and arrange themselves communicates a good deal about the structure and organization of the family. In the early days it was common for the worker to comment on the way the family seated themselves and to speculate on its meaning. But such an early and direct intervention, which comes out of a view that enhanced insight will bring about change, can be experienced as quite intrusive; it can also generate anxieties in the family and stimulate resistance.

Virginia Satir, an expert in communication, begins a family meeting by making contact with each member of the family. She shakes hands with each in turn or in some other way touches each person, establishing eye contact and calling each by name. The question of how to address family members should be settled early in the contact, and is also a matter of personal style. Satir introduces herself and states that she likes to be called by her first name, and asks the parents if she may call them by their first names as well. This is a reflection of her personal style, which is one of warm and intimate informality (1967; 1975).

In the early days of family therapy, Nathan Ackerman and his colleagues tended to call the parents "Mom" and "Dad," referring to them in terms of their roles, for the significance of role received strong emphasis in Ackerman's early work. We began with the early Ackerman style, but a story told by Satir in a workshop many years ago converted us to her preference. She reported a first session with a family in which the grandmother, a woman in her upper seventies, participated. As introductions were taking place, a family spokesman said, "And this is Grandma." Satir, after asking "Grandma" what her first name was, took the elderly woman's hand and said, "Hello, Mildred, I'm glad to meet you." Mildred's response, as her individuality was thus validated, was eloquent. Her eyes filled with tears, and taking Satir's hand in both of hers she said, "No one has called me that for years." Terms of address are not inconsequential details, but are a metaphor or a signal that contributes to shaping the relationship.

Although, as we just indicated, our style is to use first names, the major principle that we use as a guide in establishing the terms of address is that names should be symmetrical. We avoid the asymmetrical pattern used by some professionals whereby the adults in the family call the professional by surname, while they are called by their given names, since this tends to suggest that the worker is in a position of authority or in some other way occupying a "one up" position.

Haley refers to this period of introductions in the first session as the "social stage," suggesting that the best model for the worker's behavior is the kind of courtesy that would be extended to guests coming into one's home. He suggests that during this initial greeting phase, some kind of direct response be elicited from each family member in order to establish the norm at once that each family member is expected to participate (1976:15–19).

Minuchin and the structural family therapists, who believe that the ability to bring about change in a family is in part dependent on the extent to which the therapist has been able to *join* the family, describe in some detail this process of joining:

> How does the therapist join the family? Like the family members, the therapist is "more human than otherwise," in Harry Stack Sullivan's phrase. Somewhere inside, he has resonating chords that can respond to a human frequency. In forming the therapeutic system, aspects of himself that facilitate the building of common ground with the family members will be elicited. And the therapist will deliberately activate self-segments that are congruent with the family. [Minuchin and Fishman, 1981:32]

In the early contacts with the family, such joining is done purposefully and consciously, as the worker communicates "I am like you" to members of the family. Shared complaints about the weather, opinions on current happenings, and recounting of similar experiences can all serve to enhance engagement. Talk of recent sporting events can sometimes help bridge social distance. For example, one of the authors of the present study, older, white, and middle-class, finally opened communication with an angry thirteen-year-old black working-class boy through a shared interest in the Detroit Pistons.

Joining can also take place through a purposeful, open sharing of personal feelings. For example, to a family that is frightened and shy the worker can comment on his discomfort in meeting them, pointing out that they already know each other whereas he knows no one. Minuchin (1974:128–129) describes a specific joining technique called mimesis. This entails, through body position, tone of voice, or other elements of analogic communication, imitating the family member you wish to join, thereby communicating a strong nonverbal message of congruence. Minuchin, a master of this technique, may light a cigarette after a mother lights up, remove his jacket right after a father sheds his, cross or uncross his legs, or lean in a particular direction to strengthen his congruence with a particular member. Joining maneuvers are particularly important and perhaps more difficult when worker and client must bridge a combination of differences in age, ethnic or racial background, socioeconomic status, gender, or other characteristics that emphasize the estranging aspects of the worker- client relationship.

The prospect of thus sharing a part of oneself may seem difficult, particularly when one has been trained to avoid personal sharing and to maintain anonymity. This shift in perspective and the conscious use of self became evident when one of the present authors, in the course of a consultation on family work with the staff of a family agency, did a live interview with a family.

The mother and four children arrived. The stepfather (the new marriage was three years old) had been heading back from a long-distance trucking tour to attend the session but had been delayed and had called to say he would be late if he made it at all. The mother and children were seen without him. A few minutes into the session, the following joining sequence took place:

AH: "Where abouts are you from? You don't sound like you're from around here.

M: "I was born in Iowa but I lived most of my life in Phoenix."

AH: "Phoenix! What an interesting place. I was there just last year for a conference and I really liked it!"

M: "I did hate to leave! Where did you stay?"

AH: "At the Hyatt. What a beautiful hotel."

M: "Ah, the Hyatt. I worked as a waitress there for two years. In fact I met my husband in a bar at the Hyatt."

AH: (Somewhat ruefully, but with humor) "Gee, I guess I shouldn't have spent so much time in meetings!"

This interchange immediately bridged the social distance between the obviously nervous mother and the visiting consultant, forming an alliance which provided her with a sense of support throughout the interview. The professional differences in perspectives on joining in this way were apparent in the lively discussion among the staff after the session. Several were startled by the open, informal, and personal quality of the interchange.

Joining children is particularly important, for it enacts the message that the worker intends to connect with the total family. Minuchin and

Fishman (1981) suggest two maneuvers helpful in joining small children. One is to diminish the distance imposed by size. It is useful to kneel or sit on a low stool in order to be the same height as the child. The second maneuver is to communicate in the language of the child. In fact, these therapists suggest that joining preschool children is a useful way to establish contact with the family in a playful, nonverbal way (1981:39).[6]

Joining, of course, continues throughout the contact as the worker demonstrates an understanding and appreciation of the family, sensitivity to their dilemmas, and respect for the family's coherence and their efforts to survive. The worker's joining stance serves to validate and confirm both the individuals in the family and the system as a whole.

Palazzoli (1978) discusses at some length the technique of "positive connotation," which is at once a joining maneuver and an interventive strategy. As a joining maneuver, positive connotation transcends notions of good and bad, sick and well. It helps the worker avoid punctuating sequences of events with subtle investigations of blame or finding of fault. The use of positive connotation rests on the assumption that troubled behavior in the family, no matter how difficult or painful, is a part of the homeostatic tendency within the system, or its efforts to maintain itself in order to keep from disintegrating. When such behavior is given positive connotations, it is not the specific behavior that is positively defined but rather the effort implied in the behavior to protect and maintain the system. Although making a statement of positive connotation can produce a therapeutic paradox, as will be discussed later when we explore change strategies, it also communicates a respect and understanding for the family's efforts to maintain the integrity of the system.

Many of the pioneers in the family field have been highly charismatic people who seem able to engage families and to bring about change through the sheer positive force of their personalities. Watching the tapes or live sessions of an Ackerman, a Minuchin, a Satir, a Whitaker, or a Palazzoli is a compelling experience, but can leave one in despair in terms of imitating or equaling their special gifts in working with families. It is impressive and humbling to see Mara Selvini-Palazzoli, a middle-aged female physician from Italy, reach across the barriers of culture, sex, class, and age to engage a Canadian working-class adolescent boy to the point that, at the end of the session, this earlier reserved and angry youngster threw his arms around the Milanese woman and gave her a hug. Although her warmth and charisma had undoubtedly gained her a rapid connection with his family, this young man hugged her in gratitude primarily because she had understood the family's dilemma and had helped. We all have to engage families in ways which comfortably reflect our own personalities and styles; but whatever our manner, it cannot substitute for the understanding, knowledge, and experience essential to the actual giving of help.

HYPOTHESIZING

One of the most difficult aspects of interviewing families is that there is usually such a mass of information in the form of both verbal and non-verbal communications, and likewise so many paths that might be followed at any one instant, that one quickly can become overwhelmed and lose one's focus or control in the family session.

One way to avoid this potential chaos and to keep the session reasonably focused is to employ the process of hypothesizing. Several structural and strategic family therapists have suggested that a tentative hypothesis should be formulated before any meeting with a family, and furthermore that the testing of that hypothesis should provide the direction for the interview. As Palazzoli points out, it doesn't matter whether the hypothesis is proven or disproven, for either way useful information is gained (1980:4). If the hypothesis proves to be correct, one can move on to an intervention. If it is found to be incorrect, the information gained in the course of pursuing it will form the basis for a new hypothesis.

Tentative hypotheses can be developed even before the family is seen, based on information that has been gained over the phone or through a referral, and based also on past experience with families, as the following two situations illustrate:

The Ellis family called, requesting help with their nine-year-old son who had recently begun to show behavioral problems in school and at home. Seven months prior to the call, the family's younger child had been diagnosed as having a possibly life-threatening illness. A first tentative hypothesis was that the older child was acting up in order to distract the family from their worry over the younger sister. This theory was quite quickly borne out in the sessions.

Mr. Genovese called to request family counseling. He said he had been having trouble with his two boys who had remained with him after he and his wife separated the year before. He suggested that his former wife also come, since she continued to be very involved in the household and in the management of the boys. She came to the house two or three times a week, continued to do the laundry and some of the cleaning, and usually came over to help when there was a crisis. The initial hypothesis was that the boys were stirring up trouble and stimulating their father's anxiety in order to bring their mother home. Although there was some evidence that this was one of the elements in the situation, it appeared to be even more likely that the mother's and father's inability to separate had created structural problems that undermined the father's ability to take charge of the family and establish any kind of leadership. A new hypothesis was thus developed which led the exploration in a somewhat different direction.[7]

The hypothesizing process can be demanding and time-consuming, but the expenditure of time and effort in preparation for the family session will bring dividends in the usefulness of the meeting. Such an organizing approach is greatly facilitated with the use of video and with behind-the-mirror consultants, who may each see different parts of the family process.

Interviewing Techniques

The initial focus in the family interview, following the establishment of rapport, should be on the concerns which have mobilized the family to seek help. One may start in a variety of ways and each approach has its own advantages and different effects. Haley (1976) suggests addressing the family in general, while not making eye contact with any particular individual, by asking, "What has brought you?" or "Who would like to begin?" Such an approach quickly identifies who is most concerned or has taken leadership in seeking help as that person is likely to answer. It may be useful to address the parent who did not make the initial telephone call, to be sure that parent is involved early and to communicate interest in his or her opinion. At times, this way of beginning can produce a response such as "Don't ask me, this was all her idea!" This yields important information and immediately exposes the resistance, anger, and disagreement between the marital pair concerning the nature of both the problem and acceptable solutions.

Sometimes it is useful to start with a child in the family, particularly in families with older children; one may choose to begin with either the symptomatic or the nonsymptomatic child. No matter where one starts, in family interviewing it is important to facilitate interaction among family members and to begin to get a sense of the patterned sequence that occurs in the family interaction, in other words, to lead them to an *enactment* of the transactions which occur at home. Therefore, no matter who starts to tell about what is happening in the family, the next step is to discover what other members think about what the first reporter said. This step can then be followed by questions such as "Mary, do you agree with what Bill said about George's description of the problem?" This form of questioning not only elicits more information about the problem or symptom, but also reveals material about the family relationship system, exposing the nature of family boundaries, rules, and coalitions. In family systems interviewing, we are always seeking to gain information about relationships or transactions between people, between events, and between people and events; we are more interested in what people are saying and doing than in what they are feeling. The emphasis is more on process than content.

Another kind of question that allows this kind of information to surface is what Palazzoli calls "gossip in presence" (1980). In this technique, a family member is asked to describe how he or she sees the relationship between two other people in the family. Then another member will be asked to comment on the first person's view and to add his or her own. Before long, it frequently happens that families become involved in a lively interchange about relationships in the family, providing information in key areas for assessment and intervention.

TRACKING SEQUENCES

Another way of gaining important information about the family relationship system and about the function of different behaviors in the family is to track behavioral or action sequences. In such tracking, it is important to discover everything that occurred before, during, and after a particular interaction or behavior. It is through seeing the behavior in the context of a series of transactions that its function in the family system becomes clear. In tracking sequences, particularly in the realm of problematic behaviors, it is important to focus on facts and opinions rather than on feelings. Tracking is combined with asking all members of the family individually both how they saw the sequence and also their opinion of the views others hold concerning what happened. This creates a "Rashomon" effect which allows one and all to observe both the sequence of events and also the complex pattern of relationships interwoven with these events.[8]

This kind of interviewing can take a great deal of time and considerable activity and patience on the part of the worker. People often tend to relate stories in shorthand or summary form, selectively leaving out many crucial details and even altering the time sequence. One must frequently interrupt the speaker with a request to clarify, to fill in missing steps, or to tell who else was present when a particular event occurred, when that person arrived, what that person did or said, and so on. The patient tracking of the sequence retrieves the details, and it is often the most instructive details which have been overlooked. Tracking also straightens out the temporal order. Finally, after considerable information gathering, as in a jigsaw puzzle many small pieces fall into place and the picture begins to take shape, showing the coherent and purposeful pattern imbedded in what might have first appeared to be a chaotic and random family process.

To repeat an essential point, in family systems interviewing, innate or intrinsic characteristics of individuals are not the focus of our exploration; rather we are always seeking information about relationships. When we hear, for example, that Ann is "quiet," the questions that immediately come to mind are: "Compared to whom?" "Was she more quiet before Dan went to college or after?" "In what circumstances is Ann most quiet?" The behavior Ann is showing us is not seen as a characteristic which "belongs to" Ann, but as an aspect of a relationship system set in the context of and interacting with a series of people and events.

THE USE OF "COMPARATIVE" AND "RANKING" QUESTIONS

Palazzoli et al. (1980) have described in detail a number of specific family interviewing techniques particularly helpful in yielding relational information. Questions which compare, contrast, and even rank the feelings, beliefs, attitudes, opinions and behaviors of family members immediately shift the focus from the internal state of problematic behaviors of one individual to the relationship system. This process itself begins a largely unconscious redefining, expansion, or reconstruction of the family's sense of reality. The following case example demonstrates how the worker shifts the focus from the individual to the larger family relationship system. This family, which came in immediately after the Christmas holidays, opened the session with the mother's announcing, "I'm exhausted!" In the context of individual, linear, "causal" interviewing, one might pursue this lead by inquiring about the various factors which may have led to her exhaustion, and about her sleep patterns, activities, demands, stress, and so on.

However, asking a "compared to whom?" question, a question of "difference," immediately focuses on the relationship system, as the following dialogue illustrates:

WORKER: "Who else in the family is exhausted?"
FATHER: "I am."
WORKER: "Who is most exhausted?"
MOTHER: "I think I am—more than he is. In fact, I can't see why he'd be tired at all—we had *his* family over the Christmas holidays, but it was *I* who did all the work. He sat around watching TV, shooting the bull with his father and brothers!"
FATHER: (Jumps in to defend himself and to tell about all he did).

Immediately, we have advanced toward the relational meaning of mother's announcement. This statement, in fact, was her beginning effort to define the relationship system as one in which she works and serves while her husband sits around, not carrying his share.

A second and more elaborate form of the "compared to whom?" question is one which ranks. In the course of the family session, the worker may ask a family member to rank in order, or from top to bottom, everyone in the family on the basis of a particular behavior, feeling, or interaction. For example, continuing with the case of the tired mother, the worker at one point queried, "Who works the hardest?" asking each family member in turn to rank everyone in the family from most to least. After the daughter ventures an opinion concerning who works the hardest, the worker may follow up with, "Well, who would you say comes second?" and so on.

Ranking interactions tends to garner even more systematic information. For example, to continue with yet another dimension of the case cited above, the worker might ask, "When mother is working hard, who is the most likely to help her?" "Who second?" "Who third?" "Fourth?" "Fifth?" After several members have completed this particular ranking, the next question might be, "And who is most likely to help Dad?" "Second?" We see, through this kind of interviewing, that the simple opening exclamation "I'm exhausted!" can be parlayed into a kaleidoscopic picture of the family relationship system in action.

In some cases, families seem unwilling or unable to differentiate relationships, answering ranking questions with statements such as, "I don't know." Or, "Everyone is exactly the same." Or, "I feel exactly the same about each of my children!" Such answers suggest that the family may be particularly resistant to change, or to exposure of the relationship system, and fiercely protective of its current coherence.

"BEFORE AND AFTER" AND "HYPOTHETICAL" QUESTIONS

Another kind of relational question inquires as to the differences in specific behaviors *before or after* an event. For example, one may ask, "Was Johnny's trouble with homework better or worse before his grandfather died?" "Did Jean argue more or less before her father left?" "Was Bob acting more or less angrily before you moved to the new house?" This type of question can elicit valuable information concerning the timing of the onset of the problem. It may also provide information concerning the nature of the threatened change in the family which the problem behavior is warding off. Further, through this means the worker may gain insight as to how the family then organizes itself to maintain the very behavior it sees as problematic.

The *hypothetical* question can also elicit considerable relational information. Because such questions are dealing with imagined or hypothetical rather than "real" circumstances, family members often feel more free to respond. Hypothetical questions can be put in the past or the future. For example, the worker might ask, "When you were growing up, if your mother had become seriously ill, who would have been most likely to take care of her?" Continuing with a ranking question, the worker might inquire, "Who would have been the second most likely?" "Third?" "Fourth?"

A hypothetical ranking question about the future to a family with several teenagers might be, "If, many years from now, something should happen to your father, who would be most likely to stay home with your mom so she wouldn't be alone?" If the response is "No one," that is useful information, but need not interrupt the hypothetical questioning, as one can always counter, "I know, but let's just suppose someone did. Who would it most likely be?" Again, several family members can be asked to rank.

Hypothetical questions can also serve to help enlarge the unit of attention and to gain information about the parts played by extended family members in family interactions, particularly in the area of troubling behavior. The following question illustrates this technique. "If your grandmother were at your house visiting when Nancy had a tantrum, what would she do?" "What would your mother do?" "What would your dad do?"

WIDENING THE CONTEXT IN SPACE AND THROUGH TIME

Although in interviewing families exploration of the current situation should take priority, with the focus primarily on the presenting specific issue or problematic behavior, before long it may be helpful both to deepen and broaden the understanding of the current situation. This can be accomplished through exploring the extended social and physical environment which surrounds the family and also by reaching back through time to weave the historical, intergenerational dimension into the current situation. Assessment in space and through time will be discussed in detail in Chapters 8 and 10, where the use of Eco-Maps and genograms in interviewing will be presented as well.

Other less elaborate means may be used in early family sessions to expand the context but remain problem-focused. Such expansion can occur through the use of the kinds of questions described above, but with the inclusion of extended family and other important figures in the questioning. For example, in the case of the mother exhausted by the Christmas holidays, a remark was made by mother that father's family had spent the holidays with them. This immediately opened up the possibility of including these figures in ranking and other questions. For example, the worker, after learning who the guests were, might have asked father, "If you and your wife were to get into an argument over who was working harder, who in your family would be the first to jump in?" Or, a less toxic question, "Who in your family would be the most likely one to offer to help get the meal on the table?"

Bringing in the historical dimension is in some ways more difficult because of the potential danger of straying from a clear focus and becoming lost in what is often a wealth of historical data. Because timing issues are particularly important, different family therapists handle historical detail in different ways. For example, Satir reports in her early work (1967) that she routinely does a family history in initial interviews. Guerin (1976) writes that in the first session he usually constructs a genogram, or intergenerational family map.

In our own practice, we have found that an early emphasis on history can, in many situations, seem irrelevant to the family and insufficiently attuned to their current struggles. Instead of focusing on any kind of formal history-taking in the initial interview, we find that weaving the past and the present into a single fabric by moving back and forth through time can bring in the historical dimension without loss of the present focus.

There are several time dimensions that have relevance to the here-and-now system. There is the *history of the problematic behavior itself*, which can be learned by asking before-and-after questions and other relational questions that explore the context of events and relationships that existed concurrently with the onset of the problem. For example, one could ask, "Did Mary have her first tantrum before or after Grandma moved in?" "Who was home on that day?" "Was that during the period when Dad was out of work?" "Who was in the room when it happened?" "What did Grandma do?"

Second, *the history of the particular family system* currently being seen may be salient. Again, the same kinds of questions can be asked. For example, in the case of the exhausted mother, questions would naturally arise concerning loyalties and relationships with in-laws. Had they always spent major holidays with his family? When did this alliance develop? What was the nature of their connection with the wife's family of origin? As the new family was formed, was there a loyalty conflict between the two in-law families? If, indeed, the major alliance developed with the husband's family rather than the wife's, how was that decision made? What have been the outcomes of that decision for all of the members of the new family?

Third, there is family of origin or *intergenerational time*. To continue with the same example, the events and residues of the context could be recovered by asking such questions as, "Who in your family spent Christmas together when you were a child?" "Which side was most likely to come, your mother's or your father's?" "How did your mother deal with all that company?" "What did your father do?" Further questioning could be directed toward the relationship system that existed many years ago in the family of origin. For example, "When your mother was overwhelmed by company at Christmas, who was most likely to help her?" "Who second?" "Who third?" This historical systemic interviewing would elucidate those patterns which shaped the parents' childhood experiences and provided the blueprints which these architects of the new family have been reusing.

Finally, there is yet another layer of time to be explored, one which might be termed *ancient time*, a mythic fund of meanings, commitments, and rituals which can have so much power in shaping the choices, organization, and behaviors of families. Turning to the father in our case example, the worker could say, "It seems that the family gathering at Christmas has been a very important tradition in your family." The affect embedded in the father's reply would quickly signal if, in truth, the need to gather were experienced by him as a strong and ancient command coming out of generations of people who valued familiness and perpetuated it through powerful "coming together" rituals. It may be that the mother's complaint, "I'm exhausted," with its suggestion that her in-laws were a burden, was flying in the face of powerful and ancient identity and value positions held by father.

In this chapter, we have described the processes of engagement and contracting as they occur in family-centered practice. We have explored some of the special issues in engaging and contracting with family groups, and some of the principles, techniques, and skills useful in interviewing families. We now move on to the use of these and other information-gathering procedures in the complex process of assessment and intervention.

PART III

Assessment and Intervention

Now that we have reviewed the context of family-centered practice, described the kinds of agency structure and procedures which facilitate such practice, and examined the initial phases of contact with families, we turn to the heart of practice: assessment and intervention. We refer, of course, to the processes involved in understanding the situation before us and the tasks of devising and executing strategies which grow out of that understanding.

The potential arena for action is, as we have described, the family as a system, as it has developed through time, and as it is in transaction with its environment. The present, the current moment, the immediate event contains elements from recent past, historical past, and ancient or mythic past, from inner family structure and process, and from the impact of the immediate and extended environment. These elements are interwoven in complex and shifting patterns and even as we attempt to untangle and trace the threads in coming to know the present, our ordering and sorting distorts, through simplification and the creation of artificial divisions, what is by nature complex.

Nonetheless, we are practitioners, not philosophers, and as such we must take action. Action, to be reasoned and directed, must be based on working hypotheses. These hypotheses grow out of our theories about families and the specific information we have gathered about the particular family and the particular situation.

The discussion of these processes of assessment and intervention is divided into subsections: the family's relationship with its environment (chapters 8 and 9), the family's historical context (chapters 10 and 11), and the current structure and processes of the family system (chapters 12, 13, and 14).

The distinction between assessment and intervention is to a large extent an artificial one. In practice they interact together in a process of feedback, each providing information which in turn alters the other. Actually, assessment, as a shared process with individuals and families, is in itself a powerful instrument of change. Nonetheless, hampered as we are by the linear nature of the written word, we present the following seven chapters, each concentrating on a particular aspect of our unit of attention and focusing primarily on intervention or on assessment.

In the final chapter we draw upon many of the aspects of family assessment and intervention presented throughout this book, demonstrating their application in work with the aging and in health care.

Chapter 8

The Family in Space: Ecological Assessment

OF ALL OF THE MENTAL HEALTH PROFESSIONALS, social workers are perhaps the most acutely aware of the fact that individuals and families depend on many other resources in addition to counseling for their physical and emotional health, indeed for survival. Because our social work heritage reminds us that the ability to help families often depends on skill and creativity in mobilizing resources, we can make a special contribution to the development of skills in ecological assessment and intervention, skills often insufficiently utilized in some approaches to family treatment.

We have been in danger, in the family field, of shifting in our assessment from an emphasis on the "sick" individual to one on "sick" families, a trend which must be avoided if we are to develop ways of helping families build, preserve, and repair the network of relationships and resources needed for a harmonious life. Further, we have often, in the mental health professions, preferred to treat "symptoms" rather than "systems." Perhaps we can learn something from the African witch doctor, the shaman, and the healer found in many cultures. Each alike "takes into account the powerful influences and interplay of an individual with his family, his culture and his environment. All these affect his bodily states. Also he recognizes the fact that human beings are constituted of psychic and physical realities which are distinct but not separate. They interact and influence each other in all conscious and subconscious acts" (Ndeti, 1976). The shaman tries to cure his patient not only by discovering the causes of his illness and

157

administering herbs or other therapeutic medicines, but by providing the means for confession, atonement, and restoration into the good graces of the family and tribe. Such a cure might involve his assuming the roles of physician, magician, priest, moral arbiter, representative of the group's world view, agent of social control, or initiator of tribal change (Kiev, 1964).

It may be that ecologically-minded social workers are akin to the native medicine man and the shaman of other cultures in terms of their focus on the complex interrelationships among physical, social, psychological, and cultural forces; like the medicine man and the shaman, they see these as influences in the production of diseases, deviance, and dysfunction of all descriptions.

Assessment of the Family's Relationship with Its Environment

In chapter 4 we presented the principles of theory and practice which inform our perspective of the family's transactional relationships with the world around it and of those relationships as resources for change.

In this and the following chapter, we translate these principles into a set of practical strategies for assessment and intervention. We will begin with one of the most challenging aspects of this task and that is the gathering and arrangement of the complex body of information about the family–environment interface. Through this effort we hope to counteract a longtime tendency toward partialization, which in the past has frequently resulted in reductionist problem definitions and solutions.

The very fact that language is linear, except in its metaphoric or symbolic usage, imposes restrictions on our ability to describe and organize complex systems of variables. To get beyond these limitations, we have made considerable use of two- and three-dimensional models or simulations to organize data as an aid in the assessment process and in the planning of strategies for change.[1] These visual aids enable both worker and family to see the relationships within the system of variables. They also make available a more holistic picture so that major themes and patterns emerge which can order the planning process and keep both worker and family from getting lost in detail.

A simulation which portrays family-environment relationships was developed by Hartman in 1975. Called an eco-map, it was originated to help workers in public child welfare examine the needs of families. This tool is currently being used in a wide range of practice environments. Though it is deceptively simple, workers are finding that the eco-map has wide applicability as an assessment, planning, and interventive tool which can be used in any practice setting or situation.[2]

The Eco-Map

The eco-map is a paper-and-pencil simulation which maps in a dynamic way the ecological system whose boundaries encompass the person or family in the life space. Included within these boundaries are the major systems, together with all their relationships, that affect and are affected by the subject. The eco-map pictures the family in its life situation; it identifies and characterizes the significant nurturant or conflict-laden connections between the family and the world. It demonstrates the flow of resources and energy into a family system as well as depicting the outflow of family energy to external systems. In conceptualizing the family's ecological environment, a worker-family shared process, we should look to not only the more tangible and concrete life connections but to those human, personal, social, psychological, and spiritual influences which also shape our lives.

The eco-map, in portraying the flow of resources and the nature of family–environment exchanges, highlights any lacks or deprivations which erode family strength. As it is completed, then, family and worker should be able to identify conflicts to be mediated, bridges to be built, and resources to be sought and mobilized. All one needs is a piece of paper, a pencil, and a creative "world view" in terms of helping families think through and describe their particular environments. By a creative world view we mean a thoughtful understanding of both the beneficial exchanges needed to promote healthy growth and adaptation and the harmful exchanges which threaten and undermine family life, unduly stressing family adaptive capacities. It saves time to have printed, "empty" eco-maps available. Figure 8.1 illustrates an "empty" map on which some of the common systems in the lives of most families have been represented and labeled, while others have been left undesignated so that the map can be individualized for different families. It is important to be flexible in the use of a prepared "empty" map, since it is meant to serve as only a rough guide or example.

INSTRUCTIONS FOR DRAWING AN ECO-MAP

We begin with a large circle at the map's center, within which the nuclear family system or household is described (or, in the case of an adult living alone, a single person). It is common practice in mapping families to use squares to indicate males and circles to depict females. The nuclear family is mapped as in the traditional family tree or genetic chart. It is useful, at a minimum, to put the person's name and age in the center of the circle or square, although other brief information could be included also. In the process of completing an eco-map, information about inner family rela-

Eco-Map

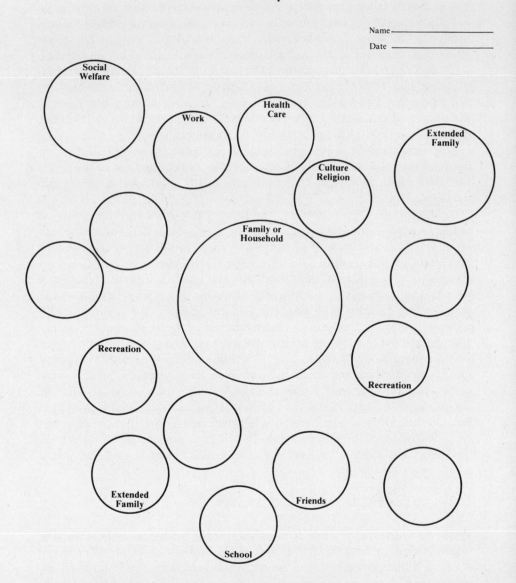

Name ————————————

Date ————————————

Fill in connections where they exist.
Indicate nature of connections with a descriptive word or by drawing different kinds of lines;
———— for strong, - - - - - - - - - for tenuous +++++++ for stressful.
Draw arrows along lines to signify flow of energy, resources, etc. ⟶ ⟶ ⟶
Identify significant people and fill in empty circles as needed.

FIGURE 8.1   Sample of Eco-Map

tionships and dynamics will naturally emerge as the family differentially describes the nature of family–environment transactions. However, it is best not to include those relationships here. Even the circles in the eco-maps are merely a convenient fiction in the sense that in a systems view we can never totally divide inner from outer; thus the eco-map has limited practicality as a tool for mapping the intricacies of the inner family system. Other tools, more suited for conceptualizing and mapping the inner family system, will be demonstrated later.

Figure 8.2 portrays a household consisting of a father, a mother, three children, and the wife's mother. The usefulness of this simple diagram becomes dramatically clear if one considers the volume of words it would take to describe this family with words alone. The mapping of more complex nuclear family systems will be demonstrated in chapter 12.

After placing the members of the household within the large middle circle, those environmental systems which affect the family's life are next identified on the map; and as soon as the nature of the family–system transaction has been determined, a line is drawn to express both the fact of the connection and the quality of it, as depicted in figure 8.3. A solid or thick line represents an important, strong, or positive connection and a broken line represents a tenuous or weak connection. Hatching across the line indicates a stressful or conflicted relationship. Along with these depictions, it is also informative to indicate the direction of the flow of resources, energy, or interest by drawing arrows along the connecting lines. The above code with its three relationship lines is an efficient shorthand in using the eco-mapping procedure as an analytic tool. Some workers have found this code too narrow or constraining and have developed their own creative codes. For example, some workers qualify the nature of the connections by writing a brief description along the connecting line, while

FIGURE 8.2

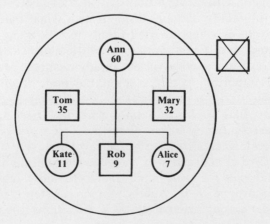

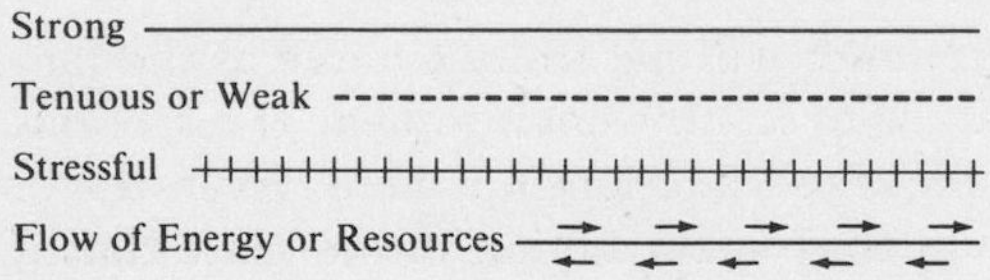

Strong ————————————————————————

Tenuous or Weak ------------------------------

Stressful +++++++++++++++++++++++++++++++++++++

Flow of Energy or Resources ——→ —→ —→ —→ —→
                             ←— ←— ←— ←— ←—

FIGURE 8.3

others have developed other types of lines or have used two different lines to describe a particularly ambivalent or complicated family connection. Figure 8.4 demonstrates one example of a completed eco-map. As a practice exercise it might be instructive for the reader to examine this map, to consider what is known about the family it depicts and to attempt a beginning assessment of the family's relationship with its world.

A quick review of John and Beth's eco-map reveals a family with rather limited connections with its world. Beth appears to be the most connected, as she has a part-time job and is involved with cultural and religious activities, friends, and a garden club. One might hypothesize, however, that John is at risk. He suffers from multiple sclerosis, and his only active connection is with the health care system. His connection with recreation is conflicted and we learn that he was formerly involved in sports. We may speculate that this has been a painful loss for John.

John and Beth share no friends, interests, or activities, and both are cut off from or in conflict with their families of origin. Of their three children, John, Jr., the eldest, is the most active, involved in college, sports, and with friends. Gwen, who appears to be socially isolated, is depicted as a "grind" in school. Joan has brought the attention of the family-centered practitioner to the family. She has been involved in some sort of difficulty, is on probation, does poorly in school, and runs with a rough crowd.

Connections can be drawn to the family circle as a whole if they are intended to portray the total family system's relationship with some system in the environment. Other connections can be drawn between a particular individual in the family and an outside system when that person is the only one involved, or when different family members are involved with an outside system in different ways. Such distinctions enable the map to highlight contrasts in the ways various family members are connected to the world. It is important to keep in mind, however, that most seemingly individual connections do indeed affect the entire family. For example, John's disability, Beth's extended family, and Joan's peer relationships all impinge on the total family system. One way some workers have handled very complex ecological portraits is by using colored pencils in addition to the code described above, choosing one color for total family connections and a different color for each family member's individual relationships with the world around them. Another important step is to draw in significant linkages among external systems. Sometimes these linkages are

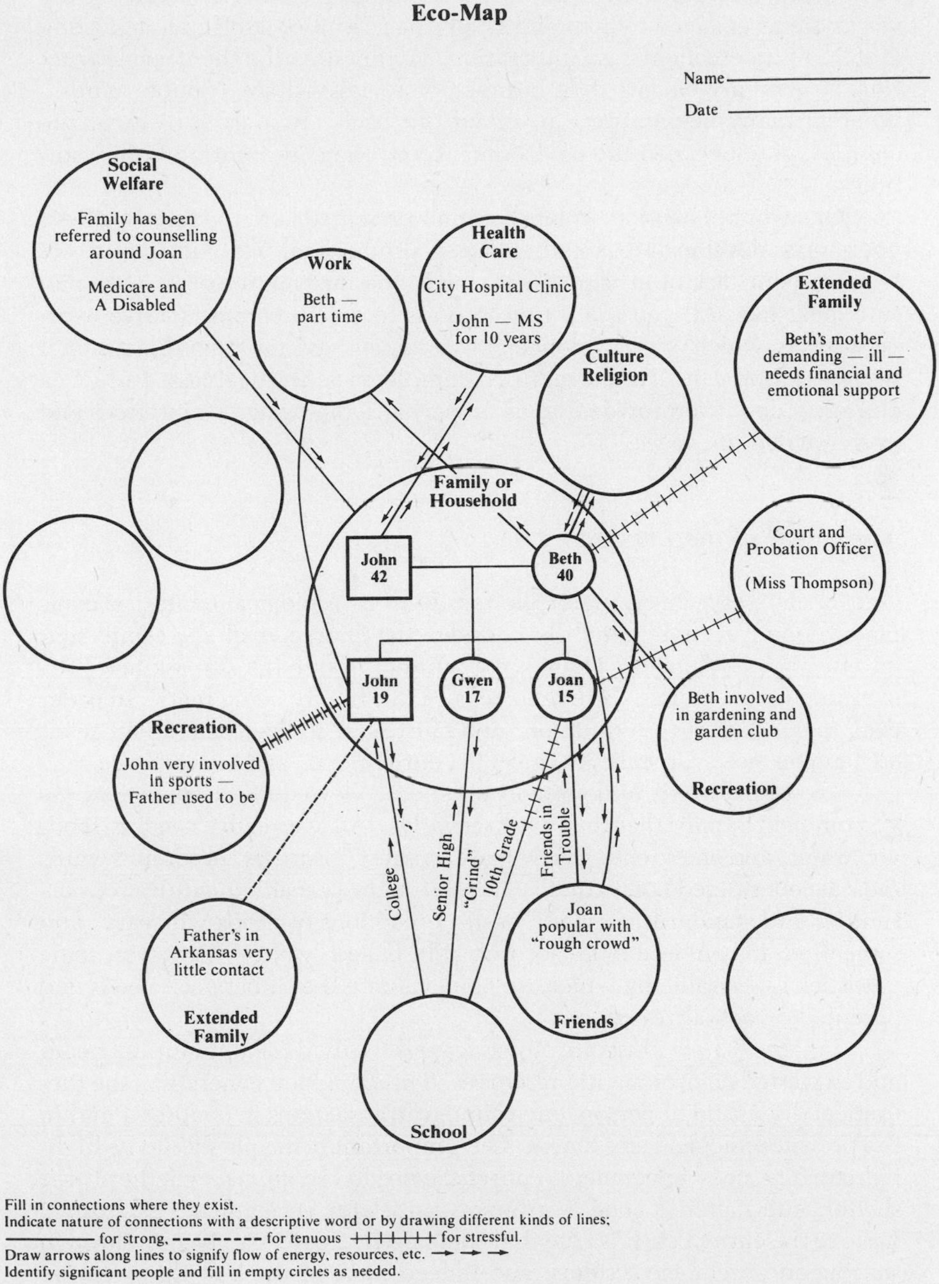

Eco-Map

Name————————————

Date ————————————

Social Welfare

Family has been referred to counselling around Joan

Medicare and A Disabled

Work

Beth — part time

Health Care

City Hospital Clinic

John — MS for 10 years

Culture Religion

Extended Family

Beth's mother demanding — ill — needs financial and emotional support

Family or Household

John 42

Beth 40

John 19

Gwen 17

Joan 15

Court and Probation Officer

(Miss Thompson)

Beth involved in gardening and garden club

Recreation

Recreation

John very involved in sports — Father used to be

College

Senior High

"Grind" 10th Grade

Friends in Trouble

Father's in Arkansas very little contact

Extended Family

Joan popular with "rough crowd"

Friends

School

Fill in connections where they exist.

Indicate nature of connections with a descriptive word or by drawing different kinds of lines;
————— for strong, --------- for tenuous +++++++ for stressful.

Draw arrows along lines to signify flow of energy, resources, etc. ➝ ➝ ➝

Identify significant people and fill in empty circles as needed.

FIGURE 8.4

tremendously influential in the outcome of problematic family situations, particularly those powerful and often conflicting connections among the very systems engaged to help and strengthen families. Hoffman and Long (1969), in an excellent case illustration, vividly describe the near destruction of a family caught in a number of social welfare "double binds," wherein many helpers were involved but each saw only a piece of the complex play between the environment and the deteriorating family stability.

One word of caution. While the map presented here is relatively clear, yours may develop into a rather messy production! Yet you should not bemoan your lack of artistic talent, for it does not matter what your picture looks like. All you are trying to do is to gain a comprehensive overview, one which shows movement as much as any two-dimensional representation can. Do not sacrifice completeness for neatness. In fact, a cluttered and overcrowded map is perhaps picturing a cluttered and overcrowded life space.

Assessment of the Eco-Map

Once a composite mapping of the family in its ecological context is completed, one can more carefully consider the character of the family–environment interchanges. There are a number of questions to ask here, the overarching one being, "Are the needs of this family being met?" In order even to consider such a question, one must have some notion about what *all* families need for stability, growth, enrichment, and competence.

The term "need" undoubtedly should be viewed in relative terms. As a prominent family therapist said recently, "All we really 'need' is food, air, water, and one friend. The rest are 'wants'!"[3] Further, needs and wants must be considered contextually, in relation to prevailing cultural opportunities and standards. Certainly self-perceptions of needs will vary, and some needs may indeed more accurately be called "wants." However, some yardstick is desirable by which we can evaluate the fit between needs and potential or actual resources.

In table 8.1 we illustrate our concept of individual and familial needs and suggested environmental resources. This depiction concretizes the theoretical discussion of person–environment transactions in chapter 4 and in the present ecological assessment. One important principle should be highlighted. The need for money to purchase needed resources, whether food, shelter, and material goods, or opportunities for enrichment, is assumed basic to the entire list. It is true that some needs clearly can be met through sharing and exchange systems, and indeed some of the best things in life may be free. In a complex society such as our own, however, money is needed to buy the free time, the peace of mind, and the leisure to meet the needs we have described.

Armed with the eco-map and a conception of needs and resources as outlined in table 8.1, we are ready to undertake an ecological assessment. This process can be divided into three dimensions, or more accurately, foci. As was pointed out in the introduction to this section, the foci of

TABLE 8.1   FAMILY NEEDS AND ENVIRONMENTAL RESOURCES

Need	*Resource*
Nutrition	Adequate and varied food Clean air Pure and plentiful water
Shelter	Housing (space, light, warmth, privacy and communality, safety)
Protection	Safe neighborhoods Police, fire, traffic control
Health	A clean environment Preventive, developmental and rehabilitative health care Adequate, responsive, accessible medical system
Belongingness, intimacy, interpersonal connectedness	Lovers, kin, friends Neighbors, social organizations, interest groups
Communication and mobility	Access to resources Telephone, public and private transportation
Education and enrichment	Schools (proficient teachers, well-maintained building, equal opportunity, support services, etc.) Other resources—vocational, adult education Family life education The arts and recreation
Varied resources for the spirit	Religious organizations Opportunities to share meanings and values Preservation of and respect for cultural, ethnic, racial, and other kinds of "difference"
Autonomy, effectance, mastery (to experience oneself as a cause)	Gratifying work in or out of home Community participation Opportunities for initiating new experiences
Generativity	To contribute to the future.

assessment are not to be thought of as discrete; the boundaries around them are artificial. One cannot, for example, examine the family's transactions in its life space without also discovering much about its inner system relationships and even how it has developed over time. Further, assessment is never a static process. It is better conceptualized as a cybernetic process in that each new piece of information is processed as it occurs, and forces some reordering of our understanding.

FOCUS I: A HOLISTIC VIEW—THE FAMILY IN RELATION TO THE ECOLOGICAL ENVIRONMENT

From the first examination of the completed eco-map, there emerges a holistic picture of: 1) what significant resources are available in the family's world; 2) what resources or supports are nonexistent or in short supply; and 3) some idea of the *nature* of the relationships between family and environment (strong, stressed, tenuous, etc.).

The following more specific questions should be asked of the map:

1. Is there income sufficient to meet basic needs?
2. Does the family have adequate food and shelter?
3. Is their neighborhood safe and a reasonably pleasant place to live?
4. Does the family have access to preventive health care and good medical resources?
5. Can family members get to needed resources, or are they cut off because of location, or lack of a telephone or of public or private transportation?
6. Does this family have meaningful social connections with neighbors, friends, community organizations? Are they part of an extended kin network?
7. Do family members belong to or participate in any group activities?
8. Does the family have the opportunity to share cultural, ethnic, or other kinds of meanings or values with others? Are their values in conflict with the surrounding environment?
9. Is the educational experience a positive one for the children? Do they and other family members have access to other vocational or cultural enrichment opportunities?
10. Do family members work? Is there any satisfaction or gratification in their work? How long has it been since family members have mastered a new experience, generated something new or different, felt proud of an achievement?

In this first look we are really asking what kinds of psychosocial supports and economic or other kinds of resources are currently in use by the family, what is needed and potentially accessible but currently lacking, and what may be required, but lacking in the community. This examination can quickly and clearly identify the most salient areas for intervention. For example, with some ecological assessments, it is immediately apparent that essential inputs are lacking and that the family is deprived of one or more life necessities, pointing to a strong brokering role for the worker. In cases where the resource is not available in the community, the worker's role may become one of advocacy in order to mobilize a needed resource on behalf of families. In other situations, it may be that the resources exist but the ties are weak. Perhaps the family needs access, or help in making better use of potential assistance from the school, the health care system, or a self-help group. In these situations, the worker may perform a mediating or counseling role. In some cases, it may be found that the family's physical and economic needs are being adequately served, but most of their ties are with remote, formal organizations, few with more informal or intimate systems. Here the task will be one of enhancement and enrichment, perhaps in helping the family join with others, strengthening extended family ties, and introducing the family to new experiences.

If, in some situations, the nature of the relationship between family and the resources of the world around it are weak or nonexistent, in others the most salient problem is rather one of overload, stress, tension, or conflict. For example, the eco-map may bring to light a number of stressful connections, suggesting that the family–environment equilibrium is in danger of becoming overwhelmed. Severe stress can result from a single event: the loss of a job, an accident, or an illness, a move from a familiar to a strange community, a natural disaster, frustrating experiences with bureaucratic organizations which themselves are frequently in conflict with each other, a developmental transition such as the birth of a new child or the leaving of a grown one. In these circumstances, the mission of the worker is clearly one of helping alleviate the conflicted or stressful situation.

Systems theory suggests that a change in one part of a system will bring about changes in all of the other parts and in the system as a whole. The most important challenge to the worker and the family is to identify the factor that appears to have the greatest, fastest, most efficient potential for change—in short, the factor that seems most salient (literally, that "jumps out" from all the rest). For example, if a breadwinner is out of work, the family may experience difficulties in housing, transportation, health, and nutrition, and probably also in their interpersonal and social relationships. Here usually a job or retraining is a first priority. In another family, the lack of any meaningful, generative, enriching involvement with others on the part of a middle-aged mother whose last child has moved away may be contributing to marital discord and to her depression and psychosomatic complaints. In yet another example, the meaningless work of a factory laborer coupled with the ever-rising cost of living and the indifference of both union and management has led the husband to excessive drinking and consequently to conflict with his foreman, the neighbors, his wife, and children. In all of these examples, positive change targeted at the point of greatest stress will reverberate throughout the system, relieving related stressful connections.

Focus II: The Family–Environment Boundary

The eco-map also reveals important information about the nature of the boundary between family and environment. This boundary is created through a series of transactions over time, and an analysis of its characteristics tells us something about the family, the world in which it is embedded, and what goes on between the two. We do not mean to imply, however, that the family–environment boundary is static or unchanging. The boundary may, to some extent, differ in relation to each individual's contact with the world, and may expand, contract, or be redefined for different activities or events.

One way to use the eco-map in order to gain a quick overall sense of the nature of this boundary is to look at the number and quality of transactions across the family–environment boundary. Is there considerable activity? Are all or most of the arrows which depict energy flow, or inputs and outputs, pointing from the family to outside systems (and thereby draining the family)? Or from outside systems into the family? Or is there a reasonable degree of exchange?

In chapter 4 we pointed out that open systems need to take in energy in the form of nourishment or in the form of new information or experiences, not only to survive but also to regenerate. If the human family, an open system, is to realize its potential, it must have the ability to take in both corrective and renewing inputs. The family which is closed off from new sources of energy is in danger of moving toward a state of entropy, that is, of randomization, disorganization, and ultimately dissolution. The degree of "openness" or "closedness" of boundaries is directly related to the family's ability to tolerate stress. While some families can exist in a relatively harmonious state for long periods of time under relatively closed circumstances (although never totally closed, which implies death), a stressful event or negative input can more easily and quickly overwhelm the semiclosed family's equilibrium. In their case, the lack of access to ameliorative resources, of escape valves for the inner family stresses, and of opportunities for corrective feedback can greatly handicap the family in dealing with stress. For example, the family with high fences, a locked gate, a sign reading "Beware of the dog," and drawn shades, whose children moreover are not allowed out of the yard, is clearly closed off from the surrounding environment. Such a family may have no one to turn to in illness, a marital upset, or the hard work of daily parenting.

Boundary questions to be asked include:

1. Is this family open to new experiences or relationships? To what extent and in what ways is it "closed"?
2. Are the family boundaries permeable and porous? Are members free to make individual connections with other people and organizations? Does the family allow others in physically or emotionally? Do in-laws remain outsiders?
3. Are the boundaries flexible, i.e., can they expand and contract adaptively in relation to the environment? Does the family protect its members when necessary and allow differentiation when appropriate?
4. Are restricted family boundaries primarily due to something about the family, something about the world, or both?

Returning to the example above, a family may be closing itself off in response to a realistically dangerous environment. Perhaps the family lives in a deteriorating urban neighborhood characterized by high rates of crime, delinquency, and drug use. Here we have a transaction between suspiciousness (or protectiveness) and danger. Or perhaps the family less realistically regards new inputs or experiences as threats to its survival and consequently encloses and suffocates its individual members. Assessment of the nature of the boundaries is essential in planning intervention, since we know that families with semiclosed, inflexible, impermeable boundaries are at risk, particularly vulnerable to various kinds of dysfunction and breakdown. Here the task of the worker becomes one of opening up their lives at the boundaries, of enhancing the nature of the transactions between the family and the world.

FOCUS III: INSIDE THE FAMILY

Chapter 12 describes tools and factors useful in assessment of the inner family system. The eco-map, however, may reveal important information about the family itself. The family's connections with its world and the nature of the boundaries cannot help but directly affect and be affected by the family's interpersonal relationships, marital, parental, and intergenerational. One may find, for example, that family members have highly unequal exchanges with the environment. A wife may work full-time, finding gratification in her job, her friends, and her extended family, while a physically disabled, isolated, complaining, and increasingly depressed husband spends most of his time watching television, drinking, and yelling at the couple's teenage daughter. In another case one may find that all but one of the children have managed to leave home in productive ways, while the youngest has been labeled emotionally impaired or delinquent, suggesting dysfunctional family relationships.

An examination of the eco-map will reveal:

1. How family members are differentially connected with other systems.
2. The fact that one or more members seem to be particularly cut off from environmental exchanges.
3. The possibility that one member seems to be more involved in stressful connections.
4. The extent to which the family is involved in joint and separate transactions with other people and systems.

While the ecological assessment cannot by itself produce enough information to explain the inner family system completely, it does give one clues concerning family dynamics and it may highlight particular areas for further exploration.

THE WORKER, THE AGENCY, AND THE SERVICE NETWORK

One further aspect of the assessment process should be considered and, in fact, is essential throughout: the nature of services extended to the family. This aspect includes the social worker, the social and family policies which frame agency practice, the structure and service delivery modes of the agency itself, and any contacts the family may be having with other agencies and professionals. The worker, the agency, and other professionals should be included in the eco-map. A series of questions should be considered:

1. To what extent do the policies informing your agency's practice conform to the needs of the families the agency is serving?
2. What is the relationship between your agency and the family? Is the agency structured in such a way that its services are appropriate to the needs of the family? If not, what can you do about it?
3. Is your agency in conflict with other components of the client's ecological environment, thereby causing additional stress?
4. How would you characterize the relationship between you and the family? Are you biased in favor of or against one or more members of the family? What is the nature of your bias and how does the family perceive it?
5. Are there other helping professionals involved with the family? What is the nature of that involvement? What is the other profes-

sional's view of the family and its situation? Does that view support or conflict with your approach?

Having presented the eco-map and discussed the process of ecological assessment, we now turn to some case examples. Our purpose in presenting these examples is to show how an eco-map is constructed and to then demonstrate how the eco-map can be used in assessment.

A Deprived or "Multiproblem" Family

The term "multiproblem," once popular in social work, has fallen into disrepute in recent years. This conception, like the "culture of poverty" notion developed by Oscar Lewis (1965), tends to be misinterpreted and misused to locate the sources of problems *within* families, leading to the effect known as blaming the victim. The term has been mistakenly used to describe something about the family system alone rather than something about the social milieu or family–environment relationships.

It is used here to suggest that families which, usually for a variety of complex reasons, are deprived of adequate physical and material resources, are likely to experience a multiplicity of problems. Significant lacks in material necessities, in educational, vocational and social opportunities, often coupled with a heritage of deprivation, cannot help but often breed hopelessness, despair, disorganization, and sometimes rebellion, reaching into every aspect of the family's interpersonal relationships. In the case of the Embree family, who are described below and further portrayed in an eco-map (figure 8.5), essential resources are in severely short supply.

CASE EXAMPLE: THE EMBREE FAMILY

The Embrees became known to protective services through a referral from the school, occasioned by concern of school personnel over high absenteeism and possible physical neglect of the children. The Protective Services worker made one visit, found no evidence of severe neglect, and considered the case a good candidate for referral to the local family agency, which had developed a demonstration project offering preventive services to families at risk. The family, more out of fear than faith in outside helpers, accepted the referral. The family agency, despite the fact that it considered the Embrees somewhat beyond "prevention," reluctantly accepted the referral as well. The project worker, Janet MacQueen, a young woman of considerable optimism and energy, had the advantage of a limited caseload and considerable agency support, resources which protective service workers sometimes lack.

The Embree family consisted of Will, aged 45, Ora, his wife, aged 39, and their six children, Will, Jr., 22, Ron, 15, Daryl, 11, Darlene, 9, Josh, 7, and Dawn,

Eco-Map

Name Ora and Will Embree

Date April 5, 1981

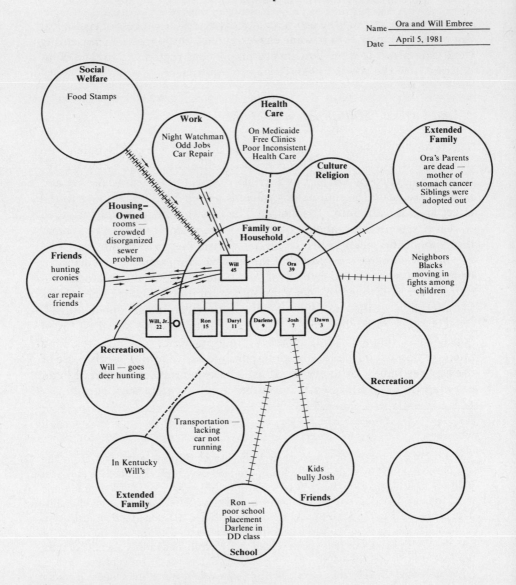

Fill in connections where they exist.
Indicate nature of connections with a descriptive word or by drawing different kinds of lines;
————— for strong, --------- for tenuous ++++++++ for stressful.
Draw arrows along lines to signify flow of energy, resources, etc. ➝ ➝ ➝
Identify significant people and fill in empty circles as needed.

FIGURE 8.5   Embree Family Eco-Map

3. The parents of both Ora Wilson and Will Embree migrated to Ypsilanti, Michigan from southern Kentucky in the late 1940s, seeking work in the automobile factories. Ora's mother died of stomach cancer in the early 1950s, when Ora was eleven years old, and her father was killed in a factory accident one year later. Ora and her younger siblings were separated, and placed in what turned out to be a series of foster homes; it has been many years since she has seen any of them. Will's parents returned to Kentucky with the younger children a few years after the end of World War II, while Will, the oldest, although only in his midteens, decided to stay in Ypsilanti. Will, Ora and their children have visited Kentucky once since their marriage, and Will has visited his family a few times by himself. Distant from their relatives, they also see little of their married son, who is barely making ends meet himself and at this point is maintaining his distance.

Ora, an anxious, tense woman, married Will when she was seventeen and he was twenty-three, their first child already on the way. She has suffered from overweight and a variety of physical problems, the most serious a form of colitis which periodically leaves her nauseous, listless, and immobilized. She also has an eye condition which makes it difficult for her to read or sew, and says she doesn't know if it is correctable. Will, a grammar school dropout as a youngster, was alternately labeled "borderline retarded" and "borderline schizophrenic," possibly as a result of discrimination against and misunderstanding of Appalachian migrants. He spent one year as an adolescent resident at Ypsilanti State Hospital. Will, an unskilled but hardworking man, has had a number of jobs over the years, usually paid at or slightly above minimum wages. Currently he works as a night watchman at a local factory. A very proud man, he has only recently and very reluctantly allowed Ora to apply for food stamps and Medicaid, feeling that a man should support his own family. He gets great satisfaction from the fact they own their own home and are beholden to nobody.

The Embree home, a somewhat dilapidated five-room cottage, is characterized by chaos and conflict, and conditions are very crowded. There have been frequent sewage back-ups and the family has often had to curtail water usage. They have complained to the township to no avail. Their old stove is nonfunctional and beyond repair, and they could not afford a new one, so for several months the meals for a family of seven had been prepared on a two-burner hot plate. The car was not running at the moment, although Will has a friend who was planning to fix it in exchange for some repairs Will had done on his house.

Meals tend to be disorganized, unscheduled affairs, since there is no space or table large enough for the family to eat together at the same time. There are piles of clothing, bits of toys and games, and other odds and ends strewn about. Ora doesn't drive and must depend on Will and the family's old, often unreliable car to get her to the laundromat, the food market, and other resources. Will, on the other hand, works long hours, from 10:00 P.M. to 6:00 A.M. at his night watchman's job, and at other times doing odd jobs such as car repairs or cleaning.

There is a good deal of conflict in the home. Will, who usually sleeps during the day, or tries to, is often tired, and often also furious at the children and Ora for not being more quiet. Ora, nervous when the children fight or make noise, resents the fact that Will "interferes" by complaining about her housekeeping, the children, and her "laziness." He can't understand where all the money goes and accuses her of poor management. She, on the other hand, complains that he doesn't earn enough, and resents the fact that he owns several expensive guns and has at least one deer hunting trip a year up north with his "cronies." Ora is often tired and depressed and sometimes ineffectual when it comes to getting the children organized for school, settling disputes, or seeing that they get their homework done. She is lonesome, and while she would never admit it, finds it both comforting and helpful to have one or more of the children stay home from school.

Both Ora and Will have been troubled about Ron's running away and blame the difficulties on the "bad" friends with whom he has been associating. As the neighborhood has become increasingly populated by blacks, the Embrees have tended to "stick to themselves" even more; and the children, who have been involved in several fights in the neighborhood, now spend more and more time in their own home.

Darlene, the nine-year-old, has been placed in a developmentally disabled class, a decision which left Ora and Will feeling extremely angry but also powerless to challenge the school's authority. Furthermore Ron, the fifteen-year-old, wanted to be trained as an automobile mechanic, but a skill training program was not available in his school district. He knew such a program existed in the neighboring district, but he had been told he was not eligible for transfer because he did not meet the academic requirements; ironically, he was confined in a program which did not interest him and was doing poorly on that account.

In terms of the family's use of space, Janet observed that the parents slept in a room near the kitchen, a room originally intended as a dining room. A curtain hung over the door between this room and the living room, where all the family regularly congregated. The very flimsiness of the curtain expressed the inadequate boundary between the parental subgroup and the children. The two younger boys slept in the large bedroom upstairs, while Ron slept on the living room sofa. Ora often watched late movies while Will was at work, comforted by the presence of Ron who would keep his mother company until he drifted off to sleep. Will seemed to sleep different hours every day, sometimes for one long stretch at random times, sometimes going to bed right after he came home from work and other times at midday or in the late afternoon. Often Will relaxed with a beer or two in the morning after he got home, allowing himself some brief time with the children before they headed for school. Ora, who often stayed up half the night watching television, generally slept until ten or eleven o'clock in the morning while Will, who had virtually been alone all night on his job, welcomed the company of one or more of the children, and was less than firm in insisting they board the school bus.

ECOLOGICAL ASSESSMENT: THE EMBREE FAMILY

Looking holistically at family–environment relationships, we may say that this eco-map portrays a deprived family. The Embrees do not have enough income to meet their physical needs adequately. While they have recently acquired food stamps, in general the family diet has been lacking in terms of balanced nutrition, probably contributing to Ora's colon difficulties, and the children's frequent colds and anemia. Housing is crowded and in a poor state of repair so that cleanliness and good hygiene is difficult, and the family's lack of privacy and competition for limited resources and space has led to interpersonal conflict. While they have recently acquired access to Medicaid, the family's relationship with the health care system has been tenuous. Preventive health care has been almost totally neglected because of lack of adequate income, accessible transportation, and child care resources, and medical care has meant waiting long hours in free clinics or in the large, impersonal, and sometimes unresponsive emergency room of the hospital.

While there is some exchange across the family–environment boundaries, the greater number of family relationships are with large, formal institutions such as the school, the hospital, the court system, and the Department of Social Services. Some of these connections, instituted for social control purposes, are ambivalent at best and conflict-ridden at worst. In sum, the most significant fact about the Embree family is that it is deprived. Further, this deprivation is contributing to their social isolation and to stress and conflict, and it is inadequately balanced by positive sources of energy and information.

About the specific nature of their boundary relationships we lack some information, but this family is probably best described as a semiclosed system. The fact that Ora's parents are deceased and the couple is geographically distant from Will's family of origin, from their "roots," means that they can rely very little on any extended kin network or mutual aid system which often helps poor families survive.[4] Uneasy and increasingly isolated in a racially changing neighborhood, their suspiciousness and self-protectiveness are growing. Thus the family's boundaries are ever less permeable, and the children are increasingly kept away from "bad" influences and home from school.

Finally, the eco-map gives us some meaningful data concerning inner family relationships. Most significantly, while none of the family has what might be termed rich connections with the world around them, Will and Ora are differentially involved outside the home. Will is at least occasionally in contact with his parents and siblings, and he has a job which, while a somewhat solitary one, does give him connections with other systems and people. His car repair work, part of the "irregular" economy, also gives him social outlets, and he has a gratifying hobby, hunting, which is not only a source of social connectedness and sometimes a bounty of food, but which also connects him positively with his rural heritage.

Ora is less connected, and has gradually become the underfunctioner in this marriage. Divested of extended family, cut off from social outlets by lack of transportation, responsibilities at home, and perhaps also by lack of knowledge or easy access to new experiences, she retreats to physical symptoms and increasingly relies on the children to meet her needs for emotional gratification. We can predict that unless there is change, the children will be vulnerable either to early, unsatisfying "leaving home" experiences as in the case of Will or may become enmeshed and unable to establish autonomous adult lives of their own.

An Overburdened Family

Many families which could be described as strong, adaptive, well-functioning families with resources adequate to meet their ordinary needs for survival and growth may become overburdened at particular times during the family life cycle. The more vulnerable periods often occur during periods of major developmental transition; these are times when the family is undergoing significant changes in organization, division of roles, living arrangements, and emotional realignments, and times when the forces for genesis or change are more powerful than those for sameness or stasis. During these transition points, such as the leaving of a child for college or marriage, or the birth of a new baby, a family may find its adaptive capacities stretched to their very limits.

The family's ability to weather these stresses and strains is greatly influenced, according to Carter and McGoldrick (1980), not only by the structure of the current system, but also by the responses learned from one's forebears, and by the degree of older, unresolved anxiety generated by particular events. Furthermore, in this age of rapidly changing norms for family life, the path for change is not always brilliantly lighted. Developmental events shake the family's homeostasis. They demand challenging and sometimes unfamiliar or painful coping responses on the part of the family members. And sometimes the family's emotional and physical energy as well as its available concrete resources may indeed become dissipated and overwhelmed. The following information led to the Rauer eco-map (figure 8.6), depicting one such overburdened family.

CASE EXAMPLE: THE RAUER FAMILY

Marta Rauer contacted the local mental health agency, indicating she had been feeling depressed, confused, and discontented with herself lately. She thought talking to a counselor might help. The worker, much to Marta's surprise (because she thought the problems were *hers*), suggested that her husband Phil also come for the first appointment and stressed that she might want to include the children or other family members at a later date.

Marta and Phil Rauer, aged forty-eight and forty-seven, respectively, have been married twenty-five years. While their marriage has had its minor skirmishes and their work its frustrations, and while they acknowledge that raising three

Eco-Map

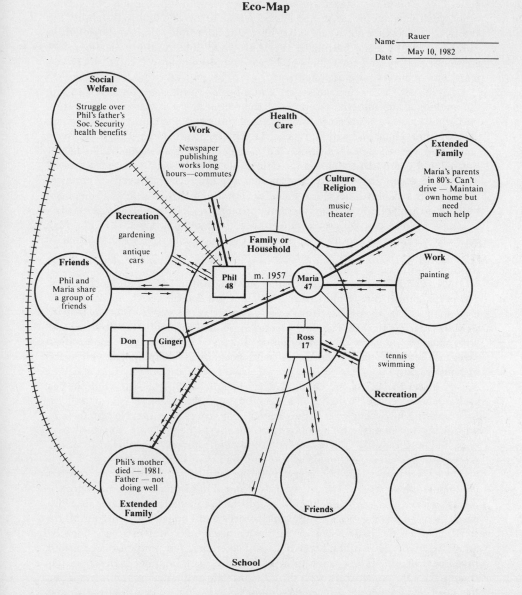

Name — Rauer

Date — May 10, 1982

Social Welfare

Struggle over Phil's father's Soc. Security health benefits

Work

Newspaper publishing works long hours—commutes

Health Care

Culture Religion

music/ theater

Extended Family

Maria's parents in 80's. Can't drive — Maintain own home but need much help

Recreation

gardening

antique cars

Friends

Phil and Maria share a group of friends

Family or Household

Phil 48   m. 1957   Maria 47

Don   Ginger

Ross 17

Work

painting

tennis swimming

Recreation

Phil's mother died — 1981. Father — not doing well

Extended Family

Friends

School

Fill in connections where they exist.
Indicate nature of connections with a descriptive word or by drawing different kinds of lines;
————— for strong, --------- for tenuous ++++++++ for stressful.
Draw arrows along lines to signify flow of energy, resources, etc. → → →
Identify significant people and fill in empty circles as needed.

FIGURE 8.6   Rauer Family Eco-Map

children has been quite a challenge, they describe their marriage as strong and close. Phil, a middle-management employee of a large newspaper publishing company, greatly enjoys his career and has been able to provide financial stability for the family. They are not wealthy but have a comfortable suburban home and a summer cabin on a northern lake; they have been able to afford vacations and ample recreation; and their three children have been able to take advantage of many opportunities for enrichment.

In the last three years, however, a number of events have combined to sap the emotional and material resources of the couple. First it was discovered that Phil's mother, always a center of strength and support in the family, had terminal cancer. After a long and painful illness, she died eighteen months ago, a loss from which they are only now recovering. Phil's father has not made a good adjustment. Retired and overly dependent on his wife at the time of her illness, his physical health and emotional stability deteriorated rapidly after her death. For some months Phil and Marta helped as much as they could, while weighing the possibility of inviting him to live in their home. Finally, with both pain and guilt, they reluctantly concluded they could not provide the care he needed. The elder Mr. Rauer now resides in a local nursing home. Family members visit him as often as possible and occasionally take him out for a walk or drive, and bring him home for Sunday dinner.

Marta's parents, now in their early eighties, are in reasonably good health except for some arthritis and rheumatism, and are determined to maintain their own home as long as possible. However, neither parent is able to drive any longer, so Marta helps with their shopping, doctor appointments, and other errands, and with some of the more demanding household tasks. Phil and Ross, the couple's seventeen-year-old son, pitch in on weekends occasionally, helping with yard work or house repairs.

Phil and Marta's oldest child, Ginger, married four years ago while in her senior year in college, and lives in a neighboring suburb. Ginger's husband Don is completing his second year of law school. The couple has survived financially with loans and grants, supplemented periodically by help from both sets of parents, and until recently Ginger worked at the public library. Ginger and Don, not wanting to postpone parenthood any longer, had their first child ten months ago, an event greatly welcomed by everyone in the family, but one which has created yet another set of strains. Ginger recently decided to begin her master's degree in library science on a part-time basis. Though she has made arrangements for child care, the plan has not been totally satisfactory, and Ginger has relied on Marta to fill in when the baby is sick or the sitter unavailable. Marta, a very talented art student when she and Phil married, unlike her daughter postponed any serious investment of time in her work until the children were in junior high school, although she enjoyed her work with the PTA and other volunteer organizations. She has been reluctant to let Ginger down and loves taking care of the baby, but is depressed about her own progress as it has become increasingly difficult for her to concentrate on her own work and to claim any consistently uninterrupted time. Until Phil's mother's illness, she had been investing more and more time in her painting, which was beginning to bring her a heightened sense of her own competence and worth, and beginning recognition in the community. As Marta began to sell a few of her paintings, both she and Phil welcomed the addition to the family's coffers.

Marta has found that the joys of grandparenthood are mixed, and that the responsibility for their own aging parents seems to be falling largely upon her shoulders. Phil, who commutes two hours every day, must be available to his firm from nine to five, and often for emergencies or evening meetings as well; but Marta's work is done at home, and therefore she is usually elected to meet the extra caretaking demands from parents, children, and grandchildren. She is literally and figuratively "in the middle." Lately Marta has found herself cross, tired, and increasingly resentful toward Phil. She and Phil seem to have little time for each other, and they have grown more distant sexually. To her dismay she has begun to find herself questioning her faith in their relationship.

ECOLOGICAL ASSESSMENT: THE RAUER FAMILY

A holistic view of the Rauer's eco-map immediately suggests that this family's energy is being drained. It is apparent that the family has many exchanges across its boundaries and sufficient access not only to material resources but to other kinds of social and cultural gratification. However, one sees that the predominant direction of energy flow is outward from the nuclear family to work, to their children, and to their families of origin.

An eco-map, it must be remembered, captures a particular point in time, and to a smaller or greater extent is constantly changing. If we had drawn the Rauers' map a few years ago or if we could look into the future, we might see a different and more even balance of resources coming into and going out of this family.

This is an "open" family. Its boundaries are permeable, its members are free to differentiate, to make new relationships, to marry. On the other hand, it is a family which has strong convictions about the responsibilities of "familiness," seen particularly in its concern for and willingness to help both its aging and its newly matured members.

If we glance inside the family, we see that all of the family members have important and meaningful connections to external systems, that no one member seems restricted or isolated, and that the family seems to have activities both shared (for example, cottage, friends, cultural opportunities) and separate (for example, school, hobbies, friends, recreation, cultural opportunities). While Phil is certainly feeling the strain, Marta is perhaps in a particularly vulnerable position at this point in the family life cycle, since the changing demands on personal time and energy have fallen more squarely on her shoulders at a time when she hoped to make a transition from a predominantly caretaker role to a career role. One can predict that the marriage will go through an increasingly stressful period unless some ways are found to alleviate the pressure.

A Socially Isolated Family

In chapter 4 it was suggested that the boundaries of living systems such as families must be permeable enough to allow the importation of energy, information, and new experiences. The alternative, as viewed by systems theorists, is increasing entropy or lack of organization and differentiation. In a family, the more closed the boundaries, the less potential exists for growth and the more vulnerable the family may be to various kinds of dysfunction, including assaults to its coherence.

Some families may meet their physical and material needs adequately yet remain cut off from potential sources of support and stimulation in the surrounding environment. Families may experience increasing social isolation for a number of reasons. Most of us have become aware of the phenomenon of isolation in aging, as growing interest in gerontological study has increased our consciousness of both the developmental needs and potential of aging people. Social workers have begun to better define the ways in which they can help this population, a topic we will examine in more detail in chapter 15. Elderly people frequently find their social and emotional resources shrinking by reason of the deaths of their friends and relatives, the moving away of their children, the deterioration of their health, the loss of paid or meaningful work, and the dwindling of their economic resources. All of these losses can imprison them increasingly within their boundaries, hastening the process of entropy and ultimately resulting in mental or physical deterioration and untimely death.

Younger families may also suffer from such social isolation, a transactional process which can eventually result not only in lack of sufficient growth and differentiation, but in physical or emotional handicaps and even breakdown. Included among the vulnerable families are those who define themselves (or more likely are defined by others) as "different" or deviant in some way, the religious family whose beliefs seem odd to others, the divorced or unmarried single parent, the lesbian couple with children, the black family in a primarily white neighborhood, the elderly Polish couple in a black urban ghetto. Some of these families experience hostility or even violence from their environments; others are set apart by a lack of mutuality or by ignorance on the part of those in whose milieu they find themselves. Such families can sometimes be recognized by the visible boundaries they erect to protect themselves. With others the boundaries are less visible but just as effective, and there is little communication with neighbors or organizations in the surrounding environment.

The following family, diagrammed in the Taylor eco-map (figure 8.7) exemplifies a middle-class, socially isolated family. While a financially secure family is presented here, it must be remembered that the fewer financial, educational, or other kinds of inputs are available to a

Eco-Map

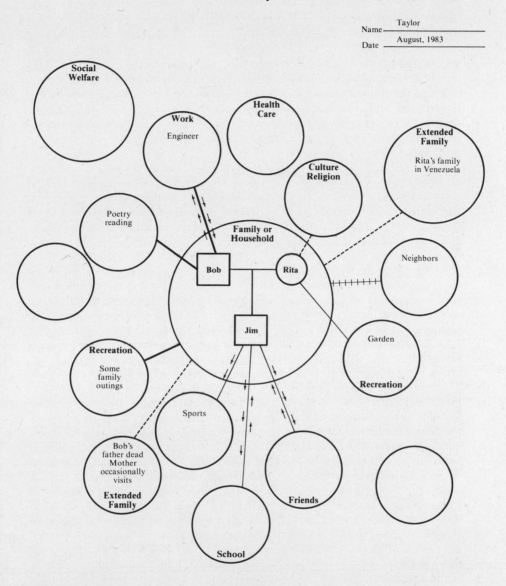

Name — Taylor

Date — August, 1983

Fill in connections where they exist.
Indicate nature of connections with a descriptive word or by drawing different kinds of lines:
———— for strong, - - - - - - - - - for tenuous ++++++ for stressful.
Draw arrows along lines to signify flow of energy, resources, etc. → → →
Identify significant people and fill in empty circles as needed.

FIGURE 8.7 Taylor Family Eco-Map

particular family, the more virulent and potentially destructive the socially isolating situation becomes.

CASE EXAMPLE: THE TAYLOR FAMILY

Rita Jimenez Taylor was brought to the emergency room of the local general hospital by her husband after a suicide attempt. She had taken an overdose of sleeping pills and been found unconscious in her bedroom by her husband when he returned from work. She was admitted for a short-term stay on the hospital's psychiatric ward, during which time the ward team, including the staff social worker, held several family sessions which involved Rita, her husband Bob, and their sixteen-year old son Jim.

Rita and Bob met about seventeen years ago when Bob, a young engineer for an oil company, was working on an oil-searching project in Venezuela and Rita was working as a hotel clerk. The two were strongly attracted to one another, and married rather quickly when they discovered that Rita was pregnant. Both families were silently disapproving. Rita's family were concerned about the ethnic and religious differences but were also upset by the fact that the couple planned to return shortly to the United States, meaning they would be distant from their daughter. Bob's family, who felt vaguely betrayed, were never openly critical of Rita, but nevertheless made it clear that they did not sanction the marriage and were not going to let Rita inside the family boundaries. They offered the young couple little emotional support or opportunity for family connectedness. Bob, shy, intellectual, socially withdrawn, and absorbed in his career, when not traveling for the company spent much of his free time in his study writing poetry. Rita, a more dynamic, lively person, devoted her considerable energy to their child, her house, and her yard. Somewhat proud, very conscious of her Spanish accent, her less than perfect English, and her lack of formal education, she would have liked to make friends with other women or couples in the neighborhood or in her church, her only potential social outlets. The neighborhood, a new east-coast suburban development near the ocean, was composed primarily of Irish and Italian families which had moved out from city apartments. Initially Rita made tentative efforts to invite one or two of the neighbors in for coffee. However, many of the women in the neighborhood worked or seemed too busy with their own activities, and all were slow to reach out to this lonely woman, while Bob showed little interest in socializing with other couples or participating in church activities. Bob was kind, introverted, increasingly absorbed in his own interests, and emotionally remote from Rita. Since he had sufficient outlets through his work for whatever social connectedness he might want, he preferred to be alone at home, and was insufficiently aware of Rita's increasing unhappiness. She hated to complain. The couple seemed to join primarily around their child, and enjoyed some family outings together, but Bob was content to leave most of the parenting to Rita. A visit back to Venezuela had left Rita saddened, since she now seemed to belong in neither world. Bob seemed to sense that he could only become closer to his family if he were to give up Rita or at least to shift his primary loyalty. He chose to remain distant.

In a gradual deviation-amplifying process, over the years Rita began to be viewed by the neighbors as "peculiar" and, in turn, to behave more and more eccentrically. She could be observed almost any day and sometimes even late at night washing down the outside of her house, her driveway, and her grass. She became increasingly upset and even enraged if a neighborhood cat or dog wandered onto her property, or if a child inadvertently picked a flower or threw a ball which landed in her yard. Gradually, the children began to dare one another to hit a ball onto her property, and to shriek back at her when she chased them out. Words like "strange" and even "paranoid" began to be used by neighbors after she accused the woman next door of deliberately encouraging her son to break her window with a baseball. The neighbors were already incensed because Rita had completely covered over her front yard with asphalt, enclosed it with a tall plastic fence which greatly limited their view of the water, and painted her cedar shingles when the entire neighborhood were uniformly allowing their shingles to bleach to a silver grey. She also modified the colonial facade of the house by adding a black wrought iron balcony on the second story and decorative iron-work on other parts of the front of the house. The building, a typical American development house, came more and more to resemble a Spanish hacienda. In the opinion of those who lived nearby, she was ruining the neighborhood. Some even speculated that she must have been the person who was poisoning cats, since two had been found dead in the last few weeks. On the morning of the suicide attempt, a woman down the street had telephoned, accusing Rita of killing her cat, and calling her "a crazy Puerto Rican."

ECOLOGICAL ASSESSMENT: THE TAYLOR FAMILY

The Taylors clearly have resources adequate to meet their physical needs, and their neighborhood is a safe, potentially positive and pleasant environment. The map indicates, however, that few emotional or socially satisfying inputs are available to this small family; they are cut off from meaningful social connections with neighbors, friends, groups, or organizations, and have become alienated from their extended families partly for geographic reasons and also because of the tensions arising out of ethnic differences and the possessiveness of their families of origin. Bob and Rita find separate consolations: Bob in his work and his solitary intellectual pursuits of reading and writing poetry, and Rita in the raising of their child and in caring for and beautifying their home—but her ethnic background has contributed to isolating rather than to enriching experiences in this environment.

The newness and instability of the neighborhood itself may well contribute to the escalating tension between Rita and those in her environment, and an analysis of the dynamics of the larger social system leads to a hypothesis that Rita is being scapegoated in the neighborhood. This newly developed area is occupied primarily by Irish and Italian families from neighborhoods where there had been a history of ethnic conflict. Initially the two groups dealt with their mutual distrust and antagonism by scapegoating the builder of the development, since everyone could share common complaints about unfulfilled promises, poor materials, or shoddy workmanship. In time, however, the builder completed his obligations and moved elsewhere. At about the same time, a popular man in the neighborhood was arrested for his connections with an extensive drug distribution ring. This incident was quickly hushed up. A review of events in the neighborhood leads one to surmise that Rita serves at least two functions in the maintenance of an uneasy stability in the neighborhood. In all likelihood she has replaced the builder as the receptacle for the shared tension, and has also provided a distraction from the disturbing arrest of a central local figure.

The Taylor family is "at risk," and is becoming an increasingly closed system whose boundaries are gradually becoming less permeable and less flexible. It appears that at the same time the family system has become less open, it has also become less able to adapt to, alleviate, or equilibrate external threats to its stability; its internal mechanisms have become too weak to adapt to the family-environment difficulties. This situation, coupled with the paucity of environmental exchanges which might increase the potential for corrective feedback, has culminated in the suicide attempt.

As Rita's desperate action shows, the members of this family have absorbed the tension unequally, and have had unequal exchanges with the world around them. Both the father and son have lives of their own which only minimally involve Rita. As Jim, the son, appropriately begins to invest far more interest in his own academic and athletic activities, and in his teenage friends rather than in his family, Rita experiences a growing sense of emptiness. Her efforts to fill this void are thwarted. Bob is also absorbed in his own interests and is insufficiently sensitive to his wife's pain, while she does not know how to penetrate the emotional barrier between them. He is content to remain cordial but distant from the neighbors and other acquaintances and thus does not help her develop needed social connections. While at this point the dysfunction in the family seems to exact its heaviest costs from Rita, one might predict that the marriage will continue to erode and that their son may become more enmeshed or triangled between the couple in order to help the family restore some kind of equilibrium.

Uses and Applications of the Eco-Map

The above three examples demonstrate the use of the eco-map in the assessment process. Obviously its value as a tool will ultimately hinge on its usefulness as a blueprint for carrying out planned change. Specific applications in the planning and implementation of ecological interventions will be found in the following chapter on the environment as a resource for change.

No matter how the eco-map is used, one of its obvious values lies in its visual impact, and another in its ability to organize and present concurrently not only a great deal of factual information but also the relationships between variables in a situation. Visual examination of the map has considerable impact on how the worker and the client perceive the situation. The connections, the themes, and the quality of the family's life seem to jump off the page, and this dynamic perception leads to a more holistic assessment. The integrative value of this very experience was aptly expressed by one twelve-year-old client who said, "Gee, I never saw myself like that before!"

Initially developed as a thinking device for the worker, it quickly became apparent that this tool is also useful in the interviewing process itself and in helping to define and develop the worker–family or individual client relationship as a shared, collaborative process. The client and worker cooperate in picturing the family's life space, a collaboration which often becomes expressed even in the seating arrangements as the family and worker sit around a table or on the floor, adult and child alike, each making suggestions, additions, and changes as the family examines, questions, and debates the nature and quality of their life. It is not only a shared process to which adult and child can equally contribute, but an unfolding, changing process, for a family's relationship with its world is rarely static. The process of mapping invites lively, active discussion. After all, it is the family's map, and no one knows their world quite the way they do. An eco-map, like a photograph, captures a moment in time. The portrait may change very quickly.

Sharing the eco-mapping process can also lead to increased understanding and acceptance of the self on the part of the client. For example, an almost empty eco-map helps the client objectify and share loneliness and isolation. An eco-map full of stressful relationships showing all of the arrows pointing away from the family may lead a client to say, "No wonder I feel drained—everything is going out and nothing is coming in!" The eco-map has been extensively tested with natural parents working toward the return of their placed children through the Temporary Foster Care Project of the Michigan Department of Social Services. Foster care workers noted that parents who were generally angry and self-protective following placement of their children because of abuse or neglect were almost without exception engaged through the use of the map. Workers were aware of a dramatic decrease in defensiveness. The ecological perspective made it clear to parents that the worker was not searching for their inner defects but rather was interested in finding out what it was like to be in the clients' shoes.

Because interventions focus attention on the client's relationship with his life space, they tend to be targeted on the family–environment fit, with both worker and client becoming active in initiating changes in the life space. Problematic conditions tend to be characterized as transactional and as a function of the many variables that combine to affect the quality of the individual's or the family's life.

In the Temporary Foster Care Project mentioned above, the worker and client moved quite naturally from the eco-map to a task-oriented contract. They talked together about the changes that would be needed in the eco-map before the family could be reunited. They identified problem areas, resources needed, and potential strengths, and planned what actions were needed to bring about change. Further, they established priorities and developed a contract describing the tasks to be undertaken by the worker and by the client.

The uses of the eco-map have multiplied in the hands of creative practitioners. For example, it has been used to portray the past and the future: In a rehabilitation program in a medical setting a social worker used eco-maps with clients to picture their world before their accident or illness; this helped clients to objectify what changes would be made in their lives following hospitalization. It helped them to mourn interests and activities that would have to be relinquished and also to recognize sources of support and gratification that would continue to be available. The mapping encouraged consideration of appropriate replacements for lost activities and of possible new resources to be tapped, both of which could expand the client's horizons. This technique was not only useful with the patient alone but was very helpful in conjoint work with disabled persons and their families.

Retrospective use of the map tends to highlight those changes in a client's life that could have precipitated current difficulties. When families and individuals seek help, a major question is always, "Why has the client sought help now?" Therefore in the months that follow, a review of the changes that have taken place may well bring to light shifts of which the client was quite unaware.

Finally, the eco-map is also a very useful tool in both presenting and recording a case situation as part of a case record, and also in evaluating the degree and quality of change in the outcome. The initial eco-map kept in the front of a case record not only tends to keep the total situation clear for the worker, but it also serves as a means of communication to others should a staff member have to respond to a client's request in the absence of the regular worker.

Now that we have discussed assessment of the family–environment interface, we will next concentrate, in the following chapter, on the environment as a target and a resource for change.

Chapter 9.

Family–Environment Transactions as Target and Resource for Change

WE HAVE INTRODUCED the Embrees, the Rauers, and the Taylors, and through the use of the eco-map we have developed an assessment of the relationships between these families and their environments. We will now discuss and illustrate a range of interventive strategies which use family–environment transactions as the arena for change. Furthermore, toward the conclusion of the chapter we will consider some of the case management issues that arise when other professionals or treatment institutions are a crucial part of the context within which the family is being seen.

An ecological perspective on change suggests that strategies may be targeted primarily toward the environment. The worker may aim primarily to help a family achieve the knowledge, skills, and confidence to make use of available resources and opportunities, or in other circumstances the worker may stand at the interface between family and environment, acting as facilitator, mediator, or catalyst in improving the nature of the transactions. Whatever the primary focus, because the family–environment complex is itself a system, intervention on any of these levels will tend to ripple throughout, bringing about changes in the other levels. However, the worker needs to identify the primary target for change, being clear whether interventions are targeted primarily toward the environment, the relationship between family and environment (in which case the environment may be construed as a resource for change), or the family system itself.

187

In some situations the major objective, growing out of our convictions concerning basic human rights, may be an alteration in the family's environment through the creation or accessing of vitally needed resources. These interventions emerge from our personal and professional values which imply that all people are entitled to such amenities as decent housing, education, nutrition, medical care, and the opportunity to work. In such cases there may not be any explicit, and should not be any implicit, expectation that the family or individual should change—an expectation which unfortunately is the hidden string sometimes attached to the provision of resources.

In other situations, the objective is an improvement in individual or family functioning, mutually understood by worker and client system, and clarified in the contracting process. Here the environment may be the resource for change, while the individual and/or family is the entity to be changed. In the past, however, a lack of distinction between these objectives on the part of both public and profession has sometimes led to the withholding of entitlements as an instrument of behavioral and social control, or else the giving of entitlements has been conceptualized as an opportunity for the giver to gain access to what are perceived as the "real" needs for change, that is individual or family behavior.

Professionals often make—consciously or unconsciously—a priori assumptions about the kinds of help people will need, based on socioeconomic class differences. We often fail to consider that wealthy or middle-class families might be in need of environmental resources or that they might be experiencing a "poor fit" with the surrounding environment.[1] On the other hand, we tend to overlook as well the fact that poor, deprived families often present highly intricate and idiosyncratic family system problems which can be helped in counseling. The family-centered practitioner must be capable of moving skillfully between both the intimate and surrounding environments.

Establishing a Nurturing and Supportive Environment

This book is not about social reform or macro-level practice. Nor do we pretend that helping individual families in a one-to-one retail approach is a route to or can substitute for social or institutional change. Many families seen by social workers and other helping professionals are struggling simply to survive under the burden of insurmountable environmental pressures and deprivations, and attempting somehow to manage and care for their families with limited access to resources considered necessary for a reasonable or adequate standard of life. Many families are excluded from the rolls of those considered eligible to work; many have children struggling through unresponsive and irrelevant educational systems which spill their graduates forth without the knowledge and skills needed to enter the social and economic mainstream. Thus a cycle of poverty and exclusion is perpetuated. The family-centered practitioner, like any other social worker, can neither abrogate or take major responsibility for social and economic injustice, but certainly at the very least must attend to the impact of the larger impinging environment in assessing the nature of family–environment transactions and in planning interventive strategies. All too often our own sense of helplessness and frustration has resulted in a "blaming the victim" outcome, leaving the family with a bitter sense of failure, of not having been understood, and of increasing alienation from society. All too often we have personified the inability of an unresponsive society to help, as we become trapped in the forlorn fantasy that the counseling relationship can substitute for concrete needs.

There is an abundance of literature describing the role of the direct service practitioner in discovering, creating, and enhancing environmental resources for clients, in coordinating such services, and in advocating for entitlement.[2] Other authors have creatively explored the mobilization and use of natural helping networks and of volunteers and paraprofessionals in meeting human needs.[3] Recently, discussion of these complex tasks and objectives has gained new momentum in the social work literature in response to the development of the "case manager" role.[4] The case manager notion has particularly taken root in community mental health agencies as an approach to serving aftercare patients, and in child welfare to deliver services to families and children at risk.

Based on an appreciation of the complexity and contradictions within the service network and on the realization that individuals and families frequently become lost in its labyrinth, the case manager role is a holistic one of system assessment, planning, coordinating, and mediating. Opinions differ, however, concerning the specific parameters and details of the case manager role: To some it is the role of a supervisor, to others that of a line worker. Questions emerge over whether the case manager should provide counseling, education, or consultative services to the family. These issues are yet to be settled. However, the holistic nature of the conceptualization, based on awareness of the impact on the family of disparate and often contradictory interventions by many discrete, uncoordinated, and even competitive or conflicting systems, promises congruence with a family focus.

A FAMILY-CENTERED CASE MANAGER AND THE EMBREE FAMILY

Chapter 7 presented the case of the Embree family, who had been referred to a family agency by protective services, and characterized as a deprived or multiproblem family.

Janet, the family agency worker, worked with the Embree family over an eighteen-month period, investing many hours and marshaling many resources. No attempt will be made to describe the step-by-step process; rather, key examples of interventive roles and strategies will be highlighted.

THE USE OF THE ECO-MAP IN ENGAGING, PLANNING STRATEGIES, AND ENHANCING MASTERY

During the second home visit, Janet and the family became involved in constructing an eco-map on a large pad of paper she had brought. The very process of constructing the map and objectifying the stresses and deficits in the environment communicated to the family more clearly than words that Janet viewed the environment, not the family, as the major problematic system and arena for change. This realization reassured the family, which had felt threatened and blamed by the referral to protective services, that she was not negatively defining them, and it was also congruent with their own perception that the major source of difficulty lay not in themselves but in an indifferent, frustrating, and depriving environment.

Upon the completion of the eco-map, Janet and the family pooled their ideas concerning the situation, and discussed its most salient factors. Janet cited Ora's lack of opportunities for connectedness and gratification. The family stressed their difficulty in obtaining needed medical care as well as their transportation problems, their conflict with the neighborhood, the lack of recreational activities for the children, an inappropriate school placement for Ron, the fifteen-year-old, and other difficulties in the school for all the children. They felt either afraid or incompetent to approach the school or any other large system to question decisions or to try to right what they experienced as wrongs.

Housing, household needs, and transportation were also identified as problem areas. In general, the social isolation, the lack of opportunities and resources, and the frustrating relationships with various outside systems were the topics of discussion. At this point, although Janet was well aware of other interpersonal difficulties in the family, she elected to keep the focus on environmental stresses.

The initial intervention was, in a sense, the construction of the eco-map itself. First the problem was reframed. Just as the symptomatic child ceases to bear the burden of being the problem when a case is reframed as a total family situation, so was the Embree case reframed from a problem family to a dysfunctional ecological system. Not only is such reframing a relief to the identified problem child or family, but it also opens up new possibilities and options for change.

Second, the eco-map led to enhanced cognitive mastery by objectifying and ordering the confusion of the Embrees' world. In it the Embrees began to see their situation as they had not envisioned it before. Such cognitive understanding is the first step in moving toward changing the nature of family–environment transactions.

Finally, the eco-map led to an ordering of priorities and a generating of shared plans for intervention. Interestingly, the family was most concerned about school problems, including the possible misplacement of Darlene, aged nine, in a special class for the developmentally disabled and Ron's ineligibility for the auto mechanic program. Additional school problems emerged regarding some of the other younger children.

Considerable discussion took place about who was going to do what. The Embrees, particularly Will, were fiercely independent, and uneasy about accepting help. Finally, they did agree that they would like Janet at least to make an initial exploratory visit to the school. Will decided to press his friend about the car and also remembered that he had heard about another member of the "irregular economy" who had been repairing used and abandoned appliances for resale and might be worth contacting. Ora did not volunteer nor was she assigned any task; but she asked if they could keep the map, and on the next home visit Janet found it tacked up in the kitchen.

INTERVENTION INTO THE EDUCATIONAL SYSTEM

The work Janet and the Embrees did with the school became the model for the work that later took place with other systems in their life. Janet took the initial steps, acting in the role of explorer, gathering information and bringing it back for discussion and planning. As a professional, she had easier access to information and could transmit and interpret it to the Embrees in a form that was useful to them. Planning and strategizing between worker and family then took place, and this action resulted in a referral for an evaluation of Darlene to determine if her placement was appropriate, in conferences with Josh's and Daryl's teachers, and in an application for the transfer of Ron to the neighboring district's auto repair program. Janet involved the Embrees every step of the way, helping them learn new advocating skills in their actions on behalf of their children. First Will and then Ora attended teachers' conferences with Janet, who acted as both catalyst and facilitator and modeled ways of dealing with bureaucratic institutions. Eventually the parents began attending an occasional PTA meeting, and once when Josh was bullied by some older children on the playground and then punished for being late back to the classroom, Ora went up to the school and "took up" for Josh. The question of Ron's admission to the auto mechanic program proved more difficult to resolve. Strong advocacy efforts on Janet's part were needed; she exposed an obvious pattern of discrimination against both poor and minority children whenever transfer applications into the more affluent school district were being considered. Interestingly enough, several other parents, three of them black, allied themselves with Janet, the Embrees, and the local school in advocating for a policy change. The Embrees and others in similar positions experienced a new opportunity for mastery and a sense of their own potential power as poor white joined with black to gain access to more resources, whereas in the past they had merely competed over limited supplies.

NEGOTIATIONS WITH OTHER SERVICE SYSTEMS

This cooperative pattern served as a guide in various transactions with other systems as Janet and the Embrees joined forces on the family's behalf. In each situation, Janet assumed a combination of roles aimed at enhancing family-environment transactions. In increasing the responsiveness of the family's environment, she acted as explorer, broker, coordinator, and advocate. Initially she concentrated on modeling competent behavior but later, in a relationship characterized by mutual respect and trust, she was able to coach the Embrees as they reached for more competence in dealing with recalcitrant community institutions.

Some problems were solved quickly—such as the defective sewer pipes, which the city finally fixed—while others were more complicated. Mobilizing health care was a central goal of the whole family and particularly important for Ora, who had been silently struggling for years with a correctable eye condition which had markedly interfered with her ability to read or do any close work. Dawn, the three-year-old, was placed in a prekindergarten program for two and a half hours a day, leaving Ora without a child at home for the first time since the first year of her marriage twenty-one years before; and although she very much wanted this experience for Dawn, initially she was so lonely with all of the children gone that frequently, at least in the first two months that Dawn was attending the program, she found ways of keeping an older child at home.

SOCIAL NETWORKING

As difficult as it was to negotiate with these large impersonal systems whose resources were so greatly needed by the Embree family, the task of informal network building was even more sensitive and difficult. It is traditional in most American families that women are responsible for mobilizing or maintaining the informal or intimate network. In the Embree family, while Will was somewhat more comfortable in dealing with people and might have been better able to negotiate this task on behalf of the family, he had not assumed the role. Ora, on the other hand, although hungry for human contact, felt painfully self-conscious, different from others, and even ostracized by them, and consequently suspicious of them.

The interaction with the school and the trial run to the PTA meeting served to give Ora just enough confidence to begin to consider making other connections. Janet had discovered while working on the eco-map that the family had occasionally attended church in the past, and the possibility of reestablishing this connection was discussed. The church had been the center of social activity for both of their families when they were children, and it seemed the most obvious source of potential opportunities for "belongingness." Ora eventually found a comfortable niche for herself at the church by exploiting one area in which she felt most competent. After her new glasses arrived, Ora, with Janet's encouragement, returned to her old interest, needlework. She was an expert at embroidery, needlepoint, and sewing. Their old sewing machine was repaired by another contact of Will's, and Ora began to sew again for the family. She was rightfully proud of her work and her ability to fashion a piece of clothing or a stuffed toy out of scraps. Smiling at Janet's amazement, she said, "That's one thing about down home. Everyone was poor and we learned to make something out of nothing."

It was through her interest in needlework that her connection with the church was strengthened. Before Christmas, a crafts fair was organized and Ora, very tentatively, became involved in setting up the booths and helping with the refreshments; she even displayed some of her own work. This led to Ora's becoming acquainted with another lonely woman from an area near where she had been born. It also eventually led to her beginning to sew for other people, a pursuit which gradually developed into a little business. Not only could she make garments and do alterations, but she knew how to reweave holes or tears in woolens, a highly valued skill.

Ora also began to work a half day every week at Dawn's nursery school, a service expected of nonworking mothers who had a child in the program. Ora was unable to do this initially, but after several months she felt brave enough to risk it and became a fringe member of the network of mothers involved with this program.

Family connections were also improved. The Embrees' young married son and his wife had cut themselves off from the parents, in part because they felt overwhelmed by the older couple's needs and demands, to which they could but minimally respond. Their staying away led to acrimony on both sides and charges of selfishness on the part of the parents; but as the Embrees were more able to manage their affairs, the younger couple felt less threatened and began to reestablish contact. Also, in completing a genogram with the family it was discovered that two cousins of Will's and an elderly aunt of Ora's lived in the area. Both Ora and Will had felt bereft of kin, and eventually they made contact with each of these relatives. Although the reunion with one of the cousins was a disappointment and temporarily a discouragement, the other cousin and her family eventually became an important part of their growing network,

and Ora's reconnection with her aunt, whom she had not seen since childhood, was very meaningful. In addition, Ora made one feeble attempt to
discover the whereabouts of her siblings, and learned that the two youngest had been adopted. She did not pursue this farther, but hopes one day
to find her brothers and sisters. In the summer, Will planned a trip down
south to see his family and for the first time in many years Ora went with
him. They not only spent a week with Will's family, but on the way back
took a detour through Ora's hometown. Ora was not ready to look up any
of the few relatives who still lived in the area, but she did find the school-
house she had attended in the early grades and a house which she thought
had been occupied by her grandparents. These were small but significant
steps in weaving together some of the fragments of her past and thus her
sense of personal identity and continuity.

The slow opening up of the boundary between the family and the
outside world, together with the building of some reciprocal connections
with that world, took well over a year. The connections, except for their
son and to some extext Will's cousin, remained relatively fragile, yet the
family's social isolation began to diminish, as did their shared perception
of the world as a depriving and threatening place. As their isolation and
suspicion gradually ebbed away, a new process gained momentum in
which each new positive experience made the family feel more competent,
more accepted, and more ready to take yet another step which might enhance their social connectedness and mastery of their environment. After
almost a year, Janet and the Embrees constructed a new eco-map, shown
in figure 9.1, which clearly depicted for them and the worker the changes
which had taken place.

TIME AND SPACE AS TARGET AND RESOURCE FOR CHANGE

Concurrently with helping the Embrees make better use of the world outside, Janet also stimulated change in the workings of the immediate household and the inner family system. She had noticed, for example, that there
was strikingly little difference between times for sleeping and times for
being awake. Will, Ora, and Ron erected few boundaries around their
times and spaces for sleep, or between eating and other family activities.
Both parents and children tended to snack intermittently in lieu of planned
mealtimes, often taking food into the bedrooms, and this habit affected
both parental control over nutrition and family cohesiveness. Janet viewed
the lack of structure in the household as an expression of the lack of structure in the family system; however, rather than define the family system
as the problem, Janet proposed that the family alter its use of time and
space in the house. Thus she conceived of the house as a metaphor for the
family system, and her change strategies grew out of her conviction that
change in household organization would be accompanied by changes in

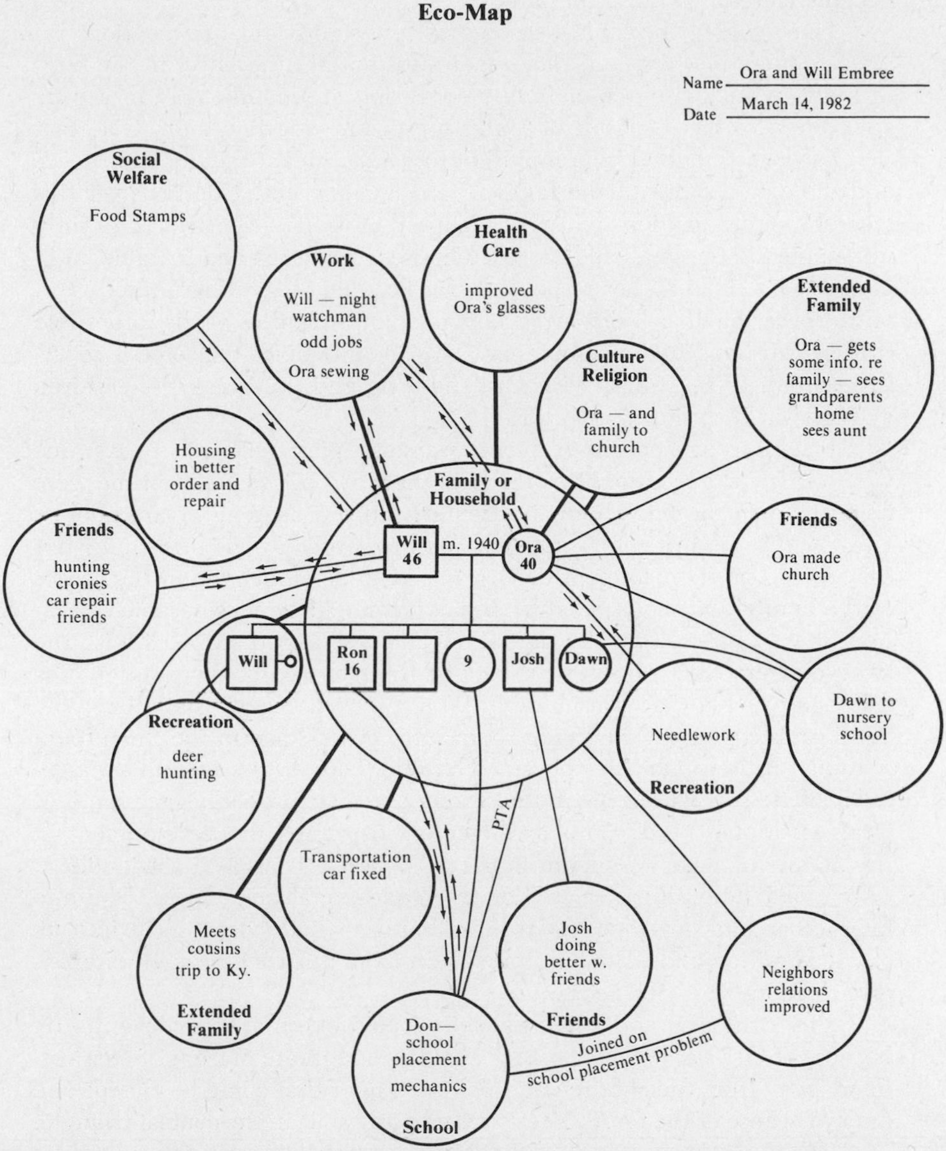

Eco-Map

Name __Ora and Will Embree__

Date __March 14, 1982__

Social Welfare

Food Stamps

Work

Will — night watchman

odd jobs

Ora sewing

Health Care

improved Ora's glasses

Culture Religion

Ora — and family to church

Extended Family

Ora — gets some info. re family — sees grandparents home sees aunt

Friends

hunting cronies car repair friends

Friends

Ora made church

Housing in better order and repair

Family or Household

Will 46   m. 1940   Ora 40

Will   Ron 16   9   Josh   Dawn

Recreation

deer hunting

Needlework

Recreation

Dawn to nursery school

PTA

Transportation car fixed

Meets cousins trip to Ky.

Extended Family

Don— school placement mechanics

School

Josh doing better w. friends

Friends

Joined on school placement problem

Neighbors relations improved

Fill in connections where they exist.

Indicate nature of connections with a descriptive word or by drawing different kinds of lines;
———— for strong, – – – – – – for tenuous ++++++++ for stressful.

Draw arrows along lines to signify flow of energy, resources, etc. → → →

Identify significant people and fill in empty circles as needed.

FIGURE 9.1   New Embree Family Eco-Map

family relationships. This hypothesis was borne out as the family system became increasingly differentiated.

Janet guided the family through a few significant interventions related to these matters, and they made substantial differences in the family's life. A major source of family confusion and conflict lay in a poor adaptation to the demands of Will's nighttime working hours. The fact that he worked nights, from midnight to 8 A.M., meant that his time needs and those of the rest of the family were incongruent. Conflict over this lack of synchronization frequently erupted as Will's sleep was constantly interrupted in the small and crowded house. Frustrated and irritable, Will blamed Ora, holding her responsible for keeping the children quiet. Ora, on the other hand, felt criticized, anxious, and resentful at the impossible task her husband had assigned her. This incongruence triggered a repetitive circuit of reactions, with Ora shouting and punishing the children and Will in turn shouting at Ora.

Janet approached this problem by encouraging the family to examine whether any changes might be made in the way both space and time were being used in the household, particularly in the sleeping arrangements. How or why the present arrangements had evolved was uncertain, but they served as an enactment of Ora's need to be embedded in the center of the family and surrounded by her children. After considerable discussion, it was agreed that the parents would exchange bedrooms with the two younger boys, who slept in one of the two bedrooms upstairs. The downstairs room was considerably larger, which meant that Ron, who had been sleeping on the living room sofa, could sleep in the same room with his brothers once they obtained another bed. Again, the old arrangement of Ron's keeping his mother company had probably met some of Ora's emotional needs. This arrangement expressed the development in this family of what Minuchin labels a "perverse triangle," a triangle or system of relationships which violates generational boundaries. Ron and his mother had developed a strong alliance, which thrust Will into an outside position and which inhibited Ron from pursuing his own interests and relationships with peers.

This structural and territorial shift took some time to achieve, partly because of Ora's ambivalence about having a separate place with her husband away from the children and behind a door that could be closed, and partly because of the family's resistance to any shift in the central triangle.

The use of time was also discussed and possible ways to work out a better synchrony explored. Families have a number of options which might be considered when the breadwinner works a night shift. The main problem with the Embrees' adaptation to Will's working hours was that there was no consistent time schedule.

The most challenging task for Janet was to help create a context in which change might be nurtured. Neither the Embrees' patriarchal family heritage, nor their own unique interpretation of it in a changed and complex environment, had promoted a marital relationship which fostered discussion, negotiation, or compromise.[5] Will's word was seen by both of them as law, a principle which suffered much in actual implementation, as many of his harangues and pronouncements were ignored or subverted by Ora. Yet they never discussed this fact, for verbal discussion and problem-solving were not part of their repertoire of skills. Under these circumstances time and space seemed to be controlling their lives, when ideally they should have been using time and space in the shaping of a life together which would better meet their needs. Mutually dependent in their relative isolation, yet curiously lacking in intimacy, neither had ever really articulated personal preferences to the other or attempted to negotiate a satisfactory resolution to conflict. Now, however, their gradual control of time and space became a metaphor or model for the establishment of a new kind of marital interaction in the negotiation of family issues. In this sense a "meta" change had taken place.

As Janet's teaching, modeling, and prescribing of tasks facilitated their discussion process, it became clear that both Will and Ora had wanted more time with each other and with the family as a whole. Will told Ora, not without a few choice words and considerable asperity, that he wished she would get up in the morning when he came home from work, and Ora bitterly complained to Will that she hated his going to bed at five o'clock, the low point of the day for her. Both wanted to try to have meals together as a family in the morning and evening, and each wanted and needed the other's help.

In time they arranged a schedule which split Will's sleep but served both their purposes. Ora began to get up earlier in the morning before Will came home, in time to make breakfast for the family. She had begun to return to her needlework, and because of her limited vision she needed daylight for most of the tasks. She had also begun to pursue some other daytime activities to which she looked forward and for which she now felt she had more time. She even began preparing a hot breakfast for Will, and after the children left for school the two of them began to have a second cup of coffee together, developing what gradually became a ritual of watching "The Today Show." Ora had shifted some of her television watching from late at night to early in the morning, and although she and Ron sometimes watched TV together in the evening, she began to retire earlier, thus freeing Ron from some of the responsibility he had formerly assumed for alleviating his mother's loneliness. The central triangle had been altered.

The end of "The Today Show" signaled to Will that it was time to go to bed, and sometimes Ora, now that the youngest child was in nursery school and they could count on some privacy, joined him there. Will usually slept until noon and then would work either at one of his many odd jobs, or around the house. After dinner he slept for a few more hours before leaving for work, although now he sometimes took that time to do something special with one or more members of the family. The family dinner, which over the months had become the most important time the entire family was together, served as a ritual which promoted the family's sense of itself as a coherent, organized unit.

Before we leave the Embrees, we should note that, quite spontaneously, this family made use of another change strategy, the ritual. Earlier, the Embrees could well have been described as an underritualized family. Their life together was largely unpatterned and "ad hoc." Not only did they lack meaningful ceremonies and symbols which expressed their sense of familiness, but they lacked also what David Reiss (1981) has called "pattern regulators"—highly routinized sequences of behavior which families use for, among other things, regulating space and distance among themselves and between the family and the outside world. Even such mundane decisions as where and when to sleep and eat were made without order and serendipitously each day. But slowly some organized, ritual-like behavior began to occur regarding times and expectations for meals, the viewing of "The Today Show", and the ways Will and Ora together sent the children off to school in the morning.

This lengthy analysis illustrates how one family-centered practitioner made use of the environment as the primary target and resource for change. Throughout the eighteen months of service, Janet maintained her focus on the environment and on family–environment transactions. The work included obtaining resources and supplies from the environment through brokering, coordinating, developing, and advocating. It included the nurturing of an informal social network and the restructuring of time and space in the family's immediate environment. As the boundaries between the family and the outside world became more open, and the boundaries inside the family better clarified and strengthened, the Embree family not only began to get some of their essential needs met, but as they experienced a number of successful encounters in which their growing competence was demonstrated to themselves and to others, a firmer sense of individual and family autonomy unfolded.

The Social Construction and Reconstruction of Reality

In the Embree case, not only did the family–environment transactions change, but the family's perception of the environment and their view of how they were perceived by that environment also changed. The deviation feedback loop which had escalated negative perceptions of self and environment's view of self was reversed. The Embrees had formerly perceived the world as an unfriendly place in which they were helpless and had little opportunity for control, a perception leading to feelings of resignation and hopelessness. Such shared constructions of reality, growing out of everyday experiences, are sometimes the primary target for change.

Work with the Rauers, an advantaged but overburdened middle-class family, likewise focused on change in family–environment transactions and ultimately on a shift in the family's construction of reality. Marta, as we noted, had been feeling depressed and discontented with herself, and an individual orientation might have resulted in long-term psychotherapy and/or the use of medication. Gary Thompson, a family-centered practitioner in a suburban community mental health clinic, found in reviewing the eco-map with Marta and Phil that although there were many stresses and demands, the family was also rich in resources. What also became apparent in studying the eco-map was that Marta was attempting to meet most of the needs and to alleviate most of the stresses being experienced by various family members, a wife-mother-daughter-caretaker role fairly typical in more traditionally structured American families.

Gary's hypothesis was that although there were stresses and burdens in this family, particularly in conjunction with the many transitions that were taking place, the major problem seemed to be the inequitable distribution of stress and demands. He further speculated that the patterns of distribution reflected the family's view of itself and of its relationship with reality. If this family was organized around a central theme, it was that mothers are to take care of the family's personal, emotional, and interpersonal needs. Phil's mother had shared this role with Marta and both women were immersed in tradition which implied that mothers were the center of the family. Great sacrifices were expected of these mothers; they were asked at all times to put the needs of other family members before their own. This construction of the family's reality was shared by all of the members, including, as it turned out, by Ginger, the oldest daughter, who, although an enthusiastic feminist, did not seem to include her mother among the ranks of the women to be liberated.

Gary asked that the whole family, including the grandparents and the baby, come in for the second appointment. This session resulted in a lively, revealing, and valuable interchange among the members of the family network. Gary opened the session by saying that Marta had been feeling pretty low, as some of them had probably realized, and that he had called the family together so that everyone could help in working out the difficulties, whatever they were.

Marta was able to express her frustration at not being able to devote enough time to her work, although she could not openly express her mounting feelings of resentment. Probably because the context had been broadened to include the larger network, Phil felt less threatened and was able to be quite supportive of Marta, moving his chair close to hers and occasionally touching her arm.

We will not report in detail the context of the session or describe the many areas of conflict which emerged, but two major related themes repeatedly surfaced: the role of mothers and of women in general, and the ways in which roles and tasks were distributed in the family. The three-generational linkages emerged with clarity as Marta's mother communicated her strong view that "family comes first," yet later expressed some sadness, now that she was nearing the end of her life, about her own lost opportunities and abandoned ambitions. She had worked as an art teacher before her children were born and remembered that phase of her life with great pride and nostalgia. Some old acrimony toward her husband entered her voice when she commented that he would never "let her" return to work.

As the issues were explored, Ginger, ruefully facing her own inconsistent attitudes toward her mother's role, became a main supporter of her mother's wish to pursue her own interests. She was soon joined by her two siblings, who agreed to take over more responsibility. At one point, the grandparents became defensive about the demands they had been making, and after some hurt protests that they did not want to burden anyone and did not need help from anyone, they turned to each other and began hesitantly to discuss ways they might simplify their lifestyle and thus be less dependent.

This total family session was followed by a meeting with Marta, Phil, and the younger generation, and the final session, a month later, included only Phil and Marta. In that session, the marital pair considered the implications for their relationship of some of the transactions currently occurring in the family. Marta was able to reveal some of her resentment, particularly now that she was feeling so much better, and Phil began to express some of his feelings of discontent with his job and with his long daily commute, as well as his sense of being overwhelmed and trapped by his struggles to meet the financial needs of the family. He had, in fact, felt just as locked into unrewarding tasks as Marta and had begun to wonder about what changes he might make. Using a very expressive metaphor, he said that sometimes he and his wife seemed to him like two oxen harnessed to a heavy load, plodding ahead side by side, but unable even to look at each other.

Marta and Phil both felt confident that they could construct new solutions on their own now that the problems had been faced and shared. Gary supported this decision but left the door open for them to return for a meeting or two sometime in the future. Toward the end of the session, the extent to which the family's construction of their social reality had been altered came to light when Marta laughingly reported that the children had given her a gift. They had wrapped up Diana Ross's record "It's

My Turn" and on the card they had written, "Whenever your resolve waivers, put this record on the stereo." She reported that she had, in fact, played it several times, and the theme had become almost a slogan which symbolized a new direction for her life. She then turned to Phil and said, "You can play it sometimes, too."

Family Network Therapy

As ecologically oriented family-centered practitioners have expanded the unit of attention and seen the family's total social network as a potential target or resource for change, family network therapy has emerged as an innovative model for practice. Developed by Uri Rueveni (1979), Ross Speck (Speck and Attneave, 1973), Carolyn Attneave (1976), and their colleagues, family network therapy sets in motion the forces of healing within the social fabric of individuals or families in distress. The energies and the resources within the network of family, friends, neighbors, and associates are focused to provide the essential supports, satisfactions, and controls required to ameliorate that distress (Speck and Attneave, 1973).

In the Embree case, worker and family intervened step-by-step together in the social network, forming linkages, mediating tensions, and strengthening connections. In family network therapy, power for change and growth is tapped in quite a unique way, as large networks of people are assembled together at one time to tap into the power available on behalf of the family. Attneave (1976) likens the excitement and force of this process to a Preservation Hall concert, a tribal healing ceremony, a wedding, a bar mitzvah, or a class reunion.

In family network therapy, a major portion of the family's entire social network is invited to the networking sessions, a group that generally includes a minimum of forty people. The selection of who should come is made by the family, which also generally is responsible for extending an invitation to those they have selected. The effort is to include as many as possible of the family's relatives, friends, neighbors, and colleagues. The extent to which service professionals, teachers, ministers, or mental health workers should be included is argued. Although they may be important parts of the family's network of resources, their relationship with the family and with the network therapists is different from that of other people, and some feel they can interfere with the retribalization power, or cohesive coming together, of the group.

During the planning session with the family, the eco-map and genogram may be used to identify the salient people in the network. Attneave (1975) has developed a network-mapping procedure that is particularly aimed at the identification of the network and its structural aspects. The team of network therapists also helps the family with the preparations, advising them about who and how to ask, making decisions about where and when to hold the meeting, and following up the original invitation.

Network therapists report that each networking session, as well as the total process (which may extend over two or three months), evolves in distinct phases (Rueveni, 1978; Speck and Attneave, 1973). The first phase is termed "tribalization," during which the group comes together and cohesiveness is established. During the second phase, termed "polarization," this cohesiveness is disrupted as disagreements and alternate views as to how the problem should be solved come to light. During polarization, network members tend to choose sides with different family members, gathering around them and offering help and advice. This phase is followed by a period of "mobilization," during which the activists and natural leaders in the network attempt to move the group toward some specific action. Frustration in attempts to reach solutions or solve problems ushers in the next phase, "depression," and the network begins to experience the same helplessness the family has felt in attempting to solve the problem. This, of course, is the most critical time in the course of each meeting and in the total course of the therapy since, for change to take place, energy must be mobilized and the group must move on.

The depression is followed by "breakthroughs." Now some steps or solutions are identified and beginning plans are made. At this point the network session comes to an end, the members often feeling both exhausted and elated. Readers who have worked with groups or studied the literature concerning the stages of group development will recognize the parallels.

The actual facilitating and interventive strategies employed by the leaders of network groups are drawn from group therapy, gestalt, encounter, and social group work methods. They include experiential methods aimed at intensifying the emotional life of the group, exercises in communication facilitation, programmatic intervention such as singing, and the organizing of focused and structured subgroups engaged in specific tasks.

A key aspect in network intervention is the development of temporary support groups which cluster around various family members. These support groups function as resources, advisors, and problem-solvers during the periods between the meetings, or, in the case of a single network assembly, as assistants in completing the work which was begun in the assembly.

Several criteria are utilized in the selection of families for network intervention. It appears that network intervention is most useful at a time of crisis, when a family is overwhelmed and desperate. It is the seriousness and awareness of the crisis as well as the desperation of the family that provide the impetus and pull the network together. A network assembly is a major and dramatic intervention and, clearly, one does not use cannons when pistols will do. The principle of parsimony dictates that one does not rely on costly, elaborate intervention if an economic, simpler strategy is possible.

A network can be utilized only if the family is able and willing to assemble a large number of friends, family, neighbors and other individuals significant in their life. Success depends in part on the availability of the network and in part on the desire of the family to call the network together. It is also suggested that network interventions be considered only after other interventive models have proved ineffective. Finally, and equally crucial, a worker planning a network must have a team of co-workers, agency support, and group leadership skills.

THE TAYLOR FAMILY: A CASE FOR NETWORK THERAPY

In the case of the Taylors, the socially isolated family described in chapter 8, it is intriguing to imagine how network therapy might be used to help such a family. Although this approach was not used in work with this family and our discussion is thus hypothetical, the dysfunctional relationships between Rita and her neighbors and the fact that the neighborhood could well be considered a target as well as a resource for change particularly suggest this approach.

As described in the previous chapter, Rita had apparently become the scapegoat in this neighborhood, having unwittingly offered herself up as the outside corner in a triangle consisting of herself and the two major factions in the neighborhood, and thus she provided an outlet for unresolved community frustration. Rita's suicide attempt, as a crisis in the family and a crisis in the neighborhood, might well provide the impetus for major change. The neighbors, caught in this escalating process, were not unusually cruel people. It is unlikely that they even were aware of the scapegoating process, and certainly had not intended to sacrifice her. In fact, it is more likely that many experienced a private twinge of guilt when they remembered their unkindnesses, and although we can speculate that a response of self-justification would begin to bloom after word of the suicide attempt spread ("See, I told you she was crazy!"), at least for some, Rita's desperate message would be heard.

Whether or not network therapy is the most appropriate strategy for resolution of this family crisis depends on several factors. First and foremost, of course, the Taylor family would have to be educated concerning the process and would have to be willing to risk the exposure and investment of time and energy such an effort requires. Secondly, the potential network resources must be assessed to determine if a large enough group of salient figures might be assembled. The neighborhood alone might form the foundation for such a mobilization, particularly if, as seems likely, some individuals are sympathetic to the troubles experienced by this family. The input of these individuals might be greatest during the "polarization" process, gathering additional strength and support. What is hoped for, of course, is that the direction of the feedback loop will be reversed, that the neighborhood will begin to organize around helping rather than scapegoating. Such a process might also enable the neighbors to confront in a more constructive way the tension, conflict, and profound alienation which exist in this and other "bedrooms of New York"—the suburban towns, villages, and neighborhoods which often fail to develop communities.

APPLICATIONS OF NETWORKING

Many practitioners probably do not have the skills or resources necessary to assemble and work with networks of fifty to one hundred people. However, if we accept the fundamental premise that bringing people together can generate new ideas and energy, applications of network therapy can be made in many situations. If we believe that the kinds of interchanges and power available in network meetings can alter perceptions, consolidate strengths, and make new solutions accessible, then it follows that the merging of multiple human resources can facilitate change.

First, partial network assemblies can be considered as an option. Moving the family to the center of our focus has expanded our conception of boundaries to include, at times, other salient figures in the life of a family, such as friends, relatives, or other helpers. Not only can additional sources of skill and strength be mobilized, but the sensitive and vital relationship between the family and the important members of the family's network can be engaged directly. The social worker who is working with an aging woman to organize supports and resources which might make it possible for her to continue to live in her own home affords us an example. Rather than slowly forging supportive links one by one, the worker might gain the client's permission to ask several people who are concerned—for example, family members, minister, senior citizen center staff members, public health nurse, attorney—to meet together with the worker and client to consider the options and the risks, and to evaluate the existing human and other kinds of resources which are available or could be marshaled.

Second, the traditional "case conference" which is called to coordinate and plan services for a client or family, usually without the client present, can be modified to include the client and other directly involved significant figures. A genuine, mutual, participatory approach to such conferences can lead to creative and valuable problem-solving results. For example, the educational planning sessions which in many states are mandated for children with "special needs," could be utilized in this way. Instead, what frequently happens is that key professionals formulate both an assessment and a strategy prior to meeting with the family; the family meeting consequently is not a "planning" session but actually an "informing" session, and parents are often left feeling frustrated and manipulated. Networks or partial networks may also make use of a ritual or a family event as a powerful strategy for change, as in the case of a wedding, a funeral, or a holiday.

The gathering together of a social network or extended family tends to expose the structure of these systems. It also leaves the professional less in control, because a group musters considerable power. In order to network, professionals must be able to risk exposure, to have faith in the healing and helping capacities of human beings, and to trust the process through which such healing and helping can emerge.

Other Professionals and Service Systems

An ecological perspective leads us to recognize that other professionals and other service systems, together with their structures, workings, and transactions, form a potent part of the context within which a family is seen and may indeed have a major impact on the course or even the possibility of treatment. In chapter 6 we described those supports we consider essential in order for family-centered practice to take place; here we will briefly consider the salience of what is known as the "referring context," together with some of the complexities encountered in working with other professionals in family-centered practice.

THE REFERRING PERSON

The referring person, the referring agency, and the meaning of the referral constitute a vital part of the assessment and intervention process in family-centered practice. The relationship between the family and the referring person, and also the messages and prescriptions attached to the referral, have important implications for the direction which the work may take. The first task is to explore the nature of that relationship and to determine exactly what prompted the referral and how it was made. Selvini-Palazzoli and her colleagues, in analyzing some unsuccessful family cases, write:

> We were able to understand that our error was very basic; we had failed to build our study of the family upon the systemic model in that we had been dealing with a family that had been missing one of its members who occupied a nodal homeostatic position in that family, the referring person. [1980:3]

For example, if one member of the family, perhaps the identified problem person, has been in long-term treatment, that member's therapist occupies an important role in the organization of the family system. If that role is not recognized, the new person working with the family may experience a "Neptune effect"—a strong force operating within the system from a mysterious and unknown source of power. Failure to understand and account for that force in the family dynamics can easily lead to grave miscalculations. Sometimes this important figure is used by one parent against the other as an ally in a central family triangle, as in the case where a mother has used a male child therapist as a stand-in for the father in parenting the child, excluding the father from participation.

The referring person may be involved in the therapeutic context in other ways. Sometimes the family is referred as an effort at social control; such referrals may be quasi-voluntary, mandated, or even coerced, as in the case of some court referrals. Or again, the family may arrive from the referring person with the nature of the problem and even the solution predetermined. For example, one family proudly announced to us in the first interview that the referring psychologist had told them that Johnny, the identified client, was the angriest boy in the city, and they challenged us to prove that we could succeed where the rest had failed. Still other families have arrived with prescriptions and instructions they claim to have received from the referring person directing how we should proceed. In cases such as these, competition can emerge between the referring person and the new worker, particularly over alternative models of practice.

Dealing with the referring person and other professionals in the family's life demands a careful systemic assessment and mutual clarification of purpose, as well as considerable self-awareness and diplomacy. Some of us who manage to control our reactivity in the most provocative of family sessions can find ourselves arguing and defending when challenged by other professionals. Bowen's theory of differentiation from the family of origin (chapter 5) is equally applicable to professional relationships.

Although the specific approaches or strategies for working with outside professionals will vary from case to case, depending on the circumstances, some principles are generic. The first principle is to avoid being triangulated by either the family or the other professionals. This means that one avoids being drawn into discussions of the family with the professional or of the other professional with the family. Further, if it is essential that the worker receive information from the other professional, then the family should take responsibility for obtaining the information if at all possible, and they should understand that some or all of the report may be shared with the family. Otherwise, if the two professionals were to share "secret" information, diagnoses, or impressions of the family, the groundwork for a potentially destructive triangle would be laid. The same straightforwardness is required when information is provided to the referring person by the family's worker, and the following case example suggests how such circumstances arise and how they might be handled.

The Doyle family, whose teenage son Bill was on probation for "borrowing" a car, had been referred for family therapy by the probation department. Early in the first session the family informed us that they had signed a release authorizing us to keep the probation department informed of our progress by telephone. We responded to the family that we did not like talking about them when they were not present and wondered if Bill would like to invite his probation officer to a family session. Bill decided not to do this. Two weeks later the family requested that a report of the therapy, required by the court, be sent to the probation officer. We thus spent part of the next family session drafting the report. After a copy of the final draft was approved by the family, it was forwarded to the probation office.

When a family is critical of previous therapists or therapy, we recognize this act as their maneuver to form a triangle against the outside professional and thus to avoid change. In such a case we "go with the resistance," agreeing that the other professional is probably right. The following is such a case:

Patricia Fox and her two young sons were being seen in family treatment. One of the sons had been, three years earlier, in child treatment for a period of some two years with a psychiatric social worker. The mother reported that the treatment had not been very useful but also urged us to send for the treatment summary. We finally acquiesced (probably a mistake!) and the former worker, upon receiving the request, called the mother. After hearing the family was in family treatment, the worker indicated she thought this was a serious mistake and recommended that her former client return to individual therapy, preferably with her, since they had already established a therapeutic relationship. During the next appointment the mother expressed great confusion and appealed to us for advice. Although appreciative of the fact that the mother's concern was genuine and her worry legitimate, we recognized her as an "overtherapized" woman who herself had previously been in individual therapy for many years and whose resistance to family work, indeed to any real effort at change, was masked but strong. We told Patricia we thought that some people were just not good candidates for family therapy; that the risks of change were too much to grapple with; that perhaps the other worker had understood Patricia's fear of change better than we had, and that having Don and maybe Dick, too, in individual treatment would be more reassuring to her. She spent the next part of the session explaining to us that we knew very well that individual treatment had not been helpful to her or her son, and that she had often felt helpless, left out, and criticized during the time Donald was seeing the worker. Now, she felt, she and her boys wanted to solve their issues as a family.

Too Many Cooks Spoil the Broth

One of the most difficult conflicts in family-centered work concerns the continuance by one or more family members of outside individual therapy concurrently with family-centered work. Although some practitioners do not find such case-sharing problematic, we have found that in most cases it has been accompanied by disappointing results. Throughout the family contact the inaccessible but ever-present force of the other therapist's "world view" operates in the system and is used by the family as a major homeostatic mechanism. As a result, when the family tiptoes close to change they may "triangle in" the individual practitioner, in order to protect the status quo by redefining the problem as an individual one which can be solved only by individual treatment, medication, institutional placement, and so on. Therefore, in dealing with such families it is our policy to recommend against family work and suggest that the family continue with individual treatment; if, however, despite our recommendation, the family persuades us they want family therapy, we reluctantly set the condition that they must interrupt the individual treatment for as long as the family work continues.

These caveats come out of bitter experience, those less than successful cases most of us would rather not write about, but which provide fertile material for learning. In the following case, therapist and family became caught up in a complex network of professional and service systems, each of which had a different agenda.

The Fallon family was referred by the court after the family had enlisted the help of the police in controlling the violent outbursts of their fifteen-year-old adopted daughter Pamela. The family was questioning whether they would be able to continue to keep this girl at home, suggesting that maybe she needed institutionalization for a year or two until she learned to control her temper. Her more severe outbursts had developed after the placement in their home of a second adopted child, a six-year-old girl. The finalization of this second adoption was pending. The parents were friendly and cooperative, informing the worker that the court wanted them to get help in learning how to control the daughter. However, it quickly became apparent that this child's behavior was in large measure a solution to other toxic family issues (the father's possible extramarital affairs, the mother's excessive drinking, an extremely troubled but superficially pleasant marriage, and the alienation of the father from their one biological child, a son now in the Navy). However, whenever the worker tried to explore any of these other family issues which fleetingly emerged despite the family's vigilance, she was met with an unmovable system. The extent to which all— worker, family members, and other agencies—were caught in a complex and powerful system of relationships eventually became clear.

One of the key links, unknown at first to the worker, existed between the court and the adoption agency. Thus the worker discovered the family's intention that she report to the court on whether they were "cooperative"; the probation officer, who was in close contact with the adoption worker, was to pass our information along, and the adoption worker would rely in part on that information in making a decision whether to approve the second adoption. Through this unexplored connection, the family worker had been invested with a role which militated against any meaningful effort to develop an alliance with the family. In the last session it also slipped out that the father was engaged in a very important course of individual psychotherapy. He had been reluctant to share this information because he thought the adoption agency might interpret it as evidence of instability. Before the family therapist could come to an adequate understanding of the complexities in the referring context, and could plan a potentially useful strategy, the family managed to precipitate a crisis which resulted in the daughter's placement in a psychiatric hospital. From their point of view the problem was at least temporarily solved and they withdrew from treatment, having convinced the community that this child, who had come to them originally with serious emotional problems, was indeed incorrigible.

SHARING CASES WITH OTHER PROFESSIONALS IN THE SAME AGENCY

One would assume that barriers to professional communication growing out of different ideologies and different organizational contexts would not be a serious problem among those working in the same service organization, particularly if they are working with the same families and individuals. Yet, in these situations, too, there is frequently a clash of perspectives. Competition may arise between individual-oriented and family-oriented practitioners, and the latter may feel lonely or embattled in settings where other service ideologies predominate. In such situations, one must attempt to maintain a differentiated professional self, to avoid triangulation, and to actively detriangulate when one finds oneself "caught"; and at all times one must try persistently to keep intraorganizational communication open and genuine.

Respect for the rights of others to embrace different conceptual frameworks can diminish competitive struggles. Yet differing conceptual frameworks may lead to contradictory definitions of problem causation and plans for solution. In such a case the danger is that clients will be caught in the middle of these ideological clashes and try in vain to respond to conflicting definitions and agendas for change. We have found it less than productive, for example, in using a team model, to include team members with radically different perspectives, since much of the energy for work becomes drained by conceptual skirmishes rather than channeled into helping the family. On the other hand, differences in ideology and experience among the staff can at times generate a rich and creative exchange of ideas in a process which may expand the conceptual resources for all.

Whether a family-centered practitioner can function well in an environment which is totally individual-oriented is doubtful, since the situation belies what we know about the power of the environmental context in shaping events. However, as the family movement grows, it will become increasingly rare that a family-centered practitioner cannot find at least a small cohort of like-minded professionals with whom to build a network of support, sharing, and mutual aid.

Chapter 10

Assessment in Time: The Intergenerational Perspective

"For thirty years I've always ironed in the dining room," Sheila explained. "My mother always did and I always did, and I never thought anything about it. A month ago, I loaned my ironing board to my married daughter who had just moved into a new apartment. I went up to the attic and brought down my mother's old ironing board. I set the board up in my dining room and as I used my mother's ironing board, I felt so close to her, so in touch with her again! I remembered her ironing and got to wondering why she had always ironed in the dining room. The answer was simple. We lived on a farm with no electricity. My mother used to have to heat the irons on the wood stove in the kitchen. She didn't iron in the kitchen because it was too hot with the stove going and thus she ironed in the dining room, which was the closest room.

And suddenly it struck me—I didn't have to iron in the dining room! I had an electric iron, and could iron in any room in the house. Since then, I sometimes iron in the dining room but I also iron in the living room in front of the television or in the kitchen. I really became free to iron anywhere I wanted to!"

THIS STORY, told to us by a woman attending a workshop on family-centered practice, exemplifies how one intergenerational prescription had contributed to her definition of herself and her accompanying behavior. It is at least in part through such family prescriptions that all of us become who we are and do what we do.

It is only with great difficulty that we shed or bury our intergenerational, psychological family heritages. In the opinion of those theorists who stress intergenerational issues in family dysfunction, change and growth occur through coming to terms with and resolving troublesome issues in the familial past. As Framo (1976) phrases it, "You can and should go home again!"

In chapter 5 we presented some of the central concepts which underpin an intergenerational perspective. In the following pages we will examine the implications of this perspective for change, and explicate the process of its assessment. Intergenerational strategies for intervention will be discussed in chapter 11.

The reader might be reminded here that, while this assessment/intervention process might be utilized as a single coherent approach in a particular case (as in Bowen family therapy), its theoretical components, assessment and intervention, may be used in many different ways. Family of origin and family history may become the main focus of the work; the perspective may be woven into the fabric of a more eclectic approach or enhance understanding of intergenerational themes in informing changes in current family structure and processes; or they may be used intermittently and peripherally. Further, an intergenerational perspective may be applied in a range of settings and with varied client populations; these applications will be discussed toward the end of this chapter.

Of key importance to the intergenerational assessment and intervention process is the use of the genogram, an intergenerational family road map which is helpful in tracing and understanding the family's history. Much of this chapter will be devoted to describing how the genogram is constructed and analyzed. But first, let us examine what an intergenerational perspective implies about the process of change.

The Nature of Change

We claimed earlier that much of the impact of one's family system and its construction of reality exists outside the individual's awareness. Just as it is difficult to observe oneself objectively, it is equally difficult to stand outside the boundaries of one's own family system and observe those very processes in which one is immersed. Yet there are a number of family theorists who are convinced that much of the difficulty people experience in their current work, family, and social roles can be linked to unfinished business in their family-of-origin relationships whether myths, prescriptions, losses, or unresolved conflicts from distant generations.

For Bowen (1978), these difficulties are related to "fusion" or to a lack of differentiation, an "emotional stuck-togetherness" which results in inappropriate emotional reactivity in current interpersonal relationships between parent and child, husband and wife, boss and employee, and so forth. In very broad terms, the goal of therapeutic change in the Bowen model is to achieve a higher level of differentiation, to "rise up out of the emotional togetherness that binds us all" (1978:371). The essence of change lies in the client's negotiation of new ways of being with, and of communicating with, key members of her family. In this process of defining a self in one's extended family,[1] it cannot be overstressed that the goal (which differentiates Bowen's therapy from more traditional modes of treatment) is not one of merely gaining insight into one's family experiences; for while such insight may be revealing, the essential need is to identify those areas where change in *one's own* behavior is needed and to design, implement and monitor, *in vivo*, hopefully with the real-life figures involved, strategies to bring about desired change. In other words, it is not enough simply to know; one must also do something. Here the assumption is that as people become more differentiated from their families of origin, they will also become more differentiated in their current love, play, and work relationships.

Boszormenyi-Nagy and Spark (1973), whose ideas were also briefly discussed in chapter 5, point out that most people repay at least part of the family emotional indebtedness to their parents by becoming parents themselves and making commitments to their own children. When destructive, undischarged commitments still exist, the practitioner's effort centers on exposing these hurtful loyalties and achieving a better balance between old and new family relationships through a repaying of the indebtedness. These therapists, like Framo (1976), make extensive use of conjoint sessions with extended family members, encouraging the reexperiencing together of unresolved commitments and unmet obligations.

Norman Paul (1965), who sees many family and individual troubles growing out of unresolved loss, believes change takes place through a corrective mourning experience which not only encourages belated grief but reveals a shift of hostility from the one lost to a current family member (usually the symptomatic member). Paul has developed several creative therapeutic techniques to facilitate what he calls "operational mourning," including sessions with extended family and family of origin and use of videotapes of work with *other* families to trigger the expression of grief by the family in treatment.

Change, then, occurs through the process of taking steps actively to differentiate oneself from prescriptions, prohibitions, projections and conflicts transmitted by one's family heritage, prescriptions which have outlived their usefulness and may be inhibiting or maladaptive in the current situation.

The first step in this process is to find a way to objectify the family emotional system, and to step outside the system far enough to identify those elements which constitute the family's "culture," and to locate one's own participation in the process. This is what happened in a small way to our friend with the ironing board as she began to realize that she could be a different person from her mother and different also from what her mother wanted her to be. It is just such a combination of closeness and empathy that can often lead to a realistic acceptance of family figures and thus to the ability to feel comfortable with one's own difference from them.

The story of the ironing board is also an example of the classic model of change. It begins with the assessment process, that is, objectification of an aspect of the family system. It contains an emotional connection with a figure instrumental in the development and propagation of the prescription being challenged. It includes the enhanced understanding of and empathy toward that key figure and ends with the family explorer having taken one more step in the process of differentiation.

A step successfully taken toward increased differentiation from intergenerational influence is often accompanied by a noticeable change in affect. Often the searcher laughs, expressing amusement and pleasure in the discovery. Some of the sense of pleasure may be related to a new and heightened sense of mastery and of freedom. The woman above was positively gleeful when she announced, "I can iron anywhere." She had freed herself, in this one area of functioning, from the control of transmitted family prescriptions and was now able to make a choice, based on her personal preferences and the circumstances of her life.

Other feelings may also be experienced. Sometimes the affect can best be described as an affectionate amusement toward the self. Of course, at other times there may be sadness and anger as a person comes face to face with the extent of tragic and debilitating constraints that have resulted from enmeshment in the family system. One young woman had been estranged from her father and his family following the bitter divorce of her parents when she was twelve. In her early twenties her father died in an automobile accident, making the cutoff complete. She struggled with feelings of depression throughout her twenties and finally sought help. It was with considerable anger and unhappiness that she realized how she had "bought into her mother's family system," questioning neither the cutoff from her father nor the characterization of her father by her mother and her mother's family.

Anger can also be directed at the self. Repeatedly, as family patterns become obvious and subject to challenge, students of their own families will exclaim, "How can I have been so stupid? How could I have not seen that before? Why didn't I question that?" Again, this response points to how completely the family world view has become a part of the self. Anxiety, of course, is almost a universal accompaniment of the search, and the stronger the prohibition against delving into family secrets, the greater will be the anxiety about finding them out. Whether the feeling involved in discovery is sadness, pain, anger, or even ironic amusement, it is almost always coupled with a sense of relief.

It is important to stress that the processes we are talking about, differentiation and fusion, triangling, multigenerational transmission, invisible loyalties, and unresolved losses are basic human interaction processes. Because of their importance in the lives of all individuals and families, an identification of these aspects of the intergenerational family system is essential in the assessment process.

Assessment of the Intergenerational Family System

Inspired by the genealogical charts used by social scientists and families themselves to trace kinship patterns and compile family history, family therapists have made wide use of the *genogram*. This paper-and-pencil simulation, which helps in the task of organizing and analyzing information about the intergenerational family system, offers advantages similar to those of the eco-map. With the aid of the genogram, an enormous amount of complex data can be organized in a way which makes it possible for important patterns and themes—which might otherwise be lost in pages of linear descriptive reporting—to become visible.

INSTRUCTIONS FOR DRAWING A GENOGRAM

The genogram, similar to the familiar genealogy or family tree, is an intergenerational map of three or more generations of a family. This intergenerational map, besides recording genealogical relationships, can chart ethnic and religious background, major family events, occupations, losses, family migrations and dispersal, identifications, role assignments, and beginning information concerning triangles, coalitions, alignments, cutoffs, and communication patterns.

As with the eco-map, all that is needed is a pencil and paper; in this case, a rather large piece of paper. We have found that large cardboard-backed desk pads with corners are ideal.

The skeleton of the genogram tends to follow the conventions of genetic and genealogical charts. As in the eco-map, a male is indicated by a square, a female by a circle, and if the sex of a person is unknown, by a triangle. The latter symbol tends to be used, for example, when the client says, "I think there were seven children in my grandfather's family, but I have no idea whether they were males or females." Or, "My mother lost a full-term baby five years before I was born, but I don't know what sex it was."

A marital pair is indicated by a line drawn from a square to a circle;

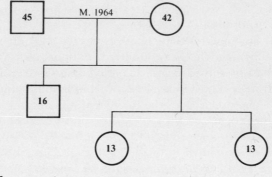

FIGURE 10.1

it is useful to write the marital date on the line. A married couple with offspring is shown as illustrated in figure 10.1. Offspring are generally entered according to age, starting with the oldest on the left. An adopted child may be identified by a small "a." The family diagramed in figure 10.1 has an older son followed by a set of twins. A divorce is generally portrayed by a line broken by two hatch marks, and again, it is useful to include dates. (See figure 10.2.) Admitted but not legally confirmed relationships may be indicated by a dotted line. A family member no longer living is generally indicated by drawing an "X" through the figure and giving the year of death. Thus, a complex, but not atypical, reconstituted family may be drawn as shown in figure 10.2.

It is useful to draw a dotted line around the family members who compose the household. Incidentally, such a family chart enables the worker to grasp who is who quickly in complicated reconstituted families.

FIGURE 10.2

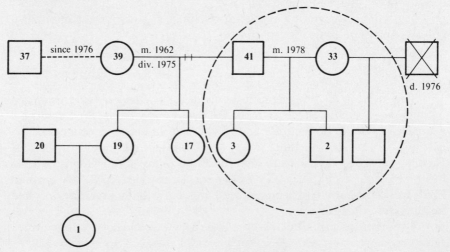

With these basic building blocks, expanded horizontally to depict the contemporary generation of siblings and cousins and vertically to chart the generations through time, it is possible to chart any family, given sufficient paper, patience, and information. (See figure 10.3.) As one charts the skeletal structure of the family, it is also important to fill this out with rich and varied data which portray the saga of the particular family being studied.

The sample genogram in figure 10.3 demonstrates the format for including salient social information in the family map. Although much data is missing, a brief examination of this genogram illustrates how easily a great deal of information can be organized and presented through the use of this assessment tool.

In the following pages, the kinds of data which may be gathered, added to the map, and analyzed, are described, illustrated with an analysis of the sample genogram and with case vignettes.

THE FAMILY EMOTIONAL SYSTEM

The fundamental goal of drawing a genogram is to objectify that intergenerational system of family projections, identifications, relationships, experiences, and events which have been influential in constructing the client's self. Worker and client together, in a sort of Sherlock Holmes and Dr. Watson collaboration, seek out family information which might help solve the family mysteries.

Most salient are experiences and relationships of the family of origin, as the searcher seeks to discover what roles he played in his family, with whom his parents identified him, what their ambitions for him were, and how he participated in the family triangles involving his parents, siblings, and other significant figures. The solution to this intergenerational mystery sometimes may be discovered only through reaching back yet another generation, where the searcher may find the explanations for his parents' adjustment and for their attitudes toward him and other family members. The searcher's travels may also take him down a horizontal path into the lives of more remote figures from whom the family has been cut off. The search for information and the assessment of that information is itself a crucial part of the intervention process.

NAMES

First, middle, and last names not only identify who family members are and suggest ethnic background, but naming patterns may help chart important identifications. In understanding where a client may fit into the family and what expectations and displacements may have affected the

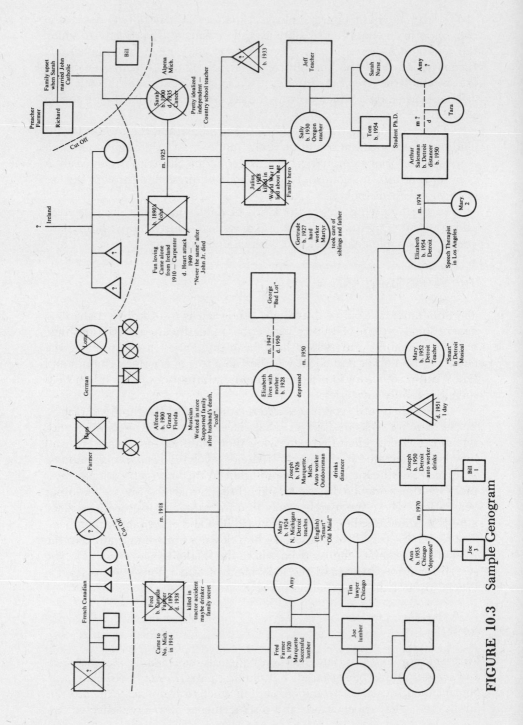

FIGURE 10.3 Sample Genogram

218

sense of self, a first step is to discover after whom, if anyone, the client was named. Once this person is identified, it is important to discover what he or she was like, what roles he or she carried, and perhaps most salient, what the nature of the relationship was between the client's parents and this relative.

In the family in figure 10.3 we see that the client Mary, born in 1952, was named after a paternal aunt and seems to be living a similar life. The next generation also has a "Mary." Mary's older brother Joseph is named after their father.

Sometimes meanings and connections are not immediately obvious and emerge only through careful exploration. The client may tell you he or she is not named after anyone in particular. You may find that it is only the first initial or sound of a name which gives you a clue, or it may be the meaning or symbolic significance of a name which is important. Perhaps a similarity will surface when you explore an ethnic or other naming tradition, as in the case of some Jews who may have both English and Hebrew names.

In one couple of mixed religion, the Jewish mother and Irish father debated for months over an appropriate male or female name for their expected child. The decision still was not made at the time of the birth, but when their son was born they suddenly arrived at a happy compromise that unconsciously embodied both of their cultural heritages. The couple named their son Aaron, which of course is pronounced Erin.

A second vignette illustrates the same theme. One of the author's nieces recently had a baby. This young woman, who comes from a family of family-centered practitioners and is also married to one, insisted she did not intend to name her firstborn son after any family member. The child was named Noah Benjamin. It happens that her brother, the firstborn child in her family of origin and a very important figure in her growing up years, had adopted the name "Ben," which he used outside of the family. Ben, at the time of the birth of his sister's child, was working for the National Oceanographic Administration (NOA).

In another example from practice, a historical inquiry into a family whose oldest son had committed suicide and whose second oldest son was showing signs of depression revealed that the father's grandmother, in her first marriage, had lost three childeren before maturity. The father claimed to know nothing about the names of these children, the circumstances surrounding their deaths, or the impact of their deaths on the family. But some detective work on his part brought to light the startling revelation that his three children had the same or markedly similar names to those who had died too soon two generations earlier. This information helped both him and the family worker understand his longtime fatalistic expectation that his children were likely to die before reaching maturity.

DATES

Dates of birth and death recorded on the genogram inform the worker of
entries and exits in the family drama. Birth dates indicate the age of family
members when important events occurred. They indicate how early or
late in a marriage a child came and the age of the parents at the birth.
In a sense, birth, marriage, and death dates mark the movement of the
family through time. In working with a client's genogram, it is helpful to
discover all of the events that took place in the period surrounding his
birth. Major losses experienced in the family around that time can be of
particular significance. The tendency to use newborn family members as
replacements for lost members seems almost universal and has even been
institutionalized in some culturally prescribed naming patterns.

One of our favorite examples of this phenomenon is illustrated in the
following story. The beloved German shepherd of a colleague's family was
killed by a car. About four days later the mother overheard her five-year-
old son Tommy talking on the phone with his uncle. Tommy was reporting
that the family's cat had given birth to a litter of kittens the night before
and, apparently in response to his uncle's query concerning what they
looked like, Tommy exclaimed, "Why, they look just like German shepherd puppies!"

This phenomenon of replacement is also graphically illustrated in figure 10.3, which shows that Joseph was born in 1950, within a year of the
death of his maternal grandfather, John. He also is the first child to be
born into his mother's family after the death in World War II of the family
hero, John, Jr.

In another case, JoAnn, a woman in her early thirties, had not married and in fact seemed to be having difficulty making any commitment
to an extrafamily relationship. Noting that she seemed to feel overly responsible for her widowed father's happiness and well-being in spite of a
conflicted father–daughter relationship, the worker discovered that JoAnn
was born three weeks after the death of her father's mother. Her father
still had intensely ambivalent feelings about his mother, who had abandoned the family during his adolescence. Apparently, JoAnn's assignment
was to balance the ledger.

SIBLING POSITION

Dates of birth also identify sibling position, another powerful source of
intergenerational identifications. Arranging the siblings in order by age
makes it easy to identify visually those who occupy the same position in
their sibships in different generations.

An individual's place in the sibship, particularly as it is discovered
who else in the family has occupied the same position, can provide clues

concerning the family's hidden "scripts" for this individual. Not only is this phenomenon often readily apparent in attributions such as the competent daughter, the responsible eldest, the caretaker, the brilliant one, the patient one, the joker, and so on, but at the same time it explains powerful affective relationships. How a mother felt about her oldest sister, the firstborn in her family of procreation, can be a weighty determinant in how she feels about her own firstborn daughter. Again, perhaps it is the middle child who for several generations has usually stayed at home, or been the most successful, or the sickly one. One word of caution: Be careful to note infant or early childhood deaths, miscarriages, and abortions. These events often represent significant losses but are also important considerations in determining sibling positions. Your client who seems to be a second-born son may actually be the product of a third pregnancy.

Turning again to the sample genogram, we see that Mary (b. 1952) not only is her aunt's namesake but in fact occupies her aunt's position of firstborn daughter (among living siblings). Moving back one more generation on her father's side, we find that Mary's paternal grandmother Alfreda was also a second-born daughter and musically gifted. Turning to her mother's generation we find that Sally, the second-born daughter in that family, is a teacher, as is Mary.

A variety of familial roles may be attached to particular sibling positions. For example, in one family, when a middle-aged, second-born daughter was feeling particularly burdened with the total responsibility for her aging and ill mother, an examination of the genogram revealed a family pattern of discordant and somewhat distant relationships between mothers and their firstborn daughters over at least three generations, while second-born daughters were closer emotionally and acted as the caretakers for their mothers. The objectification of a pattern like this can serve as the first step toward a shift of roles more satisfying for all involved. Sibling position can be linked also to dysfunctional role assignments such as the dumb one, the alcoholic, the mental patient, or the potential suicide; but again objectification of such a pattern can point the way to change.

PLACE OF BIRTH AND RESIDENCE

Place of birth and current place of residence mark the movement of the family through space. Such information charts the family's patterns of dispersal, bringing into focus major migrations and periods of loss or upheaval. Such information may also point to the fact that generations of a family have stayed within a fairly small radius except, perhaps, for a particular individual in each generation who moves away. A client who discovers that he is the present generation's "wanderer" has received valuable information from his genogram.

Picturing the family's movement through space may communicate a good deal about their norms of mobility, that is, whether they hold on or let go. It may also reflect the impact of world history, for many families have relocated in response to war, persecution, depression, industrialization, or even climatic or ecological changes.

One young man was feeling guilty about having moved to a town about thirty miles distant from his family. Indeed, he had become the target of considerable anger from his parents, who frequently urged him to come home because mother was sick, or sister was in trouble at school, and so on. The worker was initially puzzled that this move seemed to be provoking such extreme reaction. From the genogram, however, emerged the information that many generations of this family had lived within a one-mile area of a rural town. In each generation one child had left. These members had tended to develop bad reputations in the family.

The dispersal pattern is particularly interesting in the maternal branch of the family pictured in the sample genogram. Grandfather John left Ireland alone, cutting himself off from his family. Gertrude, who lives in Detroit, is separated from her only surviving sibling, who lives in Oregon. Two of Gertrude's children remain nearby, but the third, like her aunt, lives on the West Coast.

National origin, racial, ethnic, and religious background should also be included. In the family depicted in figure 10.3, we find French Canadian, German, and Irish ancestry. The maternal grandmother was of Protestant background, but her ethnicity is unknown. The religious issue, however, is crucial, since Sarah became alienated from her family when she married a Catholic. On the paternal side, the same religious mix is likely, as Fred, Sr. was probably Catholic while in all likelihood Alfreda, as a German from Grand Rapids, is Protestant.

OCCUPATIONS

Occupations of family members acquaint one with the interests and talents, the successes and failures, and the varied socioeconomic statuses that are found in most families. Occupational patterns (such as may be found in the sample genogram) may also point to identifications, and may portray family prescriptions and expectations, thus helping to determine an individual's success in identity consolidation. For example, Steven, very bright and well educated, a firstborn son, was having particular difficulty in choosing a career. Now out of college for more than ten years, he was still drifting from one temporary job to another. His family history disclosed the fact that for generations, on both his maternal and paternal sides, most of the eldest sons had become doctors. But Steven's father, a brilliant, troubled, and at times violent and cruel man, a doctor who had suffered a mental breakdown and left the family, provided an ambivalent model for identification. Further, his mother's father, also a doctor, had left Steven's grandmother for another woman and had become remote and cut off from his children, an episode which still triggered sad and angry feelings in the family.

Most of the women in this family had become teachers or helping professionals. The family saw these choices as "feminine," and altogether disparaged business careers or "making money" as an option for any of its members. Thus the family heritage strictly prescribed a medical career for Steven; but his unresolved relationship with his own father, as well as his mother's disappointment with her father, left him immobilized when it came to making a commitment to either a career or marriage.

HEALTH AND SICKNESS

Facts about family members' health and causes of death have a bearing on the way clients see their own futures, and may well have some power of self-fulfillment. While it is tremendously difficult to research relationships between emotional forces and physical illnesses, there is increasing evidence to suggest that the ways that families organize around illness or traumatic events become ritualized and are reenacted in successive generations. This process may well have implications for family health patterns.

Illness may be used thoughout the generations to keep family members close. A pattern of male family members suffering sudden heart attacks between the ages of forty-five and fifty may have important implications for the younger generation's expectations concerning how long they will live, producing an inner sense of fragility. In fact most people, based on intergenerational prescriptions, have an inner conviction concerning their own times and forms of death.

In the case of Barbara, discussed at length in the next chapter, we see the implications of family health history in the life of a young woman and follow her work in differentiating herself from painful and frightening expectations.

HEROES, HEROINES, AND VILLAINS

Information about those colorful, larger-than-life figures who are present in most families can provide clues concerning the family's values and aspirations, and, conversely, the behavior it deplores or devalues. When this aspect of the family's culture is known, the personal goals and prescribed role of the client can become more understandable.

A worker was impressed with the supreme self-confidence and very high aspirations of one young female client. Daisy, immediately upon finishing a degree in economics, had become the first woman faculty member of a distinguished, formerly all-male college. This position, she believed, was only a stepping-stone to the more illustrious career in academia or politics she envisioned for herself. Daisy is the firstborn daughter, clearly named after her mother's older brother David, a firstborn son who was the supremely gifted child of that generation. In an event reminiscent of that which befell President Kennedy's family, this family's hopes were temporarily crushed when David was killed at the age of nineteen in a plane crash. Daisy, like John, was destined to fulfill the family's mission, and no one doubted she could.

And then there was good old Uncle Charlie. . . . The family still tells affectionate stories about the practical jokes, wild escapades, and lavish spending of this huge, irresponsible man, who gradually became a heavy drinker and in later life a rather forlorn figure. Dependent on his adoring mother, who frequently made excuses for his behavior and extended innumerable "loans," he foundered after her death. But now the family is concerned about Charlie's namesake, thirteen-year-old Chad, who has been truant from school, was caught breaking into an empty house in the neighborhood, and who recently was hospitalized after "borrowing" the family car and crashing it into a tree. Before these disturbing occurrences, Mom and Dad used to describe Chad's misadventures with twinkling eyes.

LOSSES

The fact of loss is central in family development, often surfacing when one explores health, migration, naming patterns, and so on. Indeed it is frequently one of the most crucial elements in a family's behavior. Losses must be carefully assessed, not only in patterns of replacement and identification, as discussed above, but in terms of how they may influence the behavioral expectations for individuals and whole families. In some cases the tragic historical experiences of large groups of people need to be carefully considered and their impact on the particular family evaluated. For example, it was known that Eric, a young Jewish client who complained of his inability to assert himself and of his childlike feelings in relation to his parents, was the son of refugees who had escaped from Nazi Germany as adolescents but who had lost many close relatives in the Holocaust, including the father's parents. Eric's parents had never talked about their experiences to him or his siblings, had never to his knowledge read anything written on the Holocaust, and had carefully avoided seeing any of the recent films. An interview with Eric's parents revealed that both parents suffered from constant and undefined worry about whether Eric would be safe, happy, and so on. They saw him as extremely sensitive and vulnerable, but could not say why. The father, in describing his own approach to life, said he had always strived to maintain "a low profile," to avoid any overt conflict, and to not make anyone angry. Some initial discussion of his parents' painful experiences many years before was most useful to Eric (and we hope also to his parents), who is now beginning to understand the source of his anxieties and his need to avoid danger, strategies which prohibit him from achieving a richer, more satisfying life and from "leaving home" in the emotional sense.

Tragic losses echo and reecho through the family portrayed in the sample family genogram. Joseph was four when his father was killed in an accident and Gertrude was eight when her mother died of cancer. Three years after this loss, a younger sibling died; and it is interesting that this is such a painful area that the child's sex is not known to Mary, who gave the genogram information. It is mentioned that Gertrude was the caretaker of her siblings following their mother's death. One wonders whether she felt responsible for the loss of the younger child, and whether in consequence she became an anxious parent. Gertrude also lost her only brother in World War II when he was no more than seventeen, and her father four or five years later.

Another loss surfaces in Joseph's family and that is the possible suicide of Alfreda's mother, Lotte. Some of Lotte's female descendants have also struggled with feelings of depression.

CHARACTERIZATIONS, FAMILY THEMES, AND TOXIC ISSUES

In conjunction with the above objective data, the worker should also gather other important associations about family members which can greatly enrich and deepen the assessment. This information may also be added to the genogram.

One can ask, "What word or picture comes to mind when you think about this person?" These associations tend to tap deeply hidden information about the myths, role assignments, characterizations, or caricatures of family members in the client's mind. Descriptions such as lazy, bossy, martyr, beautiful, caretaker are likely to be offered, bringing forth reminiscences that have become a part of the family biography and mythology.

In assessing intergenerational families, certain themes or events may reemerge in successive generations until they become major organizing elements. It may become clear that in each generation, for example, siblings sacrifice their own education or career for that of another. One female in each generation may remain single and stay home to take care of aging parents, unaware that she has been unconsciously elected to fill this position. Fathers may leave their families or alcoholism may appear throughout the system. A family may exhibit the theme that financial success is followed by tragedy or that those in the family who "settle for less" have happier lives. Rules, life stories, role combinations, and value choices may all appear as family themes.

Toxic events may also echo throughout the generations, with painful impact on the family members. A stillborn child or the loss of an infant in the first day or two after birth, particularly if it happens more than once, may lead successive generations to be inordinately anxious throughout pregnancy.

Recently it was found in intergenerational work that the consequences of a toxic event which had occurred a hundred years before echoed through four generations of a family. The client began to notice that there were several cutoffs between groups of cousins in her parent's generation, and that these cutoffs were related somehow to weddings; the planning of weddings had been highly charged emotional processes and served to rupture ties among cousins. In doing her intergenerational work, this thirty-five-year-old woman crossed over a boundary line in order to visit the first cousins of her paternal grandfather. It was an interesting and enlightening visit. An eighty-year-old woman at the gathering, the family historian, told with considerable relish the story of the client's great-grandparents' marriage. Her great-grandmother, an orphan at the age of twelve, was taken in by her aunt and uncle following the death of her parents. Before long, she and her male cousin, two years older, became sexually intimate and there was a forced marriage. The family was shaken by the marriage between these young cousins and by the premarital intimacy. (It is unknown whether she was pregnant at the time of marriage.) After birthing five children, the couple divorced. It is easy to hypothesize that later conflicts among cousins over weddings were related to this toxic event a century earlier.

EMOTIONAL CUTOFFS

Finally, certain aspects of the family's communication structure can be indicated. Branches of the family that have been cut off become quite obvious to the worker because the client generally has very little information about them. Such cutoffs can be portrayed by drawing a fence where the rift exists, whereas tight bonds of communication can be demonstrated by drawing a line around those portions of the family that have close ties. It helps to keep things clear if a colored pencil is used for these fences and lines, so as not to confuse them with the basic genealogical structure. Cutoffs are of particular significance, as they usually indicate conflict, loss, and family secrets. Several cutoffs are apparent in the sample genogram. They generally develop to protect family members from pain and conflict, but they are nonetheless indicators of unfinished business and may leave a person out of touch with important aspects of family and perhaps of self.

It is fascinating how strong and sometimes handicapping an identification with a cut-off family member can be. Consider, for example, the heavy-drinking of the son of the alcoholic father who deserted the family many years ago; the adopted girl who becomes pregnant out of wedlock, as did her biological mother; or the daughter who is always compared to a disliked aunt on the father's side, that side of the family "we don't have much use for."

Differential Use of the Genogram in Assessment

"History taking" has long been a part of social work practice and can be approached in different ways and in greater or lesser depth. At times, it becomes a routinized, somewhat sterile affair, guided by a form, a list, or a standard outline. In some cases it is completed on the phone, at intake, or by the end of one interview. The genogram is often pressed into service for routine recording of social history and used for quick gathering of demographic, health, or other kinds of information. Although this may be an efficient information-gathering device, such routine use fails to exploit its rich possibilities. Too often we have heard social workers say, "Oh, yes, I've done a genogram; there wasn't much in it," and they will produce something not much more dynamic than the standard face sheet.

At the opposite extreme, intergenerational family study which seeks to understand in depth the significant family patterns, how they affect current behavior, and how if harmful they can be modified can take a large commitment of time and emotional energy. Some people will extend this effort over a lifetime, returning to it anew as ideas or issues emerge.

Some family-centered practitioners routinely do a genogram in the first or second session, and while this information can be very useful in developing hypotheses about what family matters are influencing the presenting problem, we suggest a more flexible use growing out of a particular situation. Otherwise, if a family is intensely and anxiously involved in a present crisis, being interviewed about the family of origin can be experienced as intrusive, distracting, or irrelevant. Of course, as family-centered practitioners we are convinced that in any situation, family history cannot help but clarify current circumstances. Nevertheless, the timing and the particular use made of the genogram are best dictated by the nature of the presenting problem and the client's readiness for intergenerational family work.

In some cases, major focus on the genogram may occur in first interview—in situations, for example, where individuals, couples, or families come for help with difficult relationships in their families of origin, the result of unresolved family conflict. Perhaps they even know that the worker is an expert in "intergenerational" work. In these cases a genogram becomes the organizing framework for the contact. However, in most family-centered helping situations, the family is seeking help with here-and-now crises. Even in such circumstances the worker may perceive that intergenerational themes should be explored, but such themes may, at this point, seem remote to the family, who are seeking immediate answers to a present difficulty. In such situations, we may begin the genogram in the first session by quickly sketching out the demographic data on the current household and other presently significant people in lieu of completing a traditional face sheet. We explain that a family map, like a family tree, helps us to keep the relationships straight and to understand how the family is organized. We say that later on we may want to work with the family in completing the genogram and in exploring family themes in more depth if it appears helpful. The genogram is kept in the case record and may be brought out as more information about the family emerges in the natural course of the work. In some cases, the situation may develop so that intergenerational work becomes an important focus; then the worker and family may analyze one segment, one theme, or one relationship for one or more sessions, later moving to other dimensions of the intergenerational picture, slowly completing the genogram, and returning often to those patterns or issues which seem most central.

SOME MANAGEMENT AND TECHNICAL ISSUES IN UTILIZING THE GENOGRAM

One question that often arises is, where should the genogram be kept? Some family practitioners suggest that the individual or family take the genogram home in order to work on it. But we find that the process of discovery can be lost this way. Clients are rather encouraged to gather information on their own and bring it to the office, where together we add it to the genogram. This process often continues throughout the entire contact. Usually, when extensive family work is being done, there are two working copies of the genogram: the client's copy and the one we work on together and keep available in the office. It is important to use a large enough piece of paper and to be as neat and clear as possible in entering material. This is not a matter of aesthetics; the advantage of a genogram over the usual descriptive narrative is that from the genogram relationships, themes, and patterns may visibly emerge. A certain amount of orderliness in the presentation therefore contributes to visual clarity and gives clients a sense of mastery over what may previously have seemed mere bits and pieces of facts.

Another management question concerns the best use of genograms in conjoint work with marital pairs and with family groups. Every marriage is, in a manner of speaking, the joining of two genograms, and the new family thus formed flows from the two extended families. Because this is so, helping a marital pair do their genograms together has the major advantage that both may share in the objectification of each family system. Such sharing leads to enhanced empathy between the couple. For example, as a wife begins to learn more about the women in her husband's family, she begins to understand the nature of some of her husband's expectations of her. One unanticipated consequence of shared genogram work can be a marked decrease in tension between the marital pair and the respective mothers- and fathers-in-law. As the extended in-law system is understood, the parent-in-law begins to be seen as a participant in a family saga. Thus tension and resentment tend to become diffused throughout the system rather than being concentrated on the in-law as the sole author of all the spouse's most difficult characteristics.

Technical problems do arise, however, in this conjoint work, and a typical example is the heightened competitiveness over time allotment for each marital partner in joint sessions. "We've talked more about your family than my family!" is a frequent comment, and indeed there never seems to be enough time for both. At first we assumed that this complaint was an expression of jealousy; however, in an unrelated adult group engaged in family work, the same intense competition developed. We eventually came to the following conclusion: Although each spouse and each group member were undeniably interested in the others' family work, they became so excited about their growing understanding of their own families that it was difficult to wait and to share time. As one young woman said, after considerable shared work with her husband on their respective families, "John's been very interested in listening to me about my family and I've been interested in his, but I guess neither of us can listen as much as each of us wants to talk about it."

Considerable negotiation must take place over the use of time in these conjoint and group sessions. Further, there must be negotiation about comments from the observing partner, whose participation sometimes irritates. A common complaint from the subject of the genogram under consideration is, "Look, this is my family." Often couples agree that the observing partner will be quiet until the other has finished making a certain point.

The more fused a couple is, the harder it is for each to stay quiet when the other is working on his or her genogram. However, attention to this part of the process can be very useful in helping the couple to see and begin to deal with their difficulties in establishing appropriate boundaries in their relationship. Even with all the complications and tension, we continue to feel that in most situations, the advantages of sharing the work outweigh other considerations. If, on the other hand, the couple's fusion and competitiveness keep retarding progress, one solution is to work with each partner alone but record the session on tape for the spouse or the couple together to hear at home. This device facilitates separateness without closing communications.

The Genogram in Different Practice Settings

The genogram is a classic tool for gathering and utilizing family data in any family-oriented practice. No matter what the setting, if the individual is to be understood in the context of the total family system, the genogram can portray that system and can move worker and client toward an understanding of its relevance to the issues at hand. In counseling regarding marital and parent–child conflict, the roots or prototypes of these conflicts may well emerge. The use of the genogram in conjoint marital counseling can increase empathy between the marital pair and help each to identify the old family issues that have been displaced in the marriage.

Genograms have been used in child welfare agencies. As part of an adoptive home study, for example, the genogram may explain why a couple experiences their family as incomplete and may also reveal what kind of identity the child is expected to assume. Charting a genogram with natural parents insures that should family ties be legally severed, there will be a full family history available to the child in the future. The issue of open adoption has yet to be settled, but in the interim the genogram can keep available the kind of information adopted children often want.

In a hospital setting, a genogram can be used to gather an expanded health history. Such a history provides information about patterns of illness and health in a family: for instance, a paternal grandmother may have died of heart disease at thirty-eight while the maternal grandmother lived an active life to age ninety-four. Further, patterns of illness as well as attitudes toward illness and ill people may appear.

In family-centered practice with the aging, as we demonstrate in chapter 15, the genogram is an invaluable tool for life review and in bequeathing the family's traditions to the generations which follow.

The eco-map and genogram are paper-and-pencil simulations that can organize and objectify a tremendous amount of data about the family system in space and through time. They can lead to new insights, to altered perceptions, and thus to new ways of bringing about change in complex human systems.

Chapter 11

The Intergenerational Family System as a Resource for Change

IN THIS WORK of defining the self in the family of origin, of coming to terms with unpaid debts, unresolved family issues, invisible loyalties, and incomplete mourning, we agree with Bowen that it must be the client who carries the responsibility for bringing about change. The worker—and this represents a major shift in conceptualizing one's role—becomes not a counselor or therapist but rather a "coach," a vital distinction which will later be elaborated. How could it be otherwise? If the worker were to take major responsibility for change, the client would by that very fact occupy a dependent position, contrary to the explicitly desired goal. More importantly, change takes place in the client's real-life relationships, with those significant people in one's life with whom ties are ongoing. While the social work relationship is one of facilitation, it is not in itself viewed as the medium for change. To use a football metaphor, while the coach helps the quarterback plan and execute change strategies, he nevertheless remains on the sidelines, occasionally sending in plays and helping with analysis and future strategies during halftime.

In chapter 10 we discussed theory of intergenerational family change and described the assessment of the family over time. The genogram and its use in a family "objectification" process was introduced. In this chapter we will concentrate on the processes of planning and intervention. We will detail a range of strategies for change, illustrated with instances from our own practice. An extended case example, the case of Peter, is presented,

231

followed by a discussion of the roles of the worker and client and the nature of the worker–client relationship in intergenerational work. The worker's own family-of-origin work, considered highly useful and in some training programs a necessary component of the training, will be examined. The chapter concludes with a discussion of the variety of ways such an approach can usefully be applied in social work practice.

The Planning of Change

The assessment process, which in this case is a family study or an "objectification" of the family system, forms a major part of both planning for change and actual intervention. Although it is time-consuming and certainly at times frustrating, it is the core of the work. Knowledge about the family system tends to dispel myths, expose secrets, and give powerful but shadowy figures substance, thus adding to the understanding both of the immediate family and of the self.

The process of assessment can bring about change in more than one way. First, as the seeker sets out to gather information about the family, lively and significant communication lines are opened, and these can become a major medium for the building of relationships. This coalescence is most dramatically seen when young adults visit aging relatives to gather family information. They may have lived in different worlds, disagreed on many subjects, and struggled with stilted exchanges for years. But the one thing they share is the same family, and as the family pictures, letters, and mementos are pulled out of storage, a genuine exchange begins to develop.

Second, the establishment of contact in the information-gathering process may itself serve to provoke family change, setting in motion a series of events which begin an alteration of the basic structure of relations. The following example illustrates this point:

Mary Lou came to the Family Center for help with a disturbed teenage son. The worker made a valiant but vain effort to persuade Mary Lou's husband and children to attend at least the first session, and finally agreed to see her alone. After three sessions of exploration and assessment, including the beginning of a genogram analysis during which it became apparent that both Mary Lou and her husband, Don, were alienated from their respective families of origin, a contract was made to continue Mary Lou's own family study and to work toward some strategies for change.

During the study process, the worker suggested that Mary Lou talk with her siblings about their relationships with each other. Reminiscing about how she at one time had thought she was "pretty close" to her brother Rob, whom she had seen very little of in the past several years, even though they lived only about fifty miles apart, Mary Lou tentatively and with considerable anxiety called him on the telephone. This call led to a plan to go out to dinner together the following week. The dinner itself was both gratifying and frustrating, and ultimately it yielded information important for further assessment and change efforts. Moreover, much to Mary Lou's amazement it seemed to generate a flurry of family activity. Her sister, Lois, whom she felt had always adopted a rather superior air with her, called to ask her advice concerning a problem with her daughter. Mary Lou's mother, who had retired to Florida and who rarely telephoned, called the very night of the dinner date. She had apparently been told of the plan for dinner by Rob and was calling to "fish" for information, but ended the conversation by suggesting that maybe next year all of the children and their familes might want to have a Christmas reunion in Florida.

In the meantime, Mary Lou pondered the fact that her husband had been in a foul mood all week. As she and the worker discussed the dinner, she commented that Don's parting shot, just as she was going out the door for dinner was, "I can't understand why you would want to spend time with that phony after all the years he has ignored you!" "And last night," reported Mary Lou, "Don mumbled something to the effect that one of these weeks he might come to one of these 'family' sessions I've been talking about."

The above vignette suggests the kinds of repercussions just one seemingly innocuous intervention can stimulate; these may herald the beginning of change in the system, or they may merely be efforts by the family to restore the status quo.

Principles Which Guide the Planning of Change

The specific nature of desired change grows out of the assessment process; it is generally a blend of the client's goals for the self and the relevant issues identified in an analysis of the genogram. Interventions are planned on the basis of the study, the identification of the targets for change, and the available resources. The discovery of significant cutoffs, for example, suggests that building new connections may be a priority. The surfacing of family secrets or taboo subjects (for example, a father's first marriage, the early death of a sibling, or an occurence of incest) suggests that family communications should be opened. The growing awareness of rigidly patterned behavior in which the client is stuck indicates the need for a strategy which can help free him or her from such role assignments. The following general principles should guide the planning process.

The first principle which guides planning is that it should be a cybernetic process in which both worker and client must learn to proceed in spite of inevitable uncertainty. In a cybernetic planning model, interventions are devised primarily through the monitoring of feedback from previous inverventions. Family systems are so complex and the interrelated variables so numerous (and often unknown as well) that prediction is difficult, if not impossible. Change strategies must be planned on the basis of both general hypotheses relating to the nature of all family systems and specific hypotheses concerning the system under study, but there will be considerable uncertainty nonetheless concerning outcome. The impact of an intervention is assessed after the fact when outcomes become observable. The more we learn about the way family systems tend to operate, the more sophisticated and useful the hypotheses we can develop to guide interventions. For example, one general hypothesis about family system functioning is that cutoffs in a family tend to keep family members caught in an unrealistic construction of family reality, unable to integrate whatever knowledge and family experience exist on the other side of the cutoff. On the basis of this theory, it is important for people to seek out family members from whom they have been alienated.

However, the specific ripple effects that may spread throughout the system often cannot be predicted. This leads to a second planning principle, namely that both client and coach should be prepared for the system's retaliation and its attempts to reestablish equilibrium. Again, accurate prediction is impossible in complex living systems, but it is possible to speculate and to watch for a variety of possible reactions.

Geri, a young woman attempting to differentiate from a large enmeshed family, determined to avoid large family gatherings and to see family members only one or two at a time. Her goal was to avoid being swept up into the system, but also to establish more fruitful and genuine person-to-person relationships. The family, however, threatened by this differentiated stance which was simultaneously promoting both separateness and the possibility of more genuine intimacy, devised elaborate countermoves. For example, while declining an invitation to attend her two-year-old nephew's birthday party, planned for one o'clock on a Saturday, Geri made arrangements to visit him and his parents at five o'clock instead, and her own parents two hours later. Although these arrangements were planned several days in advance and reconfirmed on Friday, when she called her sister on Saturday to let her know her car was being repaired and she might be a little late, she learned that in the space of twenty-four hours all of the relatives had been notified and the time of the party had been changed to five o'clock. Had she not had car trouble and called, she would have arrived just in time for the party and happy cries of "Surprise!" from her family as they won yet another round in defining the rules for family contact.

The third general planning principle which gives shape and direction to efforts at change is that a person-to-person relationship should be established with every member of the extended family system. Bowen, who sees this process as essential in the route to differentiation, describes a person-to-person relationship as "one in which two people can relate personally to each other, without talking about others (triangulating) and without talking about impersonal 'things'" (1978:540). Of course, as Bowen implies, no one could live long enough to complete this task! But the efforts to detriangulate do give direction to the change effort. And the gathering of information, as described above, is itself a valuable medium for the beginning of a person-to-person relationship.

A fourth principle is that the final objective must be a change in oneself, for changes are defined in terms of the client's own behavior. The client who sets out to change his family instead of himself is doomed to failure. For example, if a client complains that he cannot tolerate spending time with his mother because she is too intrusive and critical, he needs to discover how he reacts emotionally and behaviorally in these exchanges and to devise strategies which allow him to change his own performance. He must learn new ways of taking charge of his own reactions.

When people take the stance that they are going to "fix up" their families, chances are they have probably been caught in old patterns. The family may experience such change efforts as manipulative or hostile and they may move toward a more rigid and defensive stance. This is not to say, however, that the family will not change as a result of one or more interventions. But that change is fortuitous. Although we have emphasized the need for watchfulness in the face of family efforts to combat change, many family reactions are surprisingly positive. Family study, as we said earlier, appears to be contagious. The father of one client, a man in his seventies, responded to his daughter's search by getting reconnected to his own family, from which he had been quite cut off. "I want to do it for you and the children," he said, "but I also want to do it for me."

A fifth principle which guides planning with clients might be phrased like this: Although the shortest distance between two points is a straight line, a circuitous route is often easier to manage. We often advise clients to "work from the outside in" or to "begin with the easiest step." For most people it is their relationships with their parents (even though these are the persons perhaps most accessible and easiest to talk to) which in the end are the most difficult to change. Rarely is a client coached to begin work with the parents or with those individuals in the family for whom feelings are most emotionally loaded. Examples of highly charged situations might include an aunt who is the sister of one's mother, and from whom mother has been cut off for years (clients often believe they will lose mother if they cross this boundary), or a highly disliked relative, or someone who has been the source or target of considerable pain. Frequently the major relationships to be altered are those among client, parents, and siblings. Although client and coach may agree that these are the ultimate points of intervention, the thought of direct approaches to these persons often creates so much anxiety that the client is immobilized and quickly becomes discouraged. An oblique approach via more distant family members seems to diffuse the tension and ready the client to tackle the problem by circling in slowly on the most sensitive areas of the system.

The diffusion of tension in this manner may be a rather general phenomenon, and has consequently led us to encourage people to start family work with a somewhat remote part of the system.

A sixth guiding criterion is that of "accessibility," although lack of accessibility can usually be overcome with motivation and persistence. Some information-gathering tasks or strategies for change may be difficult to implement because the distances are great, the figures are deceased, or the relatives strongly rebuff all efforts at contact; suggestions for overcoming some of these barriers will be made below. The criterion of accessibility also dictates that clients be particularly encouraged to spend time with their grandparents and other aging relatives. Not only is there greater potential for losing these relatives and thus less time to gather information or to work on these relationships themselves, but older relatives have the perspective of long years and are frequently repositories of valuable family information.

A seventh guideline urges the identification of the relationships in the family which seem to hold the greatest promise for the client's life and goals. The choice of which relationships to examine grows out of an analysis of the genogram. In making this selection, one should ask with what figure(s) in the previous two generations (mother's and father's siblings and *their* parents) the client is most identified. Clues include naming patterns, sibling positions, and the family's own associations and identifications. We ask clients, "Which side of the family do you seem to belong to?" "Which side do you take after?" Clients often respond with such statements as "I've always been told I'm a lot like Uncle Hubert," or "My mother was always afraid I would end up in a mental hospital, like her sister Jane." Hearing more about relationships between the parents and these relatives gives one important knowledge concerning the family's emotional attitudes toward itself, and its expectations and prescriptions for the children as well.

An eighth guideline, stressed by Carter and Orfanidis (1976), reminds us that all who undertake this kind of change should avoid sharing their plans with family members. One client, it was learned, was reporting almost verbatim the content of the coaching sessions to her mother and was having difficulty understanding why nothing seemed to work as she had planned!

Finally, not only is it important that we recognize the family's resistance to change and to appreciate its power to "bite back" with ingenious maneuvers, but we must also be aware of the powerful forces within our clients (and within us) that also oppose change. The individual is, after all, a part of the family system and is subject to the family's powerful prohibitions and prescriptions. Undertaking one's own family work is indeed a humbling experience to which both authors can attest (some comments on the family of the worker conclude this chapter). Prohibitions and resistance are also expressed in the rapidity with which new insights are forgotten. Time and again clients have visited relatives, gathered information, and promptly forgotten it. A recording device, or at least note-taking during or immediately after a visit, will help outwit this defensive maneuver.

Change Techniques and Strategies

Having outlined the major principles which guide the planning of interventions, we now turn to a consideration of a range of strategies which may be utilized in bringing about change.

CONTACTS: VISITS, LETTERS, TELEPHONE CALLS

More contact, "going home again" physically and psychologically, is the key to differentiation. It is true that in some cases, when a client has a controlling and intrusive parent, the goal may become one of reducing the contact; but the point here is to make person-to-person exchanges more meaningful, comfortable, and fruitful. Such contacts should be planned in a way that the client may take better charge of the situation in order to short-circuit emotional buffeting.

In many families contacts between adults become ritualistic, dutiful, and riddled with anxiety. Altering the quality of such visits is a major interventive strategy and may be accomplished through the interruption of ritualized patterns utilized to ward off change or through the initiation of new and more expressive rituals. The use of rituals to promote intergenerational change is discussed further in chapter 13.

Visits. In some families, visits take place almost exclusively on the parents' "turf," a custom which allows the elders to maintain emotional distance and prevent their children from becoming full adults in their own right. To counteract this force, young adults are encouraged to plan social events, such as a family dinner, on *their* own turfs and terms.

One young man, in spite of the fact that he had a good income, still called home "collect," and had never given his parents a gift except at Christmas; and when the parents came to visit they always took him out to eat in restaurants and, of course paid his check. In this family, the fact that the young man had been living with a young woman for three years, though known, was not discussed. This client was, with the help (and presence) of the young woman, able to plan a dinner at their apartment, which included a birthday cake and gifts for his father and a slide presentation of the wonderful vacation trip he and his woman friend had taken the previous summer.

One of the central purposes of visits, in addition to that of gathering information, is to facilitate the establishment of more genuine person-to-person relationships. A client is often encouraged to devise ways to spend some time alone with each person in the family, a strategy which in some families requires considerable ingenuity! A daughter may plan to visit her father at work or meet him for lunch, a son may consult his mother for advice about decorating his apartment, or an older brother might ask a younger brother's advice about a career change. These strategies are at the same time often designed to make a shift in the usual role assignments which characterize family relationships. For example, in the latter instance, your client may always have been cast in the role of "know-it-all" big brother, while the younger brother may have been seen as irresponsible, roles which were surely constricting for both.

Visits during holidays or family rites of passage present a special challenge. As we suggested in chapter 5 family rituals and ceremonies serve a variety of important functions. In relation to differentiation goals, such times offer very special opportunities for change, for during such events as weddings, funerals, christenings, or bar mitzvahs, there is a heightened sense of familiness and of family emotionality. These events present the opportunity to reconnect with important family members or to connect emotionally in new ways.

Susan, who had been cut off from her father's French-Canadian side of the family, and who a year earlier "wouldn't have dreamed of going," attended the funeral of the wife of an uncle, her father's younger brother. Not only did she reconnect with her uncle, whom she hadn't seen since her childhood—an event emotionally enriching and meaningful for both—but she also discovered she had several cousins, thus widening her own previously limited sense of familiness. Further, her presence served as a trigger for helping the father and children mourn, as they eagerly shared with her their many rich memories of the lost wife and mother. This visit also stimulated her interest in the disparaged French-Canadian side of her ethnic heritage and thus further consolidated her own identity.

Not all such visits are, of course, as positive or productive as the one described above. Large family gatherings or even gatherings of the nuclear family can be distancing, alienating experiences. The valuable sense of "groupness" that ritual and reunions offer can be obtained at the expense of person-to-person closeness, and the intense power of the family system can be experienced as oppressive. These occasions are sometimes particularly difficult for the spouse, the "in-law" or "outsider," who may feel forced to compete with the family for the mate's attention and loyalty. One of our clients, a young wife in her twenties, was afraid to attend the annual major holiday reunion at her husband's mother's house, an event that stimulated a great deal of stress between the couple. She was coached to: (1) signal her husband whenever she needed time to reconnect with him (and he was to drop what he was doing and respond to her); and (2) to pretend she was an anthropologist making a careful study of the customs and organization of the husband's clan, which would greatly benefit their family work together.

What is most important in these and in fact all visits, is that they be planned in advance. The client and the worker must discuss what the client would like to accomplish during this particular visit and work out in detail the strategies for achieving these objectives. Part of the planning includes anticipating family responses, considering who may be likely to sabotage a change or effort to be different, and speculating about ways the client can then react to those responses. It may be helpful to write down some of these plans for the client to review, since they are often difficult to integrate and maintain. In some cases rehearsal or role play may be useful.

Three additional points applying to all visits should be made. First, whenever possible, visits should be brief, particularly in the initial stages or until a change has been consolidated. We have discovered that most people can "hold their own," without becoming drawn into their old, reactive family patterns, for only brief periods of time. For some, this may mean one hour, for others an overnight visit, and for others longer periods of time. One client remarked, "I did fine for the first two days, but on the third day Dad really got to me!" Second, the client should plan "time outs" or "times away" from the family. Perhaps this means visiting old friends, going for a walk, or seeing a movie alone. These "times away" are meant to gain breathing space and to assess what is happening; they should not occur reactively, that is, as a result of irritation or anger, which in most cases would mean one is again fused in the traditional way. Third, the client should try to plan time alone with each member of the family, or, in the case of large family gatherings, with one or more family members who have been singled out. This can be done simply to obtain new information, to stretch or break a rule about communication or relationship, or to change one's own habitual ways of behaving at such times.

Letters. The writing of letters, seemingly a minor way of bringing about change, can actually be a powerful intervention technique, but one which many clients are at first reluctant to use. The writing of a letter can mean violating a powerful family barrier. The classic example of this is the way correspondence usually takes place between adult children and their parents. Usually, the adult writes a letter to "Mom and Dad" as if they were one person and receives a letter back signed "Mom and Dad" but written by Mom. This communication pattern tends to continue a typical family triangle at whose center is the mother, monitoring and controlling communication with the child.

We encourage clients to try writing separately to mother and father, and we remind them that they are entitled to a person-to-person relationship with each parent. The writing of separate letters is surprisingly difficult to do, but it is a good way to begin and the reactions on the parts of parents are, for the most part, experienced as extremely positive by the clients. In most situations the parents have written back separately, and in many cases clients have been particularly delighted with and surprised by their father's responses. Many fathers, glad to have finally been asked, turn out to be the prolific and colorful correspondents, and the letters form a beginning in opening up further communication. Some results can be quite dramatic.

David, aged twenty-nine and unmarried, decided to write to his parents separately. Knowing he had recently ended an important love affair, his mother (a perennial "worrier") first assumed upon seeing the two letters that David intended to commmit suicide, and she called to urge him to consider moving back home. (David had never in his lifetime threatened or even thought about such an act.) David's differentiating move and his mother's extreme reaction served as an important step in objectifying his mother's controlling behavior and the rigid family triangle which kept father and son distanced from one another.

A letter to a distant or cut-off family member can often produce significant results. Clients are helped to compose letters which are unthreatening and which, like initial visits, begin with modest objectives. Such letters "test the waters" in a way which promises to open up further channels of communication. One client received a response for which neither she nor the worker were prepared.

Diane chose to write first to her mother's brother, whom she had met a few times during childhood. Uncle Jacob now lived on the West Coast and had not been seen or heard from by her family in a long time. Diane's mother, considered somewhat "crazy" by Diane and her brothers, had been unable (or unwilling) to give Diane much information about the family, but she did describe Uncle Jacob as "vulgar," "cruel," and even "violent." Immediately upon receiving Diane's missive, which simply expressed her wish to learn more about the family's history, Uncle Jacob proceeded to sit down and talk into a tape recorder for some eight hours. This collection of tapes, a vivid, emotional, detailed reminiscence of this Jewish family's early life in Russia, their difficult and dangerous journey to the United States, and their years on the Lower East Side of New York, punctuated with poignant descriptions of incidents about Diane's grandparents and other family members, was indeed a storehouse of family data. It also enriched Diane's limited understanding of her mother and her mother's life, which was the foundation for changing a painful and difficult relationship.

Writing a letter without sending it can serve as a kind of catharsis, initiating a process which can later be continued face-to-face. Some clients are helped, in much the same way as the Gestalt technique of double-chairing can help, to sort out their feelings and to express what inevitably needs to be said. This exercise is viewed as preparation for the more difficult person-to-person confrontations which will take place at a later date.

Telephone Calls. The telephone is also an important communication medium in family work. Even long-distance calls, which many find too expensive, can be planned for "reduced rate" times. Just as visits and letters, calls too can be meaningful in establishing person-to-person connections. Again, the classic example is the mother–father–child triangle. Here mother often functions as the supervisor of the switchboard. Many adults typically talk to all other family members through mother, who then screens all incoming communication and selects what she chooses to tell the others. Our clients and students usually report that when they call home they seem to be programed to say, if father answers the phone, "Hi, dad, how are you? Is mom there?" Or father may say, "Hello, Doug, hold on a minute and I'll get your mother." We encourage clients to discover and experiment with ways to engage their fathers (or mothers in the case of families in which the father–child dyad is dominant and mother is the outsider) in conversation. The closer parent often resists this shift, preventing or undermining these efforts by picking up the extension phone. Worker and client need to devise plans for communicating lovingly and gently the wish to speak to one or the other parent alone, combined with behavior which shows that this new state of affairs does not imply a triangling, distancing from, or rejection of the closer parent; he or she will not lose and in fact will, in the long run, gain in terms of more genuine closeness in the relationship.

Calls, like letters, can be used to make new connections with relatives from whom the client has been cut off. Such relatives (aunts and uncles are often key figures), even though the family myth may present them as unfriendly, are frequently genuinely pleased and surprised to hear from the client. The real or imagined wrongs which have led to a cutoff usually involve persons other than the client, who should not have to be deprived of these sources of identity.

Visits, letters and telephone calls, strategic communication devices in gathering information, opening up contact, and initiating change, are also the basic tools to be called upon in carrying out the more specific change strategies to which we now turn.

DETRIANGULATION

An objective crucial to the process of differentiation is that of freeing oneself from habitual participation in the powerful and sometimes rigid triangular relationships found in families, and in fact, in all relationships and groups. These triangles are maintained by an elaborate and unspoken system of rules which prescribe not only when and to whom one may communicate, but what the boundaries and content of that communication may be. Some of the case vignettes above illustrate how telephone calls, letters, and visits may be used to begin violating these often constraining or dysfunctional prescriptions. The effort here is to take charge of person-to-person relationships in a way that builds a more solid foundation, one not contingent upon the triangulation of a third person or persons.

Darlene, a black woman of 35, is destined to be the unmarried caretaker of her mother if the family has its way. She had known her estranged father only through the biased and embittered vision of her mother. Mother also tended to control Darlene's contacts with some of her siblings, particularly one sister, Ann, who lives in another state. Darlene, who had successfully reconnected with her father before his death, and now had turned her attention to her sibling relationships, reported that her mother had recently said, "Ann is very angry with you." The worker suggested that Darlene call or write to Ann herself to clarify the matter. During the next interview, Darlene mischievously reported that she has sent a giant post card to Ann, her very proper sister, with only six words written on it:

> Dear Ann,
>   F——You!!!
>   Love, Darlene.

Ann had immediately called, Darlene suggested that perhaps in the future they should communicate their business directly to each other, and the two sisters had an hour-long, very gratifying conversation, which ended with Ann's inviting Darlene to spend her next vacation with her.

The following illustration points to another subtle way triangles were being maintained in a family:

In the Bottoni family, the parents' marriage could be summed up as forty years of conflict, mutual criticism, and disappointment. The bitter feelings generated by the marital conflicts were in part dealt with by father's scapegoating of mother, mother's complementary deliberate vexing of father and also her underfunctioning, and some triangulating of the children. For example, father and youngest daughter were close but this daughter had an angry, rebellious relationship with mother, while mother was fondest of the oldest son, who in turn was on poor terms with father. The middle child, a daughter, was less involved in these two powerful central triangles, but the childhood relationships of the siblings had been characterized by constant bickering and teasing, while the adult relationships were distant at best. In fact, the hostility and competitiveness were reaching into the next generation, as the adult children competed for their parents' approval by gossiping about the others and comparing and contrasting the grandchildren.

Mark, the oldest child and in this case the client, planned two major interventions which helped release him from these routinized relationships and stimulated a complex chain of reactions (which can be described only briefly here). First, he allowed himself to be chagrined by the realization that he and his siblings sometimes tried to move closer to father by humiliating mother. He counteracted this habit during a holiday visit when all were present, as mother was timidly describing how she planned to attend a dance class and father was entertaining the group by saying, "Can you imagine someone her age making a fool of herself like that?" (followed by laughter from all). Mark suddenly said, "What a fantastic idea, Mom! I'll bet you would be terrific at that; you've always been well-coordinated. I've been thinking I might get into some exercise program myself." Both his brother and sister, who had stopped laughing, spontaneously supported his comments, and father stood in the doorway, silent and confused, not quite sure what had just happened.

In this same family, Mark followed this intervention with periodic phone calls to his siblings, and some months later he planned a visit to his sister's home. The first day was extraordinarily pleasant, as Mark became better acquainted with his brother-in-law and nieces and nephews, and began to discover that his sister and he actually seemed to like each other. That evening, however, the doorbell rang, and with a loud shout of "Surprise!" Mark's parents burst into the room, having traveled five hundred miles "as a special treat." Within half an hour, the younger generation was bickering, Mark felt a migraine headache coming on, and his sister was slumped into a chair looking disconsolate.

Mark's family system had been maintained as a rigid structure of at least three interlocking triangles. The children were involved in the destructive marital relationship in order to maintain a comfortable distance in that relationship as well as to meet each of the parent's need for an ally. One of the triangular arrangements is illustrated in the anecdote of mother's dancing class depicted in figure 11.1. This triangle consisted of father and children in the inside position, and mother on the outside. Mark's refusal to be triangulated by father temporarily altered that structure. However, that move also placed Mark in danger of slipping into the other family pattern.

This second pattern of organization in the Bottoni family consisted of two interlocking triangles (illustrated in figure 11.2). The two major triangles were Mark's father and sister on the inside positions, with both Mark's mother and Mark together on the outside position. With perfect

FIGURE 11.1

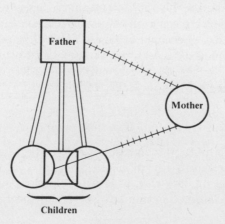

Father

Mother

Children

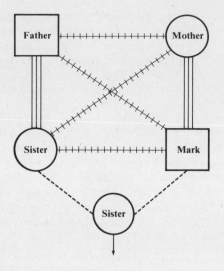

FIGURE 11.2

symmetry, in the second triangle Mark and his mother maintained a close alliance by keeping father and sister out.

Mark was now clearly in a very distressing position, as the demands of the two major triangles in which he participated were at odds. In one triangle, the "dancing class triangle," prior to his intervention he gained father's approval at the expense of his mother. In the other, he cut himself off from both sister and father by joining with mother. He found himself moving back and forth, uncomfortable in either position and dealing with the tension by emotionally cutting himself off from the system.

In order for the children to remain locked into the family triangles, it was necessary for the sibling relationships to be distant and competitive. Were Mark and his sister to develop strong person-to-person relationships, differentiating from the parents, generational boundaries would be strengthened and the father–daughter, mother–son alliances threatened.

It was, in part, for this very reason that Mark and his coach planned that he work to develop a person-to-person relationship with his siblings. However, the casual mention of "Uncle Mark's" impending visit, made during the grandparents' weekly telephone call to sister's family, alerted the system to the danger of altered coalitions. Mark's parents quickly took to the road to head off the possibility of change.

ALTERING ROLES

Another specific strategy which can have important impact on the client and the family system is for the client to change his or her role in that system. This is not an easy task, as family roles have often been carefully structured and reinforced over many years and the family members are in collusion to maintain the players in their parts. People frequently carry the roles they played in their families of origin into their families of procreation as well as into work and friendship systems. We have often found that focusing the effort of change on the relationship between the client and the family of origin can provide a powerful impetus for change in other areas of the client's life.

The use of role change as a strategy is illustrated in the following case example:

Norma, her husband Paul, and their two boys were seen in four family sessions over a period of a few months. The parents had sought help because the boys were not fulfilling their superior potential in school and the parents, who had high expectations for their sons and were very much involved in the boys' schoolwork, nagged, threatened, and cajoled to get the boys to do their homework. But the family was responsive to structural interventions and the boys began to take more responsibility for their work as the parents relinquished their control.

In the midst of this conjoint family case, focused primarily on the current parent–child issues, an episode of intergenerational work was introduced when Norma casually mentioned that her total family of origin was visiting for four days over the Christmas holidays, and that as much as she looked forward to the visit, she also dreaded it.

In response to this statement, the worker suggested that Norma come in for an appointment during that next week to see if she couldn't perhaps plan some way to make the visit different. Paul, who, because of local unemployment had taken a job in a neighboring state, was commuting weekends and would not be able to come in, but supported the idea.

Norma was the oldest in her family and had been the parental child, carrying a great deal of responsibility for her siblings throughout her growing up. Although she had been in a position of power and control she received little nurturance, care, or protection herself. She was truly the family Cinderella.

In past years, the annual Christmas family reunion had always repeated and reinforced this role as the entire family, her parents, her siblings together with their spouses, and her nieces and nephews would gather at Norma's and Paul's small house for two to four days. Norma would clean, shop, prepare all the meals, and try to keep the house in order while her family enjoyed their reunion and holiday. No one ever seemed to notice that Norma, who worked full-time, also needed a vacation.

The intervention worked out by Norma and her coach was that this year she would step out of her Cinderella role. Every detail of the shift was planned. She would make a list of all the tasks that had to be done during the reunion. As soon as the family arrived, there would be a family meeting and the group would negotiate the distribution of the work to all members of the family. She planned to ask her youngest brother to conduct the family meeting, both because he was likely to be the most supportive of her and also because it was an atypical role for him, but one she thought he could handle well.

Norma was terrified by the assignment, although determined to proceed. She was sure that everyone would be furious with her and almost undermined the whole project when she called and told her mother about it, obviously needing to obtain her mother's permission. Her mother proceeded to call everyone and tell them of the plan, and resistance was mobilized before the family gathered. In fact, Norma was faced with so many strong objections by the family that she would have given it up if her youngest brother hadn't supported her to the point of insisting they have the meeting and distribute the work. The family did come around, finally, and with some grumbling, everyone did his and her job, enjoyed the visit, and agreed that future family reunions should be organized in this way.

Norma's role change in her family of origin produced some interesting repercussions in her relationship with her current family, where she also played Cinderella. She vainly nagged her sons to do their assigned household chores and then finally did them herself to protect them from their father's anger, whose family role had been and continued to be that of "the general."

Her immediate family's response to her move was pride, as they reported how well the Christmas visit had gone. However, two weeks later, Norma called in a fury, seeking another individual coaching appointment. She was depressed, furious at the boys, who were not doing their jobs, and feeling abandoned and unsupported by Paul. After considerable discussion of options, Norma agreed to again clarify for the boys what their jobs were and then to not mention the tasks again. Because she couldn't tolerate living in chaos, she would keep the living room and her bedroom as she wanted and make those portions of the house "off limits."

The first week, the boys did not do their jobs and chaos reigned. When "the general" returned home Friday night, he "hit the ceiling," yelling at Norma about the mess. With complete calmness, even a smile, Norma responded, "It's not my problem." This signaled a real shift in the organization of the family. Norma had genuinely begun to move out of her Cinderella role in both her family of origin and her current family.

The struggle to change her role in her family of origin also had other effects. The most crucial aspect of the change strategy was that Norma, who had always complained about the role, in attempting to give it up was faced with her own need to hang on to her position. Two things became apparent to her as she began to objectify her experience. First, not only was she afraid of her family's anger, but even more important, she became aware of her fear they wouldn't like her or approve of her if she didn't do things for them. She felt she was valued not for herself, but only for what she could produce. Secondly, she also discovered the payoff she received in playing Cinderella, namely, the amount of power and control she was able to gather. She was forced to face the possibility that if she relinquished tasks to others, she would also have to give up the right to determine how and when tasks would be performed. She, who saw herself as quite helpless in both families, experienced her own manipulative power and control. This, of course, was a major issue in her struggles with her sons over their homework and school performance.

Another change strategy which can be most useful is the reversal. Both roles and other kinds of behavioral sequences and transactions may be reversed. The competent and extremely independent sister may ask for help. The radical son may take a cautious stance with his father, the pursuer may distance, the young adult who is expected to come home for a weekly ritual meal may invite his parents for dinner in his apartment. Reversals are effective, both because the client who performs the reversal has a new experience of reality and because in transactional deviation-amplifying sequences, the reversal interrupts and can even turn around the relationship.

Helen dreaded spending time with her mother, who acted toward her daughter in a competitive and critical way. Helen's response was to be defensive and sullen, and not infrequently to make subtle and demeaning remarks to herself. Although Helen was able to shrug off some of her mother's critical attacks, her most vulnerable area was her own role as a mother. Her mother criticized Helen's children, comparing them unfavorably to her other grandchildren, commenting that she couldn't understand why Helen handled things as she did. The daughter would become furious and the mother would respond that she was only trying to help, that Helen was "oversensitive."

Although this hostile transaction was expressive of a complex network of dynamics in both the nuclear family and in Helen's mother's family of origin, Helen and her coach decided to try a reversal to see if the interaction could be interrupted. Instead of being angry, hostile, and defensive, Helen decided to ask her mother for advice and help. She chose a genuine area of concern, a problem she was having with her nine-year-old son, and when her mother next visited and began listing her concerns about her grandson's progress, Helen immediately preempted the old pattern by presenting her problem and asking for help.

The grandmother rose to the occasion, admitting her own uncertainty about how the issue should be handled, and the two women were able to share ideas about the issue. The grandmother even minimized the youngster's difficulty, commenting that she thought Helen had done an exceptionally good job raising her children. Even more remarkably, as Helen was able to maintain her new position over the two-day visit, her mother, who generally presented a superior and self-satisfied facade, began to drop some of this defensive behavior, sharing with Helen her loneliness and deep feelings of disappointment in her own life. This visit initiated a new kind of interaction between Helen and her mother and, although there were times when the old patterns reemerged, they had both experienced a different kind of relationship which now became a real option for them.

Devising reversals is not difficult. Planning sessions begin with an exploration and description of the client's immediate reaction or habitual behavior in a situation, followed by the prescription, "Do the opposite." The coach and client then identify and plan exactly what the "opposite" would entail. Rehearsals and role playing can also be helpful.

Although reversals may be easy to plan, they are difficult to maintain, and therefore, as we cautioned earlier, the client should keep visits short, planning "time outs" to make the maintenance of the new stance more possible.

ALTERING THE CONTENT OF COMMUNICATION

Another strategy for change is the exposure of secrets and the open discussion of forbidden topics. Toxic events and themes in intergenerational family systems are often shrouded in secrecy, distorted by misinformation, and made even more powerful and threatening because they are cut off from the family discourse. Deaths, alcoholism, mental illness, suicide, divorce, incest, illegitimacy, illness, adoption, business failures, deviance of any kind, battles over money are all examples of toxic issues which may become skeletons in the family closet. Sometimes the oppressive presence of these avoided issues interrupts the potential for clear and open communication of any kind in the family. It is almost as if communication must be tightly controlled so the secret will not emerge.

A major change strategy which can open up the communication system and free the client from the power of the unspoken is the intentional mentioning of secrets and of forbidden topics. Usually, in time and with support and practice, the client is able to sit down with the salient figure and broach the difficult subject. Not infrequently, when the subject is finally approached, the reality is discovered to be far less devastating than were the fantasies. Often a client's response to demystification has been, "Is that all? I always thought it was something terrible."

At times the anxiety over opening up the subject is so great that a joint appointment is arranged with the client and the salient family figure. In such a situation, both participants can make use of the support of the worker in dealing with the painful or explosive issue.

The opening up of toxic subjects may be a brief but meaningful mention of the forbidden subject.

George opened Thanksgiving dinner with a prayer mentioning his mother, who had died five months previously. The family, to protect his father and the grandchildren, had colluded in a conspiracy of silence about the loss of this important person.

Other interventions may be quite elaborate.

Janet, who had been born after her parents were married only four or five months, had been burdened by the fact that her birth was a toxic issue in the family. The parents' forced marriage had been one of considerable conflict and unhappiness, for which Janet felt uneasily responsible. The circumstances of both the birth and the marriage were never discussed, the parents's anniversary never celebrated, and in fact, the shame and anger about the precipitous pregnancy were so pervasive that Janet and her siblings didn't even know the anniversary date.

Inspired by Rabbi Friedman's surprise birthday party for his mother's seventieth birthday in a family where age was a toxic issue (1971), Janet took leadership in planning and (after many complications) executing a fortieth wedding anniversary party for her parents. Not only was the shameful toxic issue uncovered, but it was celebrated.

Throughout this volume, other examples of exploring forbidden and secret topics will be presented, for this is a key strategy in many case situations, not only in work with the family of origin but also in bringing about change in the here-and-now family structure, communication patterns, and governing processes. However, the establishment and working through of the connections with a key figure in the family who is dead may be the most important and valuable portion of the work.

ESTABLISHING CONNECTIONS WITH THE DEAD

Some clients believe that work with the family of origin is either hopeless or meaningless,in situations where significant figures, particularly parents, have died or seem inaccessible for other reasons. A client may ask, "How can I ever resolve my issues with my father? He died when I was sixteen," or comment, "I have no interest in knowing my mother. She left us when I was seven and as far as I'm concerned she doesn't exist."

Some clients have lost one or both parents through divorce or abandonment and, of course, many adopted people have never known their birth parents at all. For reasons, then, of death or remoteness, these figures seem totally unavailable, and frequently clients consider them insignificant or unimportant in their lives.

It may take some time before such clients understand or are willing to acknowledge the impact these painful losses have on their lives, their current relationships, or their sense of themselves. In many situations, establishing connections and dealing with these often shadowy but powerful figures takes place after other work has been done. It may, however, be the turning point in the client's family work, the most effective strategy for change.

Barbara's work with her family of origin illustrates the value of establishing connections with lost major figures.

Barbara sought help in the early months of pregnancy. She was anxious and depressed, although ostensibly delighted to be pregnant. In doing her genogram, the source of some of her anxiety became apparent. An only child, she had lost her mother through death when she was thirteen. Her mother, too, had lost *her* mother during her childhood. In exploring this recurrence, Barbara said that she felt so sad because all she could think of was her poor child, growing up without a mother. She fervently hoped the child was a boy, both because it would break the intergenerational pattern and also because she reported that she had a terrible relationship with her mother.

Barbara, herself a sensitive, warm, and nurturing person, had no memory of her mother before the older woman had developed her final illness, and could only recall some early adolescent struggles and resentment about the demands the illness placed on her. The coach hypothesized that this was a one-dimensional view of the mother–daughter relationship and that she had, perhaps, held on to her angry and rebellious feelings to defend herself from the pain of mourning and loss.

Throughout the pregnancy, Barbara worked hard to learn about her mother. Her father had died three years earlier but some of her mother's relatives were available and Barbara visited them. Some old photographs were found of her mother as a girl, and of particular significance, she discovered among her father's possessions her own baby book in which the record of her early years had been faithfully and lovingly recorded by her mother.

The search was freeing and also painful, and Barbara's resistance was demonstrated by the fact that she "forgot" that her mother's best friend lived in a nearby community and would be an invaluable contact. Eventually, she did visit this friend, who had been their neighbor during the first eight years of her life, and who had spent many hours with Barbara and her mother. They reminisced and cried together and this visit, more than anything else, brought back memories of those early years.

This much of the work had been done before Barbara's daughter was born. By then, she was able to let herself know how she had longed for a daughter. She had also sufficiently differentiated herself from her relationship with her mother that she no longer saw the birth of a child as the harbinger of an early death.

On the first Mother's Day after her daughter's birth she sat down and wrote her mother a long letter, recording her thoughts and feelings as a daughter and, now, as a mother.

It is never too late to settle these issues, as demonstrated by a man who sought to renew emotional ties with his mother many years after her death.

The father of a client, inspired by his daughter's family work, reconnected with his mother who had been dead for almost seventy years. In his very early childhood, his father received employment abroad and moved the family to a foreign country. After four years, the mother had died and the children had returned home. They were raised primarily by their paternal grandmother. Sixty-eight years later, the client's father, without benefit of coaching, traveled for the first time to that foreign land, and although he was unable to find his mother's grave, he spent two days in the small town where they had lived, visited the school he had attended, and found the house where they had lived. Through this visit, he built a bridge across the rupture in his life that was occasioned by the death of his mother, the abrupt loss of his home, and to some extent a separation from his father. Following that trip, he reconnected with his only surviving sibling, from whom he had been estranged for a number of years.

There are many routes that may be taken by the client to reconnect with the lost person. Pictures, journals, letters, and other records which have been preserved are documents which can provide important information. Visits to old homes, neighborhoods, and discussions with friends and relatives who were close to the person furnish further data and build bridges. Visits to graves are particularly important, as such visits symbolically provide as close a connection as may be possible. One twelve-year-old portrayed this bond then he wrote a short note to his dead mother, had it laminated, and left it at her grave. Peter, whose family work we present in detail toward the end of this chapter, describes his visit to his mother's grave as the key intervention in his long and active program of family work.

Sometimes the cutoff from whole portions of the family is so complete and involves so much emotional pain that it takes considerable energy and creativity to make connections. For example, we have worked with several young adult children of people who survived the Holocaust of World War II; these children have gently but persistently worked with their parents to gain knowledge about and connection with the lost family.

In one situation, for the daughter of a survivor the path seemed completely blocked. Her father, the sole survivor in his family, had died three years earlier and had never spoken of his family. This was particularly difficult for the client, who was the child in the family most clearly identified with her father's side. In fact, she had been named after her father's mother. It seemed that her only source of information was her mother, but her mother's reports were biased by many years of an angry and bitter marital relationship. Sally, the client, did talk to one friend of her father, but her father, a reclusive person, had also shared little real communication with this friend.

Despite many obstacles, Sally began to establish a link with her father and the lost family. First, she began to learn about the history and the culture of the people and the area in Russia from which her father had come. She began to remember trips with her father to shops on the Lower East Side of New York where they would buy special cakes that he said were like those his mother had made when he was a boy. When she became acquainted with an emigré from the same area, she described this treat, obtained the recipe and with great ceremony baked this delicacy, bringing some to her coach. In her spare time, she volunteered her services in working to help resettle the new wave of Jewish emigrés from Russia and even began to study Russian.

Initially, Sally's mother was not supportive of her search. However, after some time she reported to her daughter that she had found a book of pictures that Sally's father had among his possessions. The book turned out to be a carefully put-together album, done shortly before his death, of pictures of his family—pictures she didn't even know existed.

Connections with the dead may go beyond coming to terms with one or two key figures, and may extend to one's cultural heritage and the history and experiences of one's ancestors, as in the case of Alex Haley's search for his roots. For some, reading about the family's historical and cultural heritage is enriching, and many useful volumes of fiction and nonfiction can contribute to this search process.

There are many other ways individuals and families can be helped to come to terms with the dead. Strategies which promote a more complete mourning of the loss may be needed, such as individual or family sessions which encourage operational mourning. Carefully planned rituals may be designed and executed which help to complete the mourning process, and which, at the same time, may also challenge the existing structure of the family. Such rituals will be described in chapter 13, which focuses on the inner family system as a target and context for change.

Interviews with Families of Origin

One of the most powerful and productive intervention strategies is that of interviewing the adult client with one or more members of his or her family of origin.[1] These sessions, almost without exception, prove valuable in at least three ways, in addition to the overall goal of enhancing the potential for greater differentiation. First, the opportunity to observe the client in actual interaction with parents and siblings communicates assessment information in a way that neither dozens of individual sessions nor thousands of words are likely to express.

In one mother–daughter session, as the two women were reminiscing about the client's adolescent years they began to argue about which of them had had particular experiences, felt particular feelings, or thought particular thoughts. This dramatic display of fusion in the relationship helped the worker better understand the client's depression, her sense of isolation and loneliness, and her difficulty in defining a self in relation to others or in relation to a career, and it led to the development of "I positions," that is, better definitions of herself in relation to her mother and thus to others.

In a second example, another such session also yielded important new information.

In a session with the parents and adult siblings of a young black male client who had complained of not being able to talk to his father, of always feeling intellectually inferior, and of not being "good enough," the worker noted that the father, a brilliant attorney, actually was subtly using confusing language in order to keep everyone in the family at bay and to avoid making any kind of feeling statement or taking an "I position." The mother, who had been described as "crazy" and a burden to the father, actually made far more sense than her husband, although she behaved rather childishly and seemed to have found her haven in the fusion with a retarded sibling of the client. The client, a mental health professional, began to relate his father's communication difficulties to his own sense of helplessness and inferiority and thus, armed with a better understanding and empathy for both parents, was able to plan some new ways of developing clearer communication with his parents.

Second, sessions with the family of origin provide the opportunity for obtaining a more diverse perspective on the family history and relationships, and the client's place in them, and for clarifying intergenerational confusions and misperceptions which are often holdovers from childhood. In every such session, even if the client has been able to obtain considerable data previously, new historical facts invariably surface which shed light on current family patterns and issues.

Third, and most importantly, these meetings provide a special kind of opportunity for clients to confront directly the problems they have been unable to solve abstractly.

Helen, whose husband did not wish to participate in marital work, became extremely anxious and angry whenever her husband planned a business trip, an event which occurred quite frequently because of the nature of his work, and which triggered such bitter fights that the marriage was threatened. During the course of her family-of-origin work, Helen told a story about her mother's life. It seems her mother, as a young girl of seventeen in Poland, became engaged to an older man of another religion. Her mother, Helen's grandmother, strongly disapproved. The grandmother, who it seems was unhappy in her own marriage, persuaded Helen's mother to accompany her on a visit to the United States to visit her other, elder daughter, who had emigrated. The engagement ring was pawned to help pay for the passage, with the promise that it would be redeemed upon their return. They never went back to Poland. Helen's grandmother had planned to leave both of the "undesirable" men behind. Within a few months Helen's mother's father died and thus her mother was never to see her father or her fiance again.

Helen remembered her grandmother as a fiercely dominating woman. She was certain her mother had never talked to her grandmother about her manipulation, and she could only guess at what her mother's intense but repressed feelings must have been. Helen had never been able to talk about it with her mother, since her mother would quickly close off any questions by saying, "That was in the past." During a joint session with Helen and her mother, the worker asked a rather innocuous question about the older woman's early life in Poland and her emigration to the United States. Helen's mother began to sob, and much of the session was devoted to her reliving this experience, accompanied by the still-vivid feeling of loss and rage. This operational mourning process freed Helen from carrying into her generation the grief, anger, and the anxiety connected to an earlier separation.

The proposing and planning of these kinds of meetings invariably stimulates considerable anxiety. However, there are several ways the worker can help create an atmosphere in which the client progresses toward accepting the idea and ultimately arranging family-of-origin sessions. It is helpful to suggest, even in the initial contact, as the worker describes his or her family orientation, that at some point the client may want to consider a session or two together with his parents, siblings, or other significant relatives; the worker might stress that this kind of meeting is invaluable in terms of gaining a fuller understanding of the family and the client. The client may gradually gain courage as he or she identifies the issues for work and makes beginning interventions in relationships with family-of-origin members.

Some clients of course, strongly object to the entire idea, and others are fiercely protective of their parents. Framo, who is noted for his work in conjoint sessions with families of origin, details a number of strategies for defusing the client's resistance. He "sticks to the idea tenaciously, bringing it up at every opportunity as a goal that will contribute to growth more than any other thing they can do," using persuasion, sarcasm, and even taunting. His "heavy artillery" consists of "having them imagine that their mother or father has just died and they are standing by the grave. What would they regret never having said to the dead parent? I tell them, 'But they are still alive; now you have the chance' " (1976:199).

If parents or siblings live in another community or state, we try to determine in advance when they will be visiting, preparing far ahead of time how the client will propose the session to the family, and planning the goals for the session itself. It is important to remember that the family has not contracted for therapy and the goal of the session is neither to induct them into a therapeutic relationship nor to imply in any way that they are to blame for the client's unresolved concerns. They are asked to participate because their contribution will be of great value to the client.

The client is given a large share of the responsibility for determining the goals and for planning how these goals might be achieved in the session: what questions are to be asked, what relationships or events to be addressed, what feelings expressed. Framo advises against having the spouse of a client participate because it permits and even encourages the family of origin to talk about the couple's marital or parenting difficulties, thus diverting them from the main purpose.

We heartily agree with Framo, who says, "You can and should go home again." Conjoint sessions with clients and members of their families of origin provide the opportunity for a giant step toward achieving some resolution of intergenerational family issues, unpaid debts, or, in Bowen's word, "stuck-togetherness," as family members newly experience each other in ways which may be more open and more genuine.

The Role of the Worker

The use of the worker–client relationship as a primary medium for change has long been accepted in social casework practice. Thus, reinterpreting the role of the worker as "coach" requires a shift in thinking for most practitioners, since it moves the relationship from center stage to a rather minor part in the wings. This does not mean that the worker should no longer project empathy, warmth, hope, caring, and those other qualities considered essential to the worker–client relationship, but it does mean that the revised objective is to keep the intense emotional issues among the family members and to help the client come to terms with those relationships, not through the interaction between client and professional, but in real life with the real family figures.

This brings us to transference. In general, social workers are educated at least to recognize transference issues if not to use casework as a method for resolving them. A major principle in Bowen family systems work, and in our own Bowen-inspired work, is that transference should be avoided. This is not to say that transference reactions will not occur, but rather that they are not to be exploited, not to be seen as the basic materials for work; rather they are for the most part ignored as diversionary tactics which help avoid the difficulties or anxiety inherent in one's family work. The responsibility of the worker is to keep the focus on the real-life figures, whose importance to the client tends to help keep the coach less triangulated into the intense family system and thus out of the transference. As Bowen points out, the effort is to reduce the assigned and assumed importance of the therapist:

> The more the relationship is endowed with high emotionality, messianic qualities, exaggerated promises, and evangelism, the more change can be sudden and magical, and the less likely it is to be long term. The lower the emotionality and the more the relationship deals in reality, the more likely the change is to come slowly and to be solid and long lasting (1978:345).

It would certainly seen incongruent, when the goal of the work is increased differentiation and autonomy, to consider a highly emotional, fused, and dependent relationship with the worker as the route to such growth.

While this may seem only a subtle difference in the worker–client relationship, it is often a difficult shift to make for those trained and experienced in psychodynamically oriented modes. In our own work it has proven to be a shift which is refreshing, freeing, and helpful to clients.

In making use of the family of origin as a resource for change, the coach performs several tasks. First, adopting a teacher role, or the role of expert in family systems, the coach helps the client learn about family systems and the major principles of their operation. Obviously, this teaching does not come in the form of a didactic lecture but is woven into the study of the client's own family as general principles are exemplified. Second, the coach adopts with the client the role of fellow explorer or researcher, gathering data, devising means of recovering missing information, and drawing maps of the family as it emerges. Third, the coach, again with the client, adopts the role of strategist, helping with the selection of possible entry points and interventions. This process includes detailed and specific planning in order to arrive at an objective structure which helps to protect the client from being drawn into the system. Careful planning, as we have suggested, can and often does include a day-by-day and even hour-by-hour outline of a visit home, including planned periods of absence from the family, questions to be asked, particular people to talk with, and subjects to be broached. A fourth role that the coach sometimes adopts is the role of supporter or "cheerleader." However, this role must be assumed with caution. The coach must not invest interest too heavily in the client's task, as then client and coach are moving toward fusion and the danger is that the client will begin to do the work for the coach's approval rather than for the self.

The worker may consider the following stances, which we have found useful. First, from the initial contact on, it is important to communicate one's own conviction about the meaning and importance of families. As the client discusses current conflicts and problems, the worker can comment that these may have something to do with unresolved family issues. As was mentioned in chapter 10, as family information emerges during the first interview, the worker can begin to include it in a genogram on a large piece of paper. This act tends to pique the client's curiosity and the worker can comment that perhaps later it might be helpful to complete the family map. Thus the groundwork is laid for turning to family work when the pressure of present issues has been alleviated.

Another set of messages which the worker conveys to clients is that *all* families are interesting, indeed fascinating, and of course often difficult, and that the issues the client is dealing with are issues all people encounter in their family relationships. These messages help avoid a judgmental stance on "good" or "bad" families, and also tend to stimulate whatever propensity the client may have to become a student of his or her family.

Third, it is important to take a realistic position on the difficulty of the tasks and the possibility of change. Clients tend to become both enthusiastic and overly ambitious and must therefore be encouraged to go slowly. On the other hand, when people feel hopeless about the possibility of any movement, the worker can point out that although it may be possible to make only very minute changes in differentiation or in family relationships, these tiny changes can make considerable difference in daily life.

The coach–client relationship may be described as egalitarian; it is focused on the client's autonomy and assumes his or her responsibility for the work. The coach has knowledge about family systems and experience in the coaching process, but no magic and no special authority; the client, on the other hand, is an expert on his or her own family system. Finally, the fact that the main efforts for change are occurring outside the office means that the amount of time spent with the coach can often be reduced. Once the tasks of learning, assessing, and planning have been well launched, it is often possible to see people on a biweekly or monthly basis or, even less frequently, on an "as needed" consulting basis.

Peter's Family-of-Origin Work

Family-of-origin work can perhaps best be understood in all its complexity and potential richness through a detailed examination of a single individual's protracted effort to connect with and differentiate from his family of origin. The following extensive case example summarizes the major interventions and steps taken over a three-year period by Peter.

Peter, a high school history teacher in his late twenties, sought help primarily for problems in close relationships. He wanted to get married but was having difficulty in establishing and maintaining a committed relationship with a woman; he found himself precipitating fights and separations, unable either to tolerate intimacy or to deal with separateness. Although maintaining superficial contact with his parents and siblings, he was guarded and distant with them, and his major emotion-laden interactions consisted of occasional angry exchanges with his father. He felt stalled and frustrated in his work and, although he liked teaching, found himself restless and critical of the job and of his own performance.

Peter quite quickly became involved in family-of-origin work, carrying much of the responsibility himself and scheduling an occasional coaching session when he felt "stuck" or wanted help planning or evaluating a specific intervention. His work was guided by three interrelated directives: (1) to learn as much as possible about his family system; (2) to form a person-to-person relationship with every member of the family system; and (3) to detriangulate himself from the series of interlocking triangles of which he was a part. He worked concurrently to uncover and resolve historical issues and to alter his current family relationships. Throughout his three years of effort, the course of his work was uneven. Brief periods of intense activity were often separated by months in which little or no family work was done. The demands of everyday life and the need for periods of consolidation, as well as occasional resistance to taking an obvious but difficult next step, occasioned these hiatuses. However, at the end of three years a review of his work indicated a steady and consistent process of development. For the sake of clarity,

Peter's family work will be summarized in a more orderly way than it actually took place. In reality, during that time transactions occurred simultaneously in three systems, namely, the historical family, the here-and-now family, and Peter's current social network.

The major toxic issues to be dealt with became apparent in the early contacts with Peter when he neglected to mention until he was actually working on his genogram that he grew up in a family of remarriage and that his mother, Nancy, had died of cancer when he was three. He had always referred to his stepmother, Louise, as his mother; he was devoted to her, and was almost totally cut off from his biological mother's family which, he reported, he had never particularly liked. Further exploration revealed that the new family, consisting of Peter and his sister, Carol; their father, Charles; Louise; her son by a previous marriage, Robert; and the two children by the current marriage, had been built on the myth that the two previous marriages had never happened, that Peter's and Carol's lost mother and Robert's lost father, who had died in an automobile accident, had never existed. In fact, Peter experienced intense feelings of disloyalty and anxiety even in owning the existence of his biological mother, and reported that he never thought of her, was not curious about her, and always thought of his stepmother as his "real mother." The way these two deaths and the subsequent building of the new family had been handled was expressive of a pervasive rule in the family, namely, that negative feelings or painful issues were not to be expressed. Further, as is true in many families when there is a powerful rule against communicating about a particular subject, in Peter's family communication in general was blocked and inhibited.

A second major theme which emerged was the closeness–distance issue. Peter referred to his family as very close, and strong cohesive bonds of loyalty, affection, and responsibility to the whole were indeed apparent. However, the family had some difficulty in tolerating difference or autonomy among its members, and the three older children reacted to this tension by distancing themselves both physically and emotionally.

A third issue which emerged early in his family-of-origin work concerned Peter's relationship with his father and his role in the family. Peter had been characterized from childhood on as the "bad" child and the "different" one, and had always believed that his sister and stepbrother were favored. For him, adolescence and young adulthood had been fraught with angry struggles with his father over political and social issues. After a tour in the Peace Corps, Peter had achieved more emotional distance and was more able to control his reactivity, so that the relationship became calmer. However, his father, a very successful engineer, continued to view his son's occupation with disdain, communicating to Peter the disparaging view that teaching school was no job for a man.

The information gathered on Peter and his family is portrayed in figure 11.3.

RECONNECTING WITH MOTHER AND MOTHER'S FAMILY

A major and mutually defined long-term goal in Peter's family work was to break through the maternal cutoff and to establish connections with his

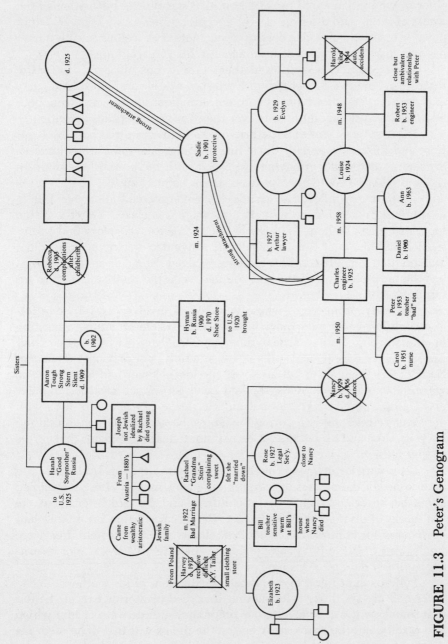

FIGURE 11.3 Peter's Genogram

deceased biological mother and her surviving family. This family consisted of his maternal grandmother in Philadelphia, his mother's two sisters (the elder of whom had cared for him and his sister during his mother's final weeks of illness and after her death) and his mother's only brother. Other possible resources included cousins of his mother as well as cousins nearer his own age, the children of his uncle and his younger aunt.

The reconnection with his mother's family took place over the entire three years and it still continuing. Each step was accompanied by anxiety and guilt on Peter's part and by subtle insinuations of disloyalty from both his father and stepmother, whenever they learned about his activities.

His first move was to write brief notes to his grandmother, his Aunts Rose and Elizabeth, and his Uncle Bill, sharing some news about himself, expressing sorrow about having lost touch with them, and holding forth the hope that he could arrange to see them before long.

All four responded. His grandmother complained about her failing health and invited him to visit. Her message was clear: "Don't wait too long, or I won't be here." His Uncle Bill's response was warm and enthusiastic. His older aunt Rose, although she responded quickly, seemed stilted and guarded in her letter. This response puzzled Peter, for he remembered her the most clearly and thought she had been the relative closest to his family.

However, Aunt Rose, whose work often involved travel, soon followed up her letter by arranging to see Peter while attending a meeting in a nearby city. In the course of their reunion, Peter learned a great deal. Rose, it became clear, had suffered considerably, not only over the loss of Nancy, her closest sister but also over the loss of Peter and his sister. She was unmarried and childless; she had been very much attached to Peter and Carol, and had taken several months' leave from her job to be with her sister and the children during the illness. He sensed that tension existed between Rose and his father, but he was not to learn until later the sources of that tension.

Peter was deeply moved by the reunion with his aunt. In this meeting he also began the process of learning about his mother. Rose reminisced about her sister and their years as children, and she told Peter about the last weeks of his mother's life. In fact, Peter learned that his mother had been cared for at home throughout the illness and that the children were finally sent to Uncle Bill's cottage during the final two weeks, not returning until ten days after his mother had died.

Perhaps most important was the clarification of his mother's illness. Peter had always thought his mother had died of uterine cancer; he felt that somehow it was related to her pregnancy and delivery of him which had taken place less than a year before the illness was first diagnosed. He learned from Rose that his mother had died of cancer of the liver. In debriefing this visit later with his coach, Peter saw at last that he had always felt he was the cause of his mother's death, that somehow he had injured her while in utero. This fantasy was reinforced by his father's disapproval and scapegoating of him.

The mystery of the cutoff from Aunt Rose was later solved, through information from both Uncle Bill and his father's genogram. After he and Bill became friends, Peter learned that his father had quite abruptly sent Rose packing shortly after his mother Nancy's death, and there were rumors that Charles (Peter's father) feared that Rose was trying to replace Nancy, not only with the children, but also with him. Rose was deeply hurt and her family rallied around her, angry that Charles was so suspicious, ungrateful, and cruel. Later Peter came to learn the probable reasons for his father's behavior and for the new family's construction of their reality. He learned that his paternal grandfather's mother had died when his grandfather was three, leaving his great-grandfather, a domineering and difficult man, with two young children, his grandfather and his infant sister. The dead wife's sister came to help out and before long, she and her brother-in-law were married. Five years later, the husband died, leaving his widow alone to care for the family, which had now grown to five. Hannah, the second wife, worked and struggled to take care of all the children. She was clearly a family heroine, by no means the legendary wicked stepmother, but rather the good and rescuing stepmother who sacrifices herself and holds the family together. When Peter's grandfather was twenty, he emigrated from Russia to the United States, worked, and sent money home to enable the whole family, including the stepmother, to follow him. In all probability, Charles saw in Rose a recreation of his great-grandmother; he feared that he might be expected to reenact this episode from his family's past; thus Rose was forced to leave. In the course of learning these facts, Peter also began to realize why he was a special favorite of this grandfather; both had lost their mothers as very young boys.

In Peter's quest for his mother, the next major move was a trip to visit his maternal grandmother Stein in Philadelphia. This was particularly difficult to do as he felt very negatively toward her and also was experiencing heightened static from his father and stepmother. But he went nevertheless, and the visit served several purposes. First, he found that his grandmother, although somewhat complaining, was a sweet and warm woman, and these qualities led him to conclude that his feelings about her had been shaped by old in-law conflicts and that he had been carrying the burden of his father's negative feelings, particularly the recriminations and accusations surrounding his mother's death. Secondly, he learned more about his mother's family, and even more importantly, about his mother. He listened to his grandmother's reminiscences with fascination, and studied pictures of his mother at every age. It was on this visit, when his grandmother cried about the death of her daughter, that Peter first experienced some of his own feelings of sadness and loss.

The next major step was, perhaps, the most difficult of all and was postponed for several months. Finally, however, Peter arranged a time alone with his father, and they talked at length about Nancy, the lost mother and wife. Peter's father reminisced about the couple's courtship at college, about their marriage, and about her illness. Peter was able to tell his father how difficult the avoidance of any mention of his mother had been, and Peter's father spoke of his own pain and devastation, his inability to talk about the loss, and his wish to protect the children. He also described his and Louise's effort to build a new family and explained their perhaps unfortunate conviction that to bury the past was best for the family. Interestingly enough, after this talk, Peter's father initiated a conversation about Nancy with Carol. Reminiscences about Nancy also began to appear occasionally in family conversations; Peter would be surprised to hear his father say, "You know, your mother used to. . ."

Peter also developed a close friendship with his Uncle Bill. Bill, also a teacher, turned out to be a sensitive and thoughtful man who shared many of Peter's interests, tastes, and political and social views. As much as he admired his father, Peter experienced a special bond with Bill and was able to interact with him in a more personal, open way. A high point in Peter's family work was a three-day camping trip which the two took together.

In reviewing his work with his mother and her family, Peter identified two major turning points, both of which had elements of ritual. The first was Peter's visit to his mother's grave. The act of finding the grave served as a partial metaphor for the entire experience, for in a dramatic example of the extent to which his father had hidden away this painful loss, Peter had been unable for many years to remember where she was buried. After calling several funeral homes he was able to obtain the information; and after considerable postponement he went, in his words, "to see my mother." He spent some time there, talking to her. When he saw the headstone he was astounded to realize that he had finally managed to get there at the very age—twenty-seven—his mother had been when she died.

The second major event was the wedding of his Aunt Elizabeth's oldest daughter, at which the entire Stein clan gathered. The wedding became, in part, a claiming ritual as the family gathered around Peter, welcoming him as the lost sheep and making him their own. Peter's only sadness was that his sister was not there; his coach had to help him understand that he could not blaze a trail for Carol; only she herself could make a decision to embark upon a similar adventure.

PETER'S WORK WITH HIS CURRENT NUCLEAR FAMILY

Peter's work with his current nuclear family took place simultaneously with his rediscovery of his maternal family, and the two events had reciprocal effects. This family was extremely cohesive and the cohesion was firmly monitored by his parents, particularly by his stepmother. Peter commented that when he was growing up the development of the family had not seemed difficult, as one might assume it would be. Each member had shoved other loyalties aside and had been captured by the strong cohesive force. Peter, perhaps more than any of his siblings, had tested the limits of the cohesiveness in his adolescence, although his teenage half brother was now showing some rebelliousness. The emphasis on the togetherness of the total group was so strong in this family that any effort to break off into dyads or other subgroups was considered divisive and greeted with suspicion. Communication in the family, including all visiting plans, was funneled through Louise, who anxiously monitored the family boundaries and screened incoming and outgoing communication. She was the switchboard.

Early interventions by Peter included strategies for bypassing Louise in establishing direct communication with each of his siblings. For example, when Louise called to tell him that his stepbrother Bob was going to be traveling nearby and wanted to see him Peter called Bob and asked him to communicate directly with him about plans. Visits were arranged with the two older siblings and Peter managed to spend time with each of them without triangulating other family members and without being drawn into old competitive struggles. The intense ambivalence in his relationships with both siblings became increasingly understandable as he recognized his father's favoritism in stimulating competition among them. Peter shared some of the factual information he had learned about the family with Carol and Bob; and Bob, interested in Peter's search, began to think about making some connections with his biological father's family.

Peter also visited his paternal grandmother, discovering animosity had long existed between her and his biological mother and her family. Grandmother Roth was extremely tied to Peter's father and had thought Nancy was not good enough for her adored son. Furthermore, she greatly objected to the fact that the Steins were less religious than the Roths. The rift was cemented when the Steins criticized the Roths for not being more helpful to Nancy during her illness. Louise, on the other hand, was a daughter of one of Grandma Roth's best friends, and, in fact, the two older women had played matchmakers.

The more Peter learned about both families, the more he became convinced that in the minds of Louise, his stepmother, and many other members of the Roth family he was seen as a Stein, resembling his mother and her family. He had clearly become the object of some of his paternal family's intensely ambivalent feelings surrounding his mother and her family. And the more he came to know his Uncle Bill, the more aware he became that he did resemble his Stein relatives in a number of ways.

As important as were the sibling and grandparent relationships, the key work was with Peter's stepmother and his father. He began with the usual assignment of writing separate rather than joint letters. Two major conversations alone with his father, one about his mother, and the other to gather genogram information, began to shift the father–son relationship, opening the way for less guarded communication in general.

The major intervention with his family, however, came about as a result of a family crisis and Peter's readiness to make use of the crisis for growth and change. Peter's father was hospitalized quite suddenly for emergency surgery. The word went out that no one was to come home. This response, of course, was congruent with the family rule that death or illness was to be denied and the children were to be protected through exclusion from emotionally painful situations.

Peter immediately flew home, arriving at the hospital to discover that there had been some complications, and that his father was critically ill and in intensive care. As he sat with his stepmother, anxiously awaiting news of his father's progress, her thoughts returned to another time when she had been called to the hospital after her first husband's fatal accident, and she remembered her terrible fear as she sat and waited while he hovered between life and death. She talked with Peter for the first time about that loss, grieving in a sense, for both husbands at once. Peter also spoke of his mother and of his recent contacts with her family, and Louise was able to recognize that in their effort to protect the children and to build a new family, and (she knew now) to protect herself and Charles from their pain, the two had cut the children off from important connections. She even admitted to Peter her deep fear that she could never really measure up to Nancy who had been so vivacious, beautiful, and creative, while she saw herself as a rather plain and humdrum housewife. Peter was able to give her reassurance of his love and his thankfulness that it was she who had become his second mother. It is possible, Peter reminded her, to have two mothers.

Peter's father recovered and, although there was no miraculous change in his relationship with his stepmother, and although she continued to lapse occasionally into controlling and intrusive behavior, Peter no longer reacted as he had in the past. The trip had another important effect. Peter, who had been characterized as the rebellious one, the selfish one, the different one, was now the one who had come to his father's and mother's side as the caring and attentive son.

Sometime later, another major event occurred which was at once an intervention and an outcome, perhaps of the family work he was doing. Peter went home to tell his parents of his plan to marry a young woman he had been seeing for over a year. He knew there would be fireworks as she was not Jewish, and fireworks there were. However, Peter was able to maintain his position without anger or reactiveness. He did not allow himself to participate in an angry and rebellious struggle nor did he storm out of the house, as was his former style. He maintained his "I" position, only slipping into a self-defensive posture when he could not resist saying, half in jest, but with a significance that was not lost on his parents, "After all, Grandma Stein's father was a Lutheran!"

Peter says this about the impact of his family work: "It has turned my life around." Dealing with the unresolved issues and "invisible" loyalties attached to the loss of his mother seemed to free him enough that he could at last form a relationship with a woman, and thus the couple is managing distance–closeness issues well. Better resolution of these issues was also facilitated, he thinks, by his scaling of the emotional wall between himself and his father. His feelings about his chosen profession have also improved, partly because he has ceased comparing himself unfavorably with his father and brother. Peter has become comfortable with the idea that there is more than one way of being a man, an idea traceable at least in part to his renewed relationship and identification with Uncle Bill.

Peter's marrying outside his faith has been a difficult issue, one which provokes crisis in many families, and which in Peter's family has reinforced the old conflict between the Roths and the Steins. Peter has not allowed this conflict to bring about a new period of alienation between him and his family, however, and although his parents are not overjoyed, they accept his fiancée and his right to make his own decision.

The Worker's Own Family

R. D. Laing has said, "Till one can see the 'Family' in oneself, one can see neither oneself or any family clearly" (1961:15). The return to the family of origin as a means for enhancing differentiation began as a part of the training program at the Georgetown Family Center, following Bowen's report of the work he did in relation to his own family (1978:486–518). The study of—and active work with—the trainee's own family of origin continues to be a part of training in family therapy at Georgetown and in other training programs influenced by the Bowen model. Reports of such efforts have appeared in the family literature (Colon, 1973; Carter and Orfanidis, 1976; Georgetown Family Symposia, vol. 2, 1977; vol. 3, 1978).

Although the issue of the need for family-of-origin work on the part of the worker is a controversial one in the field of family therapy, our experiences, both personally and through the work of students, trainees, and colleagues suggests that, if not absolutely necessary, such work can be extremely valuable in preparing one to help others. One cannot in quite any other way gain the same kind of understanding of the power of the intergenerational family system as one can in coming face-to-face with the power of one's own family. Further, there is no better way to appreciate both the difficulty and the liberating effect of differentiating oneself from the family of origin than through struggling with one's own family issues. Finally, it would seem to us artificial and somehow false to act as a coach to clients as they embark upon journeys which we ourselves have not even attempted. As we remarked earlier, it can be a humbling but also exhilarating experience which automatically enhances respect for clients and enables the worker to understand others' individual difficulties and family problems in a very different way.

A worker can approach such study in a number of ways. Most obviously one can seek the help of an experienced coach. Many of our colleagues join with other mental health professionals in family-of-origin groups led either by themselves or by an experienced practitioner. These groups can be formed from workers in a single agency, or may consist of interested colleagues from several settings. Others have simply called on friends in social work for help and ideas in planning strategies for change.

In our own work in teaching, training, and consultation, we encourage all those who would be family-centered practitioners to begin work on their family genograms. The work itself entails an opening of the family system as the trainee crosses cutoffs and engages in person-to-person discussions in the course of doing family research. For some, the search is perfunctory and leads nowhere, because the prohibitions against knowing and changing are too overwhelming. For many, however, this family study begins a process that becomes a vital part of the searcher's professional and personal life. In family classes, we offer an optional final assignment in which students begin a genogram of their families of origin, make an analysis of the genogram, and plan, execute, and evaluate one very small interventive step. Although students are warned of the difficulties inherent in this option, many elect to complete this assignment, and almost all report that it has been the most important professional and personal learning experience in their social work education (Hartman and Laird, 1977).

Family of Origin Work: A Summary

This chapter has covered in some detail the range of change strategies and intervention techniques involved in using the family of origin as a resource for change. This approach to change, inspired by Bowen's theory of family systems, can be useful to social work practitioners in a wide range of settings and in the performance of a variety of professional tasks. When one adopts the view of the family as a powerful intergenerational system and integrates the understanding of fusion and differentiation, triangles, and cutoffs, practice develops in a unique way.

The most readily apparent application of family-of-origin work is to family counseling and mental health agencies. However, intergenerational family assessment and intervention can shape social work practice in many other kinds of settings. As we have presented such work here, a full family study can become a long-term affair, but intergenerational hypotheses and strategies for change can be used in short-term work as well, and can inform or supplement other practice foci. This point will become more clear in chapter 15 which describes family-centered work in aging and health care.

It is certainly too early and the data too sparse to advance any claims concerning when, with whom, and with what kinds of problems this approach is most useful, or whether it is more or less effective than other family-centered approaches. Furthermore, it is uncertain whether it is most effective when used alone or in combination with other approaches. Different practitioners are taking different routes. As the organization of this book implies, we propose a multiple approach which encompasses ecological, family, and intergenerational dimensions. We have, however, used a family-of-origin emphasis exclusively with some clients, as well as in combination with theories and techniques drawn from other models of family therapy or from various models of social work practice.

The family-of-origin emphasis can be useful in work with couples, with total families, and with unrelated people of different ages facing different developmental and life tasks. It is further uniquely useful as a family approach in work with individuals—such as the young adult dealing with problems of identity and intimacy, the husband or wife whose marital relationship is suffering as a result of transmitted family patterns, or the older adult facing a midlife reevaluation and the aging and loss of parents.

Some clients may be enmeshed in their family systems and others almost totally cut off. And some will have lost most of their families through death, necessitating, as we discussed earlier, special creativity in designing the assessment and intervention process.

It is important to remember that differentiation is a natural growth process which begins at birth and continues, if unobstructed, throughout life. Thus problems and difficulties which are the result of interrupted growth and development are seen by us as adaptive strategies rather than as disease processes. Therapeutic intervention is aimed at removing obstacles to growth and at helping the individual to enhance differentiation through his own efforts within the family system. Life experience is the primary instrument for change. The clients work out their troublesome relationships face-to-face with the persons involved, rather than by transference in the office of the worker. The coach and the client work as partners in this enterprise, with the client carrying major responsibility for the effort at actual change.

A family-of-origin approach is highly congruent with the traditional interest of social work in the family and its emphasis on the importance of history. The skills demanded in this work, namely historical investigation, support and enabling, and development of a reality-based egalitarian relationship, are all a part of the heritage and repertoire of our profession. Finally, our reliance on the client as the primary architect and builder of the change effort gives genuine substance to the value which this profession places on the individual's right to work out his or her own destiny.

Inside the Family: Inner System Assessment

WE NOW TURN OUR FOCUS to the center of our concern, the intrafamilial system. This intimate constellation shares a history, and is a complex intertwining of relationships, patterns of behavior, rules, symmetries, complementarities, and triangles. No matter how well we might come to know each of its members separately, with all of his strengths, concerns, foibles, and styles of behavior, we would be unable to explain the family altogether. For the family is somehow a thing larger than the sum of its individual members; it emerges out of multiple sequences of permutations and combinations which it in turn works back upon, defining and shaping individual destinies. Making sense of this elusive entity is the task of assessment.

Assessment is an active process of ordering data, of seeking out connections and meanings, and of formulating hypotheses which give direction to action. Assessment of the inner family system draws upon much that has already been presented in this volume. As noted earlier, the assessment process consists of the consideration of information about a particular family in the light of theory about families; thus it is that this chapter relies heavily on the discussion of family theory presented in chapter 5, pulling out from it constructs that impart shape and meaning to particular observations. Moreover, assessment begins from the first moment of contact with a family; thus, we rely also on information presented in chapter 7, which describes the beginning phases of work with families.

269

Further, assessment is inexorably bound to the information-gathering process; it is inseparable from family interviewing which is a circular or feedback process of hypothesis-making, testing and modifying. Indeed, we have made artificial divisions in separating closely interrelated dimensions of the family in space and through time. Therefore, the information presented in the other two chapters on assessment has important implications for understanding the inner family system. For example, as we develop an assessment of a family's relationship with its environment, much about its inner system also becomes clear. The nature of the boundary between a family and the individuals in the family, who in turn interact variously with the world outside, contributes important information to understanding the family itself. Finally, a study of the intergenerational system enriches our understanding of the roles, rules, communication patterns, and beliefs which characterize the family.

In the following discussion of the assessment of the inner family system, these earlier materials will be drawn upon, but repetition will be avoided. Our main tasks in this chapter are to demonstrate through example and discussion how the theory becomes concretized through application to particular families, and to present examples of the kinds of questions we ask ourselves to guide us in family system assessment. Finally, as in ecological and intergenerational assessment, simulations will be presented which can help worker and family together achieve a more systemic view of the ongoing processes within families.

To help provide an overview of the elaborate assessment materials presented in this volume, we have arranged the major points in detailed outline form. The reader may find this "Outline for Family Assessment," which follows chapter 14, helpful in organizing her thoughts about the multiple aspects of assessment. However, we caution against using the outline as an inflexible interviewing or recording schedule. It is presented as a thinking aid for the worker confronted with a vast amount of rich and confusing data.

Family Boundaries

As one moves from outside to inside the family system, one crosses an invisible but very important boundary which differentiates the outer world from the inner family system. Perhaps the first assessment task is to determine to what extent this boundary is open or closed and to what extent it is clearly marked. This major assessment issue was explicated in our chapters on family–environment transactions as we followed the fortunes of the Embrees, the Rauers, and the Taylors. In assessing family boundaries, several family theorists have suggested that it is only at the extremes of openness and closedness that the nature of the boundary becomes problematic for a family. In fact, it may well be that the most important characteristics to assess regarding boundaries are clarity and flexibility. Clarity provides family members with clear and unambivalent messages about the regulation of members, space, distance, and relationship inside, outside, and across family boundaries. Flexibility means that the boundary may alter and shift in adaptive ways as the circumstances and needs of the family change.

Another dimension in assessing the nature of family boundaries is to note who is included within the intimate family social network. In some families, members rely heavily on nuclear family members alone to meet their needs for family connectedness and support. Other families include grandparents or members of the larger extended family. This issue has relevance in assessment since, in those situations where the nuclear family is very small, the resources in terms of sheer numbers are limited. In a relatively closed system, however, it makes considerable difference if that system includes not only a father, mother, and children, but also an extended family of some thirty or forty members.

For example, in an initial interview with a black couple who were applying to adopt a child, the interviewer, who was using the eco-map, began to be concerned about the extent to which the family seemed isolated. Friends, neighbors, community, or cultural activities were not an important part of their life space. However, when the subject of the extended family came up, it became apparent that this family was part of a complex social network characterized by active interchanges within a large and varied kinship group. In the worker's assessment of such groups, cultural norms concerning who is and is not to be trusted and included for particular family purposes are of course highly significant.

Separateness and Connectedness: Three-Dimensional Approach

Intimately connected with the issue of family boundaries, yet requiring a shift in perspective, is the assessment of separateness and connectedness in family systems. Drawing from the various views of this dual topic described in chapter 5, we would like to suggest the following rather pragmatic scheme for looking at it in families. Although our scheme is characterized by considerable overlapping, we have found it a useful approach to this central aspect of family relatedness.

The first dimension of our approach focuses on the family as a system and primarily examines the nature of the boundaries between subsystems within that system. In assessing this level, we use Minuchin's and Olson's bipolar scale from enmeshment to disengagement.

The second dimension relates to the affective component of interpersonal relationships among family members, ascertaining the extent to which people seem to care for or about one another.

The third dimension makes use of Bowen's concepts of differentiation and fusion and assesses the extent to which people in the family are able to maintain a solid sense of self in relationships with one another and with the family system.

ENMESHMENT AND DISENGAGEMENT: FAMILY SYSTEM

In assessing separateness and connectedness in the family as a system, the first question to be asked is, "Where should this family be placed on the continuum from enmeshment to disengagement?" In making this assessment, it is helpful to observe the way families verbally and nonverbally define the boundaries and relationships between each person and between different groups within the family. While conducting interviews we question ourselves: Do family members speak for each other, or do they respect the fact that the other, even a child, may have separate views? Does mother interrupt questions to her twelve-year-old son by explaining to the family worker what Bobby thinks and feels? Does Bobby look anxiously to mother or father for help whenever he is directly spoken to by the worker? Does father "worry" too much about ordinary activities and behaviors of the children? Are the parents overinvolved in every aspect or decision to be made in the child's life? Does the family tolerate differences, or must time, interests, opinions, and activities be shared?

The answers to the above questions give us clues concerning the extent to which appropriately firm boundaries exist in the family. At the other end of the continuum is the disengaged family, which may be identified by the lack of meaningful interaction and by rigid and closed boundaries between systems. If we want to learn whether a family is disengaged, we ask: Do family members seem impervious to or insensitive to one another? Do they block each other's communications or avoid close contact, either emotional or physical or both? Some families, as Bowen has pointed out, are characterized by an "emotional divorce" between the parents. Such couples may assure the worker and the world that they have no problems, they have always been happily married, they rarely disagree, but careful observation discloses that there is little or no affect or energy passing between them. They rarely look at or respond to each other in any but the most formal ways.

The way the family uses space in the interviewing room can be a valuable clue to the extent of enmeshment or disengagement in the family, as well as to the existence of powerful subsystems and triangles, family splits and alignments, and so on. Kantor and Lehr (1975), among others, have demonstrated that the family's use of physical space in their household is an aid in assessment. We ask questions such as these: Are family members allowed to close their bedroom doors? Do family members enter the bathroom when it is being used by another? Do people open each other's mail? Do family members have private places—a box, a drawer, a journal—which are respected by the others? What are the sleeping and the eating arrangements? Do children frequently spend the night in their parents' bed? Does the family have meals together? The answers to all of these questions can provide clues which lead to an assessment of the degree of enmeshment or disengagement that exists within a family, or between subsystems within the family.

When we later look at the family's organization of subsystems, we will see that the boundaries between different subsystems may exemplify different levels of enmeshment or disengagement, and that these are related to the nature of the interaction across the family's external boundaries. Just as a closed system moves toward entropy—or lack of differentiation among its parts—the highly enmeshed family has relatively closed external boundaries and is spatially isolated; and its members are not expected or allowed to make meaningful connections outside the family system. This state of affairs is understandable because, as Karpel points out, in enmeshed systems the loss of the other is experienced as the loss of the self. "Growth, change, the development of other relationships—any indication of separateness—are perceived in the other, and in oneself, as disloyalty and betrayal and generate guilt, blame, and anxiety" (1976:72).

LOVING AND CARING: INDIVIDUAL AND FAMILY TRANSACTIONS

A second dimension in the assessment of family separateness and connectedness is the individual–family transaction. Here the questions are: How much do the people in this family care about one another? Do they appreciate one another? Do they listen to one another with interest and respect and enjoy the others' efforts toward growth and change? Do family members enjoy being together? Can they also get vicarious satisfaction from the others' separate adventures? Do they smile at one another, chuckle, or laugh comfortably with each other, or at their own foibles? Do they show concern for another's pain? Do they reach out and touch?

Some families, including some of those known to protective services, at first glance may seem chaotic and uncaring. One of our colleagues, who works with families in a preventive infant mental health program, reports a visit to a home following referral from protective services based on a concern that an infant in this very disorganized household was neglected. Although the home clearly was disorganized, the baby's clothing inadequate and grey, a strong nurturant mother–child relationship quickly became evident when the worker handed the baby a spoon. The infant looked at the spoon, then looked at the mother with a broad smile, happily taking the spoon. The communication was eloquent.[1]

DIFFERENTIATION AND FUSION:
INDIVIDUAL–FAMILY TRANSACTIONS

The final dimension of separateness and connectedness to be described is
the level of differentiation and fusion that characterizes an individual's
relationship with her family system. In interpersonal relationships, a poorly
differentiated person cannot take an "I-position," clamly maintaining her
own views, but rather acquiesces or actively rebels, negotiating away the
self in either case.

The togetherness forces are so powerful for less differentiated persons
that they either slip into fusion in close relationships or protect themselves
from the anxiety of fusion through physical or emotional distancing. In
assessing the level of differentiation (or fusion) in a person's relationship
with his family of origin, we may ask ourselves the following questions.
What is the frequency and nature of the contact between the person and
his family of origin? Are contacts limited to formal or total family get-
togethers? Are there genuine one-to-one relationships between the person
and at least some members of the family of origin? To what extent does
this person have to relinquish beliefs, plans, and goals in order to obtain
love and approval from family members? To what extent does the person
need to gain distance from family members through cutting off or triangulating? To what extent does the person's self-image depend on input
from family members? To what extent can the person tolerate or even
enjoy extended intimate time with family without reactive distancing,
fighting, or bringing in a third person?

Differentiation and fusion are particularly salient matters in marital
interactions. The following assessment questions can be posed. To what
extent is each member of the marital pair able to be clear about areas of
responsibility? Does the wife feel responsible for her husband's pain? Does
the husband feel that the wife is responsible for, say, his alcohol abuse?
Does each spouse look to the other to make up for disappointments in
themselves and in their lives? Does the couple struggle with intimacy, living through chaotic cycles of blissful togetherness punctuated by angry or
even violent separations? Does the husband's sense of adequacy and competence depend on his wife's helplessness? Does the wife carry the anxiety
in the family, developing physical or emotional symptoms? Helping families and marital pairs deal with separateness and connectedness is one of
the most frequently faced challenges in family-centered practice. We will
readdress this subject in our discussions of intervention.

Other aspects of the family structure which may be assessed are the
relationships which characterize the organization of the subsystems within
the family. We must determine who are the members of these subsystems,
how firmly and clearly they are bounded, and whether there is sufficient

flexibility in the organization to allow for an adaptive rearrangement should circumstances require some alteration.

Crucial is the firmness of the boundary around the spouse subsystem. In our assessment task it is important to determine the membership of that system, for with changing family forms one cannot assume that the system automatically consists of a husband and wife. Further, once the committed adults that form the spouse subsystem are identified, the next task is to determine if that subsystem is protected by firm boundaries which afford some privacy, a life separate from the children, and freedom from interference. The nature of the boundary around the subsystem quickly becomes apparent in the couple's ability or inability to take time and space for themselves.

Other major subsystems in the family should also be identifed. These include parental and sibling subsystems and others determined by function, gender and interest. The relationships between the parental, spouse, and child subsystems are particularly important to evaluate in understanding the family and in identifying potential avenues for change. Ideally each of the children should have access to the parental subsystem without intruding on the spouse subsystem. Conversely, the parental subsystem should be able to carry out its functions in relation to the children without disrupting the sibling subsystem. The following vignette illustrates a situation in which the boundary between parent, spouse, and child subsystems are unclear:

Harry Jones came home late for dinner, having consumed a large quantity of alcohol. After some hostile and angry exchanges between Harry and his wife, Joyce, Harry went to bed. Joyce, tearful and furious, expressed her frustrations and her disappointments to her twelve-year-old daughter Janet, who had often been cast in the role of her mother's confidante and support.

In this violation of the boundary around the spouse subsystem, Janet has become a part of the marital struggle through triangulation.

Changing and Diverse Norms for the Assessment of Family Structure

By speaking of dysfunctional or maladaptive family integration we imply that we have some ideas about what adaptive or functional families might look like and some norms by which we measure the family with which we are working. However, in developing such norms we must be extremely careful to respect and indeed to help preserve the family's cultural integrity and its own notions of acceptable structure and role. We must avoid being ethnocentric or failing to appreciate the strengths of family forms. We must also avoid sterotyping sex roles, which are frequently linked to rigid norms of mental health.[2]

For example, Marianne Walters, who has studied and worked with many single-parent families, suggests that such families have special strengths. She writes:

> Single parent families are characterized by: a unilateral line of authority; *dyadic* lines of inter-generational communication; integration of management and nurturing functions; permeable inter-generational boundaries; multiple roles for individual family members; increased expectation for membership and participation in family functioning; and a task orientation. The clarity of the structural organization of the single parent family reduces the likelihood of the triangulation of adults, blurring of authority and reduction of inter-personal expectations common to family systems in crisis.
>
> As a social system, the single parent family is both more impacted by and responsible to extra-familial systems. Friendships tend to be utilitarian as well as social and affective, with extra-familial individuals and systems assuming time-limited, differentiated functions within the family. There is greater proximity between the family and the world of work for the employed single parent, with the work place and employment life of the parent often regarded as an extension of the family system. Intra-familial roles and rules tend to be prioritized with respect to real, rather than preconceived needs. Single parents tend to assign tasks which actually need doing as opposed to tasks which are created to teach one how to do. The single parent family is a system, conditioned by experiences of transition, change and redefinition of roles, rules and functions within the family. It is a system responsible to extra-familial resources and systems of support.[3]

In chapter 2 a discussion of the advantages and disadvantages of particular family forms was presented. To this we would add that families seem to get into trouble "structurally" in two main ways, namely, when the family's self-definition of its structure is unclear and inconsistent, and when the family is located in a sociocultural environment in which its definitions are in conflict with those of the mainstream. The latter situation poses a particular challenge for the family-oriented practitioner who wishes to respect the family's cultural style without supporting the enmeshment or fusion of members who may themselves be in conflict with their families, torn between two cultures. This latter issue becomes particularly salient in families of adoption and intermarriage where historical traditions and ethnic values may be in conflict *within* the family.

Two illustrations may better clarify the above points. A case in which family structure might conceivably be dysfunctional is that of the child who undertakes some of the obligations of parenting. Yet such a role, as we have implied, will not be dysfunctional in families in which, however culturally diverse, the descriptions of role are consistent, and understood and accepted by all family members. For example, in the rural family of one of the author's grandparents, there were ten children spaced out over twenty years. Each of the older children was assigned particular responsibility for one of the younger, a system which both answered the care-taking needs of large families and freed the adults and some of the older children for the demanding work inherent in farm life. This or a similar mode of adaptation is still prevalent in rural areas where families still tend to be larger (Carlson, Lassey, and Lassey, 1981:44). However, if rules concerning when and how the role will be assumed are not clear, in all likelihood it will not be understood by the designated child's siblings, and much confusion will ensue. The role of the worker here is one of helping the family establish clear, consistent definitions of the role of the parental child. Secondly, in situations where the family's values as a system may be in conflict with the community or its children, the role of the family-centered worker is less clear. For example, in the case of many Jewish families who emigrated from the East European shtetl or in the case of some Holocaust families, a number of family values concerning parent-child relationships which were adaptive, indeed crucial to individual survival and to the preservation of Jewish culture are in the contemporary context viewed as "fusing" and "enmeshing" by Jews and non-Jews alike, diffusing boundary clarity between parents and adult children and perhaps inhibiting the efforts at differentiation of young adults. Examples include the reluctance of families to allow their adult daughters to move from home except to marry, the one-directional, self-sacrificing relationship of parent to child, and strong family influences on educational and career choices (cf. Farber, Mindel, and Lazerwitz, 1976; Goldstein and Goldscheider, 1968; and Lazerwitz, 1970). Here the practitioner walks a fine line between valuing the religious, historical, and sociopolitical variables which have influenced family definitions, and supporting both the family and its individual members' efforts to redefine themselves in a changed and changing environment.

The family's culturally based ideas concerning family structure and its notions about sex-linked role relationships must be carefully gathered and evaluated, always keeping in mind our own ethnocentric views, whatever they may be. In many American families, for example, the mother–child subsystem, which traditionally has been strong during a child's infancy, may continue to take precedence over the male subsystem in the home, even when it is no longer necessarily adaptive. Frequently the task in family therapy is to strengthen the father–son subsystem. The growth of this subsystem as a strong affective alignment has often been stunted in the face of the powerful mother–child subsystem. We will continue with the themes of role differentiation and of cultural diversity toward the end of the chapter.

TRIANGLES

Another key concept in the assessment of families is that of the triangle. Bowen in particular emphasizes this organizing concept, seeing families as constructed of interlocking triangles that exist within the nuclear family system and extend back into the intergenerational family system. The assessment of family triangles brings to light special alliances, shifting coalitions, and scapegoats. Frequently, just as we saw in intergenerational work, work with the nuclear family unit may focus on the altering of triangles. In assessing family structure it is useful not only to identify major triangles but also to assess the extent to which family triangles are rigid and unchanging.

Perhaps the assessment of a complex triangular structure can best be understood through an extended case illustration. This case not only demonstrates how triangles operate, but also how generational boundaries are violated. This family is organized around a triangle that pulls a child into the unresolved tension in the spouse subsystem.

Fairly soon after Steve and Marilyn married, trouble began to brew. Even on their honeymoon, Marilyn experienced a vague sense of disappointment and loneliness but rationalized that she and Steve would grow closer in time. Steve began to doubt that marriage was really what he had wanted at this point in his life. He felt "crowded," and relieved this feeling by falling asleep or escaping for solitary walks. He rationalized that things would be better when they returned to their usual environment and picked up the threads of their lives.

Things, however, did not get better. The more Marilyn—who saw her father as distant and cold—pursued Steve, the more he withdrew, increasing his hours at work or, it seemed to Marilyn, endlessly watching sports events on TV. While Steve's distancing reenacted for Marilyn the rejection she had experienced at the hands of her father, Steve, who had experienced his mother as intrusive and devouring, felt compelled to push Marilyn away for his very survival. During the early years, the couple's relationship formed a pattern which is depicted in Figure 12.1.

After three years of marriage, they temporarily at least seemed to solve their problems through the birth of a son. Marilyn, in her loneliness, turned to the baby, investing most of her emotional energy in this relationship. At first this seemed to work well, since Marilyn's preoccupation with the baby freed Steve from what seemed the impossible responsibility of meeting Marilyn's emotional needs. Oc-

FIGURE 12.1

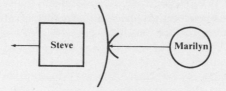

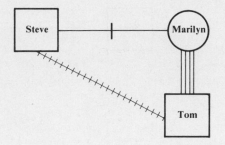

FIGURE 12.2

casionally, Steve would feel resentful toward Tommy, but for the most part the triangle of the comfortable twosome and the outsider (shown in Figure 12.2) achieved a sort of stability.

Subsequently, two other children were born, which somewhat diffused the central triangle. Everyone commented that John, the second child, was an independent youngster, and he and his father developed, if not a close relationship, at least an emotional connection. Tommy and Marilyn formed a triangle with John similar to the one they had formed with Steve, that is, with John in the outside position. John dealt with this outside position by turning more and more to his father or outside the family for relationships. Mary was the last child born. Marilyn enjoyed having a daughter and the original triangle seemed to shift and loosen somewhat to make room for the new family member. Tommy, however, when Mary was just short of two years, developed a series of undiagnosed, low-grade infections. There was even concern about leukemia at one point and thus Marilyn's primary attention was brought sharply back to Tom. (It has become clear to many family therapists that once a child is established in the inside position in a fairly rigid triangle, he or she will fight to maintain that position). Mary now turned to John and to her father in the face of Marilyn's absorption in Tom's health problems. Steve was able to be somewhat responsive to Mary, who did not pose as great a threat to him as his wife, much to Marilyn's annoyance. In the meantime, Mary and John were also developing a close alliance, shutting out Tom, whom they found to be demanding and domineering, from the sibling system. A central triangle in the family was thus preserved, and although Tom was not doing too well in school and was having some difficulties making and keeping friends, the system was fairly stable. As Tom entered adolescence, the family assumed the pattern depicted in Figure 12.3

At that point, however, the central triangle began to be stressed as developmental needs drew Tom away from his mother. Tom began to do poorly in school and was becoming involved both in behavioral difficulties in the classroom and in conflict with both parents. Although Marilyn attempted to turn to John and Mary for help, she was not very successful at pulling them in as their ties with each other, their father, and the outside world were well consolidated. Further, Tom's bad behavior became a convenient receptacle for the marital tension which kept threatening to surface whenever Steve and Marilyn connected emotionally. Thus the central triangle was sustained, despite Tom's efforts to separate himself

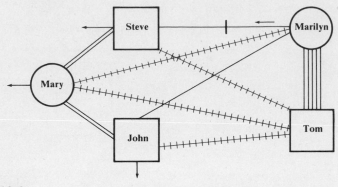

FIGURE 12.3

from it. When Steve stayed in his outside position, Marilyn blamed him for being an uncaring father. When he attempted to move toward his son, he did it awkwardly, and usually father and son ended up fighting. Marilyn would then reinstate the original triangle by siding with Tom and defining Steve (to Tom) as harsh and lacking in understanding. Tom's problems continued to escalate until finally, in his junior year in high school, after he had failed all but one subject, Marilyn sought help for him.

In assessing a family, it is particularly important to identify the central triangle in the family as it will probably be that triangle, in the long run, which will be the primary target for change. It must be remembered that the organization of interlocking triangles also extends into the family of origin. In assessing the genogram, as discussed in chapter 10, it is important to identify the key intergenerational triangles and the way these triangles are duplicated by the triangles in the current family. To return to Steve and Marilyn, there was high complementarity between their family-of-origin systems. Each had distancing fathers and intrusive mothers. That is, all four of their parents were relatively undifferentiated. Marilyn's and Steve's fathers handled the threat of fusion implicit in marriage by emotionally cutting off and distancing, as did Steve. Both mothers turned to a child for closeness. Steve, after being close to his mother as a little boy, cut himself off from her in early adolescence. Marilyn remained fused with her mother, unable to take "I-positions" on her own opinions and wishes. They continued to talk daily on the phone and to visit back and forth frequently. (It is not the extensive contact with kin which is the problem, but rather the loyalty conflicts between original and nuclear families.) In fact, a source of intense marital conflict in this family was Steve's anger at the extent to which Marilyn's mother interfered in their lives. The intergenerational triangles formed by this couple with their respective families of origin are pictured in Figure 12.4.

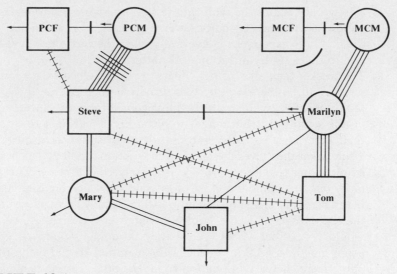

FIGURE 12.4

FAMILY SCULPTURE AS AN ASSESSMENT TOOL

The family structure can quickly and dramatically become visible through the use of an assessment and treatment technique called family sculpture.

Family sculpture is a deceptively simple but powerful exercise that has been developed by family therapists (see Duhl, Kantor, and Duhl, 1973; Papp, 1976a; 1976b). In family sculpture, a person acting as a sculptor and using living persons as a medium, portrays his or her family at a particular point in time through the construction of a tableau vivant. As the technique of family sculpture has developed, many variations in style and format have appeared including, for example, the use of fantasy and the use of movement in a technique Peggy Papp calls "family choreography" (1976b). Family sculpting may be used both with the family group, when the sculptor places the actual members of the family in the sculpture, and in family-oriented groups and training sessions, when the sculptor builds his or her family by using members of the group as stand-ins for family members. Family sculpture may also be used in case staffing or consultation when the presenting staff member sculpts a client family as a way of visualizing and communicating the complex structure of the family system to other workers.[4]

The following basic format for family sculpture is presented as a beginning model for people who want to start using the technique. As one becomes increasingly comfortable with the procedure, creative individual variations may develop.

1. The worker begins the sculpting session by giving a simple explanation of what family sculpture is, explaining that it is a way for the family to experience nonverbally what their own family is like and to share its organization and patterning.
2. The worker then asks for volunteers or specifically asks one family member to be the sculptor. It is usually a good policy to ask the family member who would be most comfortable or expressive to do the sculpture. Children, who often find it difficult to express their experience verbally, particularly enjoy family sculpture.
3. The worker then gives the sculptor instructions on how to proceed, emphasizing that the sculpture is a nonverbal process. The primary task is to build a picture of the family by placing each member in a characteristic place and position. It may be suggested that the sculptor imagine the family at home in the evening. Where would people be? What would they be doing? Chairs or other props may be used. Placement of the members should include not only where they are in relation to all the other members but also where they are looking and how their bodies are positioned.
4. As the sculpture develops, family members may object to the sculptor's portrait, because they see themselves and the system differently. For example, if a child places his father in the corner behind a newspaper, Dad may not like the picture of himself, nor what his son or daughter is communicating through the sculpture. It is important, however, to allow the sculptor to finish without interruption and to assure other family members that they will be able to sculpt the family later if they wish.
5. The worker should give the sculptor support and help as needed, encouraging him or her to take whatever time is needed and asking enabling questions like, "Do you want mom to be looking in any particular direction?" and "Is that figure just the way you want it?"
6. After the sculptor has completed the sculpture and taken his place in the tableau, the worker assumes the role of monitor and, while the actors maintain their positions, asks each member how he is experiencing his place in the sculpture.
7. The sculpting session may end after the family discusses the sculpture or after another member makes a new sculpture which more closely pictures his view of the family.

Family sculpture is a powerful assessment tool, making, in Papp's words, the invisible visible. It is a projective technique which may display a picture of the family structure and emotional system not previously realized by the family member. Sculpting one's family is usually an emotion-laden experience which offers a new understanding of the family and which often liberates its participants by demonstrating without words the possible avenues to change. The use of this technique in assessment is illustrated in the following vignette:

Gerald and Phyllis and their two children still at home, Bill, aged sixteen and Ann, aged twelve, came for help with Bill's increasing difficulty at home and at school. The older brother, George, now working in another state, had been hospitalized for psychiatric problems seven years previously when he was seventeen, a fact that increased the family's concerns about Bill. After three sessions, the worker was mystified. The family simply wasn't making sense and no useful hypothesis concerning the family's troubles had been developed. In the next session, the worker suggested sculpture and Ann volunteered with considerable enthusiasm.

She put two chairs together to form a sofa and had her father sit on one of the chairs. Then she said, "Who can play grandma?" The worker, somewhat surprised, volunteered and was placed close to father on the "couch." Mother was then placed standing up, arms crossed, looking at father, who was separated from her by grandma. Bill was placed at the edge of the family, with his body faced out but looking over his shoulder at his mother in a position that soon became physically quite painful. Ann put herself on the other side of her father, standing by him.

What became immediately apparent was that the grandmother was the center of the family and firmly located between father and mother so that their access to one another was blocked. The revelation was interesting in view of the fact that the parents had said grandmother had an apartment upstairs in their home but rarely came downstairs and had little involvement in the family. The worker had taken this at face value, failing to recognize that the absent family member who had "nothing to do with the problem" is frequently the key actor in the situation. The sculpture corrected the worker's faulty view of the family and also objectified the conflict-laden and central role of grandmother for all to observe and discuss.

FAMILY MAPPING

Paper and pencil simulations may also be helpful to the worker in the family assessment process, in planning interventions, and recording change. There are many ways to map the family. Minuchin, for example, uses symbols which provide a shorthand way of describing family coalitions, boundaries, and patterns of authority. Minuchin combines these symbols in a way that approaches mathematical formulas as may be seen in Figure 12.5. The symbolic representation in this figure means that the mother and children have formed a coalition against the father and that the boundaries between mother and children are diffuse.

In our efforts to map families we have borrowed some of Minuchin's symbols, but have attempted to construct a simulation making use of space in characterizing the family structure. In a sense, our family mapping combines some of the characteristics of the eco-map, the genogram, and the use of space as in sculpture, as well as some of Minuchin's symbols.

FIGURE 12.5

1. People are pictured, as in the other paper-and-pencil simulations, as squares and circles. Their names and ages can be included.
2. Space on the page is used as it is in family sculpture to signify closeness and distance.
3. Conflict is indicated as in the eco-map by evenly spaced hatching ($-\!\!+\!\!+\!\!+\!\!+\!\!+\!\!+\!\!-$).
4. Cutoffs are portrayed as in the genogram by a fence()) or by double hatching (-//-) through the connecting line between two people.
5. A coalition may be accentuated by a bracket.
6. Arrows may signify interest, investment, or attention, as in the eco-map.
7. A very strong tie may be indicated by a single solid line or several parallel lines (——— or ≡≡≡).
8. A tenuous connection is shown by a broken line(-----------).

Figure 12.6 shows a map of the family discussed in the example above. Figure 12.7 maps a family in which the parents are divorced and the father is remarried. We see the father cut off from the family and further blocked from access by the stepmother. The fourteen-year-old daughter is trying to invest in father but her efforts are blocked. Mother and younger sister are close, forming a triangle with the older sister in the outside position.

One of the best ways to draw a family map is to develop a mental picture of how the family would be sculpted and then translate that into the simulation on paper. We will be using family maps in conjunction with the presentation of case material at various points throughout this volume.

Family Structure and Role

Before we leave structure and move on to the assessment of family processes, it is important to examine the concept of role in assessment.

Role has long been a central concept in social work theory and was for many years the major conceptual tool in family assessment. A family tended to be evaluated in terms of the social role functioning of its members.

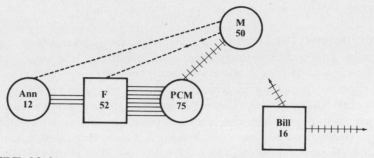

FIGURE 12.6

The problems implicit in using this norm as an assessment guide lies in the fact that the prevailing cultural norms, or worse yet, one's own, become the exclusive guidelines for assessing *all* families. Such assessment of course runs the risk of being highly ethnocentric.

Arlene Skolnick writes:

> Before the mid-1960s . . . social scientists in various fields assumed that mother, father, and child formed the basic human group, held together by interlocking needs built into human nature. The nuclear trinity was found in every society and declared to be the basis of social structure. Any attempt to tamper with its division of labor between the sexes or patterns of child rearing was said to be highly dangerous and could result in the downfall of "civilization." Family textbooks could state unapologetically that they were based on the American middle class because that was the ideal norm toward which everyone was striving. . . . Deviation from the standard nuclear pattern was attributed to psychopathology, poverty, or just misfortune. [1973:396]

Social workers have not been immune to this kind of thinking and family assessment has been an area particularly vulnerable to the projection of private norms, as if they were pictures of a universally desired reality.

FIGURE 12.7

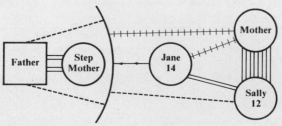

CULTURAL VARIATIONS IN FAMILY ROLE STRUCTURE

Family structure, the nature of marital and parent-child relationships, and norms for appropriate gender-linked role functioning are largely culturally determined. Although social workers learn respect for ethnic and cultural diversity in social work education, for the most part they have failed to integrate knowledge of differing cultural styles into family work. Jenkins argues in a scholarly, much needed, and very useful work, that "the social welfare field, although deeply involved in serving ethnic clients and training ethnic workers, has only recently and in peripheral ways acknowledged the need for ethnic content in therapeutic and service approaches" (1981:4).

Many social workers have come to regard as rigid and discriminatory the prevailing sex role prescriptions for men and women in American society. To some extent our own active participation in and support of more egalitarian roles for men and women presents a paradox, thrusting us into emotionally and professionally conflicting dilemmas when we work with families whose cultural traditions are different from our own and who have norms which might seem rigid, old-fashioned, or reflective of male dominance. For example, traditional Chinese-American families are characterized by "the use of the cultural ideal of a familism built around ancestor worship, filial piety, and patriarchal authority while nevertheless developing closely knit nuclear families as the central agency of socialization" (Mindel and Habenstein, 1976:124). Children are socialized to be nonaggressive, divorce is disapproved of, and external expressions of affection or demonstrativeness among family members are atypical, particularly between adults.

Chinese-American family structure is far from uniform, as acculturation proceeds at varying rates, some families and family members embracing the new and others clinging to the old. The traditional family in China was strongly patriarchal, with wives sometimes viewed as little more than slaves and female children regarded as being of questionable value, as the following poignant reminiscence from Maxine Hong Kingston portrays:

> But I am useless, one more girl who couldn't be sold. When I visit the family now, I wrap my American successes around me like a private shawl; I *am* worthy of eating the food. From afar I can believe my family loves me fundamentally. They only say, "When fishing for treasures in the flood, be careful not to pull in girls," because that is what one says about daughters. But I watched such words come out of my own mother's and father's mouths; I looked at their pen and ink drawings of poor people snagging their neighbors' flotage with long flood hooks and pushing the girl babies on down the river. And I had to get out of hating range. I read in an anthropology book that Chinese say, "Girls are necessary too"; I have never heard the Chinese I know make this concession. Perhaps it was a saying in another village. . . .[1975:62]

Huang, however, points out that in many contemporary Chinese-American families, the roles have been changing and the husband is not always boss. She says, "A product of traditional values . . . [the China-town-based husband] . . . is characteristically puzzled and disillusioned by the activities of a spouse who often no longer shares those values, but he tries to be reasonable and make the best of a difficult situation . . . ." (1976:130).

As family-centered social workers working with families in the midst of major cultural change and conflict, perhaps our most important task is to help such families seek resolutions to these value conflicts, helping them in their efforts to fashion family forms which are both expressive of their rich cultural traditions and adaptive in a changing environment.

Are we as family-centered workers to encourage long-subservient Chinese women to become more autonomous, to contradict their parents and husbands, to stand up for themselves?

In many Mexican-American families, the authoritarian role of machismo on the part of the father and a more passive homemaker role on the part of the mother are strong and valued traditions. Such families have a firm sense of family identity and high levels of mutual responsibility and group interdependence, while "opportunities for individual expression, autonomy, self-sufficiency and a differential identity are reduced" (Falicov and Karrer, 1980). Immigrant families, however, may be characterized by different levels of acculturation, depending on the opportunities individual members have for exposure to a new language and differing cultural values and practices. Falicov and Karrer point out that "the discrepancies between stages (of the life cycle) give rise to conflicting expectations and norms within families. Intrafamilial dissonance is usually expressed through heightened conflict between the generations or between the sexes and will affect developmental transitions" (355). An example from the field of education clearly illustrates how additional conflicts will be created for the transplanted Chicano child and his family when cultural factors such as machismo are not adequately understood or respected:

> What makes the Spanish-speaking child appear "uneducable" is his failure in an educational system that is insensitive to his cognitive styles and cultural and linguistic background. An example of this would be the suppression of the male-dominant image that Mexican-American boys bring to school. In school he is confronted by Anglo female teachers (unlike in Mexico where the majority are male). If he is to succeed in school he becomes a feminized male, if he retains his *macho* characteristics he more than likely becomes a failure and a discipline problem. He is rewarded only for behavior accepted by the teacher. [Ballesteros, 1971:5, quoted in Jenkins, 1981:14]

In some communities, Mexican-American parents have been protesting their children's educational experiences and the resulting effects on family life. One school principal replied:

It is true that we have a different set of values . . . Mexican-American families have an authoritarian system and what father says goes. But we teach the children to question and they end up questioning father. [Quezada, 1973:23, quoted in Jenkins, 1981:15]

Are we too expected as social workers to help children question their parents' values, to help wives liberate themselves from their husbands' authority? If in the past we were often guilty of helping husbands and wives to adapt to their socially prescribed roles (comfortable that we knew what they were), today social workers with strong convictions about changing roles for women and "differentiation" goals for children may feel particularly critical of traditional family structure, and biased against families in which principles such as male authority are the norm. This issue is often at the very core of work with ethnic families, and with other families as well.

On the other hand, the lives of weaker family members, like the relationships of the weaker group to the dominant in any social system— whether peasants to landholders, workers to owners, or blacks to whites— may be less than satisfying and indeed oppressed, as the function of unequal and exploitative distributions of power. Weaker family members, typically women or children, may be exploited or oppressed in *any* family, ethnic or not. The assessment task in relation to these issues is most delicate, to understand and respect the family's normative role structure and its cultural heritage, while at the same time assessing the impact of this structure on difficulties for which the family is seeking help. The goal, of course, is to achieve an adaptation workable for the family as a whole, one which does not cost the dysfunction or alienation of particular family members. As we said earlier, the solution of some ethnic families to such culturally based intergenerational conflict or marital turbulence is to cut themselves off through emotional and/or physical distancing. The social worker's role may often be one of helping such families learn how to resolve these dilemmas without self-destructing.

Another characteristic of many ethnic families and of many black families, an issue insufficiently understood or taken into account, is that of "extendedness." Relationships with kin, role constellations which involve considerable sharing of material goods and parenting roles among a kin network (Stack, 1974), and mutual support networks are often unfamiliar modes to family workers who have little idea how to tap into these rich sources of help. Recently Staples (1976), Hill (1972), Ladner (1971), and Scanzoni (1971), among others, have concentrated in their writing on the strengths of black families, emphasizing the historical and contemporary importance of family and kinship in these families as functional, adaptive, and necessary to survival. The black family has been a source of affection, companionship, and self-esteem in the face of hardship.

Given such widely varying norms for role behavior, how can the concept of role be used in family assessment without conjuring up the role stereotyping that has been so critical of cultural and personal variety in life-style? First, in the use of the concept of role in family assessment, two different kinds of roles must be distinguished. There are formal roles which are built into the biological and traditional structure of the family, such as father, mother, husband, wife, son, daughter, mother's sister, stepfather, godmother, and so on. Secondly, there are informal roles that are ascribed to members of the family system. These roles are also clearly linked to the ongoing maintenance and functioning of the family system and include such ascriptions as caretaker, explorer, jester, and family historian. These roles require specified behavior and are frequently passed on intergenerationally in very patterned ways.

ASSESSMENT OF FORMAL ROLES

In assessing the family as a network for formal, reciprocal roles, there are several aspects to consider, namely, (1) role congruity, (2) role continuity, (3) role conflict, (4) role ambiguity, (5) role complementarity, (6) role competence, and (7) role flexibility.

In addition to these assessments we must also ask how the carrier of a role would describe that role, as well as what the expectations of others in the family are for the person carrying that role, and we must note discrepancies as they emerge. For example, it is just as important to know how the mother in the family describes her duties and behavioral expectations as it is to know how the others in the family describe their expectations of her. Knowing how the various family members understand and define a particular family role helps lead to an assessment which is not as likely to suffer from ethnocentricity.

ROLE CONGRUITY

Are the family's role prescriptions for the mother congruent or incongruent with the picture of the role held by the mother herself? Changing norms concerning the roles of women as well as an increase in the numbers of marriages across cultures have increased the potential for role incongruence. Role incongruence often emerges as a major issue in marital conflict when each marital partner criticizes the other for failure to occupy the marital or parental role as expected, and at the same time feels guilt for not living up to the other's expectations. Such norms of proper role performance are usually developed in the family of origin, and the more different the two sets of original families, the more likely it is that role incongruence will occur.

An amusing example of how different or incongruent cultural norms generate marital reactiveness was reported recently by a cross-cultural marital pair who had been dealing with considerable cultural dissonance. They laughingly described a time early in their marriage when the husband had to go on a business trip for several days. Arriving home around midnight, he (the son of a matriarchal Jewish family) tiptoed into the house in a state of anxiety, certain that his wife would be enraged because he had gone away and left her alone with all of the household responsibilities, and then was late getting back. At the same moment, she (the daughter of a partiarchal Irish family) lay awake upstairs in an equal state of anxiety, expecting anger and reproach from him because, busily involved in some of her own projects, she had "let the house go" in his absence.

ROLE CONTINUITY

It is also important in assessing roles to examine the extent of continuity or discontinuity. Ruth Benedict (1938) pointed out that role discontinuity occurs when preceding roles in the life span do not prepare one for successive roles. Again, the more rapidly society changes, the more likely people will experience role discontinuity. Women in particular have struggled with issues of role discontinuity in recent years. Although more educated and more career oriented, most women still carry major responsibility for the care of the home in addition to their paid employment, and those who are not employed outside the home sometimes think despairingly, while scrubbing the floors, "And I went to college for this!" Men, on the other hand, find themselves poorly prepared for child rearing and home care, roles they are increasingly asked to share with their wives in egalitarian marriages.

ROLE AMBIGUITY

Role ambiguity is yet another concept useful in assessment. This state exists when there is lack of clarity of expectations concerning the prescriptions for a particular role. As family forms change and vary, the new family roles that are occasioned can be extremely ambiguous. For example, role ambiguity is often a major issue in families of remarriage. The role prescriptions for stepparents are often not only diffuse but even negative (the wicked stepmother). The role of parent is already occupied at least psychologically by the biological parents, and there are no widely accepted models for stepparents.

This particular case, the occupation of a parent role by adults other than the biological parents, becomes even more ambiguous in the case of nontraditional families. One of our colleagues has been meeting with a group of lesbian mothers and their partners. The single most complicated and conflictual issue the group raises is the ambiguous role of the live-in lover in relation to the other's children. While many such couples have worked out solutions comfortable and adaptive for themselves and the children, in some instances the confusion over the definition of the parenting roles on the part of the children, the couple, and the surrounding community can become a major strain. The often ambiguous response on the part of mental health professionals to such nontraditional families is dramatically expressed in the title of an article on lesbian families which appeared in recent years. The author inaccurately and insensitively exaggerated role ambiguity by entitling the work, "My Stepfather Is a She."

ROLE COMPLEMENTARITY

Complementarity exists when reciprocal roles "fit" with each other or are in a harmonious balance. For example, a high degree of complementarity may well exist between traditionally oriented spouses. The husband may see his role as providing for and protecting his wife, while the female wishes to be provided for and protected. On the other hand, she may see her role as nurturing and taking physical care of her husband and children and in maintaining a comfortable and attractive home. He does the outside work, she does the inside work, and so on. This kind of comfortable balance exemplifies complementarity and can be maintained as long as external events and family or individual developmental changes do not generate disruption or disharmony. Referring again to the changes in women's roles, in some families we see a growing lack of complementarity, as many women are becoming less satisfied with traditional definitions of the roles of homemaker, wife, and mother, and the husband or children may resist a new definition, sometimes finding ingenious ways to maintain the existing equilibrium. As such couples move toward discomplementarity, dissatisfaction, and open conflict, the prognosis for the marriage may well depend on the capacity of the marriage to tolerate efforts at differentiation on the part of one member, to mediate stress, and gradually to evolve a changed but newly satisfying balance.

ROLE COMPETENCE

It is also useful to assess the extent to which people have had the opportunity to master social role behaviors. Role prescriptions and role competences are learned; they are a part of the socialization process. Social workers encounter some families in which the parents have never had the opportunity to learn some social roles many would take for granted. People who have been deprived of the opportunity to grow up in families, for example, have had little chance to learn or integrate either spouse or parenting roles and may become overwhelmed when faced with the demands of a marital relationship and the complexities of family life. McBroom (1970), Polansky (1972), and Bandler (1968) are social workers who have taken leadership in identifying ways of understanding and working with such families.

ROLE FLEXIBILITY

The final concept to be discussed in assessing formal role structure is flexibility. It is important to ascertain just how flexible the role structure is under the stress of all the vicissitudes that families face. In times of illness or crisis, can role responsibilities be shifted? Can family members assume roles normally carried by others? The family with a rigidly fixed role structure will have less ability to adapt to crisis or to change.

In summary, a knowledge of the role structure in a family can serve as one organizing framework in assessment. The assessment task, however, is not to apply a set of inflexible norms to determine if the family's roles are proper or appropriate, but to look at the functional and transactional aspects of role relationships. The assessment develops from a joining of the worker's impressions with those of the family, so that the expertise of the professional merges with, as anthropologists might say, "the native's point of view." Further, it is useful to discover whether these role allocations are congruent or incongruent, clear or ambiguous, and whether the family is carrying incompatible roles which are stimulating excessive conflict. One should also examine the reciprocity of roles within the family, that is, the extent to which they are complementary and meet the needs of the family. Finally, it is useful to examine the extent to which family members have been prepared for role assumption, both in the process of socialization and in circumstances which call for continuity.

ASSESSMENT OF INFORMAL FAMILY ROLE ASSIGNMENTS

Beyond the formal role structure just discussed, families are also characterized by a structure of informal roles. These roles and their importance in the functioning and maintenance of the family system are a vital part of family assessment.

Informal role prescriptions are not necessarily verbally identified, since family members themselves are not aware of their own "assignments." Such role prescriptions may surface only from a careful observation of family members in a series of situations or over a period of time. Questions such as these are designed to uncover informal roles: What is happening in the family during the periods before, during, and after Julia refuses to eat? Or David goes on a drinking binge? Or Pamela makes another suicide threat? Or Bobby shoplifts? Or in the session, when Susan starts noisily banging the Lego blocks? Or Missy kicks her sister? Or Peter starts acting silly? In the history of this family, who is the one typically called upon when someone needs to be picked up at the airport, is ill, or needs a loan? Who is blamed for the family misfortunes? Who has been defined as "no good," "crazy," the "freeloader", or the "bad seed"?

In more general terms, the following questions are helpful in guiding the practitioner: What are the major informal role assignments in this family? How are they defined? Who carries them? What are their specific functions in this family system? Who carried these roles in previous generations, and what happened to them? What is the impact of the person carrying this role?

A brief case example demonstrates how these questions were answered in one situation.

Martha, an unmarried woman in her forties and a second-born daughter whose mother and mother's mother were also second-born daughters, was identified as carrying the role of family caretaker. She had asked for help because lately she had been feeling tired, drained, and somewhat resentful, sensations which she attributed to possible menopausal symptoms or midlife crisis. It seemed to her that her job in the family was one of rushing to the rescue of all in trouble. For example, if any of her married sisters or brothers or any of their children experienced any sort of misfortune, Martha would quickly leave her own demanding work and social activities to be at the bedside, to keep things running smoothly and to pick up the slack, both for her siblings and for her widowed father, all of whom lived in other cities. Of late she had been called on several times to help out her sibling's children, now reaching adulthood. After a good many years of this pattern, and acutely aware that her father was becoming increasingly frail and would be needing more and more attention, Martha was beginning to rebel, wondering if anyone would help *her* out if she needed it, and questioning whether she was really appreciated, but then feeling less than noble about these thoughts.

A genogram of the family disclosed that her mother and her maternal grandmother had both been the caretakers of their parents and siblings in their generations. Other family roles of "mental patient," of "slow" sister, and of "wanderer" could be traced intergenerationally to resemble the current informal roles assumed by some of Martha's brothers and sisters. Her assumption of the caretaker role provided some rewards for her. For one thing it seemed to insure her a "special daughter" status in relation to her father, and she seemed to have the admiration of her siblings. While Martha obviously liked being needed and wanted, she was beginning to feel that her life did not count; that since she was not married and did not have a family "of her own" she was the obvious choice to help out in times of need; and that family members were interested in what she could give but not in her as a person. Her carrying of this immense responsibility in fact seemed to insure that her siblings would be free to pursue their own lives and activities, at the expense of keeping them somewhat distant from each other but especially from father, and protecting them from having to come to terms with longstanding family tensions.

The assessment dimensions we explored in relation to formal roles may also be applied to informal roles. In such circumstances the expectations for the informal role assignment sometimes conflict with other role expectations. For example, children who play the role of caretaker or mediator in relation to their parents or their parents' marriage may find it extremely difficult to leave home, to become autonomous adults, and to direct their primary loyalties to a wife or husband in a new family. In the case of a married couple, the informal role of one spouse may become less complementary over time to that of the other, as seen in the following vignette:

At first it seemed that the marriage of Norma and Joe was highly complementary. Joe, a "charmer," good-looking, convivial, the "life of the party," had grown up in a chronically depressed family in which he was assigned the role of cheering up, of bringing liveliness into the system. Norma, on the other hand, provided order and stability in a fun-loving but chaotic family. Joe was originally attracted by Norma's "sensible" attitude toward life, and her concern and dedication toward her own family. Here was a woman who would love her hearth and home. Norma found Joe's outgoing, flamboyant personality the perfect contrast to her own shyness. But after six years of marriage, he is becoming increasingly bored with what he calls her "stick-in-the-mud" approach to life, her reluctance to socialize, while she has become increasingly angry about his drinking, flirting, and late nights out.

Informal roles should be as flexible as possible. For example, if the family's "camp counselor" falls down on the job, can someone else help plan and direct family activities? Can the "sickly," overdependent wife who cannot drive and never learned to manage a bank account support herself and the children if widowed? These are just a few examples of the many informal roles that may be adopted by family members, and which often become important targets of change because of their tendency to maintain the status quo. Nevertheless, the consequences of role change must be carefully predicted, insofar as it is possible to do so, since when central roles are altered or dropped the effects reverberate throughout the system.

Forces for Stability and for Change

Up to now we have been primarily mapping the topography of the family structure. But if we were to leave it at this, our map would be too static.

Therefore we will now examine the family as a dynamic, living system, a field of powerful forces and continuous processes.

In chapter 5 we presented at some length differing conceptualizations of the transactional forces for stability and change that exist within a family. One of these forces is family boundaries, which we will now discuss in relation to the family's potential for change.

FAMILY BOUNDARIES, ADAPTABILITY, AND CREATIVITY

As we have seen above, the capacity or ability to change and to develop more differentiated adaptive mechanisms depends on the family's capacity to receive and to exchange information. This capacity in turn is related to the nature of the family-environment boundary and the boundaries between various family members or subsystems. An assessment of family boundaries will reveal the way a family receives and processes information, and thus will reveal its capacity for change. Figure 12.8 illustrates modes through which new information and change can enter a family.

Input is received from the outside as people, ideas, and experiences are allowed into the system. We are reminded here of Kantor and Lehr's (1975) description of the family with the open windows and open doors. In chapter 7, both the Embrees and the Taylors initially exemplified families with opaque boundaries or families with closed doors and windows, which cut them off from needed resources for growth and change. The

FIGURE 12.8

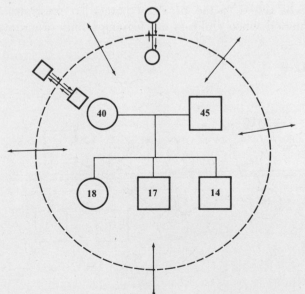

impact of the lack of information between Rita Taylor and the neighborhood was dramatically illustrated when both neighbors and family responded increasingly to each other with suspiciousness and eroding esti-
mations of reality.

On the other hand, in Figure 12.9 we depict a person who is allowed
to move outside the family system, partake of new experiences, and gather
new information. She is then readmitted to the family, which shares these
new experiences and information through open exchange, and consequently grows and changes. This process is exemplified as young people
in the family begin to mature and then to move out into a world of new
ideas and experiences. The family must grapple with these new ideas, often
with considerable tension, and if they are adaptable they will incorporate
some of these changes. In the 1960s and early 1970s, the intergenerational
conflicts that churned as many young people embraced a variety of an-
tiestablishment views eventuated in various kinds of change in their parents' generation; even the middle-aged began to let their hair grow.
Clearly, if the family does not recognize change in the younger generation,
tensions between subsystems are bound to increase.

Change can also occur in a family through the epigenetic development of its members—depicted in Figure 12.10. Epigenetic changes include the growth, development, and the eventual launching of the children
in the family and also, although less obvious, the many developmental
changes and transitions that take place throughout the family life cycle.
If these changes come gradually, the family's adaptive tasks are less overwhelming. Stress is particularly likely to develop when change occurs rapidly, as it often does during adolescence, when the family's morphostatic
forces may be tested to the breaking point. To illustrate, during the
launching period when children are leaving home—a stressful time for

FIGURE 12.9

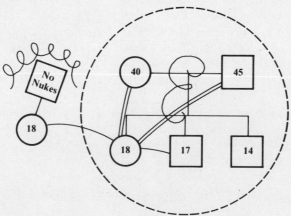

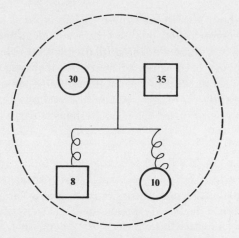

FIGURE 12.10

many families—the children may become emancipated and simultaneously marital conflict may arise. Or, in even more morphostatic families, a young person's efforts to establish a separate life may be blocked or even sabotaged because his or her presence is experienced by the family as essential to the maintenance of the marriage. In some such situations, the youth may develop serious symptoms and may fail to leave home, remaining entangled in the rigid family system (Haley, 1980). A major assessment question, then, is whether the family's external boundaries are sufficiently open to allow for the admission of information and for the movement of family members and others across those boundaries. In an ideal situation, the exchange of information is encouraged, and the bearers of useful change are ultimately welcomed.

THE FAMILY RULE SYSTEM

Coherence, stability, and synchrony are maintained in the family through a series of rules which direct the family's life. These rules govern the elements we have already discussed, such as role, structural arrangements, the family's use of space and time, and the nature of boundaries. They also direct the flow and nature of communication, confer status and power, define family rituals, and express meaning and value systems. The sources of family rules are many and are probably not fully understood. They arise in part from family experiences and intergenerational history, and in part from the family's adaptive efforts to respond to the changing world.

We do not take the strict functionalist position that *all* rules serve some purpose in the maintenance of the family system; some, we believe are principally matters of style. For example, many families have emotionally charged rules about Christmas rituals, such as whether gifts are to be opened on Christmas eve or Christmas morning. There are even family customs about how the gift-opening ceremony is to be conducted—whether gifts are distributed one at a time or all at once, who does the distributing, and in what order the gifts are opened. These seemingly minor customs become permeated with intense feelings of family loyalty, pleasant memories, and ties to the familiar, and they continue although they do not necessarily have any particular functional importance for the survival of the current family. Glen's experience clearly illustrates this latter point.

Glen had always fried bacon in a metal ice-cube tray. Although a relatively minor rule, it did direct his behavior. An exploration of the source of that family rule was enlightening. Glen was a descendant of eastern European Jews who had emigrated at the turn of the century, and he grew up in a second-generation family which began, with considerable conflict, to turn away from the old ways. By the time he was half grown, his grandparents were dead, and his mother stopped keeping a kosher home. Eventually even pork, although only in the form of bacon, began to be served, but his mother could not bring herself to fry bacon in a pan used for anything else. She thus kept aside one metal ice-cube tray, a perfect size and shape for frying the traditionally forbidden meat. Glen continued to do automatically what he had always seen done.

Such aspects of the family's culture can dictate one minor style of behavior or a complex activity. For example, one of the author's grandfathers, born and raised on a farm to a family that had been farmers for many generations, determined that he would break with the farming tradition and make a different kind of life. However, despite his verbalized hatred of the farm, which he left at the age of sixteen, he spent every free minute thereafter working in his vegetable garden. Moreover, most of his children, grandchildren, and great-grandchildren continue to be devoted gardeners. To paraphrase an old saying, it seems that "You can take a family out of the country, but you can't take the country out of the family."

It is likely that none of these rules, values, and ceremonies may be essential for survival or maintenance. However, some accumulation of shared meanings and ceremonies is an essential ingredient of family cohesion, sense of continuity, and individual identity. Hoffman (1981) suggests that some families may be underorganized, having too few ceremonies, rituals, or shared meanings, as exemplified by the Embrees. It is important to identify such families so that an interventive strategy may help them construct new rituals and ceremonies or to rediscover and reinstitute old ones. One of the demanding tasks faced by marital pairs from very different cultural traditions is the development through sharing and negotiation of a body of ritual and ceremony which provides each with an adequate sense of continuity.

Rituals and ceremonies have been recognized by anthropologists as both embodiments of continuity and instruments for change in societies. The function of these social forms in families is beginning to be studied, creating not only a new area for assessment but a resource for change.

In assessing a family's rules we ask, What are the major tenets of the family's belief system? Are there pervasive themes that seem to organize the family's perception of itself and its construction of reality? How are these themes expressed in the life of the family? Does the family build cohesion, communicate meaning, and handle transitions through the use of rituals and ceremonies and if so, what are these rituals? Does the family appear to be immobilized in rigid and repetitive ritualized behaviors? Does it appear to be underritualized and lacking in ceremonies? Through such questions we accomplish a central task in the assessment process—an understanding of the idiosyncratic culture of the family.

SYMPTOMS AND FAMILY RULES

The most vigorously and rigidly protected rules in families are those that are deemed essential to the survival of the family system. It is usually these rules which must be identified in developing change strategies for dysfunctional families; and the purpose they serve for the maintenance of the family system must be determined as well. For example, if the behavior of a family member or members appears to be odd, troublesome or even destructive, the question is not so much what is its origin but rather what is its purpose. This epistemological stance totally alters one's thinking in assessment and opens up new options for treatment. For example, when a marital pair appears in the office seeking help because of constant fighting, the question is not why they are fighting, but how the fighting helps to maintain the system. This approach takes the view that the arguing is not the problem but rather an attempt at a solution, and it leads us to the question, "Then what *is* the problem?"

This assessment process, which the Milan group calls hypothesizing, and which grows out of the interviewing processes described in chapter 6, should result in a theory about the possible function of the problematic behavior in the maintenance of the family system. For example, in one family situation, a colleague asked for a consultation on a family with whom he was working.

After seeing Barbara's family for several unproductive sessions, the therapist began to see the twenty-year-old "identified patient" alone, as she had moved out of her home, was living in a college dorm, and seemed to be making steps toward appropriately separating. Almost as soon as she moved out, however, things began to deteriorate. She became increasingly depressed and withdrawn, vaguely threatened suicide, dropped out of college, and moved home.

The following information emerged. There were three children in this family, two boys, two and three years younger than Barbara. Both were doing well. The father worked long hours in a responsible position in a large industrial firm and also had maintained a liaison with another woman for the past seven years. The mother did not work and had been very involved in the rearing of the children and the maintenance of the home.

The initial hypothesis sought to identify what function Barbara's symptoms were performing in the family. We speculated that Barbara's symptoms were somehow related to the maintenance of the three-cornered marriage. It appeared that Barbara, by remaining "sick" and thus a needy "child" in the home, kept mother involved in caretaking, a role that she had missed as it had become less and less required by her family. Barbara's return home also provided mother with a companion; moreover, it freed father to spend time at work and with his girlfriend, and also freed the younger brothers to pursue their task of growing up.

Palazzoli, whose work has been primarily with very dysfunctional families in which there is an anorectic or schizophrenic member, has found such families, as did Jackson, to be highly morphostatic, that is, caught in a complex network of rigid rule-governed relationships and transactions of which the pathological behavior is a key part. The task of assessment in dysfunctional families such as these is to identify the fundamental rules in the family of which the pathological transaction is a part. Once they have been identified, interventive strategies may be designed to alter them.

RULES ABOUT RULES

In assessing the family rule system it is essential to gain some understanding of the family's rules about rules, or metarules. These rules prescribe whether rules can be talked about and, of particular importance, how they may be changed. In a very rigid, homeostatic family, there is a powerful metarule that rules may not be commented upon or altered. In fact, a major change strategy may consist of commenting upon a family rule, thus violating the metarule that prohibits this action, and bringing the rule itself up for discussion; at the very least, it may be possible to remark that the family seems to have a rule against talking about rules.

Power in Families

In the presentation of family theory (chapter 5), differing views concerning the location of power in the family system were outlined. Our position continues to be that power may reside in several locations at once within the family system: in the body of rules, in individual family members by virtue of their control of resources or their own higher levels of differentiation, and in the family's meaning or value system.

In assessing power in the family, it is often important to ask how power is distributed throughout the family. For example, do some members appear to have a greater stake than others in the protection and maintenance of the family game? If so, their identities may emerge when a particular rule is challenged in work with the family. Who skillfully and with considerable power moves to preempt the process of change? If some people in the family have more personal power than others they will demonstrate it by their ability to take "I positions" with the family and to stay out of certain patterned familial transactions. It is not always easy to identify the most powerful among family members; one member may appear to be very much in control, but through careful tracking and observation another member may be unmasked as the secret holder of real power.

However, one must be cautious in attributing helplessness to an adult except in cases of illness or forced dependence of some kind. Most situations of seemingly unequal distributions of power among adults in families have been negotiated by those adults, and the apparently powerless member has relinquished control in one area in order to gain benefits in another.

Children are less powerful than adults in families because of their dependence on the adults. This does not mean that a child cannot tyrannize a family. Nevertheless, as Minuchin puts it, if a child is dominating a family he is standing on the shoulders of the adults. His domination is serving some purpose; it is the solution to some other more threatening problem.

Sometimes power is found to reside in the system of rules or in the game, and all of the family members feel helpless in the face of repetitive processes that seem to have taken over and developed a life of their own. The family members' fear of change empowers the repetitive transactions and no one in the system seems able to mount a successful challenge.

Finally, the family's system of shared meanings and values can be the repository of considerable power to mold or change the family. This power may be evoked by the appeal of a family member to a shared principle, and in assessing families one may determine what some of these principles are and how effective they are in directing the family. The power of the meaning system may also be mobilized in family rituals and ceremonies; learning about these and their impact on the family further contributes to an assessment of the distribution of power.

In summary, in dealing with complex issues of power in the assessment process, one should attempt to identify its presence in the family game, evaluate the extent to which it is distributed in a variety of ways among family members, and attend to its expression in the family belief system. However it is described and no matter where it is located, the accumulated power of a family is formidable and must be understood and faced by everyone seeking to facilitate change in a family system.

COMMUNICATION AND FAMILY ASSESSMENT

Communication is a salient part of the assessment process in two respects. First, communication is the medium through which we learn about families. Secondly, the communication patterns in the family are themselves a target for assessment.

Families tell us about themselves in many ways; what we "hear" or learn depends on our sensitivity to their varied ways of teaching us what they are like and how they perceive the world. We must of course attend to the basic content of their messages; we have all been taught to understand communication on this level.

But the more difficult task in learning to understand families is to reach beyond the verbal content of their communication to their other languages, which can in time become quite clear to the careful observer. Facial expressions, gestures, and positioning of the body are all eloquent means of communication and may offer more information than spoken words. The significance of nonverbal communication in family systems had led to the practice of videotaping family sessions as a recording and assessment aid. A very useful way to enhance one's sensitivity to nonverbal communication is to observe a videotape of a family with the sound turned off.

On still another level we learn about the structure of a family through the observation of repeating patterns of communication. Using interviewing techniques described in chapter 6, by tracking communication we learn who talks to whom about what, and how often, who are the "senders" and who the "receivers," who is not included in the communication network, who interrupts the communication when two family members begin an interchange, and so on. Bermann (1973) monitored the frequency of communication between different family members, and from this information was able to construct a picture of the family relationship system. In a home study, as simple a question as asking a potential adoptive couple with whom they have discussed their intentions to adopt will contribute information about the family's relationship system.

Observing communication patterns also clarifies the nature of the boundaries between family members. We can find out, for example, whether boundaries between family members are violated as people speak for one another or assume knowledge about how the other feels or thinks; or, on the other hand, whether boundaries between family members are rigid and impenetrable, as demonstrated by frequent disqualification, a lack of empathic response, and imperviousness in communication patterns.

MONITORING AND ASSESSING CYBERNETIC PROCESSES

Tracking the paths of communication processes as cybernetic or feedback systems leads to an understanding of the family's rules and the governing processes that maintain those rules. In chapter 6, when we discussed interviewing family groups, we described this tracking process and how it may lead to an hypothesis concerning the family's morphostatic efforts or regulating processes.

In observing the family's cybernetic processes, we may realize, for example, that when John, aged thirteen, attempts any move toward autonomy, he is immobilized by a quick and effective double bind. When Mary attempts a rather accurate observation concerning what is happening in the family relationship system, she is told she is wrong or stupid, and is ridiculed. When Jeff makes a remark about the conflict in the parents' marriage, he is silenced either by being told he is crazy or by being completely ignored.

In these examples, children in the family are making efforts to alter the family's stance. On the other hand, children may also contribute very effectively to the maintenance of the status quo. For example, a child may be an expert at providing static or distraction which obscures another family member's attempt to broach a painful subject. Or, two siblings may stage a fight when they sense that the tension between the marital partners is escalating or might be expressed verbally.

In identifying such situations we are making use of both digital and analogic communication as a source of information about the family's concerns, structure, and process. There is, however, yet another aspect of communication which is important in assessment and that is the quality and the nature of the family's communication as communication. First, we may ask, what are the rules that govern communication in this family? What are the communications about communication? What topics may be explored and what subjects are taboo? What feelings may be expressed? Some families cannot communicate sadness. For others, anger is beyond the pale. And still others seem to possess few comfortable means for the expression of affection.

Secondly, in the assessment of communication per se, we question the quality of the family's exchange. Is communication clear? Is there congruence between digital and analogic communication? Do family members have difficulty in translating analogic communication? Do family members listen to one another and validate each other's statements, or do they interrupt the process of communication by invalidating their own communication, by repudiating the other's statements, or by disconfirming the other as a source of communication? How do family members punctuate the communication in the family? Is there a persistent theme of blaming in that the family's major effort is to assign the fault for an event? Do family members punctuate interactive sequences by generally experiencing their own behaviors or feelings as being caused by another?

Many marital couples and families seek help with the specific complaint that they have "communication problems," an amorphous description which must be carefully assessed. Some family therapists center their interventive goals and strategies on helping families communicate better. Satir (Satir, Stachowiak, and Taschman, 1967), for example, emphasizes improvement in communication as a path to family change, and in her work with families assumes the role of teacher of good communication through modeling, communication exercises, and other cognitive and experiential means. Another interventive approach which stresses enhancement of interpersonal communication is found in the marriage encounter movement, and the learning of more effective communication behavior is also often central in behavior modification approaches to marital and family therapy (cf. LeBow, 1976; Liberman, 1976; Thomas, 1977). Whether a central focus of intervention or an auxiliary change strategy, understanding and enhancing communication in family systems is generally a part of any interventive plan.

In this chapter, we have discussed the assessment of the family as a system. We have identified some of the key aspects of family structure and process which can provide a framework for assessing families in the initial phases of contact and thereafter for identifying targets of change, selecting interventive strategies, and evaluating outcomes.

These key aspects include the nature of the family's external boundary and the degrees of separateness and connectedness inside the family. Separateness and connectedness are considered to have several components, namely, the quality of enmeshment or disengagement which characterizes the family as a system, the extent to which family members care for and about one another, and the extent to which individuals in the family are differentiated from or fused into the family emotional system.

Another important aspect of assessment is the organization of the family. It includes the nature of the boundaries between subsystems, the membership and arrangement of subsystems, and the central family triangles. It includes also the distribution of formal and informal roles within the family.

Specific family processes were examined as well. These include the family's system of rules and metarules, its values and meaning systems, and its ceremonies and rituals. The distribution of power is an important process, too, and the process of family communication is not only a potential target for assessment but also the major route to understanding the family system.

Chapter 13_____

The Family Unit as Resource and Target for Change

WE NOW TURN to examine interventive processes where the family unit itself is defined as the "unit of work" and the object or resource for change. The purposes of such work vary. They grow out of the family's identified problem or need, the nature of the setting, and the function of the agency.

The goal of such intervention is an enhancement of family system functioning. Family meetings may be initiated to help a family deal with a crisis, to aid in its problem-solving efforts, or to increase its competence as a functioning group. Such problem-solving efforts frequently occur, for example, in settings where the family seeks help in providing care for an ill or aging member, as in health care settings, or in the face of some other life event which strains its adaptive capacities. In other situations, such as in protective services, the total family unit may be functioning far below its capacity because of its disorganization. In these cases, the social worker can help the family to make use of its strengths, remove obstacles to growth and change, and alter destructive patterns. Often a family requires help specifically for difficulties in relationships or because one member is exhibiting disturbing or dysfunctional behavior. In such a situation, the target and resource for change may be the entire system, but the goal is the enhanced functioning of an individual member.

We have seen that any aspect of the complex ecological system or of the family of origin can be selected as a focus of change, and this principle applies to the current family as well. In fact, one way the major schools

305

of thought in family therapy may be distinguished from each other is by their particular focus. In our view, any of the aspects of family structure and process described in the previous chapter may be targets for change in helping families. Boundaries, informal or formal roles, communication patterns, organization, structure, meaning system, and family rules may all be involved in the change process. Further, since these aspects are all interrelated, a change in one may well reverberate throughout the system, bringing about change in other parts of the system.

In discussing intervention, it must be remembered that therapeutic change in families comes about, not spontaneously through the use of a single technique or strategy, but over time through a sequence of interventive moves, each one growing out of information gained, in part, through observing the outcomes of the previous intervention. Thus a family worker may utilize many strategies and target many aspects of the family system as the case develops.

In the next chapter we exemplify how a family counseling situation develops over an extended period of time, and in the final chapter we will describe a sequence where multiple interventions are used. Our primary purpose in this chapter is to describe a considerable number of specific interventive strategies, recognizing that in practice they overlap or are often utilized simultaneously.

Learning and Experience as Agents of Change

A wide variety of interventive strategies may be considered to fall under the category of teaching. By "teaching" we do not imply didactic instruction but rather those modeling, demonstrating, and experiential strategies which help family members gain new competencies, a new view of their situation, or novel ways of understanding events and processes.

The first teaching the worker does occurs during the assessment process itself, since this process demonstrates the worker's systemic epistemology. Family interviewing, the careful tracking of transactional sequences surrounding problematic events, the systemic or circular questioning designed to show comparisons and relationships rather than intrinsic characteristics of individuals, all these provide the worker with information and at the same time provide the family with a new understanding of what it means to be a family and a changed conception of the family problem.

The very way the worker asks questions and makes comments can reframe the family's concerns and begin to alter its epistemology. Similar examples of the change potential of assessment occur in the use of the eco-map and genogram, since these devices not only organize extensive information about relationships, patterns, and transactions, but in the process communicate a new framework for understanding the family and its world. The Milan team has speculated that the systemic assessment process in work with families may be sufficient in and of itself to achieve desired change, even without the final strategic intervention for which they have become known (Palazzoli et al., 1980).

Powerful messages are conveyed to a family through the systemic interviewing and assessment process. In this process the context is widened and the view that events are outcomes of a sequence of complex transactions is demonstrated, primarily because the notion of simple linear cause-and-effect relationships is abandoned and with it the effort to assign blame. The interruption of the search for blame and of self-blame, a search which grows out of linear cause-and-effect notions, is in itself a major change. Moreover the assessment process models an ecosystemic epistemology; and through participating in that process, family members are taught to be systems thinkers. Such teaching often takes place through the use of metaphor and analogy as well as through experience, thus influencing the way family members organize, construct, and symbolize reality.

REFRAMING

The practitioner not only reframes the family's situation through assessment, but also makes direct reframing statements to the family, which can alter their views of events. First, "the gentle art of reframing" may change what systemic therapists have termed the family's "punctuation" of events. By the punctuation of events is meant the placement of the period which ends a sequence or defines the beginning of a series of transactions. Events are in fact often simultaneous, with participants involved in circular transactions; thus when they are described in digital language and conceptualized in linear terms, punctuation must be selectively inserted to give structure to the statement. This structure, which often is truer to language than to reality, usually implies a beginning, middle, and end, as well as a subject and an object.

Intervening into a family's punctuation of their sequences of behavior may alter their concept of causality, either reversing the causal relationship or, more frequently, converting what the family interprets as a linear causal relationship into a circular one. For example, in the complementary dyad of Mary, the chronic invalid, and George, the caretaker, everyone may punctuate the relationship by believing that George takes care of Mary because she is ill. A reverse punctuation would be, Mary is ill so that she can provide George with someone to take care of. A more circular or systemic understanding might be that Mary and George have established a relationship in which each meets the other's need. The fit is perfect.

A second kind of reframing alters the view of the purpose of behavior. One example of this kind of reframing, suggested by Palazzoli, is called "positive connotation." This reframing positively connotes all behavior in the family, no matter how apparently destructive, as an effort to benefit and to preserve the family system or to rescue another family member. An adolescent son's nasty and abusive behavior toward his mother can be reframed as his effort to help her with his leaving home. A mother's nagging can be seen as an expression of her loving concern. The eruption of acting-out behavior on the part of a teenage boy following his sister's departure for college can be reframed as an effort to occupy his mother when she is feeling so sad and depressed about her daughter's leaving.

Related to positive connotation is the reframing of the problem as a *solution to another problem*, particularly a problem which is threatening to the family. For example, when meeting with a marital pair who identify constant bickering as their problem the worker might reframe the fighting by asking, "I wonder how this fighting is helping you two in managing your relationship?" Symptoms may be very accurately reframed as efforts to solve other problems.

Reframing the problem may also take place through expanding its meaning, that is, by setting the problematic behavior in the context of the total family or in an historical context. For example, one family's major concern was that their teenage son Tom was antisocial, spending most of his time pursuing solitary interests. It soon became clear that both the parents and older sibling were also loners, each very much interested in his or her own work. The worker expressed surprise that the family believed Tom's lifestyle was problematic, since he seemed to be following an important family tradition and was actually behaving much like the rest of the family. This discovery released Tom from being defined as the problem, but also brought to light the entire family's isolation, discomfort in social situations, and difficulties in establishing connectedness.

Another "family tradition" reframing took place in the case of a boy who was refusing to do his work in school and had been involved in some rather serious trouble in the community. In time it was discovered that when his father was a teenager, he had been a good student but had been involved in some minor escapades. The mother, on the other hand, had behaved very conventionally but had not applied herself in school. The worker commented that the youngster seemed to be following family tradition and was, in fact, taking after both of his parents. This observation was particularly useful, for it cast light on the fact that the parents, although presenting a united front of concern, felt very differently about the boy's difficulties. The father was furious and intrusive over the schoolwork but rather casual about the acting-out behavior; the mother, on the other hand, was panicked over the behavior, attempting to monitor and control it, while the schoolwork problem bothered her much less.

Another kind of reframing can take place through the use of metaphors which may integrate information or intensify its meaning. For example, one young alienated and frightened marital pair reminded the worker of Hansel and Gretel wandering hand in hand, lost in the woods. Another family seemed like Wendy and the boys who never grew up in *Peter Pan*. A surprisingly effective reframing is made simply through drawing such an analogy with the family. It has been our experience that an accurate and colorful analogy tends to reorganize the family's self-conception and expose hidden rules and patterns. Families will recall an effective analogy time and time again, examining its assumptions and implications. We include reframing as a "teaching" strategy because it imparts new information and a new way of thinking. It challenges the family's construction of events and behavior, offering a new context for understanding and thus stimulating altered responses and new options.

TEACHING ABOUT FAMILY SYSTEMS

Through working together as a unit, families, with the intercession of the worker, can learn to become experts on their own family, independently capable of recognizing, commenting on, and thus interrupting dysfunctional patterns. This learning, as we mentioned earlier, can take place through the assessment process; but the worker can also contribute comments and observations that help family members identify rules, roles, and patterns.

Sometimes, information contributed by the worker pertains to systems in general and alerts a family to some of their patterns in a very unthreatening way. Take, for example, this comment: "Triangles are hard. One person always seems to be on the outside trying to get in.'" Such words help the family better understand and deal with triangulating processes among parents and children, siblings, or others. At other times a comment from the worker may address specific behavior exhibited by family members: "Has anyone noticed that whenever people in the family get sad, Mary tries very hard to cheer them up?" Or, "It seems to me that whenever Judy and Bill [the parents] try to talk about anything important you two kids start fighting!" Such comments can be useful in teaching about how the family is functioning, particularly because they describe the behavioral sequence as it is happening and as it is experienced by everyone in the session. Reflective comment on the family system's patterns can be made more powerful if coupled with a positive connotation. The worker may comment, "I think it's probably a good idea you kids begin to fight every time your folks start to talk. Who knows what might happen if they *really* got into discussing things!" This comment may be further strengthened as an intervention by adding a "command" level to the message, such as "I want you kids to continue to start fights when your parents begin to talk, because I am worried about what might happen if they really talked about things!" Such a comment, which is a form of the often-used prescription "Don't change," will be discussed at greater length when we deal with paradoxical interventions in the following chapter.

The above example describes very simple observations made about a single behavioral sequence in the session. More extensive learning about the family system can be achieved if the worker's hypothesis about the purpose of the major problematic behavior in maintaining the family system is shared with the family and positively connoted. Such a positively connoted statement of the circular hypothesis may be enough to begin the process of change.

EXPERIENCE AS A MAJOR RESOURCE FOR CHANGE

Most of those who work with family groups rely very heavily on experience within and outside the family meetings as a resource for change. These techniques are based on the view that actually experiencing the family in a different way, experiencing altered relationships, or doing things differently, stimulates a change process. Once a new experience takes place, things are never quite the same again. "Doing" engages more of the person than "talking about," for it breaks habitual patterns of "the way things are done." It demonstrates that other ways are possible and interrupts transactional sequences by providing new input. In conjoint sessions, the very fact that the family is in the room together thrusts them into bold relief and makes them available for processing and for change.

A major strategy for utilizing experiences within the family session is through what Minuchin and others call "enactment." Families may enact their problems in the session and then go on to enact various solutions. Enactment may be as simple and subtle as the family's spontaneously seating itself in a session and thus modeling the organization of the family system. Or it may entail an entire session in which, as demonstrated in Peggy Papp's widely used training tape, "Making the Invisible Visible,"[1] the family portrays through family sculpting the many facets of its inner organization, and then enacts options for change. The worker may use family sculpting, role playing, and other experiential techniques to clarify a problem with which the family is struggling. The worker may also highlight a spontaneous family enactment so that it can be dramatized. For example, a sixteen-year-old with an overconcerned and intrusive mother is sniffling in a session and the mother hands him a tissue. The worker comments rather lightly, "What good care your mother takes of you. Look at the way she knew what you needed and gave it to you without your even asking!"

Sometimes an enactment may be orchestrated by the worker specifically in order to test a hypothesis. In one family, the worker developed a hypothesis that the father, although superficially charming and glib, didn't really know how to approach his son, and tested it by asking the father to talk with the boy about an issue that had just come up in the meeting. Initially they seemed to be managing all right, but as the worker extended the sequence by asking the pair to keep going, the conversation degenerated; the father blamed and criticized his son and the son angrily defended himself, and thus they enacted their painful and problematic relationship.

Sometimes a structural difficulty may be dramatically portrayed through enactment. In another episode of difficulty between a father and son, the mother, father, and son seated themselves with the mother in the middle. As the worker asked about a recent crisis precipitated by the son's cutting school, the father made a few angry comments which the mother modulated and interpreted. As the scene continued, the mother acted as a negotiator between the father and son, ostensibly keeping things smooth between them. The structural issue was particularly obvious in that father and son couldn't even see each other around mother unless they leaned forward. And, in fact, when the father leaned forward to say something, the son was able to shift slightly backward, keeping mother as a shield.

Enactment is also used to enable the family to experience a new way of doing things, a new approach to organizing the family. In the episode described above, the mother was asked to move into a chair on the other side of the room and father was moved into mother's chair. When it was suggested that father and son talk together about what was going on, Bill, the son, sat with his head down. Initially father expressed his anger directly to Bill, who began to cry. Father sat in helpless silence, obviously anxious and frustrated. Mother, seeing Bill cry, began to cry herself. The following sequence then took place:

FATHER (turning to worker after a long silence): "I really would like to be close to Bill . . . but I don't know, it just doesn't work out."
WORKER: "Could you tell that to Bill, do you think?"
FATHER: "He knows."
WORKER: "Perhaps, but could you tell him anyway?"
FATHER: "Bill, I really would like to be closer to you. I don't really know why we can't be."
(Bill keeps head down, doesn't respond.)
WORKER: "Bill, do you have any idea about what the obstacles might be that keep you two apart?"
(Bill shakes his head.)
WORKER to MOTHER: "Virginia, do you have any ideas about that?"
MOTHER: "Maybe I'm the obstacle."
WORKER to MOTHER: "How is it for you to be over there?"
MOTHER: "It's not too bad . . . "
WORKER: "Do you think you could let them struggle with their difficulties without moving in to help?"
MOTHER: "I think so, at least here."

This brief and rather simple sequence served to enact the dysfunctional triangle that entangled these three family members, with an over-close and protective mother–son relationship on the inside and the father on the outside. It also portrayed and allowed the family to experience a shift in the triangle and thus to experience the potential of a new organization. Of course one intervention will not permanently alter this enduring aspect of the family structure, but it can begin the process by providing a blueprint for change.

Enactment in the session with the family can delineate and strengthen the boundaries between subsystems. For example, the children may be given a task on one side of the room while the parents discuss an issue between them on the other side. Alliances may be strengthened and, as in the above examples, triangles altered.

Enactments may also be used to teach skills and to help a parent experience mastery or competence in dealing with a child. In the tape entitled "A Family with a Little Fire"[2] Braulio Montalvo orchestrates an enactment of the problematic relationship between the mother and the little girl who has set a fire. He suggests that the child read and, while she does so, the mother criticizes and disparages her efforts, while the parental child joins with the mother in the negative interaction. Later in the session, after having joined the mother and gained her confidence, Montalvo first models and then enables the mother to teach her daughter how to build a carefully controlled fire and subsequently to put it out. While the mother is teaching this skill to her daughter, the therapist praises the mother for being such a good teacher and for having a smart child who learns so fast. As the mother and daughter share a positive interaction with feelings of enhanced competence, the boundaries around the dyad are secured as Montalvo gently, but firmly, intercepts the parental child's efforts to join and interrupt the mother–daughter interaction.

Enactment may also be used for improving communication. Problem-solving sessions which engage all or part of the family and which enact the making of a decision or the resolving of a specific issue may reveal communication problems, and even identify ways these might be overcome. In such sessions, the worker can act as both coach and model. These sessions can also encourage family members to reflect on their own family processes and to learn to observe dysfunctional patterns that obstruct good interchange. It is sometimes useful to give the family a special opportunity to observe themselves either by inviting some members to sit behind a one-way mirror, or by showing a portion of a videotape which particularly exemplifies their patterned interactions.[3]

The Use of Assignments

In working to bring about change in family systems, it is often useful to extend the change effort into the daily life of the clients by devising ways for them to continue their work in the period between family meetings. In fact, the development, delivery, and processing of family homework assignments is the core of family work for many family practitioners.

Any intervention begun within the session may be followed up by an assignment which gives the family the opportunity to continue it in the time between family meetings. Montalvo, in the fire-setting case, for example, gave mother the assignment to continue fire-building lessons on a regular basis throughout the following week. In the case discussed above of the overly close mother–son dyad with the excluded father, the session ended with the assignment that the son should take his father to the electronic game center and teach him the game of Pac Man. This assignment had many components. Not only did it give the father and son a chance to be together, but it also put the son in the teaching role (in this family there had been many battles over father's helping with homework), and at the same time it exposed father to the electronic game center which he had considered, sight unseen, a den of iniquity.

THE TECHNIQUE OF GIVING DIRECTIVES

Jay Haley (1976), drawing on the work of Milton Erickson, specifies methods and techniques of giving directives which markedly increase their likelihood of being followed. Directives should *not* be conceived of as suggestions or advice casually and informally mentioned by the worker in the course of the family session. On the contrary, directives should be formally intoned with considerable seriousness and, if possible, a little drama.

Usually there should be only one assignment given at a time, or perhaps two at the most, and they should be given toward the end of the session so that the family leaves the session carrying the task with them. Generally, families react rather positively to being given an assignment, experiencing it as a gift from the worker, as a concrete response to the often-repeated question, "What shall we do?" The task assignment also gives the family a way to move ahead on its own and to act on its own behalf.

The first step in giving a task is to gain the family's attention. This may be done through tone of voice, through waiting while everyone is attending, or in a playfully teasing way. The playful approach is illustrated in the following sequence:

> WORKER: "I have something I would like to ask the family to do." (One or two people begin to attend.) "It involves everyone in the family, and I don't know if we should try it." (The family begins to quiet down.) "It's sort of a strange idea . . . I just don't know . . . " (Johnny, aged eight, continues disruptive behavior.)
> KEN (aged twelve): "You shut up, Johnny. I want to hear this."

WORKER: "Well, it seems kind of silly, perhaps strange, but it might be very important."
MARY (aged fourteen): "Come on, tell us, what is it?"

In time, the giving of the assignment toward the end of the session becomes almost a ritual as the family awaits and expects it. Sometimes there is an interruption in the session while the worker alone or with a consulting team fashions the assignment. This very dramatically frames the assignment, enhances its importance, and commands the family's attention. This method also has the advantage of giving the worker time to think, if she or he is working alone, or to seek the help of a colleague or team members.

Secondly, steps must be taken to motivate the family to do the task and to preempt its moves to discount or invalidate the assignment. Some families will be activated by a challenge. In these situations it is important to present the task as difficult. The worker may stimulate motivation by saying, for example, "I know it may seem simple, but this is really extremely hard to do. Many families couldn't even attempt it!" Here the worker is appealing to the family' courage and its willingness to take risks. With other families, particularly families which may be frightened and overwhelmed, it may be more efficacious to present the assignment as a simple and minor task. Further, no matter how it is presented, except in unusual circumstances, the task should be manageable and not overly demanding. For example, in the situation of an extremely alienated couple with two severely dysfunctional young adult children still at home monitoring and protecting the parental dyad, it was clear that some sort of connection had to be built between the parents. Although for many couples, an assignment to go out for an evening or out to dinner is useful, that would have been too much for this couple. They were assigned to go out in the car and get something to eat together—an ice cream cone or perhaps even take-out food from a drive-in restaurant. They were cautioned not to attempt a whole meal in a dining room.

The task should also be suited to the family's life-style, preferences, and resources. If a task fits the family's general style, it will stimulate much less resistance. On the other hand, if a task is given which is inappropriate to the family's interests or financial resources, the members will experience the worker as unreasonable and lacking in an understanding of the family's life. One way to assure that the task is appropriate to the family lifestyle is to involve the members in a discussion and decision-making process concerning the details of the task. For example, the worker may want to strengthen the parental alliance by giving the couple an assignment to go away from the home and do something together that they would enjoy. Discussion in the session of what they could manage and would like to do can be revealing as well as enabling. One couple decided on a weekend camping trip. They had not been camping without their children since the first two years of their marriage, and became quite nostalgic in planning the trip. Another chose an overnight stay in a local motel with a swimming pool. Sometimes the first assignment can include the making of, but not actually executing, a plan. In the following session the plan and the planning process are reviewed and an assignment may then be given to execute the plan. Although family members may be involved in planning the details of the assignment, before the session ends the assignment should be clearly repeated by the worker, with every step included, in the form of a directive.

Even the smallest task must be clearly specified. For example, if the worker wants the mother and father to spend fifteen minutes three times a week alone, discussing a specific matter, she may involve the couple in negotiations concerning where is a good place and when is a convenient time. This matter should be completely settled before the session terminates so that the family leaves with an agreement as to when and where the fifteen-minute talk will take place. Of course an exception is made when part of the task is to give the couple an opportunity to solve a problem creatively by themselves. In this case, they might be asked to spend five minutes as soon as they get home deciding when and where the future fifteen-minute discussions are to take place.

In another variation of this kind of assignment, Haley (1976) describes a directive in which the husband is asked to do something for his wife which she would not expect. This, of course, means that the husband initiates something novel in the marriage but it also requires him to think about his wife. Another open-ended assignment is to ask an estranged father and son to find something they would each enjoy doing together. This encourages them to think about what the other would like, and to express their needs or desires to one another. In this case, however, even with the lack of definiteness as to outcome, the worker should specify exactly when, where, and how they will carry out this plan.

Frequently it is useful to start homework in the family meeting, giving the family an opportunity to practice within the session, and then to prescribe that the activity be continued at specified times between the sessions. The fact that the task has been rehearsed in the family session tends to make it more likely that the family will be able to continue it.

Finally, the task should be given slowly and with repetition and, after it is given, the family members should be asked to repeat their particular assignments. Sometimes the instructions for a task are also written out and given or mailed to the family, particularly if a family member has missed the session. This is sometimes a way of involving a member of the family who is refusing to participate.

In constructing a directive for a family, it is important to include everyone, even if one person's role in the family task is to "stay out" or not interfere. When the task is for the parents, for example, it is often useful to give the children another task to be performed separately at the same time. They may be assigned to stay in the living room and watch TV, or simply not to involve themselves in the parental task. This directive can be framed as a part of the family assignment by saying, "And you may have the hardest job of all, and that is to stay out."

The task may be structured like any piece of work. Some members will be given an aspect of the task to do directly, and another member may be given the job of helper. The role of supervisor may be assigned to one member, and another may be asked to record the events.

TYPICAL TASKS AND ASSIGNMENTS

Although every family is different and the details of tasks must be tailored to those differences, there are also some frequently encountered family problems, so that similar tasks and directives with individualizing adaptations may be utilized with many families. The following are examples of the kinds of tasks that may be used in commonly occurring situations.

In many families, the boundary between the spouse system and the children is insufficiently clear or is too permeable. The parents allow the children to intrude into their privacy and seem unable or unwilling to draw an appropriate protective boundary. An assignment which directs this couple to spend private time together and to exclude the children fortifies the generational boundary. This kind of assignment has many forms. It may entail a rearrangement of time and space in the family home. It may be one simple boundary-strengthening action, as in the case of a directive which states that the children are not allowed to come into the parental bedroom without gaining permission after nine o'clock at night. It may be the development of the rule that the den is off limits to the children after nine o'clock. Or the assignment may entail the parents' going out together for an evening or spending a weekend away.

The outcome of such an assignment quickly provides information about whether the marital pair is triangulating the children between them in order to maintain distance or to moderate conflict, or whether this boundary problem originated out of earlier issues and is now being maintained in a transactional process which no one has identified or knows how to interrupt. It may be a pattern which is self-sustaining but no longer serves an important function.

If the family finds a way not to do the task, we can hypothesize that the children's involvement in the spouse system is still required. The processing of how the task was interrupted can give further information about the issues that could emerge should the generational boundary be defined and strengthened. Sometimes the parents are able to risk being alone despite the current threat that remains and, through this experience, begin to face what it is they have been avoiding.

Other boundary-building tasks may also serve to reinforce and strengthen the parent–child boundary. In one case where two teenage boys were in a struggle over homework with their mother, the mother was given the task of not mentioning the homework to either boy. The younger son was given the task of keeping a written record of every time the homework was mentioned. This task identifies the homework as the boys' territory and places them in charge of monitoring the boundaries.

Another kind of assignment is geared to the strengthening of alliances or detriangulating triangles. Such assignments tend to involve a subsystem of the family in a shared activity which has a positive meaning to the participants and helps to build an alliance between them.

Some tasks are tailored to break a stalemate or circumvent a power struggle, as illustrated in the case of John and Dolores:

John and Dolores were caught in a stalemate in which neither would nor could define the relationship. They had been going out together for several years, and they continually spoke of marriage but seemed to be unable either to part or make a commitment. When John moved toward marriage, Dolores would flee. As soon as John distanced himself in response to her flight, Dolores would begin to pursue. They sought help in coming to a decision about their future. After considerable work with the couple brought them no closer to a decision, their worker gave them the following prescription, designed to preempt the power struggle. The assignment was planned ahead of time and delivered in a very ritualized way. The couple were told to go to their favorite restaurant. After dinner, they were to ask for a brandy snifter, which they were to place between them. Each was then to take a small piece of paper and write on it either the word "separate" or the word "together." They were to fold the messages and place them in the glass. After shaking the snifter, they were then to unfold and examine the words written on the paper. If there were two "Togethers," that night they were to set a wedding date. If there were two "Separates," they were to separate immediately. If each paper carried a different message, they were to try once more. If after three trials, they still did not agree, they were to separate.

In the above example, the couple found the assignment both humorous and challenging, and they subsequently were able to part without guilt and on friendly terms. When a similar assignment was given in a marital case in which part of the husband's game was to threaten continually to leave, he quickly refused to consider doing the assignment, because, he said, "Then there would be no out!" For him, the assignment threatened finality. The significance of such a task lies in its dramatic ability to expose and comment upon the family game. The inability of the players to act it out does not necessarily imply it has been an ineffective strategy.

Palazzoli and her colleagues (1978) have devised an assignment which interrupts a conflict between parents over management issues in dealing with the identified problem child. This assignment, called "Odd Days and Even Days," or a variation of it, may be used whenever there is a competitive tug-of-war over responsibilities and decisions. It dramatizes and highlights the split while it disengages the protagonists. When this prescription is used, for example in a case where the mother and father are in a struggle over the management of the identified problem child, the mother is assigned the task of taking complete charge of the child on Monday, Wednesday, and Friday between the hours of 6:00 P.M. and 9:00 P.M. (or whenever everyone is at home). Father, in the meantime, is to behave as if he were not there, making no comment or contribution to the handling of the behavior. On Tuesdy, Thursday, and Saturday during the same time period, father is to take complete charge of the child while mother pretends she is not there. On Sunday, they are to behave spontaneously. Further, on the days assigned to them, the father or mother is asked to keep a record of any infringement of the arrangement by his or her spouse.

The authors have used a variation of this assignment, putting each parent in charge for alternate weeks. In one situation, the conflict between the parents over handling issues had been submerged by mother's taking most of the parenting responsibility and father's opting out. In the session after the assignment was given, the parents' conflict over parenting issues surfaced, having become explicit in their attempt to follow the assignment. During mother's week, she was aware of wanting help in making parenting decisions and of feeling alone and burdened. Father claimed to have enjoyed the "vacation." During father's week, mother was lured back into the parenting role by the son's provocation, father's abdication, and her own anxiety. Most important, father accused mother of "taking over" but began to look at the way he encouraged her to do so. Mother began to realize how arduous it was for her to resign her supervisory role and trust father to manage.

Task assignments may also be utilized to intervene in a troubled relationship of complementarity which continues to reinforce itself in a circular and escalating fashion. For example, in the marital situation where the husband repeatedly criticizes the wife and gives her unsolicited advice, and the wife is resistant and defensive in regard to any suggestion made, the more he gives advice, the more she resists; and the more she resists, the more he gives advice. One may intervene in this situation by prescribing a reversal. The husband is to give no advice to the wife—in fact, he is to ask *her* for advice concerning how to manage his life. The wife, on the other hand, is told to solicit advice interminably from her husband.[4] This kind of task is generally assigned in individual meetings without the knowledge of the other member. A reversal can begin to interrupt the escalating circular process and give each of the partners a new experience of each other and the relationship. The same kind of intervention can be used in any cybernetic process, for instance, the distancer and pursurer, or the teenager who is trying to achieve independence and the mother who is trying to hang on to his childhood.

Another kind of assignment, in some respects the opposite of the reversal, exaggerates or intensifies the problematic behavior until the exaggeration creates a recoil and an abandonment of the behavior. As a case in point, in a complementary marital pair consisting of the chronic hypochondriac and the caretaker, the hypochondriac may be encouraged to take to his or her bed while the caretaker is assigned the task of intensifying solicitous behavior. Hastening the escalation may bring the couple more quickly to the point where the transaction is truly intolerable, provoking a crisis out of which change can be considered.

The Use of Rituals as Instruments and Resources for Change

In chapter 5 we described the dimensions of ritual, its multiple definitions and characteristics, and some of the purposes it serves in family life. As analogic and metaphoric enactments, rituals speak to the nonverbal part of the self, and may provide a new way of integrating family relationships. Reiss (1981) suggests that at the center of family life is a set of ceremonials which are episodic and highly prescribed sequences of behavior rich in affect and symbolic meaning. These family ceremonials in turn shape and are shaped themselves by a set of pattern regulators, the daily, utterly routinized sequences of family life which are invested with little emotion and which regulate responsibility, space, and distance. Both ceremonials and pattern regulators are themselves shaped by, and in turn help to shape, the family's intergenerational view of itself.

In the following pages we examine how rituals may be put to use in interventions designed for maintenance, adaptation, or change in work with families.

RITUALS ADD FORCE TO DIRECTIVES AND ASSIGNMENTS

Almost any assignment given to a family may be strengthened and given more meaning by the addition of ritualized components. If the effort is to strengthen the boundary around the spouse system, for example, helping the couple develop private times together which include elements of ritual such as repetition, symbolic enactment, public communication, and regularity as to time and place will increase the importance of the activity and render it more difficult for others to disrupt it. Aside from their general use in any assignment, rituals may be used as specific change strategies in a variety of family situations.

UNDERRITUALIZED FAMILIES

Underritualized or underorganized families are families which may have lost once-meaningful ceremonies and traditions or lack everyday ritualized, regulatory patterns which help consolidate family identity and provide structure and cohesiveness. In some situations, rituals and ceremonies are lost through larger cultural or social influences, such as cutoffs from tradition occasioned by migration. Pressures to conform may have influenced families of ethnic and racial minority to relinquish once-cherished traditions. The following example illustrates the creative use by a young couple of a familial and cultural ritual to reaffirm their sense of continuity and identity.

Albert and Joyce had moved to a northern industrial area from their East Texas home upon Bert's graduation from a small black college. An excellent math student, he had been recruited by a northern company, had received additional training through the firm, and was now well established in a good job. Bert and Joyce had two children, Joyce had a part-time job in a local library, and the couple had recently bought a small home which they enjoyed. While this upwardly mobile young couple was pleased with their economic success, they at times felt isolated and alienated from the larger community.

Their ties with home, however, continued to be strong. They had grown up in the same small town in a rural area, surrounded by family and friends and nurtured by a close social network and rich traditions of family and community. Bert and Joyce went home as often as they could, particularly around holidays, but found it difficult to establish a similar network in their new community, or to transplant many of the family and local customs in what they sometimes felt to be inhospitable northern soil. The family and community tradition Bert particularly missed was "Juneteenth Day," the nineteenth of June, which was celebrated by blacks in his hometown and throughout the southwest to commemorate the emancipation of the slaves. He and Joyce remembered with nostalgia and pride the parades, the floats, the political speeches, the pit barbecue, and especially the afternoon baseball games. Only once since moving north had they managed to return home for Juneteenth Day, but they were delighted when their parents wrote that a bill had been passed in the Texas legislature proclaiming the nineteenth of June a legal holiday in the state of Texas.

In 1982, June nineteenth fell on a Saturday. Bert and Joyce had, with time, become acquainted with the black community and had met some other emigrés from the area of western Louisiana, Texas, and Oklahoma who also reminisced about this special celebration; and so the couple organized a Juneteenth Day picnic. It was held in a local park and attended by ten families; there were no floats, bands, or parades; but there was a barbecue, a baseball game, and the coming together and sharing of stories of Juneteenth Days each had experienced. There was even what might be called a speech when Bert told the children about Juneteenth Day, its origin and meaning. All of the families agreed to plan another such festival the next year. To other groups gathered in this northern county park, the group looked like any other church picnic or family reunion. They didn't know it was a Juneteenth Day Celebration nor had they ever heard of such a day.

For some families, extended experience with poverty, discrimination, social oppression, and continued lack of opportunity have contributed to anomic responses and family disorganization. The Embree family described earlier in these pages, is an example of such a family. Ceremonials, rituals, and even regularity in the patterns of daily life were lacking. As a change strategy, the worker and the Embree family developed mealtime, bedtime, and recreational rituals which served to better synchronize family activity and bound the use of space and of time.

CONFLICTING FAMILY TRADITIONS

When two people make a life together, the norms, rules, and prescriptions of the two families of origin must be integrated into a new paradigm. If the individuals come from very different families, they may experience considerable difficulty in forging new family traditions. This is often the situation when people from very different religious, racial, or ethnic backgrounds marry, in an atmosphere of conflict between the two families. The resolution may be to cut off rather than to attempt some integration of the old traditions into the new system, as described in the following situation:

Anthony, considering a separation from his wife Patricia, complains that the marriage is bland and lifeless. He has concluded that he and his wife are basically two "very different" kinds of people, poorly matched in "basic personality, interests, activities, and styles." Anthony, the youngest son in a Sicilian Catholic family which migrated to New York in the 1930s, disavows any interest in the Catholic religion or in his family's cultural heritage. He is proud of his own educational and financial success and his earlier athletic achievements, and he tends to disparage what he calls his father's rough language and uncouth manners and his mother's lack of formal education and strong Italian accent. He has little in common with his family anymore, he says, and has become increasingly alienated from his parents and "less successful" siblings. Anthony met Patricia, the daughter of a Southern Baptist family, while both were in college, and remembers being attracted by her sweet, refined, feminine manner, and her "cultured ways." The couple's two children are being raised Baptist, and the family spends Christmas and most other major holidays with Patricia's family in Knoxville, Tennessee. While Anthony denies feeling like an outsider on these occasions, neither does he participate enthusiastically in his in-laws' religious or family rituals. He complains that he is "bored silly" and feels particularly distant from his wife at these times. Neither Patricia nor her family are very warm, exciting, or vibrant people, according to Anthony, who recently complained to the worker, "Hell, they never even have a good fight!"

Lately Anthony has begun to reminisce about the lively, exciting, warm holidays in the district of Little Italy, the midnight mass on Christmas Eve, and the large family gathering for delicious and sumptuous meals, noisy conversation, and good-humored teasing. Unwittingly, Anthony resents his wife for all he has lost.

By helping individuals and families reminisce and recapture forgotten, lost, or abandoned rituals, the direction for the development and integration of new rituals or the reinstatement of old ones in a modified form will become clear. A couple such as Anthony and Patricia may be helped to design their own family rituals which preserve treasured traditions and experiences from both families of origin but creatively transform them in ways which fit their changed religious views and sociocultural lifestyle.

Recently a Jewish colleague in a Jewish–Christian marriage described how her three-year-old daughter had forged such an integration. When she arrived home from nursery school to question whether the Easter Bunny would be coming to her house, the mother carefully explained that in their family they did not believe in the Easter Bunny nor in the various customs associated with the Easter celebration. A few days later, on Easter Sunday, the couple and their three-year-old set out on their usual Sunday morning foray to buy the paper and to stop for freshly made bagels. When they reached the bagel store the child suddenly exclaimed, "I know what we do in our family! We get Easter bagels!" Another Jewish–non-Jewish intermarried couple seen in our practice celebrates Christmas as a national, nonreligious holiday, but the Jewish husband began to acknowledge to himself his sense of loss and his feelings of being an outsider during these times. This past Christmas, with the support and encouragement of his wife, he planned and gave a Chanukah party, which was attended by many friends and relatives, and this is a ritual he plans to repeat and one which may help compensate for his lost traditions. Integrating the competing demands of different cultural traditions in a new marriage can become a metaphor for dealing with intergenerational family issues and a theater for the enactment of changing relationships. Further, family rituals and holidays provide a forum and an opportunity for individuals in family-centered treatment to rework intergenerational conflict.

RITES OF PASSAGE

A major function of ritual in societies and in families is to mark life transitions, to dramatize change, and thus to help people experience and incorporate new roles and statuses with their altered social relationships. Weddings, funerals, graduations, christenings, and bar mitzvahs are all examples of familiar rites of passage.

Life transitions are often accompanied by increased tension and stress as well; these events bring new demands for families. It is often at such times that families seek help for family problems or individual symptoms which have developed in response to the unsettling challenges that such transitions bring.

Sometimes a family has not made use of a ritual in completing the transition, and in other situations a ritual may have been performed but without sufficient emotional investment or meaning. When an individual or a family has been overwhelmed by or is avoiding a culturally prescribed transition, the planning and executing of a ritual may be an effective strategy for change. For example, in situations of incomplete mourning, families may be helped to enact a ritual to bring some resolution to the process. This ritual may be something as simple as a prayer, poetry reading, planned reminiscence at a holiday dinner, and visit to the cemetery, or something as elaborate as a large memorial service.

In other situations there may have been an elopement or a city hall wedding, one insufficiently celebrated by family and friends. Perhaps one or both families of origin objected to the marriage, in which case a couple may continue to experience their union as illicit or unsanctioned. The unresolved intergenerational issues, the family of origin's anger, and the younger generation's alienation from family may be dealt with through the planning of an anniversary gathering in which the marriage is celebrated and the vows repeated, this time witnessed by family and friends.

Other life transitions exist in our society for which there are no prescribed or familiar rituals, either because the transition has been relatively uncommon in the past, as in the case of divorce, or because old forms no longer appropriately enact the change. For example, many societies have various rites of passage which mark entry into adulthood and departure from the original family. In our society, marriage, particularly for girls, once enacted this transition as the father "gave" the daughter to the husband. Today young people often leave home gradually, beginning the process long before marriage, and occupying for extended periods of time a liminal status in which they are still partly or even totally financially dependent on their parents. Families may develop considerable conflict during these periods. Leaving home is rarely a completely smooth process; rather it is often fraught with ambivalence and pain around separation and a time when some young people develop serious psychological symptoms. Such conflict may drive the young person to cut off or may hinder her appropriate departure. Families in the leaving home phase may be helped to deal with the leaving home of their children through the use of a ritual which includes communication of feelings about the change and a contracting process whereby new rules and boundary definitions are constructed and expressed.

Some individuals and families have created their own ceremonies to mark divorce, remarriage, childbirth, retirement, or other important transitions. For example, one young, recently divorced, woman planned a "name changing" ceremony, followed by a party, while a student of one of the authors described the "shower" her parents gave for her when she rented her first apartment.

Social workers in child welfare, where separations and changed statuses are such an important part of the lives of the families and children with whom they work, may help their clients make use of rituals in the resolution of loss or separation. Adoption, which is a major life transition for families and children, is a case in point. Although christening has sometimes been used to celebrate adoption, and adoptive families frequently commemorate a child's adoption day as well as birthday, the finalization of adoption itself is rarely marked by a meaningful ritual.

A claiming ritual, modeled after marriage, can be fashioned by the family, complete with an exchange of vows, the expression of sentiments by extended family members, a party, pictures, and gifts. Such an event helps the extended family as well as the adoptive parent or parents claim the new family member, and communicates in word and deed a sense of belonging to the child. In the case of open adoption, the natural parents and other family members may also have meaningful parts to play in this transition ritual.

Using Rituals to Change Rituals

We have described the sustaining, adaptive, and transforming capacities of rituals but it must be remembered that rituals also may be used in rigid, repressive, and degrading ways in families to preserve the status quo. Some families employ ritual to avoid contact, to suppress information or communication, to forestall change, or to control the expression of affect. In the following case example ritualized interaction is used to avoid pain, shame, and guilt, which threaten the fragile cohesiveness of a family.

Carol and Richard McNaughton's adolescent son Bobby had committed suicide three years before the family sought help for the second child in the family, who was acting depressed and ruminating about suicide. The family's coping style leaned heavily on avoidance and denial. The family had been devastated by the suicide of the oldest son, and the event was so painful and so fraught with conflict that it was never discussed. In fact, the son's name was almost never mentioned. In the course of inquiry about extended family connections, an interesting ritual was revealed which was being used to avoid pain and maintain equilibrium. There had been considerable bitterness and blaming over the death, particularly from the father's parents, who had refused to attend the funeral. The paternal grand-parents, however, stayed in contact with the family in the following way, which the worker hypothesized managed to maintain a rigid sort of continuity but at the same time forbade any mention of the terrible event and constrained any oppor-tunity to resolve the loss. It also protected the couple from any real examination of Carol's disappointment in the marriage and her unexpressed blaming of Richard for the son's unhappiness. On the second Friday of every month, the younger cou-ple drove the forty-five miles to the grandparents' home, called for the older cou-ple, and then took them out to the same local restaurant for dinner. They usually sat at the same table. Immediately after dinner, the four would return to the grandparents' house. Richard and his father would then spend approximately twenty minutes in the living room discussing the national economy, while Carol, excluded from the men's conversation, listened to her mother-in-law complain about her father-in-law while making coffee in the kitchen. After another few minutes of small talk over coffee, the ritual visit ended with the son saying, "Well, I guess we'd better hit the road; we have a long drive. See you next month." It seemed as if all the pain and anger was contained in the repetitive structure of these events. If anything were changed, the edifice might crack and all the unex-pressed emotions and unresolved issues would come pouring out.

The worker through slowly altering the repressive ritual helped the two generations come together in an acknowledgment of their common grief. Beginning with minor innovations which would precipitate a shift in the rigid pattern, the worker assigned Carol and Richard the task of bringing a surprise picnic supper and later planning an extra visit. Richard was coached to stay in the kitchen with Carol while his mother made coffee, and he discovered that his isolated father quickly joined the three-some. The four gradually began to touch tentatively upon the sorrowful and forbidden topic and to express some of the hidden anger, making the marriage and intergenerational issues more available for change. It is the worker's speculation that the eventual development of a memorial ritual in which the grandparents participate will play a significant role in con-tinued family change.

In the previous pages, we have described a number of strategies for promoting change in families. Many of these strategies have been exem-plified in situations where families are willing at least to try a prescribed task and to entertain the possibility of doing things in a different way. Such families, if our expectations are appropriate to their goals, congruent with their values and life-styles, and not beyond family capacities, will move to reorganize their structure one step at a time.

What, however, of families who cling to their problematic patterns and will not or cannot respond to the worker's efforts for change?

Chapter 14

Persistence, Coherence, and Paradox

CHANGE CAN BE FRIGHTENING. In some families, any change is perceived as an enemy which must be warded off—a threat to coherence, stability, or even continued existence. And although such a family may approach a mental health professional or social agency for help with a particular problem, their implicit message is often this: "Change our problem, but don't change anything else!" The problem that such a family wants resolved is usually some upsetting or seemingly dysfunctional behavior on the part of one of its members, and they are certain to repudiate any indication on the part of the practitioner that the total family system has a stake in the problem. Such families are generally called "resistant" or "stuck" and their power can be defeating to any worker hoping to overcome the resistance and somehow push the family to change.

A therapeutic response to such families requires a reframing of the meaning of resistance. First, it is important to remember (and it has been stressed throughout this volume) that families over a period of time propagate rules and patterns of behavior which gain a certain coherence and which serve to preserve the family. "Symptoms" or problematic behaviors are often an essential, indeed a key part, of the family's effort to maintain itself. The family is not resisting so much as trying desperately, in Lynn Hoffman's language, to persist. The symptom should be understood, then, not as a problem but rather as a solution to another more grievous or threatening problem, one which might expose a feared secret, threaten

326

the family with dissolution, or otherwise shake its very foundations. Such a family is in a paradoxical situation in the sense that they want the disturbing symptom to change but they do not want, or rather are afraid for, the family itself to change. Yet one cannot happen without the other.

The Therapeutic Paradox

The therapeutic response to the family's paradoxical situation has been termed the "therapeutic paradox" or the "counterparadox." The therapeutic paradox, sometimes referred to as the therapeutic double bind, contains the following elements. First, it is assumed that the symptom or identified problem serves an essential function in the maintenance of the family system. Second, a hypothesis is developed which describes how the problem or symptom serves the family. Such a hypothesis, to be truly systemic, should include the responses to or participation in the symptom of every member of the family. This hypothesis is stated to the family in positive terms, or in terms which describe how the behavior may be helping the family. Third, the family and the symptom bearer are cautioned *not* to change and very specific reasons are given concerning possible detrimental outcomes to the family should change be attempted. This leaves the family members facing their own paradoxical situation. In responding to the family's paradox with a counterparadox, the practitioner may achieve several aims. The family's paradox is dramatized; and moreover the practitioner has respected the family's efforts to preserve its coherence. The worker *joins* rather than pits herself against the family's resistance. The statement of the therapeutic paradox also breaks the metarule that tends to exist in double binds, that is, the rule that no one is allowed to comment or make explicit the conflicting commands.

The family has three avenues open in response to the therapeutic double bind. One is to accept their troubles as inevitable and unsolvable. Another is to accept the possibility of change, and a third is to attempt to disqualify or invalidate the family-centered practitioner as a source of help. The family's efforts to disqualify, however, may be preempted in some very specific ways. For example, as the Milan team suggests, the counterparadoxical message may be delivered by the worker at the very end of the session, thus precluding all discussion (Palazzoli et al., 1978). This strategy effectively leaves the family without the opportunity to argue, negotiate, or disqualify; it forces them to confront the challenge to change or not change.

Another mechanism which adds drama and power to the intervention is that of having the counterparadoxical prescription sent from behind the mirror from a consultant or members of the therapeutic team. The message is thus not subject to repudiation. In this case, the practitioner may even take a position different from the unseen consultants, or as Papp (1980) has named them, the "Greek Chorus." For example, the worker may say in introducing the message, "The team and I really got into quite an argument today, and although I promised to give you their message, I don't really agree with them." Frequently the team takes the position against change while the worker believes that the family is strong enough to take the risk. When worker and team take different positions, the paradoxical prescription cannot be invalidated by disagreeing with the worker.

Many practitioners wanting to do strategic family work do not have the luxury of a one-way mirror, video equipment, or an observing "Greek Chorus." However, adaptations can be made to capture some of the power of a team, even without these arrangements. For example, a worker may use a colleague or a supervisor between sessions to plan an intervention and then may return to the family with the outside authority's prescription. The worker may agree with the prescription or, as with the team behind the mirror, may set up a contest or challenge. She may report, for example, that she and the consultant saw the situation quite differently and present both points of view, or she may use the outside consultant as a challenger in the following way. "The consultant and I really disagreed about whether you could stand up to your father. In fact, we have a bet on it—he bet you can't and I bet you can!"

There has been considerable debate in the professional literature concerning the definitions and uses of paradoxes, and there have been differing views as to when they should or should not be used (Fisher, Anderson, and Jones, 1981; Haley, 1973; Hare-Mustin, 1976; Hoffman, 1981; L'Abate and Weeks, 1978). Paul Dell has termed paradoxical therapy "a set of techniques in search of a theory" (1981:41), while Palazzoli (1981) states that the complexities of a systemic approach prove too great a challenge for the limitations of our minds. In her view we should take a simplifying and above all pragmatic approach. Some therapists, particularly those outside the field of family therapy, have been highly critical of paradoxical interventions, characterizing them as manipulations or "tricks," as "lying," or as playing false with the client or family. Undoubtedly some tricks have been played on families in treatment in the name of paradox and as such, may have given paradoxical interventions a bad name. A true counterparadox, however, is neither trick nor lie. It is an honest restatement of the family game or the family's own paradoxical situation, accompanied by a genuine cautionary prescription which supports the family's coherence and warns the family of the potential threats to its stability, should change be attempted.

The counterparadox is often surprising and sometimes produces anger or amusement. The surprise generally comes from the fact that the practitioner is not taking the stance that "helpers" are supposed to take, that is, against the symptom and thus, by definition, against the family's coherence. The anger or amusement is the response to the accuracy of the hypothesis, to the fact that the family has been caught at its game. Perhaps the counterparadox can best be understood through illustration. In chapter 10 we developed a hypothesis concerning Barbara, the twenty-year-old who had become depressed, left college, and moved back home. The hypothesis suggested that Barbara's failure to grow up was related to the need her parents had for her to help them maintain a marital triangle. The following counterparadoxical message was read to the family at the end of a session.

We believe that Barbara is playing a very important and helpful role for her entire family. By remaining a child, she provides an ongoing permanent relationship for her mother. This helps to maintain the marriage by involving mother and at the same time freeing father to devote himself to his work and his relationship with Virginia (his mistress). It also helps Pete and David to move out and to pursue their own interests. We feel that in order for the family to continue in its present form, Barbara must continue in this role in the family. Should she really change and abandon her childlike position, we have great concern about what would happen to the total family.

The counterparadox thus consisted of a statement of the hypothesis, positively connoted, coupled with a warning restraining the family from change. The family's response to being faced with the logic of its own system was immediate. The father looked at his wife and said, "We can't let this happen." Following this session, the parents took responsibility for initiating marital therapy.

In another case we used an adaptation of a counterparadoxical prescription used by Palazzoli and her team and presented at a Toronto conference in 1979. We have dubbed this intervention "The Unusual Marriage Prescription."

Janet and Fred, who hoped to get married, had been dating for about three years. Each had previously been married for approximately twenty-five years, and each had three children. Fred's marriage had been annulled by the Roman Catholic Church, but Janet's husband had refused to agree to an annulment. When the annulment request was approved over his objections by the bishop of the diocese, the husband filed a new challenge which meant, Janet and Fred informed the worker, that the case would now proceed up the Church hierarchy to Rome, a process they mournfully explained might take at least three years. To further complicate things, Janet's fourteen-year-old daughter, Marcie, who was extremely tied to her mother and who had spent much of her childhood meeting her unhappy mother's emotional needs, was adamantly opposed to the new marriage and was threatening to go live with her father. Janet felt she could not risk losing her daughter.

At the end of the second session, the following "unusual marriage" prescription was given:

It looks to me as if it will not be possible for you two to be married for a very long time, because in many ways Janet is already married to you, Marcie. Janet, you and Marcie formed this unusual mother–daughter marriage a long time ago when you became increasingly unhappy in your marriage to Marcie's father. Marcie, you have made many sacrifices for your mother by taking the place of your father and giving her the affection she so desperately needed. Now your mother has found a new person to love and you feel betrayed because you have given so much in the past. I think until you, Janet, and you, Marcie are able to get an annulment too, it will be advisable to postpone the marriage to Fred.

Janet and Fred set a wedding date the following week.

A COUNTERPARADOXICAL THERAPEUTIC STANCE

The Milan team model requires that the counterparadoxical prescription emanate from the team behind the mirror at the end of the session. This is a very powerful intervention and many family therapists who utilize it reserve it for families that have failed to respond to other therapies or interventions, or families which are clearly caught in rigid and repetitive symptomatic patterns. Other applications of this approach are possible, however, in less intractable situations, or when a person is working alone with a family, without the benefit of co-worker, team, or consultant. For example, we have found it quite useful to maintain a counterparadoxical position throughout our work with some families, and to make occasional interventions emanating from this stance throughout the course of a session. Such a stance is maintained by keeping constantly in mind that persistent, problematic behavior may be serving an important maintenance function for the total family, and accordingly by warning against change. The following case highlights how such a stance might be used.

Jennifer's school work in her senior year in high school began to deteriorate seriously. Her stepfather of several years, who had kept himself (and had been kept by his wife) quite remote from Jennifer, was drawn into the problematic situation because he was ostensibly more qualified than mother to help with homework, particularly with math and science, Jennifer's special areas of difficulty. The worker commented, "It is very smart of you, Jennifer, to figure out a way to help Harry be a father to you, particularly since it won't be long before you will be growing up and leaving home. Then he might never have a chance!"

When Jennifer's grades improved very quickly, the worker expressed concern, suggesting that perhaps she should not improve her school work quite so rapidly. "If you cease to need Harry's help, Jennifer, your relationship might again deteriorate."

Perhaps the most difficult stance for social workers to adopt, since they have been educated to be supportive and to praise change enthusiastically, is that of the doubtful or worried counselor. Yet it is a role worth playing, for not only does it communicate to the family an appreciation of their efforts to preserve stability and coherence, but it avoids a contest in which the worker pushes for change and the family members anxiously and stubbornly defend their position.

Further, some families, which Papp (1980) defines as "defiance-based," become challenged by the worker's cautions and concerns about change and are stimulated to prove the worker wrong or to defy her by making some change. For example, when a defiant family announces they neither need nor want family therapy, it is often useful to agree with them, and to add, "While we have concluded that family therapy is the choice of therapy for your family, we think family therapy is really difficult. Your family may not be ready for it yet." Such a comment is experienced by a defiant family as a challenge they find difficult to resist. Sometimes the combination of both support and caution is useful. For example: "It's really amazing how much you have been able to accomplish in these few weeks . . . But it worries me . . . Things seem to be changing awfully fast, and I think so much change so fast may place too great a strain on the family."

Predicting a regression is also a useful technique. For example, it is often helpful to say that there will have to be at least one and probably two occasions in the next two weeks when the problematic behavior will recur. If the family takes a defiant stance and proves the worker wrong, well, so much the better, and the therapist need only express amazement and own the mistaken prediction. If the problematic behavior does recur, the family need not be disappointed or fearful that all is lost, because the regression has been framed as an expected part of progress.

Novel Solutions to Chronic Difficulties

Watzlawick, Weakland and Fisch (1974), Rabkin (1977), and other members of the Palo Alto group descend from the same tradition as does the Milan group, namely the work of Bateson (1956; 1972; 1978). However, their concepts and interventive strategies, although also systemic and cybernetic, have taken a somewhat different turn.

The Palo Alto group suggests that problematic behaviors exist in families not necessarily because they have important functions for maintenance (although they may have begun that way), but because the behaviors themselves are maintained by the environment's response and most frequently by the very responses which are called upon to control or change the behavior. These inadvertently symptom-maintaining responses are found within the family, in the surrounding environment, and within the helping community. These theorists argue with considerable logic that if familial and professional solutions had been effective, the family would not still be in need of help. Examples of such deviation-amplifying transactions have appeared throughout this volume and include the wife who attempts to reach her emotionally elusive husband by pursuing him (which of course stimulates him to distance himself farther) or the family and school which attempts to deal with a rebellious adolescent by the institution of more authority and control.

Understanding this process by which problematic behavior is maintained or even exacerbated leads to the notion that the intervention must be novel—in fact sometimes even the exact reverse of existing family and community responses to the problem. For example, the pursuing wife may be taught to distance herself from her husband, or the rebellious adolescent given his or her freedom. During this process, the members of the family and social environment are credited for their efforts to bring about change but at the same time they are told that their approaches were understandable and well-meaning but mistaken.

Novel solutions which interrupt and turn around deviation-amplifying (or in Bateson's term, schismogenic) processes may be in the form of reversals, as described above, or may be new responses. One novel intervention which may be utilized is the prescription to intensify or exaggerate the very pattern which has been exacerbating the problem. Such intensification may create an escalation to the point that family members "get sick of" the interactions and recoil from them, or else it may precipitate a crisis which disturbs the equilibrium enough so that the patterned behavior breaks down, and new behaviors or solutions are demanded. In the following example, a crisis is precipitated:

The Vanderwaters' response to their adolescent daughter Amy's sexual involvement with her boyfriend and her occasional violation of curfew was constantly to threaten out-of-the-home placement. Amy, locked in a power struggle with her parents, was an outstanding student, a violinist in the school orchestra, captain of the girls' soccer team, in every way the closest to fulfilling the parents' high aspirations for their four children.

When the worker's efforts to resolve the power struggle and to reestablish a workable family hierarchy through the use of direct interventions and tasks was unsuccessful, she decided to "go with the resistance" and, in fact, to push the parents to follow through with their threats. The worker proceeded to encourage the family to select an appropriate institutional placement from among the resources she had explored. When the parents began to retreat, she insisted it was the only viable solution. As the threat of placement became a reality, a crisis was precipitated and the family began to propose alternative means for coping with their daughter's differentiation efforts.

Case Management and the Selection of Intervention Strategies

The adoption of an eclectic systems approach has both advantages and problems. One is presented with a wide array of options and a variety of assessment and interventive strategies which may be mobilized in understanding and helping a family. On the other hand, one is also faced with the difficult challenge of integrating various perspectives and of selecting from among the many alternatives those most appropriate to the situation at hand. Most of the originators in the family therapy field do not help us with these tasks, since they are devoting themselves to the development, elaboration, and evaluation of their particular approaches, and often to demonstrating how a particular theory of intervention differs from others, rather than searching for similarity, integration, and complementarity. Similarly, the current state of evaluative research in the family field does not furnish us with much definitive data concerning the effectiveness of the various interventive approaches in particular situations.

Some leaders, are beginning to address themselves to these issues. Peggy Papp (1980), for example, attempts to distinguish those circumstances when she employs direct interventions from those when she turns to the use of paradox. Lynn Hoffman (1981) defines as a major task for family theorists and practitioners the integration of historical perspective and the use of historical material with the focus on systems transactions in the present. For the time being, however, each family therapist or family-centered practitioner must contend with this issue alone. It is a comforting fact that as one becomes increasingly experienced, one is more easily able to integrate a varied array of approaches to change.

Our own efforts to master this task are still in process as we attempt to make differing use of ecological, structural, intergenerational, strategic, and paradoxical resources for change. The task is extremely difficult, for new knowledge in this field appears at what often seems an exponential rate of speed; throughout this volume, the extent to which we are currently both failing and succeeding in this task in undoubtedly evident to the reader. Some principles continue to guide us, however. First, and most importantly, as we have repeatedly emphasized, interventive plans should grow out of both an initial and ongoing assessment process. This circular, cybernetic assessment–intervention–assessment process entails both a comprehensive understanding of the family and its situation and a careful monitoring of the family's response to interventive efforts.

Second, we tend to be guided by the principle of parsimony, that is, the notion that the *least* intervention which will bring about the desired change is the best. This principle is in direct opposition to the assumption so often made in psychotherapy that if a little intervention is good, then more must be better. Yet because of the ever-present possibility of unforeseen consequences and iatrogenic effects, we try to limit rather than to expand our role in the life of a family. This does not necessarily mean that we shy away from the use of powerful interventions, such as paradox. Papp, as we said above, suggests that paradoxical interventions be utilized primarily with defiant, resistant families who are caught in intractable, repetitive cycles. We have found, additionally, that the use of therapeutic paradoxes with motivated and better-functioning families is both powerful and pragmatic, hastening change and making the contact more focused and thus briefer.

We do, however, in the interests of economy of time and effort, make use of the team for families on whose behalf the support, the objective observation, and the power of the unreachable Greek Chorus are truly required. These families are generally identified by the severity of the symptoms of their "identified patient," by obvious evidence of resistance to any kind of change, or by a history of failed attempts to get help.

The principle of parsimony also pertains to the use of time in that we favor brief over long-term intervention and, in most cases, the spacing of appointments at least two weeks apart. Time between appointments is often required for the intervention to work, like yeast in bread dough, or for the clients to complete their tasks. Third, we tend to be highly pragmatic in our approaches. If the intervention strategy is working, we continue it. If it is not, we are ready to admit our errors and adopt another.

Finally, we do not hesitate to draw upon a variety of models from case to case or to move from one approach to another within a single case, as different phases of the work develop or as different issues emerge. The use of a variety of strategies may also be called for in planned short-term treatment, which will be illustrated in chapter 15 in work with the Marzikian family. In the long-term, open-ended work with the Gray family, described below, we demonstrate the integration of a number of interventive approaches.

The Family Case of a Mental Patient Who Achieved a Midlife Career Change

---

Jerry and Edith Gray, ages forty and thirty-eight respectively, were referred for family therapy by the local psychiatric hospital where Edith had been seen on both an inpatient and outpatient basis. Family counseling had been suggested by the psychiatrist, who continued to treat Edith with psychotropic medications, because he felt that the family needed help in "coping with" and "adapting to" Edith's illness. Edith had been hospitalized a number of times throughout her marriage and before, and had been diagnosed at various times as "manic depressive," "unipolar depressive," "chronic depressive," or "suffering from agitated depression." It was learned that she had first been taken by her parents to a psychiatrist at age eight. Thus Edith had successfully occupied for much of her life and in both her family of origin and current family the role of mental patient.

Jerry and Edith have three children: Ann, aged thirteen, Bill, aged eleven, and Alice, aged nine. Alice, like her mother before her, is a youngest child and second daughter. She also was taken to a therapist at the age of eight. Alice's symptom was that she was afraid of electric storms. The family was seen in family sessions for nine months on a biweekly basis and then once a month for a year. The worker seeing the family was supervised by one of the authors, who also studied some of the videotapes and consulted from behind the mirror on a number of occasions. In the course of the almost two years of contact, many interventions were employed and a number of complex themes were woven into the fabric of the work. It will be impossible to describe the development of all of these themes; rather, the major phases, strategies, and shifts that marked the process will be identified and described.

SOCIAL HISTORY

Historical information was shared at various times throughout the course of the family work. Some of the more salient facts are assembled here. Edith, the youngest of three children, grew up in an upper-middle-class family. Her father, an aggressive and successful businessman and an alcoholic, favored his youngest daughter. He died four years before the Grays began family work. Edith's mother was described by her as unaffectionate and anxious, showing interest primarily in what she considered to be Edith's psychological problem. Edith was clearly the child who was most triangled into the parent's marriage, becoming a major preoccupation for her mother, a buffer between her parents, and a distraction which helped to divert attention from her father's alcoholism.

Edith was defined very early as fragile, sickly, and needing special care. This early identification was probably in part encouraged by the fact that she had a serious, almost fatal bout with pneumonia at age three and it was given intergenerational emphasis by the fact that Edith's aunt, her mother's youngest sister, was the dysfunctional member of that sibling group.

Jerry was the eldest of two boys and one girl in a working-class family of Polish descent. His family name had been anglicized shortly after his grandparents had emigrated to Cleveland, Ohio when his father was ten years old. Both his grandfather and father had worked in the steel mills. Jerry's younger brother, Greg, was as ambitious as the rest of the family, and though lacking a college education, had worked his way up into a middle management position and was quite successful. Greg is married and also has three children. Jerry's frequently repeated memory of growing up was that his brother, although younger than he, could always "beat him up." Jerry's mother was a frail and sickly woman and Jerry, who occupied a parental caretaking role with her, was her favorite. He was named after her father, who had died in her childhood.

The first member of the family to go to college, Jerry majored in business and accounting. His plan to go on to graduate school, however, was interrupted first by a tour in the army during the Vietnamese War, which he spent in ordnance in the United States, and then by marriage. He felt trapped in a routine job in a large, bureaucratic firm where he neither earned a high salary nor had much opportunity to move ahead. His job was a constant source of frustration and discontent, and the shortage of money and his seeming lack of success were constant points of contention between him and Edith.

Jerry and Edith met on a blind date in Baltimore, Edith's home, when Jerry was in the service. They subsequently met on his furloughs and corresponded regularly while Jerry was shipped around the country. Shortly after his discharge they were married and within a year Ann was born. Since marriage, Jerry has become increasingly alienated from his family of origin.

INITIAL SESSION

The Grays arrived late for the first meeting, but quickly and actively involved themselves with Glen, the worker. Mental health agencies and professionals were clearly not a new experience for the Grays. The two younger children were intrigued by the one-way mirror and the video equipment, and enjoyed seeing themselves on tape.

Much about the structure and nature of the processes in this family began to emerge in the initial session. Edith looked rather bizarre in her dress and appeared to be somewhat agitated, smoking one cigarette after another. She rarely looked at Glen but did occasionally contribute to the conversation. Jerry was resigned and careworn. He appeared to shepherd the family into the session and immediately attempted to set up an alliance with Glen as cotherapist, talking about Edith and her illness in quasi-professional language. Ann now and then joined him in this endeavor, sat near her father, and frequently reprimanded the younger children, particularly her brother. Jerry and Edith sat on opposite sides of the room, while Alice pulled a chair over to sit close to her mother, was clinging and affectionate with her, and occasionally nestled on the edge of her mother's chair. Edith's pleasure in the attentiveness of Alice was obvious. Billy danced around the room, creating distractions, exploring, and occasionally making an unsuccessful attempt to break into one of the two fixed dyads in the family, Jerry and Ann, or Edith and Alice. By the end of the session, the family had demonstrated their structural arrangements (see Figure 14.1).

Jerry and Edith seemed distant and estranged, with Jerry playing the role of burdened caretaker and Edith the role of fragile patient, although occasionally she would attempt to reduce the power differential by mak-

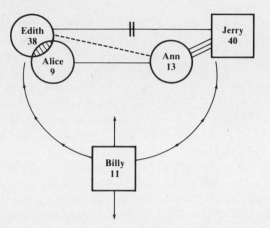

FIGURE 14.1

ing remarks about Jerry's lack of success and the family's financial difficulties. Ann was clearly not only the parental child who had assumed much
of Edith's role with her siblings, but was also Jerry's adult companion.
Alice was fearful and adhering to her mother, although she could become
lively and playful with Billy and was able to leave mother to experiment
with the video. However, even when occupied elsewhere, she usually kept
a keen eye on mother and when Edith seemed sad or withdrawn, returned
to cheer her up or keep her in contact with the family. Other layers of
organization would emerge as the case developed, but this initial vision
of the main outlines of the family structure most characterized the family.

The second primary area for investigation in the first session concerned the function of the symptom—Edith's depression—in the maintenance of the family system. The children were most helpful, as they often
are, in illuminating the patterns. When the topic of mother's depression
arose almost immediately, Glen reframed this symptom as "sadness" and
used the technique of circular ranking questions to ask each person to rank
everyone in the family in terms of sadness. All members ranked Jerry, not
Edith, as the saddest person in the family. This ranking question helped
Glen begin to validate the first portion of a circular hypothesis, namely
that Edith's illness was serving some protective function in relation to
Jerry's sadness. It also reframed and normalized heretofore pathologically
labeled depression as sadness, an emotion experienced by every member
of the family. Thus began the task of moving Edith out of the patient role.

ALTERING THE FAMILY'S STRUCTURE

The initial focus of Glen's work with the Grays was on restructuring the
family, and it continued intermittently throughout the contact. The ul-

timate goals were to strengthen the boundaries between the generations, to replace Ann with Edith in the roles of parent and wife, and to strengthen the relationship between the spouses. Later in the work, the extent to which Jerry was distancing himself from all of the family members became apparent, and so Glen worked with the family to help Jerry relate more effectively as a father to his children, particularly to Billy, who was estranged from him and who tended to occupy an outsider's role as observer, commentator, and distracter. Glen did not expect that the achievement of these structural shifts would be a simple task or come about rapidly, but a carefully maintained image of the reorganized family provided him with a road map as he worked with them.

In the second and third sessions, the suppressed marital conflict began to emerge although the children quickly moved to restore the status quo by diverting and separating the parents. It became obvious that the family was terrified about what might happen should the parents really fight. However, before they were successfully interrupted, father expressed some anger at Edith about how her illness was ruining their lives and Edith attacked Jerry with a "laundry list" of disappointments and complaints, unfavorably comparing their economic lifestyle with the one her father had provided. It was at this point that Ann quickly moved in to protect her father. Edith also mentioned her wish for a career, which Jerry immediately disparaged, pointing out that since she couldn't even manage a house, she certainly couldn't manage a job. Almost as an aside he added, "A woman with three children should stay home and take care of them."

Glen intervened into the family structure throughout the sessions, attempting to block the children's interference in the marital dyad and to demarcate the generations, giving the parents an opportunity to communicate directly. This resulted, as expected, in escalating conflict and even more active efforts on the children's part to stay in the middle. When Edith withdrew into depressed silence and Jerry distanced himself, the family peace was restored, but at considerable cost.

Careful interviewing concerning the events surrounding Edith's most recent hospitalization revealed the possibility that the hospitalization served to bring the family together. Jerry spent much less time at work, everyone pitched in to run the household, and the whole family gathered to visit Edith regularly, often combining these trips with a family treat or excursion. It became clear that the family functioned better and was more intimately involved when Edith was in the hospital, a fact which led Glen to think that contrary to the view of the referring psychiatrist, it was not managing the illness with which the family needed help, but rather adapting to her improved functioning.

The first restructuring homework assignment was given following session three. Glen divided the family into its male and female subsystems and involved them separately in planning an activity which each subsystem would do separately before the next family meeting. This strategy was considered a less threatening one than a more direct approach to the marital dyad and to Ann's involvement in it. The hope was that a beginning shift could be made by giving Ann and Edith an opportunity to be a mother and daughter rather than estranged competitors.

Surprisingly, the females did better than the males. Edith and the girls went out for lunch and shopping. But Jerry and Billy could not think of anything to do, and finally went to a movie which neither liked, then stopped for ice cream afterward. They both shrugged when asked how it had gone.

In the following session, more conflict emerged between the parents. Edith was furious after overhearing Jerry talking to his parents on the phone, in one of their rare contacts, about her hospitalization; she did not like the way he spoke about it. This episode was reframed by Glen, who commented that Jerry needed help in learning how to talk about and express his feelings, to his family or anyone else. A hopeful sign emerged when Ann attempted to involve herself in the argument between her parents and Jerry told her that this issue was between "me and my wife."

The consultant behind the mirror during this session sent the following message to the family. "The children in this family are very good at expressing their feelings, but it seems more difficult for the adults, particularly for Jerry. Perhaps it would be too frightening for the family if Jerry talked about his sadness and his fears. We think Jerry should go very slowly in learning to do this."

In the following session, it was Edith who responded to this injunction against change by announcing that things in the house were hopeless and that she had to get out and do something with her life. The whole family reacted to this startling announcement with all of the reasons why it would be impossible for her to do so. By the next meeting, the old balance had been restored. Edith was agitated, Jerry was definitely in charge and long-suffering, and the children were quiet, feeling secure that mother's push toward potentially disruptive change had subsided.

This reinstatement of the old balance was only temporary, however, as Glen continued to help the family strengthen generational boundaries and alliances by blocking the children's involvement in the marital dyad, thus readjusting the hierarchy. One of the most moving sessions occurred when Jerry confessed that he didn't know how to talk to the children or to encourage them to talk to him. In a delightful enactment, which targeted many aspects of the family's structure, Jerry and Billy pretended to be riding in a car. This was suggested by Edith, who said that it was when driving that she had the best talks with the children. Jerry continued to have trouble with the conversation and Glen suggested that Edith, in an altered version of the backseat driver role, sit behind Jerry and coach him. The rigid marital balance of functional husband and dysfunctional wife was temporarily altered, as Edith, by helping Jerry, assumed the competent role of teacher.

At the end of this session, the parents hinted that they wanted to talk about their relationship without the children, which led to a scheduling of the next appointment for the parents alone. Interestingly, instead of focusing on the marital pair this session resulted in an episode of work on family of origin issues. The session began with the shared complaint that the marriage seemed dead, although in responding to an assignment the previous week they had gone out as a couple for the first time in over two years, and had had a good time. Edith then began to talk of the death of her father four years before. She expressed her ambivalent and intense feelings about this larger-than-life, tremendously assertive, and successful figure. She said that although he was unpredictable, distant, and verbally abusive at times, he had been the only person with whom she could really be herself; he thought she was all right, even special. It was apparent that Edith had not been allowed to mourn her father. In fact, her family and Jerry, so certain that she could not sustain the loss, had protected her by cutting her off from information about his final illness, and from participating in his illness or death. There had only been a brief trip to the funeral, with tight control maintained to prohibit any open expression of feeling.

Jerry also spoke of his family, his parents' unhappy marriage, and his fears that his marriage was following the same pattern. Following this meeting with Jerry and Edith, family of origin work became a recurring focus throughout the contact. Edith began to mourn her father, wrote him a letter telling him all the things she had wanted to say to him before he died, and finally, for the first time, visited the grave. She initiated correspondence with her mother's youngest sister and invited her for a visit, discovering that much about her aunt that had been defined by her family as "disturbed" could more accurately be described as independent, different, and at most eccentric. Finally, toward the end of the first year of treatment, when Edith's mother was visiting, Glen and the two women met for a very meaningful session.

Jerry, too, began to reconnect with his family. His primary goal was to get better acquainted with his father. The two boys in his family had been so clearly "assigned" to the different parents, he to his mother and his brother to his father, that he had never, within his memory, spent any time alone or had a one-to-one conversation with his father. Much to his amazement, his father was responsive to his approach, and eventually Jerry felt safe and comfortable enough to talk over his job frustration with him, obtaining both suggestions and support concerning how to deal with his work situation in a manner that might enhance his freedom and power and expand his options.

Later on in the course of treatment, Jerry also began to reconnect with his younger brother, about whom he had particularly conflicted feelings. The brother, Greg, larger and outwardly more aggressive, had, as noted, been able easily to best Jerry physically when they were boys; and Jerry had learned that the only way to win and to gain control with his brother was to withdraw and refuse to fight, a tactic he now used with Edith, and one which his mother had also used with his father. In talking with his brother, he was stunned to learn that Greg had always looked up to *him*, particularly because of his school achievements, and in fact often felt inferior. As Jerry experienced more genuine communication with his father and brother, he found himself more able to connect with his son. Furthermore, as Edith and Jerry began to confront their family of origin issues more directly, there was a marked de-escalation of tension in the marriage.

After about four months of contact, and despite some efforts on the part of the family to sabotage the improvement, Edith (whose almost exclusive contact with her ecological environment for years had been with mental health systems), began to make tentative efforts to establish new connections. She collected contributions for the cancer drive in her neighborhood, which was a considerable achievement, and gave her structured practice in approaching people as well as at least minimally connecting her with her neighbors. Finally, with great anxiety, she signed up for a course at the local college, planning, perhaps, to finish her bachelor's degree.

In the eleventh session, after Edith signed up for her class and announced her resolution to finish school, Glen intervened with a major metaphorical reframing of Edith's symptoms that marked a turning point in the case. Edith was quite agitated, expressing fears that she could not manage the schoolwork, while the family showed their ambivalence about her attempted change by alternate supportive and undermining responses. Glen ended the session by predicting that this was going to be a difficult time for the family. Edith, he said, was now embarking on a midlife career change, always a big undertaking for any person. She had been deeply involved for many years in a full-time career as a mental patient and now was considering retiring from that career to take on some new role, for example, that of student. This reframing clearly hit the mark, and Edith said in enthusiastic agreement, "And it's been my main career for thirty years! My mother launched me on it when I was eight when she took me to a psychiatrist because I wouldn't sit still." "Thirty years is a long time on one job," Glen responded. "It seems to me retirement after so long deserves a gold watch or something."

Glen and his consultant hypothesized between sessions about the possible ways the family might respond to the "midlife career change" reframing. Glen was prepared for increased conflict between the parents, especially for depression in Jerry or problematic behavior among the children. In the following session, Glen attempted to preempt such consequences by predicting these and other possible responses. The family discussed possible outcomes if Edith really managed her career change, and Edith commented that perhaps Jerry's career might begin to worsen because he always seemed to do better when she was in bad shape!

In the following two sessions, there was considerable tension and a sense of excitement. It was apparent that things were shifting, but it was difficult to track exactly what was happening. The family reported various events that had occurred between sessions. Edith complained that she could not study. The family had received a call from school advising them that Alice was not handing in her assignments. Jerry had been vaguely ill with some gastrointestinal complaints and Edith told him quite sharply to do something to take care of himself. "If it were I," she said, "you would make it a federal case and drag me to the doctor." At one point Billy commented that it was boring when his mother was home because she cooked meals and they didn't get to go to Taco Bell and besides that, they had to go to bed on time.

In the next session, the limitations of preemption were confirmed, as the family once again managed to outwit the therapist by managing to do something that Glen had failed to predict. As Glen told the consultant, "It was the most obvious thing. I should have predicted it." Edith had been rehospitalized over the weekend; but, marking her shortest hospitalization ever, she returned home in three days.

Glen reframed the hospitalization for the family by commenting that perhaps after thirty years, a complete job change all at once could not be expected. Edith agreed, saying that things were happening too fast. "If I'm not being the sick person in the family, I don't know what else to do." Discussion centered on the fact that early retirement from her full-time job as mental patient really necessitated many new adjustments. Edith would have to find other ways to fill her life. Perhaps one college course was not enough. Toward the end of the session, Glen commented in an offhand way, "It's too bad Blue Cross doesn't cover a three-day stay at a resort hotel."

The next few sessions confirmed slow but continued change in the family's former paradigm, that of a family organized around the care of a sick mother. Initially Alice escalated her fears and problems in school and Edith temporarily began thinking that she should stay home and devote herself full-time to the children. The consultant was behind the mirror when the issue of Alice's escalating problems came up and a message was sent to the family praising Alice's efforts to slow down the changes in the family and to attempt to fill mother's life with yet another role, that of mother to a child in trouble. She was following a family tradition, as

Edith had kept her mother busy the same way for many years. The message recommended that Alice continue to present the family with problems until mother found some other ways to fill her life.

In the following weeks, Edith began to involve herself more outside the home. She joined a woman's discussion group, which initially alarmed the children because there were several divorced women in the group. They discussed their fears that their parents were going to get a divorce. This very usefully put the threatening marital issue on the table and required each parent to take a position by defining their relationship. Jerry looked nervously at Edith, waiting to hear what she would say, and was visibly relieved when she said with considerable firmness that she was staying in the marriage. Jerry then followed suit with a similar, although more equivocal, commitment. Following this meeting, the parents seemed more able to argue openly, although tight controls on the expression of anger continued in force, and the children relinquished their task of monitoring the parents' interactions and preempting their fights.

As Edith began to feel better, Jerry began to appear more depressed. Edith commented that now that she was stronger, he could afford to let himself be sad. She told him it was time he began to face his life and the difficult things instead of ignoring troubles and hiding in a rut as she had done. Jerry talked about how badly he felt about himself as a provider, father, and husband. At one point he commented that now that he had lost his job taking care of Edith, he didn't know how to fit into the family. Edith concurred that her retirement meant changes for him, too. It was around this time that Jerry began to put more energy into a reconnection with his father and brother, which defused the intensity within the family and further increased the potential of drawing on outside resources. Jerry began to cope with his work situation more assertively, and he and Billy went away for a weekend camping trip.

Jerry also experimented with new ways of "taking care" that didn't depend on illness or dysfunction. In one session Glen and the family discussed the fact that there were few family rituals that were planned or celebrated together. In fact, the Taco Bell trip, which had occurred only when Edith was in the hospital, was one of the few that had been celebrated. Coming from such different backgrounds, they had not only been cut off from family, but had also failed to adapt from their separate families modified versions of rituals and celebrations that each could enjoy. One item on Edith's list of complaints had always been that they never did anything together as a family that was fun or had any meaning. Ann agreed, saying, "It's like we don't have any family traditions!" To correct this situation, Jerry and the children planned a surprise celebration for Edith's birthday, which had considerable meaning for her.

At this point, the case was refocused primarily on the marital pair and their relationship, and the children stopped attending the sessions.

Meetings were arranged on a monthly basis and Jerry and Edith continued to attend for almost a year. Edith obtained a part-time job which she managed quite well. The marital themes revolved around fears of too much closeness, of expression of anger, and of loss and abandonment. The marriage of Jerry's parents had been silent and cold. That of Edith's parents relationship had been unpredictable, tumultuous, and even violent. Both feared a repetition of their parents' marriages; but it was almost as if they thought that only these two choices were available to them. They maintained a tight control on affect, which tended to keep the marriage flat, but they felt compelled to avoid potentially threatening expression which they feared might get out of control.

In the course of the year, their focus on the marriage and their performance of a variety of assignments which intensified their intimacy served to "heat up" the relationship but, predictably, these raised the level of conflict and anxiety as well. The new situation was expressed in the following sequence. Jerry began to have a drink Friday nights with his fellow workers at a bar near the Gray's home. Edith agreed that this was important to Jerry, for he had been quite socially isolated at work. One Friday, Jerry was considerably later than usual and Edith walked down to join him, and, clearly, to check up on him. She found him with a group as she had hoped, but to her consternation deep in conversation with an attractive woman who worked in his office. Edith made a scene in the bar, even giving Jerry a hard slap across the face. Then she stormed home and proceeded to throw his clothes out on the porch. When Jerry came home, they had an angry confrontation, but then were able to make up, with Jerry making a stronger commitment to the relationship than he had in the past. Their sexual relationship improved and they began to be more expressive in general. They had fortuitously discovered that when they ceased keeping such tight control of their feelings, nothing so terrible happened.

Shortly after this, although the quality of the marriage had improved, Edith began to have bouts of anxiety when Jerry left for work, and frequently throughout the day became obsessed with the thought that he was having an affair with the young co-worker. To help her, Glen gave the following intervention. Rather than attempt to control or ignore her fears, she was to act on them, with Jerry's cooperation. She was to drive Jerry to work every day. After he went inside she was to wait in the car. In a few minutes he was to come out and reassure her that he was at work and was not going to leave her. Next, Edith was to bring lunch to him at work and then they were to eat it together; and she was to pick him up after work. It happened that Jerry worked on the ground floor of an office building and his desk could be seen through a window on the street. Edith was told that if she became anxious at any other time, she was to go and look through the window and see what Jerry was doing. After a week, Edith called Glen and told him that the anxiety had disappeared. Glen insisted that they continue with the assignment until the next appointment, but Edith, after two more days, rebelled and quit because it was interfering too much with her life.

Jerry and Edith began to focus more on how to express themselves to one another and how to be both close and yet maintain boundaries. They had become active in church again and decided they would attend a marriage encounter group offered through the church. Glen supported this wish on their part to seek help through other than mental health organizations.

Their final appointment came two months after the encounter weekend. Jerry and Edith indicated that things were going fine between them and with the children. Both parents felt they were now ready to try life on their own. The case was terminated with the understanding that they could contact Glen in the future if they felt the need.

Outline for Family Assessment

I. PRESENTING PROBLEM OR NEED

   A. What needs and/or problems have led to the contact?
   B. Who recognizes these needs or problems?
   C. Who initiated contact?
   D. How do the various members of the family define the problem?
   E. How do others (school, court, etc.) define the problem?
   F. What are your initial impressions?

II. THE FAMILY IN SPACE: ECOLOGICAL ASSESSMENT

Major Data Collection and Assessment Tools: Interviewing, the Eco-Map

   A. BASIC NEEDS

   1. Is their income sufficient to meet basic needs?
   2. Does the family have adequate food and shelter?
   3. Is their neighborhood safe and a reasonably pleasant place to live?
   4. Does the family have access to preventive health care and good medical resources?
   5. Can family members get to needed resources, or are they cut off because of location, or lack of public or private transportation or telephone?
   6. Does this family have meaningful social connections with neighbors, friends, community organizations? Is it part of an extended kin network?
   7. Do family members belong to or participate in any group activities?

8. Does the family have the opportunity to share cultural, ethnic or other kinds of meanings or values with others? Are their values in conflict or congruent with the surrounding environment?

9. Is the educational experience a positive one for the children? Do they and other family members have access to other vocational or cultural enrichment opportunities?

10. Do family members have an opportunity to experience effectance and enhance their competence? Do family members work? Is there any satisfaction or gratification in their work? How long has it been since family members have mastered a new experience, generated something new or different, felt proud of an achievement?

B. INDIVIDUAL FAMILY MEMBER'S RELATIONSHIP WITH ENVIRONMENT

1. Is one member more "cut-off" from environmental exchanges?

2. Is one member more involved in stressful connections?

3. Do family members always have "together" transactions with other people or systems or do family members tend to relate to environments separately?

4. Do family members have differential access to and exchange with the world around them?

C. AGENCY–WORKER CONTEXT

1. Are the helping agencies or systems involved with the family pursuing similar or conflicting goals and actions on behalf of the family?

2. Is the family caught between different and confusing sets of expectations?

3. Is the effectiveness of your goal(s) being undermined by conflicting or unclear norms or goals?

4. What is the relationship between your agency and the family? Are the agency's services appropriate and available to meet the needs of the family?

5. Is your agency in conflict with any other important systems in the family's ecological environment?

6. What is the nature of the relationship between you and the family? How do they view you?

D. FAMILY–ENVIRONMENT BOUNDARY

1. Is this family open to new experiences or relationships? Are members free to make individual connections with

other people and organizations? Does the family allow others in physically or emotionally?

2. Are the boundaries flexible, i.e., can they expand and contract adaptively in relation to the environment and the changing developmental needs of the family? Does the family protect its members when necessary and allow differentiation when appropriate?

E. OVERALL ASSESSMENT OF THE FAMILY'S RELATIONSHIP WITH ITS ENVIRONMENT

1. Has this family achieved an adaptive balance with its surrounding environment?
2. Is the family in a state of disequilibrium or in danger of being overwhelmed?
3. Is most of the energy being drained from the family?
4. Is the family only "taking in" from outside systems?
5. Are essential supports or resources to meet basic needs potentially available in the environment or are they lacking? In what particular areas?
6. Does the family need help or enhanced skills in tapping and making use of these resources?
7. What sources of strength, support, or resources could be activated or enhanced?
8. Are there particular sources of stress or conflict?
9. How would you characterize the most salient aspects of the family-environment relationship? For example, family is deprived, socially isolated, overburdened, etc.

III. THE FAMILY IN TIME: INTERGENERATIONAL ASSESSMENT

Major Data Collection and Assessment Tools: Interviewing, the Genogram, Documents, Letters, Visits, Photos, etc.

A. FAMILY PATTERNS

1. What are the most significant family patterns emerging from a study of the genogram?
2. Has the family experienced any major losses through untimely or tragic death, migration, separation?
3. Are there particular themes or events which are "toxic" or around which there is shame, pain, or secrecy?
4. What are the family intergenerational patterns of health?

B. FAMILY DEFINITIONS: THE FAMILY PARADIGM

1. How does the family define itself? What are the major

themes which contribute to its identity, sense of itself, and its particular coherence or construction of reality?

2. What are the major family stories, myths, heroes, and heroines?
3. What family traditions or events evoke pride? How are they marked or celebrated?
4. What rituals and ceremonies are important to the family? What is their meaning?
5. What role does ethnic, racial, cultural, or religious heritage play in the family's identity?
6. How has ethnic or religious intermarriage influenced family relationships and identifications?

C. INDIVIDUAL IDENTIFICATIONS

1. With whom are current family members associated or identified by the family? In what ways? What are the clues? (Names, occupations, sibling position, etc.)
2. What formal roles do individuals carry and how are they similar to and different from those of past generations?
3. What informal roles do they carry? Who else has carried these in the past?

D. CURRENT FAMILY RELATIONSHIPS

1. Are there close ties and open communication with extended family? On both or only one side? (Maternal and paternal.)
2. Is there a significant emotional cut-off from either the maternal or paternal side, or among parent-child or sibling relationships?
3. What is the family's explanation for the cut-off? How did it come about? Who is really maintaining it?
4. What effect does the cut-off have on the family or on particular individuals?

E. SOURCES OF DIFFICULTY

1. Are there serious unresolved intergenerational family issues? How are they being transmitted?
2. Are one or both parents handicapped by too great a degree of fusion with *their* parents?
3. If there is a serious emotional cut-off, what effect does it have on the family or on a particular member?
4. Is much of the family's energy devoted to avoiding intergenerational toxic issues or to maintaining secrets?
5. What dysfunctional roles transmitted from the past are family members carrying?

IV. INSIDE THE FAMILY: STRUCTURE, ORGANIZATION
AND PROCESS

Major Data Collection and Assessment Tools: Observation, interviewing (tracking patterns), family mapping, family sculpture, family drawings, eco-map, observations of families' use of their habitat.

A. FAMILY STRUCTURE

  1. *External boundaries (see linkages to ecological assessment)*
    a. Permeability:
      1. Are the boundaries relatively open, for example, clear but permeable?
      2. Are the boundaries relatively closed, for example, opaque, relatively impermeable?
      3. Are the boundaries random, for example, inadequate, little cohesion?
    b. Variation:
      1. Do some members have more or higher quality or less stressed exchanges with the outer world than others? Why?
      2. What effect do these differentiated exchange relationships have on the individual? On the family as a whole?
    c. Membership:
      1. Where are the external boundaries drawn? *Who* is included within the intimate family network?
      2. Is the family isolated from extended family or family of origin?
      3. Does it welcome and embrace new members, for example, through courtship or marriage?
      4. Are outsiders welcome to "share a common table"?
  2. *Part-Whole Relationships: Separateness and Connectedness*
    a. Enmeshment or Fusion
      1. Are the parents overinvolved in their children's lives?
      2. Does the family tolerate difference?
      3. Do parents "worry" too much about the children? Each other?
      4. Can members make meaningful connections outside the family system?
      5. Are individuals' efforts to individuate experienced by the family as disloyalty or abandonment?

      6. Are family members able to take "I-positions"?

  .b. Disengagement, Emotional Cut-Off

      1. Do the parents fail to attend to important emotional or physical needs of the children?

      2. Do family members seem impervious or insensitive to one another?

      3. Is close emotional or physical contact avoided?

  c. Loving, Caring, and Attachment

      1. How would you characterize this family's affective relationships?

      2. What is the quality of family member's attachments to one another?

      3. Are family members able to be affectionate, nurturing, validating, and appreciative of one another?

      4. How do family members show that they care and care for? How are they unable to show and why?

3. Sociocultural Themes and Values

  a. How is the family's structure influenced by its particular ethnic and religious history? (See linkages here to intergenerational assessment.)

  b. What is valued or not valued?

  c. What are the implications of cultural ethnicity for family-environment boundaries, individual variation in family-environment exchange and in family-membership? (See linkages here to ecological assessment.)

  d. What are the implications for separateness and connectedness? For example, are there cultural norms which influence expectations for family loyalty and the degree and quality of involvement?

  e. Do these norms mesh or conflict with the surrounding cultural milieu? For the whole family? For particular family members? (See linkages here to ecological assessment.)

B. FAMILY ORGANIZATION

1. *Internal Boundaries*

  a. How is the family system organized?

  b. What are the relationships among subsystems?

  c. Is there a clear boundary between the spouse subsystem and the children subsystem?

  d. Do both adults and children have clearly demarcated time and space for themselves?

  e. Is the parental subsystem marked by clear boundaries

in terms of membership, function, consistency of roles, and lines of authority?

f. Is the parental subsystem accessible to the children?

g. Do the spouses offer each other mutual aid and support?

h. Is the sibling subsystem characterized by mutual aid or competitiveness and rivalry?

2. *Triangles*

a. What are the central triangles and what purposes are they serving?

b. What role is triangling playing in the current problematic behavior or issue?

3. *Roles*

a. Familial Roles

1. Are family roles clear and consistent?

2. Are they complementary? Symmetrical?

3. Do family members possess the skills and competence needed to carry out their familial and social roles?

4. Is there rigidity or flexibility in assigned roles? Conflict?

5. How are role assignments influenced by the family's sociocultural heritage?

6. Is the role structure contributing to the problem or dysfunction?

7. Is the family's solution to the role problem contributing to new or additional problems?

8. What is the role of grandparents or other extended family members?

b. Informal Roles

1. What are the major informal role assignments, for example, caretaker, scapegoat, distracter, family switchboard?

2. How are they defined?

3. Who carries them and how did they get selected?

4. What are their specific functions and effects in this family?

5. Who carried these roles in previous generations? What happened to them?

6. What is the impact on the person carrying this role?

Note: Informal roles may also be assessed in terms of clarity, consistency, conflict, complementarity, etc.

C. FAMILY PROCESSES

1. *Adaptive and Regulating Forces*
   a. What is the function of the family's or an individual's problem in the maintenance of the family system?
   b. What homeostatic or morphostatic forces are helping to maintain stability?
   c. What morphogenic forces are promoting adaptation and change?
   d. What is the family's capacity to receive and exchange new inputs and information?
   e. What developmental and/or transitional forces are currently operating? How is the family adapting to and processing these transitions?

2. *Power and Authority*
   a. What is the hierarchy of and distribution of authority and power in the family? Where is the seat of power?
   b. How are family rules enforced?
   c. What happens when a rule is challenged?
   d. What part does power play in the family's game?
   e. What is the role of power in the relationship between practitioner and family?

3. *Family Communication Processes*
   a. What is the nature of family communication?
   b. What are the rules that govern communication and communication about communication?
   c. What topics can be explored? What subjects are taboo?
   d. What feelings may be expressed? What emotions or thoughts may not be expressed?
   e. Who talks to whom? Where? When? About what?
   f. Are some members left out?
   g. Do some talk for others?
   h. What does the nonverbal communication demonstrate?
   i. Is there congruence between verbal and nonverbal communication? Between digital and analogic communication?
   j. Are communications understandable, clear?
   k. Do members validate each other's statements, or even their own?
   l. How is communication "punctuated"?

4. *Meta Rules (They are rules about the development, maintenance, and alteration of the family's rule system.)*

    a. Can the family's meta rules be commented upon? Is there a process for change?

    b. What are the meanings, values, rituals, ceremonies, myths, pattern regulators which maintain the family rules?

    c. How are these pervasive themes and behaviors contributing to the family's construction of reality? How are they expressed?

    d. Is the family immobilized, caught in rigid, repetitive, ritualized behavior?

    e. What purpose(s) is this behavior serving?

    f. Is the family lacking in ceremonies? Underritualized?

    g. What rules are maintaining the family problem or dysfunction?

Chapter 15.

Family-Centered Practice in the Fields of Aging and Health

WE BEGAN OUR EXPLORATION of family-centered practice with a brief review of the historical links between social work and the family, followed by several chapters which sketched the context in which such practice takes place. In this section we have presented separately the various foci for assessment and intervention, the family-environment interface, the intergenerational family system, and the internal structure and processes of the family.

All of these dimensions are important for an understanding of any particular case. In this chapter we bring these threads together through an application of family-centered practice with the aging and in the delivery of health care. These two topics are presented together, not because aging is considered a disease process, but because there are many parallels in the two fields of practice. In both aging and health care the family's role as a provider of social services may become salient, and in both fields it is often through the crisis of illness or the growing incapacity of an aging person that the family or its elderly members come to the attention of social workers.

The Family and the Aging

For some years a myth concerning the aging was widespread among mental health professionals as well as in the population at large. This myth, which still claims some adherents, proclaimed that the family was abandoning the aged, that filial responsibility and concern were dying, if not dead, and that the aged were isolated and alone. This notion was itself part of a larger mythology which suggested that the extended family had been destroyed by industrialization, urbanization, and mobility, and in fact that the family was no longer a viable social system.

In the last twenty years, social scientists have been challenging these myths, and meanwhile the family, although changing over time in both form and function, continues to survive and even, in the opinion of some, to flourish. Social scientists have been examining the relationships between the aging and their families with results that are of considerable interest to family-centered practitioners. Recent research has found that most old people are strongly tied to a network of kin and are involved in ongoing relationships of reciprocal support and care. For example, Butler and Lewis (1973) and Puner (1974) find that in the United States 75 percent of old people live in the same household or within thirty minutes of adult children, and 85 percent live within one hour's drive. Townsend (1968) reported that contact between older people and their kin tends to be regular and frequent, and in the Cleveland Study (U.S. General Accounting Office, 1977), it was discovered that 88 percent of a sample of 1400 elderly people indicated that kin were available to them for assistance and support.

The view that intergenerational households are necessarily problematic has also been questioned by Newman's (1976) study of three-generational families, which reported that 60 percent of the adult children who had an aging parent living with them said that the addition of the older member of the household had caused no major changes in the family's life, and although 40 percent of the respondents stated that there was increase in strain, 90 percent of the older people and their children indicated satisfaction with the living arrangement. Many of these families were providing considerable personal care to their aging family members.

Most studies indicate that the bulk of personal services are provided old people by family members and, in fact, one researcher found that between 70 and 80 percent of care to old people was being provided by the kinship system.[1] Moroney (1980) reminds us that the family is a major resource to the social welfare system in providing care for the elderly, the ill, and the handicapped, and suggests that it is inconceivable to speculate on the public costs that would be involved were families to cease carrying this burden. It is possible that one reason myths of the neglected old are perpetuated is to remind families of their responsibilities, or to create social pressure to keep families from demanding assistance with this burden.

Even most old people in nursing homes, who—contrary to popular belief, comprise only 4 percent of the population over sixty-five (Sussman, 1976)—continue to be in regular contact with family members. Over 60 percent receive weekly visitors and only 11 percent have no visitors at all (Zappolo, 1977).

The meaning of these statistics is clear and compelling. First, families are very much a part of most older people's lives and the elderly are very much a part of most families. This conclusion has major implications for family-centered practice with the aging, as well as for all families in need of help. In each situation, the enhancement of the relationship between the family and its elderly member or members may be a major goal. Such intervention may be preventive when the potential for intergenerational conflict is recognized or it may be rehabilitative in situations where such conflict is already a central part of the family's dysfunctional patterns.

Although the statistics reporting the continued strong connections between the elderly and their kin are reassuring, it also must be remembered that in almost every study, at least 10 percent of the respondents reported otherwise and it is just this 10 percent that is most likely to comprise a social agency's case load (Puner, 1974). Eleven percent of nursing home residents receive no visitors, 10 percent of families and old people sharing a home are dissatisfied with the arrangement, and 13 percent of the elderly in the Cleveland study could identify no one who could help them should they need assistance.

VARIATIONS IN THE AGING AND THEIR FAMILIES

In serving families and their aging members, we should recognize that there is great variation in this population. First, the age range considered under the category of "the aging" comprises a full generation: from youthful, tennis-playing sixty-five-year-olds who continue to work full-time to the growing numbers of aging who, although perhaps frail, are living well into their nineties and even past a hundred. Clearly, the capacities and needs of these two groups are vastly different, and gerontologists have begun thinking about this long period in terms of different stages with differing tasks.

Moreover, as the span of life increases, more and more families consist of the elderly and their children who themselves are well into their sixties. Four-generational families are increasingly common, and the "sandwich generation," as Miller calls them (1981), fulfill simultaneously the roles of grandparent, parent, and child. There is a further complication as well in the great variety of rates and styles of aging, both physical and psychological. It is impossible to generalize based on age alone; each situation requires a careful assessment.

Another variable that must also be considered in planning services for the aging and their families is cultural difference. Different ethnic and racial groups vary considerably in their views of the meaning of aging, the structure of intergenerational family systems, and the norms concerning intergenerational relations. The ideal of filial piety professed in Asian-American families is different from the Anglo-Saxon American emphasis on individualism, independence, and separation among the generations (Palmore, 1975). There is also evidence that blacks have higher expectations of filial responsibility than do whites (Hill, 1971; Schorr, 1960; Seelbach and Sauer, 1977). The respect for the aging found in many cultures is very much at odds with the disparagement of age and idealization of youth so prevalent in this country. The family-centered practitioner is of course subjected to prevailing cultural values concerning aging and influenced by her own ethnic and familial traditions and experiences with aging. Practitioners should make every effort to be aware of these variables, since they influence the planning and delivery of services and are expressed in direct practice with families.

DIFFERING VIEWS OF INTERGENERATIONAL RELATIONSHIPS

In a very useful study of family–state relationships and the potential for shared responsibility between the family and social service systems, Moroney (1980) studied and developed a typology of the views of professionals concerning the family's role with a handicapped member, including the frail elderly.

In the first view, the professional considers the family as a part of the problem. The family is conceptualized, if not as a causal agent, at least as an obstacle to the care of the member and the delivery of service. This view is perhaps most dramatically demonstrated in the old, happily almost defunct, practice of sharply limiting family visits to pediatric wards because seeing family members "upset" the children. In the case of the institutionalized elderly such an attitude on the part of professionals stimulates guilt, leads adult children to feel incompetent and unable to assume appropriate filial roles, and subtly encourages them to break off communication and to leave the care and decision-making to the professionals.

In the second view the family is considered a resource. Professionals of this persuasion keep control of the planning and decision-making process but make use of the family as needed for concrete help. This professional stance can have unhappy outcomes. First, expecting the family to provide services without being involved in the planning can cause them to feel manipulated, angry, and resentful. Second, using the family as resources without at the same time making any kind of assessment of their needs can lead to inappropriate demands which create stress and intensified guilt on the part of family members because they were unable to do enough. Or else they may attempt to comply with excessive demands and experience system overload and breakdown.

A third conceptualization considers the family as part of the team. It implies active participation in planning and decision-making on the part of family members. The effect on the family of this approach depends on how it is implemented and on whether the family is closely involved in decisions or only cursorily, as in the second view.

In the fourth view, the professional considers the family as the object of intervention. Here the total family system, including the aged members, is identified as the client and potential recipient of service. Moroney points out that this is the only one of the identified perspectives that does not focus primarily on the aged or handicapped member but rather on the total system.

There is yet another attitude that we have seen operating which, although more benign than the one that considers the family as part of the problem, may be just as destructive, and that is the view of the family as irrelevant. This opinion, sometimes held by those who operate institutions for the elderly, is expressed in subtle possessiveness of the aged person who is seen as belonging to the nursing home. Such an attitude undermines familial connectedness and interest, and frustrates family efforts to deal with impending loss, contributing to premature mourning and disengagement from the aging loved one.

SOCIAL POLICY, THE FAMILY, AND THE AGING

The support and care of dependent populations, the chronically ill, the handicapped, or the frail elderly, cannot be borne alone by families over an extended period of time without stressing them to the breaking point. Increasingly, some portion of responsibility has been transferred to the state, although in fact some of the transfer is illusory. For example, although children are not now *directly* responsible under the law for the financial support of their parents, the working population is carrying a major share of the responsibility for supporting the aging through their old age, survivors, and disability insurance payments.

Most leaders in the study of social policy regarding the aging seem to agree that a partnership between the family and the social welfare system is needed in caring for dependent populations. Social policy issues revolve around the question of which institutions should provide which services and how this partnership can be managed in such a way that the family is supported rather than undermined (Moroney, 1980). Up till now, however, public policy regarding support to families with frail elderly members has been similar to the policy regarding preventive support to families and children at risk. In both cases, under the guise of not interfering in family life it has called for support to strangers and institutions rather than support for families enabling them to care for dependents. This position is currently being questioned and there is a growing emphasis on in-home services. Innovative programs are now being attempted as well, modeling the ideal of a state–family partnership in which services and other incentives are made directly available to families for the care of their frail elderly members.[2] Family-centered practice with the aging can only be truly effective if such services and supports can become available to families.

A *Family-Centered View of Practice with the Aging*

This study defines the unit of attention in work with the aging as that ecological system which includes the aging person, his or her current family system, the physical, social, and cultural environment, and the intergenerational family system. Any aspect of that system may be the target or resource for change in serving this population.

Further, our perspective assumes that family connectedness is important for people of all ages, and that cutoffs from significant relationships leave them unresolved, thus contributing to pain and dysfunction. There is no one model for intergenerational relationships, as Brody (1974) has pointed out, but we agree with Shanas (1979) and many other specialists in the field of gerontology and the family that continued intergenerational involvement is usually in the best interests of everyone in the family.

We will not, in the following pages, attempt to take the reader through every step of the family-centered model as it applies to serving the aging and their families, but will illustrate some specific concepts and skills that have special relevance for work in this area.

After a brief discussion of assessment and intervention in work with the aging, we will explore the ways in which family-centered practice can help the aging to master their developmental tasks. We will end with an analysis of the three- and four-generational family system as a target and a resource for change.

THE AGING, THE FAMILY, AND THE ECOLOGICAL ENVIRONMENT

Growing isolation, unavailability of resources, and the diminution of meaningful interchanges with the environment become major concerns as people age. The loss of family and friends through illness and death, the lessening of mobility, and the insufficiency of resources geared to the needs of the elderly can begin to close the boundaries between the older person and the surrounding environment, bringing the all-too-familiar situation of loneliness, loss of opportunities for effectance and competence, and deprivation. Much of our work with the elderly is located at that boundary and is concerned with the reestablishment of a flow of contact and resources.

Sussman (1977) has conceptualized the family as occupying a coordinating and mediating role between older people and the bureaucratic social structures set up to meet the needs of the aging. He suggests that frequently family members perform many such transactions, with or without professional help. This role suggests that the eco-map could be an invaluable tool to help aging persons and their families clarify complex person–environment exchanges, identify needs and resources, specify areas for intervention, and plan connections to formal and informal support systems.

Such a mapping session, which should whenever possible include both the aging person and members of the family, can facilitate the development of a clear plan or contract which specifies the roles and tasks that different family members can assume.

THE AGING AND THEIR FAMILIES: PAST AND FUTURE

Aging is a developmental stage in the life cycle and not, as has often been assumed, the "end of the line" or simply a process of attrition. Erikson (1959), in his elucidation of the life cycle as composed of a series of developmental crises, defines the task of aging as the evaluation and ultimate acceptance of one's life, one's history, and the uniqueness and yet inevitability of one's life cycle. The successful mastery of this life crisis leads to integrity; a negative resolution leads to despair, a sense of meaninglessness, and a feeling that one's life has been wasted or should have somehow been different.

Peck (1968) and others have expanded Erikson's rather poetic conception by distinguishing the specific tasks involved in successful aging. Peck, for example, divides aging into three critical tasks. The first task is the achievement of ego differentiation as opposed to preoccupation with one's role in work. The aging person must establish varied activities and interests to provide a sense of usefulness, competence, and satisfaction in the face of the loss of work through retirement and the relinquishment of other accustomed roles. The second task is the achievement of body transcendence as opposed to body preoccupation; this requires the ability to rise above the limitations of the aging and ailing body and to find gratification in human interaction, intellectual pursuits, or creative activities. The third is ego transcendence versus ego preoccupation. The mastery of this crisis involves the ability of the aging person, through the valuing of children, grandchildren, and future generations as well as other contributions to the future, to extend the significance of life beyond her own lifetime.

LIFE REVIEW AND THE FAMILY

One of the processes that contributes to the achievement of integrity is life review, considered by Butler to be a "naturally occurring, universal mental process characterized by the progressive return to consciousness of past experiences, and particularly, the resurgence of unresolved conflicts; simultaneously, and normally these revived experiences and conflicts can be surveyed and reintegrated" (1968:487). The awareness of the importance of life review has led to the conscious use of reminiscence with the aging person as a therapeutic tool.[3] However, the research about the universality and the usefulness of reminiscence is equivocal, and Merriam (1980), following a review of studies in this area, suggests that more careful groundwork is needed for a clear understanding of this phenomenon.

An adaptation of the Bowen model of family of origin work to the aging provides both a structure and a vehicle for reminiscence and for life review. The genogram, for example, has been found to be a very useful tool in working with the aging. In constructing an intergenerational family chart, the older person finds himself in the middle of the family tree; three or four generations of family of origin and two or three generations of descendants appear, so that the continuity of the family and the aging person's part in that continuity is graphically portrayed.

The construction of the family of origin portion of the genogram offers an opportunity for a reassessment of family themes, relationships, and prescriptions. For most people, much of life occurs in the context of intimate family relationships, and thus as each important figure is described and memories and associations are shared, the life review process unfolds. Relationships, dates, and major events are specified. In fact, the order provided by the structure of the map is important for the older person in clarifying any confusion about people and time sequences and it keeps the worker, too, from becoming lost in the detail. The goal in life review is to reassess and to reintegrate, to come to terms with one's own life cycle and with conflicts that may reemerge, and to complete any unfinished life business. The example of Anna illustrates how such a process might occur.

Anna was a lonely and despairing woman of eighty-three who lived in a home for the aging. She complained bitterly about the home, the staff, and about her life in general. Turning to the use of life review via the genogram, the worker learned that Anna had never married and had given up her own aspirations to devote her life to her parents. As she talked about her life and her regrets, describing the "might have beens", her anger at her parents, although thinly veiled, remained unexpressed. Clearly, Anna could not confront those feelings and instead spoke of her parents in an unrealistic, idealizing way. The worker did not press Anna to voice the anger but rather continued with the construction of the genogram, enlarging the context beyond the triangle of Anna and her parents. Anna spoke of her parents' childhood in Russia and the series of painful losses experienced by them. Not only had they lost their own parents and siblings and their homes when they emigrated, but they had lost Anna's two older siblings, before she was born, in a tragic New York tenement fire. As Anna talked about her mother's life, she began to wonder how it must have been for the young mother, cut off from her parents and her culture, in a strange and often hostile land, losing her two babies with no family or friends to comfort her. "No wonder she needed me so much," Anna commented.

The enlarging of the context and the reminiscence that took place through the use of the genogram led Anna to reexperience her mother in a new way, to envision how both she and her parents were a part of a larger family context, itself part of a pageant of history. This process took her a few steps closer to an understanding and acceptance of her own life. One of the sources of Anna's anger at the institution in which she resided was that she felt that she was not reaping the rewards of what she had given. She had taken such good care of her parents and now no one was there for her. As the worker continued with family of origin work, unrealistic complaints about the present situation diminished.

This case identifies a common theme in the aging experience, namely that one's attitudes and expectations about aging tend to be closely related to one's parents' experiences with aging. For the professional, then, it is valuable to learn as much as possible about the course of the parents' aging, about how they lived, who, if anyone, took care of them, and when and how they died. This knowledge can bring to light the sources of some of the client's attitudes and expectations, and identify new opportunities for differentiation.

THE FAMILY AND INTERGENERATIONAL WORK WITH THE AGING

Most of the literature about the use of reminiscence and history with the aging assumes that it is the professional who conducts the process, although there is an occasional report of the professional teaching and encouraging the family members to construct genograms and to reminisce with their aging kin (Ingersoll and Silverman, 1978).

Anthropologist Barbara Myerhoff (1978) reports the very moving experience of the use of reminiscing techniques in her "living history class" held in a senior center, while Ingersoll and Goodman (1980) report the therapeutic use of such groups with institutionalized elderly. These were undoubtedly meaningful encounters for participants and leaders alike; nevertheless a family-centered practitioner would ask, "Is there some way that other family members as well might share this experience?"

Reminiscence is life review for the aging person but it is also a legacy for and a gift to the younger generation. This is movingly depicted by Ingersoll and Goodman when they write, "The group leaders were seen as vessels through which participants' memories and knowledge might be conveyed beyond their own finitude. One woman expressed the hope that her memories would live on, by saying to them, 'Some day you'll think back to the old woman in the group'"(1980:315). In this situation, the workers became surrogate descendents, especially because no kin were available.

However, in our experience it is even more beneficial if the legacy can be passed on to family members. Such a transaction between the generations exhibits a perfect complementarity. One vehicle through which older persons may achieve ego transcendance is in the giving of their history to the safekeeping of future generations. The younger family members in turn need this information in their own life in order to consolidate their identities. Further, the history and the genogram are things the generations of a family have in common. No matter how great the distance between their views and their lifestyles, they belong to the same family and they share the same familial traditions. We have had considerable experience with the positive effects of this shared process between the generations. Over a period of some fifteen years we have been sending members of the younger generation to their aging parents and grandparents to establish or renew contact and to learn about family history. Often the younger family members will ruefully comment, "She had been trying to tell us about all this for years, but no one would listen." Now, not only were grandchildren listening, they were recording the stories and the information for posterity!

One young woman, for example, traveled to California to see her isolated and ailing grandmother. One of the purposes of the trip was to gain some information about her family. Photo albums and letters had been carefully saved and the grandmother, with great relief and pleasure, gave them to her granddaughter. "I thought no one was interested," she said, "I was so afraid that when I died all this would just be thrown out and then it would all be over."

NEVER TOO LATE

Too frequently social workers and other mental health professionals assume that old people cannot change, and consequently limit their interventions to the delivery of concrete services and emotional support, assuming that counseling or psychotherapy would not be useful. Change is an option at any age, however, if one takes the position, as does Erikson, that human beings go through a series of developmental crises throughout life; each crisis offers an opportunity to readdress and master earlier unresolved tasks and raises new challenges for coping and adaptation.

In chapter 11 we reported briefly on the case of a septuagenarian who, primarily stimulated by his children's family of origin work, reconnected with his mother, who had been dead for 68 years, by visiting for the first time the small town in a foreign land where he had lived as a child and where his mother had died and been buried. Interestingly enough, the daughter had sought help for a depression following the death of her mother, and her father had come to two of the sessions with his daughter to help her resolve her difficulty. As father and daughter helped each other mourn their shared loss, he began to reconnect emotionally with his own mother, whose loss he had incompletely integrated. It was after this meeting that he resolved to visit his mother's village.

In another family situation, two sisters in the course of a few meetings were able to make some crucial decisions and plans and to deal in a new way with some old family issues.

Elizabeth, a widow in her late sixties, requested help in planning for her younger sister, Ellen, who was currently visiting but who lived in another community and could no longer, the older sister felt, continue to live alone. Elizabeth was trying to decide whether she should invite Ellen to come live with her. An appointment was arranged for both women to be seen together.

It soon became clear that the sisters were locked into circular family patterns that had been enacted repetitively for over sixty years. The older, the "responsible firstborn," had been playing the overfunctioning caretaker of the "little sister" since their childhoods. The younger sister had consistently played the complementary role of helpless and incompetent younger sister. The more the older sister took care, the more dysfunctional the younger sister would become. The more dysfunctional the younger sister would become, the more burdened and angry the older sister would feel. She responded to her anger, however, by increased guilt and renewed efforts to take better care of her sister.

Ellen had never married and, until her retirement for health reasons some ten years ago, had worked as a legal secretary. Further, over the years Ellen had spent most of her vacations and holidays with Elizabeth and Elizabeth's husband and children, even though the two sisters lived some distance from one another. In fact her sister's family served as the major resource for her social connectedness. The younger sister had experienced periods of depression since her teenage years and although in the past she had quickly bounced back, now that retirement, health problems, and a shrinking social network had left her more vulnerable and with fewer resources, these periods of sadness were more serious and of greater duration.

Although initial sessions with Ellen and Elizabeth included an ecological assessment and a mutual effort to evaluate the feasibility of Ellen's remaining in her own apartment and to consider what supports could be made available should she remain alone, the major focus was on the sisters' relationship in the context of the intergenerational family. Of particular interest was the growing understanding of their respective roles in preserving an uneasy equilibrium in their parents' marriage. Each had been drawn into it in particular ways and in a sense had been played off against one another. And each had been jealous and resentful of what was perceived as the other's place, feeling divided as the parents themselves were divided. Elizabeth, the older, had been charged with Ellen's care, since their mother was almost invariably ailing or preoccupied. Ellen had felt inferior and incompetent in comparison with Elizabeth and, moreover, was hurt and angry that Elizabeth was favored by their father, a distant figure whom Ellen worshiped from afar. The family's concerns over Ellen's health, whether or not they were based on reality, precluded her going away to college. Thus Ellen remained home with her mother, ostensibly to be taken care of but in reality to supply her mother with a companion and a reason for being. This family solution in turn freed her father to pursue his career unrestrainedly and at the same time allowed the other daughter, Elizabeth, to separate, marry, and raise a family. Elizabeth felt guilty about the opportunities that she had had that Ellen had missed, aware on some level that Ellen had been sacrificed to maintain the family. Perhaps now Elizabeth could balance the ledger.

Constructing the intergenerational family history with Ellen and Elizabeth helped them objectify the family system of which they both had been a part as they identified the intergenerational themes and role assignments that had contributed to the patterning of their relationship. Both women were able to recognize the dysfunctional balance that took over in their transactions, particularly in times of stress. Elizabeth was able to relinquish her controlling caretaking role enough to let Ellen return to her own community to live and Ellen was able to let go of her hostile demanding "you owe me" stance enough to realize that she gained more gratification from being autonomous, despite the sense of justice and pleasure in exacting payment for ancient debts.

The Children and Grandchildren of the Aging

For most older people and their families, transition to old age, with all of the accommodations and adaptations required, is accomplished without professional help. Family networks remain intact, younger family members offer appropriate help and support as needed, medical problems may emerge but are often manageable and not catastrophic, extrafamilial human and economic resources are sufficiently available, and needed progressive care is available through familial and social arrangements.

For those aging people who come to the attention of social workers, however, these transitions are not being smoothly accomplished. The professional's challenge is to help the aging person and family to resolve problems generated by illness, increasing need for care, social and emotional isolation, and lack of appropriate resources. Family systems respond in a variety of ways to the increasing stress and even crises that may be precipitated by the needs for changed relationships, planning, and care that accompany the aging process.

An understanding of the dynamics of family systems and of aging can help a worker deal with the complex and often highly intense transactional sequences initiated in such situations. Bowen has hypothesized that families become more fused and more caught up in reactive patterns when faced with increasing stress. Dependence is intimately connected with fusion. It is difficult to take an "I-position" when one is realistically dependent for survival on the very person or system from which one is attempting to differentiate; it is probably to this issue some refer when they liken the conditions of aging to those of childhood.

As we have discussed earlier in this study, one way to defend against intensified threats of fusion is to cut oneself off emotionally. Not infrequently the aging client and family which come to the attention of a social worker are each responding in this way. The older person, fearful of the potential loss of autonomy and selfhood, cuts off, refuses to ask for help, and takes a pseudo independent position. The younger generation, fearful of being pulled back into a fused relationship with the older, creates as much distance as possible. Cutoffs can also be stimulated by other factors. The anticipation of frailty, illness and death may provoke parents and adult children to move away from one another in order to protect themselves from the painful experience of loss. Premature mourning on the part of the younger generation may insulate them from pain but it also means that they are emotionally unavailable to their aging relatives. Further, as the parents age, the children must face the prospect of their own mortality and may seek to avoid this anxiety-provoking confrontation. On the other hand, rather than cutting themselves off, some families slip into fusion, reenacting unresolved and intense emotional patterns, conflicts, and triangles. In either situation, the worker is often faced with tremendously complex emotional systems in which the levels of tension and anxiety are high.

Each family situation is different, but certain guidelines are useful in working with the aging and their family members. The obvious objective is that the needs of both the older person for care, support, protection, stimulation, and opportunity for creativity—and the needs of the family in helping the older person be met as appropriately as possible. Implied in this overarching goal, however, are related objectives concerning how these needs are to be met.

First, the needs of the entire family system should be met in such a way that the older person's autonomy is respected and preserved as much as possible. As one older person was quoted, "I may need help crossing the street but that doesn't mean I don't know where I'm going" (Miller, 1981:421). This perspective is very closely related to the notion of the "least restrictive environment" which is used as a guide in decision-making in child welfare.

The complementary goal to be achieved by the children (and grandchildren) of the aging person has been termed by Blenkner (1965) "filial maturity," or the ability to accept the parents' dependency as appropriate and to take whatever responsibility is indicated by the situation of the older person and the situation of the total family. What this may be will vary from family to family.

In family systems terminology we may reframe these goals by suggesting that we would help the older person and his intimate family members maintain a differentiated relationship, connecting in an intimate but autonomous manner, and relating to one another in terms of the realities of the situation rather than reactively to old issues in the family system. In structural terms, despite the realistic dependency of the older person, appropriate boundaries should be maintained and the family hierarchy supported. Hierarchical issues are particularly salient in this situation. Intergenerational relationships have long been distorted by the myth that a reversal of roles occurs between the generations, that the old person becomes the child and the child becomes the parent. This myth sometimes has the effect of a self-fulfilling prophecy when a transaction develops in which old people are patronized and in turn assume childlike behaviors and attitudes. The myth distorts the reality that the parent, no matter how frail or even deteriorated, is always the parent; and in fact, one of the myth's functions may well be to disarm the parent who continues to be experienced by younger family members as a powerful and controlling person.

How, then, may the practitioner draw on family-centered skills to identify obstacles and to help with the achievement of the goals described above? Any of the strategies of assessment and intervention presented in this study may be adapted for use with the aging and their families and, if successfully mobilized, may make this transitional stage an opportunity for growth and change, as exemplified in the following case.

Matt, a fifty-year-old father and husband, had been emotionally cut off from his seventy-nine-year-old mother for a number of years. She had retired to Arizona and Matt had moved to New England, about as far away as he could get. Pro forma letters and gifts at Christmas were exchanged but emotional and physical distance was firmly maintained. Matt experienced his mother as an extremely controlling and intrusive woman who was an expert at utilizing guilt to pull him back into the emotional system in which he had replaced his father, who had abandoned the family when Matt was six. Matt had struggled to leave home, had married late, and had finally successfully established himself separately from his mother, at least geographically. However, although cut off, he remained emotionally caught in the old system, reacting to his wife or any other woman who made demands or who tried to get close by distancing himself. A year or so before seeking help, Matt, an only child, had received a call from his mother's doctor in Arizona reporting that his mother had suffered a stroke. In the next months, he became more and more involved in planning for the older woman. Although she made an excellent recovery, some residue remained and it was clear that she would not be able to return to her apartment.

Concurrent with this situation marital problems began to escalate and it was in relation to the marriage that Matt and his wife Jean sought help. The family-centered practitioner quickly identified the unresolved situation with Matt's mother as a key precipitant of the marital conflict. Focusing the work on Matt's relationship with his mother soon made it clear that Matt was terrified that his mother was once again going to take over his life. In the course of work with Matt, his family, and Sallie, his mother, a variety of family-focused interventions were utilized. Initially, working primarily in a Bowen framework, Matt was encouraged to move toward rather than away from his mother. He was helped, in the process, to set boundaries, to take "I-positions," and, while attempting to get to know his mother better, to plan nonreactive ways of staying out of the system. For example, after some exchanges of letters in which Matt communicated more openly with his mother and even asked her advice about how to handle an issue with Matt, Jr., he planned a visit to Arizona. The boundary difficulties and his mother's overwhelming demands were dramatically enacted during his visits to the rehabilitative hospital where his mother was now in care. No matter when he visited, it was too late, and no matter how long he stayed, it was not long enough; thus his mother attempted to control him by assuming an injured and abandoned position. Matt, however, anticipating some of these maneuvers, and with the help of his coach, developed some new strategies for his own behavior, including a proposed schedule for the times and durations of visits with his mother. His ability to maintain these boundaries with his mother was crucial to their future relationship and his success led him to consider asking her if she would like to move to a facility in the city in which he lived. Also, although he limited the time spent visiting his mother, he found, since he felt more in control, that he could more comfortably move toward his mother and be more attentive to her. Thus the quality of the time spent was much improved.

After considerable planning, discussion, and joint sessions with his coach and Jean, the decision was made to invite his mother to move to their community. The invitation was eagerly accepted and Sallie was ensconced in the nearby convalescent care center.

There were many struggles the first year as Sallie felt she should have a greater part in Matt's and the family's life. However, careful boundaries were established and maintained. Sallie, when she was able, spent alternate Sunday afternoons with the family, and regular visits to the center were planned by various family members. Matt's three children had hardly known their grandmother and, as is often the case, Sallie was able to establish a far better rapport with her grandchildren than with her son. In fact Ginny, the thirteen-year-old granddaughter, and Sallie developed a quite special relationship. At times Matt felt that they united as coconspirators against him and Jean, whom they saw as the middle generation and common "enemy," a not unusual occurrence in family systems. Ginny became quite interested in family history and spent several Sunday afternoons recording Sallie's reminiscences and accounts of the family's historical adventures.

Occasionally Matt found himself enmeshed in the old transactions, but when this began to occur, he was usually able, with the help of his coach, to quickly reestablish his more differentiated position.

Two and a half years after her move east, Sallie suffered a second, and this time fatal, stroke. When Matt saw his coach, he reported that they had decided not to have a funeral service since Sallie really didn't know anyone in town except the family. As they discussed this decision, it soon became apparent that Matt, responding to the loss and attendant stress, had again opted for an emotional cutoff. He was gently encouraged to consider other ways of dealing with his mother's death; and in response to this intervention, Matt and his family planned a small and meaningful memorial service.

In the case of Matt, an only child, current marital conflict was heightened with the resurfacing of unresolved intergenerational issues. In other families, sibling issues among the adult children, issues that have long lain dormant, are fanned into flame. Competition about who is closest to the aging parent may emerge or bitter quarrels about who has sacrificed the most may erupt. The accomplishment of filial maturity can be obstructed by any of these reactions.

For example, the possessive and overprotective daughter who was always mother's caretaker may take on too much, complaining about the burden but not really allowing the other adult children or grandchildren to participate in the care of the older person. In such a situation, the caretaker is likely to report that her siblings are neglectful and uninterested, not recognizing that she, too, has had a part in the way the family has distributed roles and tasks. The worker who concurs, accepting a single family member's assessment of the feelings and attitudes of other family members, has been caught in the family system and will thus unwittingly cooperate in maintaining the system as it is.

In some cases the crisis generated by the aging parents' needs can be utilized as an opportunity to shift a family's dysfunctional organization. The overprotective daughter can be helped to allow other family members to participate, and the "neglectful" family members can take the opportunity to assume some responsibility and establish meaningful contact. The middle generation can be encouraged to stop blocking and controlling transactions between the grandparents and the grandchildren. Sometimes these structural changes can be made with a focus entirely on the present, with change occurring as family members enact new roles and move out of rigid, dysfunctional triangles.

Occasionally, however, old family conflicts continue to undermine the intergenerational relationships and it is necessary to deal with them directly. For example, family sessions which include all of the adult children of the aging person may be used to explore the history of some of the current conflicts and to detoxify old issues. It is sometimes useful to include the adult children's spouses, as they too have often become involved in and have a stake in the complex network of relationships.

In some chronic situations, the ways the family has devised to care for the aging parent may at the same time mask and become solutions to other problems in the family. In work with such families, it is essential for the practitioner to develop a hypothesis concerning how these arrangements are maintaining the family system. For example, if the family seems to scapegoat an aging member to protect a fragile and mutually destructive marriage, and if tracking and circular interviewing discloses the fact that when the aging family member attempts to take a step toward autonomy the system reacts in a subtle way to counter that movement, there is some evidence that this "problem" of the aging family member is a solution to other problems located elsewhere in the system. In such a situation, more dramatic interventions such as reframing, positive connotation, and paradoxical prescriptions may be needed to unlock the system and to open up possibilities for change.

Family-Centered Practice in the Delivery of Health Care

Many of the issues and principles explored in the discussion of the family and the aging find their parallel in the family's response to the illness of one of its members. Despite the tremendous growth of the health care system, the family continues to provide a large proportion of the health care in the nation. The role of coordinator and broker of services frequently falls to the family, which often finds itself negotiating between large bureaucratic health care systems and the ill person. And, as with the aging, the social worker must understand this complex ecological system and aid patient and family in these coordinating and brokering tasks.

The family's brokering role in relation to a member's illness may begin with seeking appropriate health care and other resources at the onset of illness. A sudden illness or accident may push a family into crisis as emotional and material resources are stretched to the limit and the family's usual adaptive capacities are overwhelmed. In such a situation, an ecological assessment and careful examination of needs and resources can help the family toward a cognitive mastery of the overwhelming situation, enabling step-by-step planning to develop.

The impact of serious illness on the family structure may also overwhelm the family. If the ill member is a central and powerful member in the maintenance of the system and the carrier of crucial roles, the family's structure and role distribution will have to be dramatically altered. This is particularly true when a parent becomes ill, and even more devastating when a single parent is the patient. The caretaking, planning, nurturing, and administrative roles of the parental subsystem must be supplemented and supported through the flexible shifting of roles within the family system and the mobilization of an expanded social network.

The enforced dependency of the patient and the family's response to this dependency may give rise to fears of fusion or loss, reactive cutoffs, or oversolicitous and intrusive behavior on the part of families, just as with aging family members. These reactive responses must be assessed in the context of both the current and historical family. The family and the patient must be helped to maintain both emotional contact and appropriate boundaries. The ill person, just as the aging person, must be helped to maintain as much autonomy and decision-making power as is possible within the limits of the illness, and the family often needs help in enabling the sick member to accomplish this difficult task.

At the same time, out of the dread of loss, families often need help in maintaining emotional contact with the ill person, as the pain of the contact may stimulate the family to distance. The emotional distancing, in turn, is experienced by the ill person as an abandonment at a time when he or she most needs to be surrounded by caring people. Silverman and Brahce (1979) suggest that families sometimes avoid their aging relatives because they do not understand the aging process, what it is the aging person needs, or how they can help, and that such families often feel incompetent and helpless. These authors have organized groups of children of aging parents to help them understand what their parents are going through and how they may help.

In the same way, particularly when an ill member is hospitalized and the family has had little experience with the mysterious world of medicine, the efficient professional in white, and the increasingly elaborate medical equipment, the family may feel awkward and uncertain how to deal with visiting a patient in this alien environment. If the social worker can help family members feel more comfortable in the hospital setting and aware of what they can do to help, the important sustaining relationship between patient and family can be protected and nurtured.

Just as the fact of aging takes on meaning according to the family's intergenerational experiences with growing old, so does illness become defined and experienced in terms of the family's history with illness. The genogram may be used to great advantage in gathering the family history of health and illness, and in seeking out how the family organizes around illness and makes it part of its system of meaning and belief. Patterns of family illness, family responses, and the outcomes of illnesses not only alert the family and the professionals to the possibility of hereditary health patterns and problems but also draw a picture of the family's experiences and expectations. When hereditary patterns of illness are uncovered family members can identify risks and institute preventive measures. They can also come to differentiate current situations from the historical context and to cope with the present in more objective and realistic ways.

Finally, the issue of "secondary" gain is as crucial for families as it is for individuals. An illness or a handicap may come to play an important role in the maintenance of the family system or the avoidance of other, more threatening problems. Illness may draw the family together, or may give a failing marriage new life as a couple shares care and concern for a child. Illness, just as emotional dysfunction, may keep a family member from leaving home or shift the power structure in a way that certain family members, who now have more control and power in the system, are loath to relinquish. When the illness has become a solution to other problems in the family, it may well be prolonged by the collusion of both family and patient.

This issue is particularly salient in the area of rehabilitation. Although the family discourse identifies the illness or handicapping condition as the "problem," if appropriate steps toward rehabilitation are not taken, it is important for the worker to hypothesize that the handicapping condition and the maintenance of the patient's role has become part of the family's organization and perhaps a solution to some other problem. If it has, this fact may be brought to light by circular and tracking interviewing which details familial responses to the patient's rehabilitative efforts, before-and-after questions which define the differences in family structure and process prior to the onset of the illness, and hypothetical questions which stimulate the family to speculate about what could happen should the patient begin to function more fully. If evidence demonstrates the family's persistence in maintaining the illness, paradoxical interventions may well be utilized: The advantages to the family of the illness may be pointed out and positively connoted, the selflessness of the patient's sacrifice for the family praised, and the family and patient cautioned against too rapid a rate of change.

In work with the aging and their families and in the delivery of health care, we have seen that the ecological environment, the family of origin, and aspects of family structure and process may all be utilized as targets and resources for change. The following case of family-centered practice in the health care arena illustrates the integration of a range of strategies.

The Marzikians: The Case of a Vigilant Family

The Marzikian family, consisting of Barbara and Joe, a couple in their mid-thirties, and two sons, Jeffrey, eleven, and Peter, eight, became known to the social worker in pediatric hemotology after Jeffrey was diagnosed as having leukemia. Throughout the initial crisis, the family was able to mobilize its considerable strength to support Jeff and each other through a grief-ridden and highly anxious time and the elaborate, debilitating, and sometimes painful diagnostic and treatment procedures. It was after Jeff was in remission, discharged from the hospital, and back in school, that the parents began to suffer sleeplessness, irritability, and depression. Jeff continued to be followed and treated on an outpatient basis.

Jeff's father, Joe, had taken a very active role with the hospital staff, monitoring his son's progress, reading extensively about leukemia and its treatment, and asking for detailed explanations of every step and decision in the treatment. Although initially the physicians were sympathetic and cooperative, they began to experience Joe, polite and pleasant though he was, as demanding and intrusive. They began to avoid him and to end conversations abruptly, tactics which cut Joe off from information and control and made him feel increasingly anxious and helpless. Those feelings led him to intensify his pursuit of the medical staff who, in turn, distanced themselves even more. The social worker who had been seeing the family occasionally attempted to mediate the growing dysfunctional relationship between Joe and the hospital staff but no amount of reassurance or information appeared to be sufficient.

When Jeff came home, Joe was at first somewhat relieved because he felt more in control, but he soon became intolerably anxious again. Now he felt entirely responsible for Jeff's welfare and his monitoring increased to the point where even his sleep was interrupted several times each night because he would awaken to check on Jeff. He also found it very difficult to refrain from restricting Jeff's activities unnecessarily.

Barbara, Jeff's mother, felt equally helpless, but retreated into passivity, alternating between denial and resignation. Joe had accused Barbara of being neglectful and insufficiently watchful, and Barbara in response to her husband's criticism had taken a leave from her job in an advertising firm, a job that she had acquired shortly before Jeff got sick. An unspoken accusation hung in the air, one which implied that if Barbara had been home and not pursuing a career she might have noticed sooner that Jeff was listless and pale and taken him to a doctor for an earlier diagnosis. Barbara was particularly vulnerable to this unspoken insinuation, for she was the first working mother in either her own or Joe's family, and she had experienced some uneasiness about this departure from family tradition. Her mother had been quite disapproving, believing that Barbara should wait until the boys were older to pursue a career. This had also been Joe's feeling, although he had not directly expressed any strong objection to Barbara.

Margaret, the social worker, met with Barbara and Joe for a few sessions to help them in their dealings with Jeff, the illness, and the medical staff. Both were able to express their terror, their guilt, and the conflicts that were emerging between them over the illness. Barbara found Joe's constant watching and worrying extremely unnerving. She felt she could not get away from the illness for a moment, and was becoming increasingly depressed, particularly since leaving her job. She also felt that Joe was overprotective, controlling, and too involved with Jeff, hardly letting the boy breathe. Joe admitted he was overanxious but nevertheless expressed his anger toward Barbara, charging that she was leaving it all up to him. He said he knew she really was upset about Jeff, but that she was acting so remote that it was almost as if she did not care.

What became dramatically apparent was that this couple had become locked into a schismogenic escalation. The more Joe worried and watched, the more Barbara retreated and denied the threats in the situation; and the more Barbara utilized denial, the more frantic Joe became in his constant worry and anticipation of the worst. Interestingly, Joe had initially been attracted to Barbara because she was so happy-go-lucky, and Barbara had admired and felt secure with Joe because he was so thoughtful, serious, and responsible. Margaret commented on the escalating process and attempted to divide up the worrying and the monitoring more evenly between the two of them with a structural intervention.

Joe was reluctant to let go, however, and unable to trust anyone but himself. Barbara at one point commented that Joe's whole family was like that, always preparing for the worst and worried about health. "They still worry about Joe," she said. "Not only about his being sick, but about his being in an accident whenever he travels."

In order to understand the intergenerational themes which might have played a role in the way the family was organizing around the illness, a genogram was completed on both families of origin. Joe's intergenerational history (see Figure 15.1) was particularly helpful in casting light on the current situation.

In each of the two generations before Joe, a tragic loss of the firstborn son had occurred. Joe's grandfather's older brother had been killed by the Turks in the massacre of 1909. Joe told the story of the miraculous escape from Turkey of his grandfather (also a Joseph) after the death of his brother, and his subsequent emigration alone, at the age of sixteen, to the United States. This family patriarch and hero had gone from factory and farm labor to building a major rug-importing firm. Yet his cutoff from his family was almost complete, despite his efforts to bring them to America. World War I, continued Turkish repression and massacres, and political upheaval led to the destruction of the Armenian communities, and, except for one sister, the loss of his family.

This man's firstborn son was called Joseph, Jr., and he was the joy of his parents' life. But the child died from complications following a routine tonsillectomy recommended by the family physician, who had assured the family that it was a minor procedure. The grandfather never forgave himself or the doctor for the loss, and he was depressed for a long time on account of it. It seemed to him that the one time he had failed to expect the worst and had turned the care of his family over to another, he lost his beloved son. Paul, his surviving son, and John, born a year and a half after Joseph's death, were some consolation; but in the following generation Joseph III, Jeffrey's father, became the true replacement for his namesake, often being told that he resembled Joseph, Jr.

The historical experiences of Joe's family helped clarify his response to the current situation. He saw that his fear and expectation of the loss of his firstborn son, his distrust of the doctors, his need to monitor and control, and his anxiety about health were all firmly rooted in a series of tragic events in his family of origin.

The explanation and sharing of this history enabled Joe to differentiate his experience from his grandfather's and he began to allow Barbara to share the caretaking and the worry. Slowly, they began to feel safe enough to allow Jeff to become involved in normal activities and Margaret knew that considerable movement had taken place when, following an appropriate check on available nursing and emergency health care, they were able to let Jeff and Peter go to camp for two weeks.

Jeff remained in remission and, although he continued to be followed by the pediatric–hematology outpatient department, Margaret did not see much of the Marzikian family for over a year. Then she received a call from Joe. He and Barbara had recently become concerned about the behavior of Peter, who was constantly fighting with Jeff and creating chaos both at home and in school. Joe wondered if Margaret would see him or if she could make a referral. He was certain it had nothing to do with the leukemia but Margaret was not so sure, and she suggested they come in

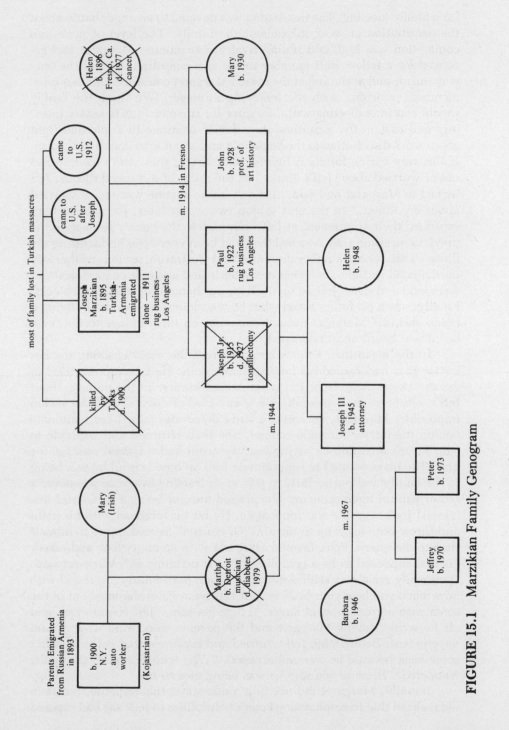

FIGURE 15.1 Marzikian Family Genogram

for a family meeting. The first session was devoted to an angry battle about
the distribution of work throughout the family. The level of noise and
commotion was high and sibling rivalry was intense. Margaret had arranged for a fellow staff member to act as a consultant behind the one-
way mirror and at the end of the session Margaret consulted with her team
member, returning with the following message: "We think the family
should continue meeting with Margaret for three or four biweekly meetings and that in the meantime they should continue to argue and fight
about work distribution in the household and about who does what chores.
If this very caring family is fighting and angry, they won't have to feel
sad or worried about Jeff's illness." In the midst of a stunned silence, Jeff
turned to Margaret and said, "I didn't know anyone was sad or worried
about my illness." In the next session two weeks later, Joe and Barbara
expressed their amazement at Jeff's response to the team's message in the
previous meeting; they assumed they had been very open in discussing the
illness. Throughout a rather disjointed and frustrating session, neither boy
participated verbally, but their metaphoric and analogic communications
were loud and clear. Jeff sat on the floor busily building with Lego blocks.
Finally, when his father asked what he was doing he replied, "Building a
bomb shelter!" Margaret did not comment on this message to the team
but it was heard and understood.

In the meantime, Peter whirled around the room enacting the behavior that had caused his family to seek help. He interrupted, tried to
get the Legos away from Jeff, complained bitterly to the parents about
Jeff's selfishness, and generally made any kind of discussion in the session
impossible. Margaret, becoming a little desperate, joined her teammate
behind the mirror for some counsel. She then returned and was able to
gain Peter's attention by saying that the team had a special message for
him. The team wanted to congratulate him on how helpful he was being
to the family and particularly to Jeff by distracting everyone whenever a
sad or painful topic came up. She praised him for being a wonderful distracter! Joe's response was immediate. He hit his forehead with his palm
and threw both arms up in the air, "Of course!" he said, more to himself
than to the group. Peter favored Margaret with an angry look and asked,
"Is that supposed to be a compliment?" "It certainly is," Margaret said,
"you really are a very skillful distracter. I am particularly impressed with
how much you help your brother." At this point Peter slammed out of the
room with a great show of anger. "I'll go get him," Jeff volunteered, and
off he went, leaving Margaret and the parents wondering what would
happen next. Before long, Jeff returned and explained that Peter wouldn't
come back because he was embarrassed. "Why embarrassed?" the adults
wondered. "Because you said he was being nice to me."

Initially, Margaret did not fully understand this response, but then
she realized that in emphasizing Peter's helpfulness to Jeff, she had exposed

his concern and tender feelings about his brother. This undid the great show of rivalry and began to alter the public definition of their relationship, which had been one of anger and dislike. A red-eyed Peter shortly returned and announced that no one was to talk to him at all.

When scheduling the appointment for two weeks hence, Joe reported that his father, Paul, was going to be visiting from California and they wondered if they could reschedule. Margaret asked instead if they would bring him to the session. The family meeting with Paul was the major turning point in the case and illustrated with great drama both the power of intergenerational transmission and the rich resources for change which can be found in intergenerational family exchanges. The major themes in this emotionally moving session can only be summarized.

Margaret hoped that she could muster the courage to ask Paul about his brother Joe. But she need not have worried, for Paul had come to the session determined to help his family and to talk about important issues. "I was raised in a family that swept everything under the rug," he said, "and now I know it wasn't good. In fact Martha and I raised Joe and Helen the same way. Martha was always cheerful and never wanted to complain. She had serious diabetes and went through so much, but until the end she was sure she'd be all right."

Early in the session, Paul spontaneously began to reminisce, telling the story of his brother's death. He remembered sharing a room with Joe, Jr., and how much he had idolized him. When his brother died, he was never told what had happened, but he had a vivid memory of someone coming in, stripping Joe's bed, and taking his bed pillows away. His parents had been devastated, and now he knows, as he looks back, that his father was very depressed for a long time, and emotionally unavailable to the family. Paul was sent away right after his brother's death to stay with his mother's sister—he wasn't sure for how long but he knows that it was for at least six months. He described Joe, Jr., as the "perfect" boy, tall, handsome, outgoing, athletic, and an excellent student. "As for me," Paul said, "I was short, homely, and poorly coordinated, I did all right in school, but not like Joe." Paul, becoming tearful, remembered that as a youngster he had always felt it should have been he, not Joe, who died. "I spent my life trying to make it up to my parents, particularly my father, but I never felt I could." He also talked about the family history, about his father's escape and his grandfather's previous warning to both sons of the impending danger. The elder man, despite a decade or more of tense quiet between the Turks and the Armenians, had increasingly expected a new eruption of violence, and believed that his sons were particularly vulnerable. The older son had disregarded the grandfather's warning, sure that he was exaggerating the danger; but Joe hid out with a rural family. When the inevitable violence came, the older brother was killed, but Joe, Sr. survived and at his father's insistence made his way out of Turkey and ultimately, to the United States. The details of this story dramatically reinforced the subsequent family paradigm, which warned, "The only way to survive is to watch carefully, anticipate the worst, and plan accordingly,"

Toward the end of the session, Paul talked about the recent loss of his wife, of her long illness, her strength, and of how much she had loved her grandsons. Everyone in the room became tearful as Paul spoke of grandma. Joe was the most moved; the two men, with obvious emotion, openly shared their grief. During this enactment, Barbara's face registered a range of emotions which communicated her sharing of their sadness but also her own uneasiness, as she kept glancing with protective concern at Jeff and Peter, who had been mesmerized by their grandfather's story and the coming together of the father and grandfather.

When the family arrived for the next session two weeks later, Margaret was impressed with the dramatic change in Peter. Peter had always seemed a little bedraggled, a less attractive child than Jeff. Today, however, he was so handsome and engaging that Margaret realized how angry and depressed he must have been before. The meeting was primarily one of feedback, of processing and enacting the changes that were taking place in the family. Barbara reported that on the way home from the previous meeting, she had asked Peter if he ever felt the way grandpa had felt when he was little, that is, that it would be better if it were he rather than his brother who was ill. After a thoughtful silence, Peter had answered, "Not exactly." When asked if the family had anything they wanted to bring up from the meeting before, Jeff said that grandpa talked too much. "He didn't have to tell all the details," said Jeff. "Yeah," Peter rejoined, "like about the pillows."

During most of the session, the boys played together fairly quietly and the parents talked about how things were going. Barbara tentatively wondered about returning to her job, and immediately Joe began to look tense and annoyed. Then Jeff lay down on the floor, complaining he was tired and did not feel well. This act immediately drew Joe's attention but then he caught himself, and said to Margaret and Barbara, "It's hard to tell when he really feels bad." Jeff became angry, went over to the other side of the room, and lay down again. Peter went over and invited Jeff to come back and finish the game, which he finally did, but with much sighing and sullenness. Joe and Barbara continued to glance over at Jeff, who had so successfully diverted attention from the conflictual issue between the parents. At the end of the session, Margaret and her colleague consulted and agreed that the parents should be seen alone for one or two final meetings.

Margaret made this plan with the parents, assuring the boys that she wanted to talk with the parents about some "grown-up" business that had nothing to do with them. Peter asked what it was and Jeff, adopting a very adult tone, said, "Oh, you know, it's probably about their fights." Both parents looked stunned. Barbara said, "What do you mean?" "We hear you in your room," Jeff replied. "Those aren't fights," Joe responded, "they're just discussions."

The final two sessions were with the parents alone. Major themes included Barbara's returning to work, which Joe was able to accept once appropriate arrangements were set up for after-school child care. The second theme was the extent to which the couple had allowed the children and the illness to inundate their relationship. They had almost entirely ceased to protect the boundaries around the marital system, and had planned no activities alone without the children in months. As a metaphor for this new family structure, both their own and the children's bedroom doors were left open at night so they could hear Jeff, should he awaken.

Margaret gave them a restructuring assignment after the first marital session, intended to nurture the couple's relationship. They were to plan one block of time each week away from the children doing something they would both enjoy. Barbara was to plan the first and Joe the second.

The fact that they were easily and willingly able to do this assignment by the next meeting and to enjoy themselves indicated the extent to which the change in the marriage had been reactive to the illness. In the second session, the focus was on whether or not to close the bedroom door, accompanied by a careful exploration of all of the issues connected with this, including Joe's need to monitor and Barbara's need to have some respite. The problem was one of assessing just how much watching was realistically necessary. Barbara's dependence on Joe's monitoring, the couple's anxiety, and their uncertainty about neglecting Jeff if they pursued their own lives, the extent to which they had allowed the children to control their lives and disrupt their intimacy were all held up for examination in the context of whether or not to close the bedroom door. By the end of the session, they decided they would try it.

The Marzikian family came to the attention of the social worker in a medical setting in the context of helping the family cope with a life-threatening illness in one of the children. Contacts with the family made clear that the meaning of illness and the family's adaptive and maladaptive responses could be seen and understood on many levels. Further, a variety of interventive measures were utilized to bring about change. Intergenerational prescriptions, the family's transactions with the environment, its structural arrangements, and its regulatory and communication processes helped shape the family's strategies for dealing with the problem and, similarly, each level or area became a part of the process of change.

What is particularly evident in the case situation with which we end this book is the extent to which variables located in different dimensions of time and space were transacting. This fact, in turn, dramatically demonstrates the limitations necessarily inherent in any written description of family-centered practice. For clarity's sake, the multiple directions for family assessment and intervention have been presented separately and consecutively. In an actual case, however, even in a relatively brief episode of service, the worker and family are traveling together through several dimensions of space and time at once. Yet all the while a part of the conscious professional self is standing back and analyzing the shifting scene.

Notes

Preface

1. Olson (1975) terms behavior modification approaches with families "quasi-interactional." Much of the family behavioral literature is centered around such issues as parent training, dyadic communication, or child management, or is symptom-focused around such family problems as sexual dysfunction.
2. See, for example, A. S. Gurman and D. P. Kniskern, "Research on Marital Therapy: Progress, Perspective and Prospect," in S. Garfield and A. Bergin (eds.) *Handbook of Psychotherapy and Behavior Change*, 2d ed, New York: Wiley, (1978); W. S. Pinsof, "Family Therapy Process Research," in A. S. Gurman and D. P. Kniskern, *Handbook of Family Therapy*. New York: Brunner/Mazel, (1981); R. A. Wells and A. E. Dezen. "The Results of Family Therapy Revisited: The Nonbehavioral Methods." *Family Process* 17 (1978):251–274; and A. S. Gurman and D. P. Kniskern, "Family Therapy Outcome Research: Knowns and Unknowns," in Gurman and Kniskern, ibid. In this last cited work, Gurman and Kniskern argue that " . . . what is needed, in our opinion, is not a re-mastication of what already has been digested, but a re-direction and re-focus toward identifying what needs to be studied in the future, and toward the identification of the clinically most relevant questions needing answers" (1981:743).

Chapter 1

1. Bertha Reynolds believed that social work should be available where people conduct the regular business of life, not exclusively in conjunction with the

identification of problems. This position is developed in her classic monograph "Between Client and Community" (1934).

2. An analysis of social work functions as institutional or residual appears in Wilensky and Lebeaux (1965). Alfred Kahn (1973) has elaborated this analysis in his approach to social policy and program development, and Carol Meyer (1970; 1976) has described an institutional-preventive approach to direct practice.

3. The discussion and debate on these complex issues has been continuous throughout the history of the profession. See Gordon (1965), Hardman (1975), Levy (1973), Miller (1968), and Tillich (1962).

4. Webster includes several definitions of a model and lists the following synonyms: "Archetype, copy, pattern, sample, specimen, example, type, mold, design." *Webster's New Twentieth Century Dictionary*, 2d ed. For a discussion of model definitions and model building in social work, see Fischer (1978), Hearn (1958), and Meyer (1973).

5. For a discussion of this issue, see Stein (1960).

6. This division continues to affect the delivery of services. See Laird (1978).

Chapter 4

1. The works of sociologists Talcott Parsons and Robert Merton have been particularly influential. The new developments in the social sciences were made readily available to social workers through the book *Social Perspectives on Behavior* (Stein and Cloward, 1958), which was a widely used text.

2. For a review of this theory see Strean (1967).

3. Some theorists proposed that "social role functioning" could be a unifying concept for social work. See Boehm (1959).

4. See, for example, the work of psychiatrist John Speigel (1957) on complementarity, sociologist Otto Pollak (1956) on social interaction and family structure, and social worker Carol Meyer (1959). Meyer was pioneering the effort in casework to integrate interactional concepts from the social sciences in a "quest for a broader base for family diagnosis."

5. Bateson's influence has not only continued unabated but has become even more widespread in recent years. Many major family therapists and theoreticians acknowledge their debt to him and continue to return to his work for further applications in understanding and bringing about change in families. For example, in a recent issue of *Family Process* (March, 1982), in which a series of articles dealing with family theory was published, themes from Bateson's work weave throughout. Lynn Hoffman, in her book *Foundations of Family Therapy*, presents a useful analysis of Bateson's role in this field. Bateson's influence is particularly interesting since, according to Haley, who worked side by side with Bateson for ten years, "Bateson was an anthropologist to his soul and an anthropologist doesn't believe you should tamper with the data or change it in any way. The task of an anthropologist is just to observe. For Bateson, the idea of stepping in and changing something was kind of personally revolting" (Simon, 1982:22).

6. For full discussion of general systems theory, see the work of Ludwig von Bertalanffy (1962), who founded the movement. Overviews may be found in Gray,

Duhl, and Rizzo (1969) and in Buckley (1968). For a detailed examination of general systems theory as an epistemological platform, see Sutherland (1973).

Chapter 5

1. There have also been a number of efforts to summarize, categorize, and classify family theories and the work of leaders in the field. See, for example, Beels and Ferber (1969), who emphasize therapeutic style, Guerin (1976), who classifies by theoretical disposition, Ritterman (1977), who looks at the ideal categories or philosophical assumptions which underlie theory, and Laird and Allen (1983) who categorize by the conception of and target for change.

Chapter 6

1. For a more complete discussion of some of the variables which shape worker notions about causation and thus diagnostic thinking, see Hartman (1969). She asks: "Could it be that irrelevance develops when our diagnoses—which are, after all, our ideas about what is amiss—reflect our values, our knowledge gaps, what we like to do rather than what is going on out there?"
2. Workshop led by Murray Bowen, North Shore Hospital, Long Island, New York, 1972.
3. See Hartman (1974) for an application of Auerswald's concept of the "explorer" to social work practice in a family agency.
4. For further consideration of how the issue of physical and spatial arrangements affect practice, see Seabury (1971) and Walz, Willenbring and DeMoll (1974).
5. A review of the literature and the reactions of family therapy trainees to live supervision may be found in Gershenson and Cohen (1978). The structural family therapists, led by Salvador Minuchin, are known for their wide use of the one-way mirror, not only for supervision, but as part of the therapeutic process itself. One or more family members observe other family subgroups from behind the mirror as a way of altering dysfunctional generational boundaries or powerful alignments. See Minuchin and Montalvo (1967) and Montalvo (1973).
6. For particularly provocative discussions of professional value dilemmas, see Miller (1968) and Hardman (1975).
7. Broadly conceptualized views of the school social worker's role may be found in Aponte (1978), Gitterman (1971), Radin (1978), and Vinter and Sarri (1965).

Chapter 7

1. In this case, or in any situation in which the worker is mandated by law to perform particular functions such as child protection or probation supervision, the worker's "contract" is actually with the community or the agency. At this

stage, the client may be considered "involuntary" or, to use Pincus and Minahan's (1973) conception, a *potential* client. See chapter 6 for further discussion of this issue.

2. Some protective agencies support the notion of surprise initial visits, in order to "gather evidence" which might be useful in supporting a neglect or abuse petition in the court; the rationale for this action is that the client might otherwise hide or temporarily correct the situation. In our experience, such an approach is disrespectful of the client's autonomy, is rarely necessary to protect a child, and establishes an initial relationship centered on the investigative function, which can all but completely undermine the worker's ability to help.

3. Family-centered individual counseling in such situations is often targeted at helping people differentiate successfully from their families of origin. See Bowen (1978), Carter and Orfanidis (1976), and Minuchin (1974) for discussions concerning the early tasks of marriage and the important influences of parental relationships on the prognosis for successful marriage. Many of the unsuccessfully married we have seen have inadequately resolved important issues with their families of origin and have insufficiently "left home" emotionally; their current marital relationships are undermined by, to use Boszormenyi-Nagy and Spark's terms (1973), unpaid debts and invisible loyalties to earlier generations. A family-centered approach useful in working with such individuals is elaborated in chapters 10 and 11.

4. In a workshop attended many years ago by the authors, Murray Bowen remarked, "I don't keep secrets, but I'm not a blabbermouth." One of the major hazards of individual work with family members or one of a marital pair (even if the couple is seen by separate workers) is that the worker may become privy to information which the other family members or spouse may not know. This "secret" then burdens the flexibility of the worker, solidifies the resistance, and can effectively strangle progress. The worker can avoid being triangled by: 1) cautioning that he or she should not be told things that cannot be shared with others in the family (given certain qualifications, of course. We don't advocate discussion of the parent's intimate sexual practices with the children present. This would violate an important generational boundary); and 2) avoiding the encouragement of secrets.

     The Milan team, for example, is not particularly interested in the content of family secrets and will even discourage families from "spilling" them in treatment, but it is very definitely interested in the way the family processes or organizes around a secret.

5. Great caution should certainly be exercised in the use of paradoxical or other such techniques which enhance the worker's power. However, the worker who dismisses such interventions as "unethical" or "manipulative" should consider that more direct methods which have been tried repeatedly in earlier helping relationships, or have failed in earlier sessions of the present work, only continue the family's pain, frustration, and disillusionment at encountering yet another unsuccessful therapeutic experience. The use of such techniques, discussed further in chapter 14, is based on a careful assessment of the family's accessibility or resistance to change.

6. These techniques may be seen in several videotapes available for rental from the Philadelphia Child Guidance Clinic. Especially fine examples of joining

children can be seen in Braulio Montalvo's work in "The Family With a Little Fire" and in the work of Minuchin in the tape entitled "Taming Monsters."
7. This case example comes from our work with Harry Aponte who consulted to the staff and conducted a live family session in a 1981 workshop at Ann Arbor Center for the Family.
8. The work of Peggy Papp exemplifies the artistry involved in tracking family patterns. See Papp (1977; 1980) for descriptions of her work with families, and for an application of similar principles to work with groups of married couples, see Papp (1976).

Chapter 8

1. The notion of mapping personal networks, first introduced by J. A. Barnes (1954), has been used extensively in anthropological research, and has been drawn upon by some family therapists, particularly those identified as "network" therapists. Carolyn Attneave (1975), for example, has developed a "family network map" on which can be depicted relationships between an individual and the significant family, kindred, and nonfamily persons with whom he or she comes into contact. The map depicts a nesting of concentric circles, at the center of which is the household, and beyond which are emotionally significant, casual, and distant person-to-person relationships. Attneave's map is accompanied by a questionnaire which is useful in assessing kin and social network relationships.
2. The eco-map was developed in 1975 by Ann Hartman as a part of the Child Welfare Learning Laboratory, a project of The University of Michigan School of Social Work Program for Continuing Education in the Human Services. The project was supported in part by a grant from Region V, Social and Rehabilitation Service, U.S.D.H.E.W., Section 426, Title IV, Part B of the Social Security Act. Lynn Nybell, Coordinator of the Family Assessment Module, offered many helpful ideas and criticisms. (See Hartman, 1978).
3. Remark made by Elizabeth Carter, while leading a workshop entitled "Mothers and Daughters" sponsored by Family Therapy Associates, Ann Arbor, Michigan, October, 1981.
4. For example, Carol Stack (1974) describes the elaborate "swapping" system and intricate mutual obligations and supportive kinship networks of the black urban poor in a midwestern city. It has been suggested that "Appalachians lack the church organizations, distinct language, and racial characteristics that often define an ethnic group. What group consciousness they have comes from their distinctive kinship system, religion, dialect, and music. Their group identity is only partial . . . " (Thernstrom et al., 1980:125).

Chapter 9

1. Mannino and Shore (1972) demonstrate the effects of ecological forces in a well-presented case of a middle-class family which has moved to a new and different environment.

2. The reader may find the following sources particularly useful: Brager and Holloway (1978); Grinnell, Kyte, and Bostwick (1981); Grosser (1979); Hartman (1974); Maluccio (1981); Middleman and Goldberg (1974).
3. See in particular Collins and Pancoast (1976); Sobey (1976); Swenson (1979); and Swenson (1981).
4. The role of the case manager is discussed by Stein (1981). See Regional Institute of Social Welfare Research (1977) and Community Research Applications (no date) for more complete discussion.
5. Kai Erikson found that Appalachian families were profoundly patriarchal: "Fathers are the source of final authority within the family nest and exercise at least the theoretical right to dictate their every whim to wife and mother as well as children" (1976:89). But it is an obligatory, ritualistic patriarchy, one which maintains the proud sovereignty of the man and one around which the women usually learn to maneuver.

Chapter 11

1. While they are not technically correct in terms of the language of kinship, we use the terms "family of origin" and "extended family" or "kinship network" interchangeably. When we talk about intergenerational work, we mean work with the family of origin rather than with the current family of commitment or marriage. The family of origin includes both vertical and collateral relatives. This work does not preclude strategies for change in one's current family, and of course, at the very least, its effects should be felt there.

Chapter 12

1. Personal communication from Vivian Shapiro, assistant professor of social work, University of Michigan, 1981.
2. One of the frequently heard concerns in the family therapy field is that we are without well-researched, operationalized definitions of the "healthy" family, particularly definitions which account for cultural and ethnic diversity. Beavers (1977) has attempted a typology.
3. This quotation is excerpted from a mimeographed handout distributed by Marianne Walters at a workshop on "Single Parent Families," Ann Arbor, Michigan, May 7, 1982.
4. We have used family sculpture extensively in teaching family-centered practice. Students, in completing papers on families, have illustrated them creatively with photographs and drawings which portray the family structure and emotional system. One student even submitted a diorama he had constructed, depicting a client family. In working with individuals in a family systems context, in situations in which no other family members may be available, clients can draw their families or portray them by using dolls, blocks, tinker toys, or other objects.

Chapter 13

1. Papp's videotape is available for rental from the Ackerman Institute for Family Therapy, 149 East 78th Street, New York, N.Y., 10021.
2. The videotape entitled "A Family with a Little Fire" may be rented from the Philadelphia Child Guidance Clinic, 34th Street and Civic Center Blvd., Philadelphia, PA., 19104.
3. Virginia Satir was a pioneer in the use of this technique, which is beautifully demonstrated in an early videotape entitled "A Family in Crisis." Information concerning purchase or rental of this tape is available from Science and Behavior Books, Inc., P.O. Box 11457, Palo Alto, California 94306.
4. Papp (1976) reports the use of the reversal technique in brief therapy with couples groups. For a particularly provocative description of the use of reversals, see Friedman (1971).

Chapter 15

1. Shanas (1960); Shanas and Streib (1965); and Sussman (1959) have researched this issue. Brody's research described in Lebowitz (1979) seems to concur with the predominant conclusion that families are assuming some 70 to 80 percent of the needed care.
2. For research and program development on the state-family partnership, see Dobrof and Litwak (1977); Gross-Andrew and Zimmer (1978); and Sussman (1977).
3. Useful discussions of this issue may be found in Boylin, Gordon, and Nehrke (1976); Havighurst and Glasser (1972); Ingersoll and Goodman; Kaminsky (1978); and Lewis (1971).

Bibliography

ACKERMAN, NATHAN. "The Diagnosis of Neurotic Marital Interaction." *Social Casework* 34 (Apr. 1954):139–146.

_____. "Interpersonal Disturbances in the Family: Some Unsolved Problems in Psychotherapy." *Psychiatry* 17 (1954):359–368. Reprinted in *Family Therapy: An Introduction to Theory and Technique*, edited by Gerald D. Erickson and Terrence P. Hogan, New York: Aronson, 1976, pp. 34–47.

ACKERMAN, NATHAN; BEATMAN, FRANCES; and SHERMAN, SANFORD. *Expanding Theory and Practice in Family Therapy*. New York: Family Service Association of America, 1967.

_____, eds. *Exploring the Base for Family Therapy*. New York: Family Service Association of America, 1961.

ALVAREZ, R. "The Psycho-Historical and Socioeconomic Development of the Chicano Community in the United States." *Social Science Quarterly* 53 (Mar. 1973):920–942.

APONTE, HARRY J. "The Family School Interview: An Ecological Approach." *Family Process* 15 (Sept. 1976):303–311.

APTEKAR, HERBERT. "The Essential Function of a Family Agency." *The Family* 20 (Nov. 1938).

ATTNEAVE, CAROLYN L. *Family Network Map*. Available from 5206 Ivanhoe, N.E., Seattle, Wa, 1975.

_____. "Social Networks as the Unit of Intervention." In *Family Therapy: Theory and Practice*, edited by Philip J. Guerin, Jr. New York: Gardner Press, 1976.

_____."Therapy in Tribal Settings and Urban Network Intervention." *Family Process* 8 (Mar. 1969):192–210.

AUERSWALD, EDGAR. "Families, Change and the Ecological Perspective." *Family Process* 10 (Sept. 1971):263–280.

———. "Interdisciplinary VS Ecological Approach." *Family Process* 7 (1968):202–215.

BALLESTEROS, DAVID. "Understanding the Bicultural Child." Paper presented at the Early Childhood Special Education Manpower Needs Conference in Washington, December 1971.

BANDLER, LOUISE. "Family Functioning: A Psychosocial Perspective." In *The Drifters*, edited by Eleanor Pavenstedt, Boston: Little, Brown & Co., 1967, pp. 225–253.

BANE, MARY JO. *Here to Stay: American Families in the Twentieth Century*. New York: Basic Books, 1976.

BARBARO, FRED. "The Case Against Family Policy." *Social Work* 24 (Nov. 1979):455–457.

BARNES, J. A. "Class and Committees in a Norwegian Island Parish." *Human Relations* 7 (1954):39–58.

BARTLETT, HARRIETT M. "Characteristics of Social Work." *Building Social Work Knowledge*. New York: National Association of Social Workers, 1964, pp. 1–15.

BATESON, GREGORY. *Naven*. Rev. ed. Stanford, Calif.: Stanford University Press, 1958.

———. *Steps to an Ecology of Mind*. New York: Ballantine Books, 1972.

BATESON, G., and JACKSON, DON P. "Some Varieties of Pathogenic Organization." *Disorders of Communication* 42 (1964):270–283. Reprinted in Don D. Jackson (ed.), *Communication, Family, and Marriage*. Palo Alto, Calif.: Science and Behavior Books, 1968, pp. 200–215.

BATESON, G.; JACKSON, D.; HALEY, J.; and WEAKLAND, J. "Toward a Theory of Schizophrenia." *Behavioral Science* 1, no. 4 (Oct. 1956):251–264.

BECK, DOROTHY FAHS, and JONES, MARYANN. *Progress in Family Problems: A Nationwide Study of Clients' and Counselors' Views of Family Agency Service*. New York: Family Service Association of America, 1973.

BEELS, C., and FERBER, ANDREW. "Family Therapy: A View." *Family Process* 8, no. 2 (Sept. 1969):280–318.

BENEDICT, RUTH. "Continuities and Discontinuities in Cultural Conditioning." *Psychiatry* 1 (May 1938):161–167.

BENNIS, WARREN G., and SHEPARD, HOWARD. "A Theory of Group Development." In *The Planning of Change*, edited by W. G. Bennis, K. D. Benne, and R. Chin. New York: Holt, 1962, pp. 321–340.

BERGER, PETER L., and LUCKMANN, THOMAS. *The Social Construction of Reality*. New York: Doubleday, 1966.

BERMANN, ERIC. *Scapegoat*. Ann Arbor: University of Michigan Press, 1973.

BERTALANFFY, LUDWIG VON. *General Systems Theory*. New York: Braziller, 1968.

———. "General Systems Theory, A Critical Review." *General Systems Year Book* 7 (1962):20.

———. "The Theory of Open Systems in Physics and Biology." *Science* 3 (Jan. 1950):23–29.

BIESTEK, FELIX P. *The Casework Relationship*. Chicago: Loyola University Press, 1957.

BILLINGSLEY, ANDREW. *Black Families in White America*. Englewood Cliffs, N.J.: Prentice Hall, 1968, pp. 155–166.

BIRDWHISTELL, RAY L. "The Idealized Model of the American Family." *Social Casework* 51 (Apr. 1970):195–198.

BLENKNER, MARGARET. "Social Work and Family Relationships in Later Life with Some Thoughts on Filial Maturity." In *Social Structure and the Family: Generational Relations*, edited by Ethel Shanas and Gordon Streib. Englewood Cliffs, N.J.: Prentice-Hall, 1965.

BOEHM, WERNER. *Objectives of the Social Work Curriculum of the Future*. New York: Council on Social Work Education, 1959.

BOSZORMENYI-NAGY, IVAN, and SPARK, GERALDINE. *Invisible Loyalties: Reciprocity in Intergenerational Family Therapy*. New York: Harper and Row, 1973.

BOULDING, KENNETH. *Beyond Economics*. Ann Arbor: University of Michigan Press, 1968.

BOWEN, MURRAY. "Family Psychotherapy." *American Journal of Orthopsychiatry* 31 (Jan. 1961):40–60.

———. *Family Therapy in Clinical Practice*. New York: Aronson, 1978.

———. "Theory in the Practice of Psychotherapy." In *Family Therapy: Theory and Practice*, edited by P. J. Guerin. New York: Gardner Press, 1976.

BOYLIN, N.; GORDON, S. K.; and NEHRKE, M. J. "Reminiscing and Ego Integrity in Institutionalized Elderly Males." *Gerontologist* 161 (1976):114–118.

BRADBURY, K., ET AL. "The Effects of Welfare Reform Alternatives on the Family." U.S.D.H.E.W. Special Report Series. Madison, Wisc.: University of Wisconsin Institute of Research on Poverty, 1977.

BRAGER, GEORGE, and HOLLOWAY, STEPHEN. *Changing Human Service Organizations*. New York: Free Press, 1978.

BRIAR, SCOTT. "In Summary." *Social Work* 22 (Sept. 1977):415–418.

BRODERICK, CARLFRED B. "Beyond Five Conceptual Frameworks: A Decade of Development in Family Theory." *Journal of Marriage and the Family* 33 (Feb. 1971):139–159.

———. "Power in the Governance of Families." In *Power in Families*, edited by Ronald E. Cromwell and David H. Olson. New York: Wiley, 1975.

BRODEY, WARREN M. "The Need for a Systems Approach." In *Expanding Theory and Practice in Family Therapy*, edited by Nathan Ackerman, Frances Beatman, and Sanford Sherman. New York: Family Service Association of America, 1967.

BRODY, ELAINE M. "Aging and Family Personality: A Developmental View." *Family Process* 13 (Mar. 1974):23–37.

BRONFENBRENNER, URI, ET AL., *American Families: Trends and Pressures*. Hearing before U.S. Senate Subcommitee on Children and Youth. Washington.: U.S. Government Printing Office, 1974.

BRUNER, JEROME; GOODNOW, JACQUELINE; and AUSTIN, GEORGE A. *A Study of Thinking*. New York: Wiley, 1962.

BUCKLEY, WALTER, ed. *Modern Systems Research for the Behavioral Scientist*. Chicago: Aldine, 1968.

BURGESS, ERNEST W.; LOCKE, HARVEY J.; and THOMAS, MARY MARGARET. *The Family from Traditional to Companionship*. New York: Van Nostrand Reinhold, 1971.

BUTLER, ROBERT N. "The Life Review: An Interpretation of Reminiscence in the Aging." In *Middle Age and Aging.* edited by B. Neugarten. Chicago: University of Chicago Press, 1968, pp. 486–496.

BUTLER, ROBERT N., and LEWIS, M. I. *Aging and Mental Health.* St. Louis: Mosby, 1973.

CANNON, WALTER B. *Wisdom of the Body.* New York: Norton, 1932.

CAPLOW, THEODORE, ET AL. *Middletown Families: Fifty Years of Change and Continuity.* Minneapolis: University of Minnesota Press, 1982.

CARLSON, JOHN E.; LASSEY, MARIE L.; and LASSEY, WILLIAM R. *Rural Society and Environment in America.* New York: McGraw-Hill, 1981.

CARTER, E. A., and McGOLDRICK, M. "The Family Life Cycle and Family Therapy: An Overview." In *The Family Life Cycle: A Framework for Family Therapy,* edited by E. A. Carter and M. McGoldrick. New York: Gardner Press, Inc., 1980, pp. 3–20.

CARTER, E. A., and ORFANIDIS, M. "Family Therapy with One Person and the Family Therapist's Own Family." In *Family Therapy: Theory and Practice,* edited by P. J. Guerin. New York: Gardner Press, 1976.

CLOWARD, RICHARD A., and OHLIN, LLOYD E. *Delinquency and Opportunity.* New York: Free Press, 1960.

CLOWARD, R., and PIVEN, F. "A Strategy to End Poverty." *Nation* (May 2, 1966).

COALITION OF FAMILY ORGANIZATIONS. *COFO Memo* 3 (Winter/Spring 1981): 1–12.

COLLINS, ALICE, and PANCOAST, DIANE. *Natural Helping Networks.* New York: National Association of Social Workers, 1976.

COLON, FERNANDO. "In Search of One's Past: An Identity Trip." *Family Process* 12 (Dec. 1973):429–438.

COMMUNITY RESEARCH APPLICATIONS, INC. *Protective Services for Abused and Neglected Children and Their Families: A Guide.* New York: Community Research Applications, Inc. n.d.

COMPTON, BEULAH, and GALAWAY, BURT. *Social Work Processes.* Rev. ed. Homewood, Ill.: Dorsey Press, 1979.

CONFERENCE ON FAMILY DIAGNOSIS, PROCEEDINGS. *Social Service Review* 34 (Mar. 1960):1–50.

COSTIN, L. "The Historical Context of Child Welfare." In *A Handbook of Child Welfare,* edited by J. Laird and A. Hartman. New York: Free Press, forthcoming.

COYLE, GRACE L. "Concepts Relevant to Helping the Family as a Group." *Social Casework* 43 (1962):347–354.

DEGLER, CARL. *At Odds.* London: Oxford University Press, 1980.

DELL, PAUL F. "Some Irreverent Thoughts on Paradox." *Family Process* 20 (Mar. 1980):37–41.

DEMOS, JOHN. "The American Family Past Time." *American Scholar* 43 (Mar. 1974):422–446.

DOBROF, ROSE, and LITWAK, EUGENE. *Maintenance of Family Ties of Long Term Care Patients: Theory and Guide to Practice.* Washington: U.S. Government Printing Office, 1977.

DONZELOT, J. *The Policing of Families.* New York: Pantheon Press, 1979.

DUHL, FREDERICK J. "Intervention, Therapy, and Change." In *General Systems*

Theory and Psychiatry, edited by W. Gray, F. J. Duhl, and N. D. Rizzo. Boston: Little, Brown and Company, 1969.

DUHL, FREDERICK; KANTOR, DAVID; and DUHL, BUNNY S. "Learning, Space and Action in Family Therapy: A Primer of Sculpture." In *Techniques of Family Psychotherapy*, edited by Donald Bloch. New York: Grune & Stratton, 1973.

DUNCAN, G. J., and MORGAN, J. N., eds. "Introduction, Overview, Summary, and Conclusions." In *Five Thousand American Families: Patterns of Economic Progress*. Ann Arbor: University of Michigan Institute for Social Research, 1976.

ELIOT, T. S. *Four Quartets*. New York: Harcourt, 1943.

ERIKSON, ERIK. *Identity and the Life Cycle*. New York: International Universities Press, 1959.

_____. *Identity: Youth and Crisis*. New York: Norton, 1968.

ERIKSON, KAI. *Everything in Its Path: Destruction of Community in the Buffalo Creek Flood*. New York: Simon and Schuster, 1976.

FALICOV, CELIA J., and KARRER, BETTY M. "Cultural Variations in the Family Life Cycle: The Mexican American Family." In *The Family Life Cycle*, edited by Elizabeth Carter and Monica McGoldrick. New York: Gardner Press, 1980.

FAMILY IMPACT SEMINAR, March 31–April 1, 1977. Summary Report of Third Meeting.

FAMILY SERVICE ASSOCIATION OF AMERICA. *Range and Emphasis of a Family Service Program*. New York: F.S.A.A., 1963.

FANSHEL, DAVID, and SHINN, EUGENE. *Children in Foster Care: A Longitudinal Investigation*. New York: Columbia University Press, 1978.

FARBER, BERNARD; MINDEL, CHARLES H.; and LAZERWITZ, BERNARD. "The Jewish American Family." In *Ethnic Families in America*, edited by C. H. Mindel and B. Farber. New York: Elsevier North Holland, 1976, pp. 347–378.

FELDMAN, HAROLD. "Why We Need a Family Policy." *Journal of Marriage and the Family* 41 (Aug. 1979):453–455.

FERREIRA, ANTONIO J. "Family Myth and Homeostasis." *Archives of General Psychiatry* 9 (Nov. 1963):457–463. Reprinted in *Theory and Practice of Family Psychiatry*, edited by John G. Howells. New York: Brunner/Mazel, 1971, pp. 358–366.

FISCHER, JOEL. *Effective Casework Practice*. New York: McGraw-Hill, 1978.

FISHER, L.; ANDERSON, A.; and JONES, JAMES. "Types of Paradoxical Intervention and Indications, Contraindications for Their Use in Clinical Practice." *Family Process* 20 (Mar. 1981):25–36.

FRAMO, JAMES L. "Family of Origin as a Therapeutic Resource for Adults in Marital and Family Therapy: You Can and Should Go Home Again." *Family Process* 15 (June 1976):193–210.

FRANKLIN, PAUL, and PROSKY, PHOEBE. "A Standard Initial Interview." In *Techniques of Family Psychotherapy: A Primer*, edited by Donald Bloch. New York: Grune and Stratton, 1973, pp. 29–38.

FRIEDMAN, EDWIN H. "The Birthday Party: An Experiment in Obtaining Change in One's Own Extended Family." *Family Process* 10 (Sept. 1971): 345–359.

FURSTENBERG, FRANK F. *Unplanned Parenthood: The Social Consequences of Teenage Childbearing*. New York: Free Press, 1976.

GEERTZ, CLIFFORD. "Religion as a Cultural System." In *Anthropological Approaches to the Study of Religion*, edited by Michael Banton. A.S.A. Monograph no. 3. London: Tavistock, 1966, pp. 1–46.

GENNEP, ARNOLD VAN. *Rites of Passage*. Introduced by Solon Kimball. Chicago: University of Chicago Press, 1960.

GEORGETOWN FAMILY SYMPOSIA. Vol. 2, edited by Joseph P. Lorio and Louise McClenathan (1973–74). Washington: Georgetown University Family Center, 1977.

GEORGETOWN FAMILY SYMPOSIA. Vol. 3, edited by Ruth Riley Sagar (1975–76). Washington: Georgetown University Family Center, 1978.

GERMAIN, CAREL B. "Casework: An Historical Encounter." In *Theories of Social Casework*, edited by R. Roberts and R. Nee. Chicago: University of Chicago Press, 1970, pp. 3–32.

———. "An Ecological Perspective in Casework Practice." *Social Casework* 54 (June 1973):323–330.

———. "Social Study: Past and Future." *Social Casework* 49 (July 1968):403–409.

———. *Social Work Practice: People and Environments*. New York: Columbia University Press, 1979.

———. "Time: An Ecological Variable in Social Work Practice." *Social Casework* 57 (July 1976):419–426.

GERMAIN, CAREL B., and GITTERMAN, ALEX. *The Life Model of Social Work Practice*. New York: Columbia University Press, 1980.

GERSHENSON, JUDITH, and COHEN, MARTIN S. "Through the Looking Glass: The Experiences of Two Family Therapy Trainees with Live Supervision." *Family Process* 13 (June 1978):225–230.

GIELE, JANET. "Social Policy and the Family." *Annual Review of Sociology* 5 (1979):275–302.

GIL, DAVID G. "The Ideological Context of Child Welfare." In *A Handbook of Child Welfare*, edited by J. Laird and A. Hartman. New York: The Free Press, forthcoming.

———. "A Systematic Approach to Social Policy Analysis." *Social Service Review* 44 (Dec. 1970):411–426.

———. *Violence Against Children: Physical Child Abuse in the United States*. Cambridge, Mass.: Harvard University Press, 1970.

GITTERMAN, ALEX. "Group Work in the Public Schools." In *The Practice of Group Work*, edited by William Schwartz and Serapio Zalba. New York: Columbia University Press, 1971.

GLAZER, NATHAN. "The Limits of Social Policy." *Commentary* 52 (Sept. 1971): 51–58.

GOFFMAN, ERVING. "Interaction Ritual: Essays on Face-to-Face Behavior. New York: Doubleday, 1967.

GOLDSTEIN, HOWARD. Social Work Practice: A Unitary Approach. Columbia, S.C.: University of South Carolina Press, 1973.

GOLDSTEIN, JOSEPH; FREUD, ANNA; and SOLNIT, ALBERT J. *Beyond the Best Interests of the Child*. New York: Free Press, 1973.

GOLDSTEIN, SIDNEY, and GOLDSCHEIDER, CALVIN. *Jewish Americans: Three Generations in a Jewish Community*. Englewood Cliffs, N.J.: Prentice-Hall, 1968.

GOMBERG, ROBERT. "Family Diagnosis: Trends in Theory and Practice." *Social Casework* 39 (Feb. 1958):3–10.

GOODE, WILLIAM. *World Revolution and Family Patterns*. Glencoe, Ill.: Free Press of Glencoe, 1963.

GOODY, JACK. "Against 'Ritual': Loosely Structured Thoughts on a Loosely Defined Topic." In *Secular Ritual*, edited by B. Myerhoff and S. Moore. Amsterdam: Van Gorcum, 1977, pp. 25–33.

GORDON, WILLIAM E. "Basic Constructs for an Integrative and Generative Conception of Social Work." In *The General Systems Approach: Contributions Toward an Holistic Conception of Social Work*, edited by Gordon Hearn. New York: Council on Social Work Education, 1969, pp. 5–11.

_____. "Knowledge and Value: Their Distinction and Relationship in Clarifying Social Work Practice." *Social Work* 10 (July 1965):32–39.

GRAY, WILLIAM; DUHL, FREDERICK; and RIZZO, NICHOLAS. *General Systems Theory and Psychiatry*. Boston: Little, Brown and Company, 1969.

GRINKER, ROY. *Toward a Unified Theory of Human Behavior*. 2d ed. New York: Basic Books, 1967.

GRINNELL, RICHARD M.; KYTE, NANCY S.; and BOSTWICK, GERALD J. "Environmental Modification." In *Promoting Competence in Clients: A New Old Approach to Social Work Practice*, edited by Anthony Maluccio. New York: Free Press, 1981, pp. 152–184.

GROSS-ANDREW, SUSANNAH, and ANNA H. ZIMMER. "Incentives to Families Caring for Disabled Elderly: Research and Demonstration Project to Strengthen Natural Support Systems." *Journal of Gerontological Social Work* 2 (Winter 1978):119–125.

GROSSER, CHARLES F. "Participation and Practice." In *Social Work Practice: People and Environments*, edited by Carel B. Germain. New York: Columbia University Press, 1979.

GUERIN, PHILIP. "Family Therapy: The First Twenty Five Years." In *Family Therapy: Theory and Practice*, edited by P. Guerin. New York: Gardner Press, 1976, pp. 2–22.

GURMAN, ALAN S., and KNISKERN, DAVID P. "Family Therapy Outcome Research: Knowns and Unknowns." In *Handbook of Family Therapy*, edited by Alan S. Gurman and David P. Kniskern. New York: Brunner/Mazel, 1981.

_____. "Research on Marital Therapy: Progress, Perspective and Prospect." In *Handbook of Psychotherapy and Behavior Change*, 2nd ed., edited by S. Garfield and A. Bergin. New York: Wiley, 1978.

GURMAN, ALAN S., and RICE, DAVID G. "Emerging Trends in Research and Practice." In *Couples in Conflict: New Directions in Marital Therapy*, edited by Alan S. Gurman and David G. Rice. New York: Jason Aronson, 1975.

HALEY, ALEX. *Roots*. Garden City, N.Y.: Doubleday, 1976.

HALEY, JAY. *Leaving Home*. New York: McGraw-Hill, 1980.

_____. *Problem-Solving Therapy*. San Francisco: Jossey-Bass, 1976.

_____. *Uncommon Therapy: The Psychiatric Techniques of Milton H. Erickson, M.D.* New York: Norton, 1973.

HALL, A. D., and FAGEN, R. E. "Definition of a System." In *Modern Systems*

Research for the Behavioral Scientist: A Sourcebook, edited by Walter Buckley. Chicago: Aldine, 1968.

HARDMAN, DALE G. "Not With My Daughter You Don't." *Social Work* 20 (July 1975):278–285.

HARE-MUSTIN, R. "Paradoxical Tasks in Family Therapy: Who Can Resist?" *Psychotherapy: Theory, Research, and Practice* 13 (1976):128–130.

HARRIS, L., and Associates. *The Myth and Reality of Aging in America*. Washington, D.C.: National Council on the Aging, April 1975.

HARTMAN, ANN. "Anomie and Social Casework." *Social Casework* 50 (March 1969):131–137.

———. "Bowen Family Systems: Theory and Practice." In *Models of Family Treatment*, edited by E. R. Tolson and W. Reid. New York: Columbia University Press, 1981.

———. "But All Knowledge Is One: A Systems Approach to the Dilemmas in Curriculum Building." *Journal of Education for Social Work* 16, no. 2 (Spring 1980):100–107.

———. "Diagnosis: The First Step in Providing Casework Services." In *Community Focused Social Services*. School of Public Health. Chapel Hill, N.C.: University of North Carolina, 1969.

———. "Diagrammatic Assessment of Family Relationships." *Social Casework* 59 (Oct. 1978):465–476.

———. *Finding Families: An Ecological Approach to Family Assessment in Adoption*. Beverly Hills, Calif.: Sage, 1979.

———. "The Generic Stance and the Family Agency." *Social Casework* 55 (Apr. 1974):199–208.

———. "To Think About the Unthinkable." *Social Casework* 51 (Oct. 1970):467–74.

HARTMAN, ANN, and LAIRD, JOAN. "The Use of the Self in Learning and Teaching Family Practice." Presented at the Annual Program Meeting, Council on Social Work Education, 1977. Mimeographed.

HAVIGHURST, ROBERT J., and GLASSER, R. "An Exploratory Study of Reminiscence." *Journal of Gerontology* 27 (1972):245–253.

HEARN, GORDON A. *Theory Building in Social Work*. Toronto: University of Toronto Press, 1958.

———, ed. *The General System Approach: Contributions Toward an Holistic Conception of Social Work*. New York: Council on Social Work Education, 1969.

HELLENBRAND, SHIRLEY. "Client Value Orientations: Implications for Diagnosis and Treatment." *Social Casework* 42 (April 1961):163–169.

HILL, ROBERT. "Strengths of the Black Family." Study presented at the Annual Conference of the National Urban League, Detroit, July 1971.

———. *The Strength of Black Families*. New York: Emerson Hall, 1972.

HOFFMAN, LYNN. "Enmeshment and the Too Richly Cross-Joined System." *Family Process* 14 (Dec. 1975):457–468.

———. *Foundations of Family Therapy*. New York: Basic Books, 1981.

HOFFMAN, LYNN, and LONG, LORENCE. "A Systems Dilemma." *Family Process* 8 (Sept. 1969):211–234. Reprinted in Allen Pincus and Anne Minahan, *Social Work Practice: Model and Method*. Itasca, Ill.: F. E. Peacock, 1973.

HOFFMAN, W., and MARMOR, T. "The Politics of Public Assistance." *Social Service Review* 50 (Mar. 1976):11–22.

HOLLIS, FLORENCE. *Women in Marital Conflict*. New York: Family Service Association of America, 1949.

HUANG, LUCY JEN. "The Chinese American Family." In *Ethnic Families in America*, edited by C. H. Mindel and R. W. Habenstein. New York: Elsevier North Holland, 1976, pp. 124–47.

INGERSOLL, BERIT, and GOODMAN, LILI. "History Comes Alive: Facilitating Reminiscence in a Group of Institutionalized Elderly." *Journal of Gerontological Social Work* 2 (1980):305–319.

INGERSOLL, BERIT, and SILVERMAN, ALIDA. "Comparative Group Psychotherapy for the Aged." *Gerontologist*, 18 (1978):201–6.

JACKSON, DON. "The Question of Family Homeostasis." *Psychiatric Quarterly Supplement* 31 (1957):79–90.

————. "The Study of the Family." *Family Process* 4 (Dec. 1965):1–20.

————, ed. *Communication, Marriage and the Family*. Palo Alto, Calif.: Science and Behavior Books, 1967.

————, ed. *Therapy, Communication, and Change*. Palo Alto, Calif.: Science and Behavior Books, 1968.

JANCHILL, SISTER MARY PAUL. "Systems Concepts in Casework Theory and Practice." *Social Casework* 15 (Feb. 1969):74–82.

JARRETT, MARY. "The Psychiatric Thread Running Through All Social Case Work." In *Proceedings*, National Conference on Social Walfare, 1919.

JENKINS, SHIRLEY. "Duration of Foster Care—Some Relevant Antecedent Variables." *Child Welfare* 46 (Oct. 1967):450–456.

————. *The Ethnic Dilemma in Social Services*. New York: Free Press, 1981.

JENKINS, SHIRLEY, and SAUBER, MIGNON. *Paths to Child Placement*. New York: Community Council of Greater New York, 1966.

JOSSELYN, IRENE M. "The Family as a Psychological Unit." *Social Casework* 34 (Oct. 1953):336–343.

KAHN, ALFRED J. "Service Delivery at the Neighborhood Level: Experience, Theory and Fads." *Social Service Review* 50 (Mar. 1976):23–56.

KAMINSKY, M. "Pictures from the Past: The Use of Reminiscence in Casework with the Elderly." *Journal of Gerontological Social Work* 1 (1978):19–32.

————. *Social Policy and Social Services*. New York: Random House, 1973.

KANTOR, D., and LEHR, W. *Inside the Family*. San Francisco: Jossey-Bass, 1975.

KARPEL, MARK. "Individuation: From Fusion to Dialogue." *Family Process* 15 (Mar. 1976):65–82.

KENISTON, KENNETH, and the CARNEGIE COUNCIL ON CHILDREN. *All Our Children: The American Family Under Pressure*. New York: Harcourt Brace Jovanovich, 1977.

KERR, MICHAEL E. "Family Systems Theory and Therapy." In *Handbook of Family Therapy*, edited by A. S. Gurman and D. P. Kniskern. New York: Brunner/Mazel, 1981.

KIEV, A., ed. *Magic, Faith and Healing Studies in Primitive Psychiatry Today*. London: Collier–Macmillan, 1964.

KINGSTON, MAXINE HONG. *The Woman Warrior: Memoirs of a Girlhood Among Ghosts.* New York: Vintage Books, 1977.

KLUCKHOHN, FLORENCE. "Variations in the Basic Values of Family Systems." *Social Casework* 39 (1958) :63–72.

KLUGMAN, JEFFREY. " 'Enmeshment' and 'Fusion'." *Family Process* 15 (Sept. 1976):321–323.

KRESTAN, JO-ANN, and BEPKO, CLAUDIA S. "The Problem of Fusion in the Lesbian Relationship." *Family Process* 19 (Sept. 1980):277–289.

KUHN, THOMAS S. *The Structure of Scientific Revolutions.* Chicago: University of Chicago Press, 1962.

LADNER, JOYCE. *Tomorrow's Tomorrow: The Black Woman.* Garden City, N.Y.: Doubleday, 1971.

LAING, R. D. *Self and Others.* London: Tavistock Publications, 1961.

LAIRD, JOAN. "Ecologically Oriented Child Welfare Practice: Issues of Family Identity and Continuity." *Social Work Practice: People and Environments,* edited by Carel B. Germain. New York: Columbia University Press, 1978, pp. 174–209.

LAIRD, JOAN, and ALLEN, JO ANN. "Family Theory and Practice." In *Handbook of Clinical Social Work,* edited by Diana Waldfogel and Aaron Rosenblatt. San Francisco: Jossey-Bass, 1983.

LASCH, C. *Haven in a Heartless World.* New York: Harper, 1977.

LASZLO, ERVIN. *The Systems View of the World.* New York: George Braziller, 1972.

LAZERWITZ, BERNARD. "Contrasting the Effects of Generation, Class, Sex, and Age on Group Identification in the Jewish and Protestant Communities." *Social Forces* 49 (1970):50–59.

LE BOW, M. D. "Behavior Modification for the Family." In *Family Therapy: An Introduction to Theory and Technique,* edited by G. D. Erickson and T. P. Hogan. New York: Jason Aronson, 1976, pp. 347–376.

LEBOWITZ, BARRY D. "Old Age and Family Functioning." *Journal of Gerontological Social Work* 1 (Winter 1978):111–118.

LEE, PORTER. "The Fabric of the Family." *Proceedings,* National Conference on Social Welfare, 1919.

LEE, PORTER, and KENWORTHY, MARION E. *Mental Hygiene and Social Work.* New York: Commonwealth Fund, 1931.

LEICHTER, HOPE J., and MITCHELL, WILLIAM E. *Kinship and Casework: Family Networks and Social Intervention.* 2d ed. New York: Teachers College Press, 1978.

LEIK, ROBERT K., and HILL, REUBEN. "What Price National Policy for Families?" *Journal of Marriage and Family* 4 (Aug. 1979):457–459.

LESLIE, GERALD R. "Family Breakdown." *Encyclopedia of Social Work.* National Association of Social Workers, 1977, pp. 369–382.

LEVY, CHARLES. "The Value Base of Social Work." *Journal of Education for Social Work* 9 (Winter 1973):34–42.

LEWIS, C. N. "Reminiscing and Self-Concept in Old Age," *Journal of Gerontology* 26 (1971):240–243.

LEWIS, HAROLD. "Morality and the Politics of Practice." *Social Casework* 53 (July 1972):408–417.

LEWIS, OSCAR. *The Children of Sanchez.* New York: Random House, 1961.

————. *Five Families: Mexican Case Studies in the Culture of Poverty.* New York: Basic Books, 1959.

————. *LaVida: A Puerto Rican Family in the Culture of Poverty—San Juan and New York.* New York: Random House, 1965.

LIBERMAN, R. P. "Behavioral Principles in Family and Couple Therapy." In *Couples in Conflict,* edited by A. S. Gurman and D. G. Rice. New York: Jason Aronson, 1976.

LIDZ, THEODORE. "The Family: The Developmental Setting." In *American Handbook of Psychiatry,* 2nd ed., edited by S. Arieti. Vol. 1: The Foundation of Psychiatry. New York: Basic Books, 1974, pp. 252–263.

————. *The Person.* New York: Basic Books, 1968.

LIPPETT, RONALD; WATSON, JEANNE; and WESTLEY, BRUCE. *The Dynamics of Planned Change.* New York: Harcourt, Brace, and World, 1958.

LITWAK, EUGENE. "Extended Kin Relations in an Industrial Democratic Society." In *Social Structure and the Family: Generational Relations,* edited by E. Shanas and G. Streib. Englewood Cliffs, N.J.: Prentice–Hall, 1965.

LOWRY, FERN. "Problems of Therapy in Family Case Work." *Social Service Review* 10 (June 1936): 195–205.

LUBOVE, ROY. *The Professional Altruist.* Cambridge, Mass.: Harvard University Press, 1965.

LUTZ, WERNER. "Concepts and Principles Underlying Social Casework Practice." *Social Work Practice in Medical Care and Rehabilitation Settings.* Monograph III, Medical Social Work Section. Washington, D.C.: National Association of Social Workers, 1956.

LYND, ROBERT S., and LYND, HELEN MERRELL. *Middletown: A Study in American Culture.* New York: Harcourt and Brace, 1929.

MCADOO, HARRIETTE PIPES. "Factors Related to Stability in Upwardly Mobile Black Families." *Journal of Marriage and the Family* 40 (Nov. 1978):761–776.

————. *Black Families.* Beverly Hills, Calif.: Sage, 1981.

MCBROOM, ELIZABETH. "Socialization and Social Casework." In *Theories of Social Casework,* edited by Robert W. Roberts and Robert H. Nee. Chicago: University of Chicago Press, 1970.

MALUCCIO, ANTHONY N. *Learning from Clients.* New York: Free Press, 1979.

————. *Promoting Competence in Clients.* New York: Free Press, 1981.

MANCINI, JAY A. "Family Relationships and Morale Among People Sixty-Five Years of Age and Older." *American Journal of Orthopsychiatry* 49 (Apr. 1979): 292–300.

MANNINO, FORTUNE V., and SHORE, MILTON. "Ecologically Oriented Family Interaction." *Family Process* 11 (Dec. 1972):499–505.

MANSER, ELLEN, ed. *Family Advocacy: A Manual for Action.* New York: Family Service Association, 1973.

MASLOW, ABRAHAM. *Motivation and Personality.* New York: Harper, 1954.

MERRIAM, SHARON. "The Concept and Function of Reminiscence: A Review of the Research." *The Gerontologist* 20 (1980):604–609.

MERTON, ROBERT K. "Social Structure and Anomie." In *The Family: Its Function and Destiny,* edited by Ruth N. Ansher. New York: Harper and Brothers,

1949. Reprinted in *Social Theory and Social Structure*. Rev. ed. Glencoe, Ill.: Free Press, 1957.

MEYER, CAROL H. "Practice Models: The New Ideology?" *Smith College Studies in Social Work* 63 (Feb. 1973):85–98.

———. "Quest for a Broader Base for Family Diagnosis." *Social Casework* 40 (July 1959):370–376.

———. *Social Work Practice: A Changing Landscape*. 2d ed. New York: Free Press, 1976.

———. *Social Work Practice: A Response to the Urban Crisis*. New York: Free Press, 1970.

MEYER, JOHN E., and TIMMS, NOEL E. *The Client Speaks: Working Class Impressions of Casework*. Boston: Routledge and Kegan Paul, 1970.

MIDDLEMAN, RUTH, and GOLDBERG, GALE. *Social Service Delivery: A Structural Approach to Social Work Practice*. New York: Columbia University Press, 1974.

MILLER, DOROTHY. "The 'Sandwich Generation': Adult Children and the Aging." *Social Work* 26 (Sept. 1981):419–423.

MILLER, HENRY. "Value Dilemmas in Social Casework." *Social Work* 13 (Jan. 1968):27–33.

MILLER, JAMES G. "The Nature of Living Systems." *Behavioral Science* 20 (Nov. 1975):343–365.

MINDEL, CHARLES H., and HABENSTEIN, ROBERT W. *Ethnic Families in America: Patterns and Variations*. New York: Elsevier North Holland, 1976.

MINUCHIN, SALVADOR. *Families and Family Therapy*. Boston: Harvard University Press, 1974.

MINUCHIN, SALVADOR, and FISHMAN, H. CHARLES. *Family Therapy Techniques*. Cambridge, Mass.: Harvard University Press, 1981.

MINUCHIN, SALVADOR, and MONTALVO, BRAULIO. "Techniques for Working with Disorganized Low Socioeconomic Families." *American Journal of Orthopsychiatry* 37 (1967):880–887.

MINUCHIN, SALVADOR; MONTALVO, B.; GUERNEY, B. G., JR.; Rosman, B. L.; and Schumer, F., eds. *Families of the Slums*. New York: Basic Books, 1967.

MONTALVO, BRAULIO. "Aspects of Live Supervision." *Family Process* 12 (Dec. 1973):343–359.

MONTALVO, BRAULIO, and HALEY, JAY. "In Defense of Child Therapy." *Family Process* 12, no. 3 (September 1973):227–244.

MONTEIL, MIGUEL. "The Social Science Myth of the Mexican-American Family." In *Voices*, edited by O. Romano. Berkeley: Quinto Sol, 1971, pp. 40–47.

MOORE, MADELINE. "The Treatment of Maternal Attitudes in Problems of Guidance." *American Journal of Orthopsychiatry* 3 (Apr. 1933):113–127.

MOORE, SALLY F., and MYERHOFF, BARBARA. "Introduction: Secular Ritual: Forms and Meanings." In *Secular Ritual*, edited by S. Moore and B. Myerhoff. Amsterdam: Van Gorcum, 1977, pp. 3–24.

MORONEY, ROBERT. *The Family and the State: Considerations for Social Policy*. London: Longman, 1976.

———. *Families, Social Services, and Social Policy: The Issue of Shared Responsibility*. Rockville, Md.: National Institute of Mental Health, 1980.

MOYNIHAN, DANIEL. "Foreword" to Alva Myrdal, *Nation and Family*. Cambridge, Mass.: MIT Press, 1968.

―――――. *The Negro Family: The Case for National Action*. Washington: U.S. Government Printing Office, 1965.

MYERHOFF, BARBARA G. *Number Our Days*. New York: E.P. Dutton, 1978.

―――――. *Peyote Hunt: The Sacred Journey of the Huichol Indians*. Ithaca: Cornell University Press, 1974.

MYERHOFF, BARBARA G., and TUFTE, V. "Life History as Integration: An Essay on an Experimental Model." *Gerontologist* 15 (1975):541–543.

NAPIER, AUGUSTUS Y., and WHITAKER, CARL A. *The Family Crucible*. New York: Harper & Row, 1978.

NATIONAL ASSOCIATION OF SOCIAL WORKERS. "Conceptual Frameworks II." *Social Work* 26 (Jan. 1981):entire issue.

NATIONAL ASSOCIATION OF SOCIAL WORKERS. "Special Issue on Conceptual Frameworks." *Social Work* 22 (Sept. 1977):entire issue.

NATIONAL COMMISSION ON CHILDREN IN NEED OF PARENTS. *Who Knows? Who Cares? Forgotten Children in Foster Care*. New York: National Commission on Children in Need of Parents, 1979.

NATIONAL CONFERENCE ON SOCIAL WELFARE. *Families and Public Policies in the United States: Final Report of the Commission*. Columbus, Ohio, 1978.

NATIONAL RESEARCH COUNCIL ADVISORY COMMITTEE ON CHILD DEVELOPMENT. *Toward a National Policy for Children and Families*. Washington: National Academy of Science, 1976.

NDETI, KIVUTO. "The Relevance of African Traditional Medicine in Modern Medical Training and Practice." In *Medical Anthropology*, edited by Francis X. Grollig and Harold B. Haley. The Hague: Mouton Publishers, 1976.

NEWMAN, SANDRA. *Housing Adjustments of Older People: A Report of Findings from the Second Phase*. Ann Arbor: Institute for Social Research, University of Michigan, 1976.

OLSON, DAVID H.; SPRENKLE, DOUGLAS H.; and RUSSELL, CANDYCE. "Circumplex Model of Marital and Family Systems: I. Cohesion and Adaptability Dimensions, Family Types, and Clinical Applications." *Family Process* 18 (Mar. 1979):3–28.

ORTNER, SHERRY B. *Sherpas Through Their Rituals*. Cambridge: Cambridge University Press, 1978.

OSMAN, SHELOMO. "My Stepfather Is a She." *Family Process* 11 (June 1972):209–218.

PALMORE, E. *The Honorable Elders*. Durham, N.C.: Duke University Press, 1975.

PAPP, P. "Brief Therapy with Couples Groups." In *Family Therapy: Theory and Practice*, edited by Philip Guerin, New York: Gardner Press, 1976.

―――――. *Family Therapy: Full Length Case Studies*. New York: Gardner Press, 1977.

―――――. "The Greek Chorus and Other Techniques of Family Therapy." *Family Process* 19 (Mar. 1980):45–58.

PARSONS, T., and BALES, R. F., eds. *Family, Socialization, and Interaction Process*. New York: Free Press of Glencoe, 1955.

PAUL, NORMAN L. "The Role of Mourning and Empathy in Conjoint Marital Therapy." In *Family Therapy and Disturbed Families*, edited by G. Zuk and I. Boszormenyi-Nagy. Palo Alto, Calif.: Science and Behavior Books, 1967. pp. 186–205.

PAUL, N. L., and GROSSER, G. "Operational Mourning and Its Role in Conjoint Family Therapy." *Community Mental Health Journal* 1 (Winter 1965):339–345.

PECK, ROBERT C. "Psychological Developments in the Second Half of Life." In *Middle Age and Aging*, edited by Bernice Neugarten. Chicago: University of Chicago Press, 1968.

PERLMAN, HELEN HARRIS. "Intake and Some Role Considerations." *Social Casework* 41 (Apr. 1960):171–177.

―――. *Persona: Social Role and Personality*. Paperback ed. Chicago: University of Chicago Press, 1976.

PHILLIPS, JOHN L. *The Origins of Intellect: Piaget's Theory*. San Francisco: W. H. Freeman, 1969.

PIKE, VICTOR, ET AL. *Permanent Planning for Children in Foster Care*. Portland, Oregon: Permanent Planning Project Regional Research Institute, Portland State University, 1977.

PINCUS, ALLEN, and MINAHAN, ANNE. *Social Work Practice: Model and Method*. Itasca, Ill.: F. E. Peacock, 1973.

PINSOF, WILLIAM S. "Family Therapy Process Research." In *Handbook of Family Therapy*, edited by Alan S. Gurman and David P. Kniskern. New York: Brunner/Mazel, 1981.

PIVEN, F., and CLOWARD R. *Regulating the Poor: The Functions of Public Welfare*. New York: Pantheon Books, 1971.

POLANSKY, NORMAN, ET AL. "Assessing Adequacy of Child Caring: An Urban Scale." *Child Welfare* 57 (Jul.–Aug. 1978):439–449.

POLANSKY, NORMAN; BORGMAN, ROBERT D.; and DE SAIX, CHRISTINE. *The Roots of Futility*. San Francisco: Jossey-Bass, Inc., 1972.

POLLAK, OTTO. *Integrating Sociological and Psychoanalytic Concepts*. New York: Russell Sage Foundation, 1956.

PUMPHREY, MURIEL W. "Mary Richmond's Process of Conceptualization." *Social Casework* 38 (Oct. 1957):399–406.

PUNER, M. *To The Good Long Life: What We Know About Growing Old*. New York: Universe Books, 1974.

QUEZADA, ADOLFO. "Innovative School Losing Pupils." *Tucson Daily Citizen*, October 3, 1973, p. 23.

QUINN, WILLIAM H., and KELLER, JAMES F. "A Family Therapy Model for Perserving Independence in Older Persons: Utilizing the Family of Procreation." *The American Journal of Family Therapy* 9 (Spring 1981):79–84.

RADIN, NORMA. "A Personal Perspective on School Social Work." *Social Casework* 56 (Dec. 1975):605–613.

RAINWATER, L., and YANCEY, W. *The Moynihan Report and the Politics of Controversy*. Cambridge, Mass.: MIT Press, 1967.

RAMEY, J. "Experimental Family Forms—The Family of the Future." *Marriage and Family Review* 1 (1978):1–9.

RAPPAPORT, ROY A. "The Obvious Aspects of Ritual." In *Ecology, Meaning and Religion*, edited by R. A. Rappaport. Richmond, Calif.: North Atlantic Books, 1979, pp. 173–222.

RED HORSE, JOHN G., ET AL. "Family Behavior of Urban American Indians." *Social Casework* 59 (Feb. 1978):67–72.

―――. "Family Structure and Value Orientation in American Indians." *Social Casework* 61 (Oct. 1980):462–467.

REGIONAL INSTITUTE OF SOCIAL WELFARE RESEARCH, INC. Vol. 1: Case Management: Concept and Process. Vol 2: The Case Management Model: Implementation Requirements. Athens, GA.: Regional Institute of Social Welfare Research, Inc., 1977.

REID, WILLIAM J. "Social Work for Social Problems." *Social Work* 22 (Sept. 1977):374–381.

REIN, MARTIN. "Equality and Social Policy." *Social Service Review* 51 (Dec. 1977):565–587.

————. "Social Policy Analyses as the Interpretation of Beliefs." *Journal of American Institute of Planners* 37 (Sept. 1971):297–310.

REISS, DAVID. *The Family's Construction of Reality*. Cambridge, Mass.: Harvard University Press, 1981.

REYNOLDS, BERTHA. "Between Client and Community." *Smith College Studies in Social Work* 5 (Sept. 1934):entire issue.

————. "Can Social Work Be Interpreted to a Community as a Basic Approach to Human Problems?" *The Family* 13 (1933):336–342.

————. "A Changing Psychology One Year Later." *The Family* 13 (June 1932):107–111.

RICE, ROBERT. "Child Welfare in the Context of Child Welfare." In *A Handbook of Child Welfare*, edited by J. Laird and A. Hartman. New York: Free Press, forthcoming.

RICE, ROBERT M. *American Family Policy: Content and Context*. New York: Family Service Association of America, 1977.

RICHMOND, MARY. *The Long View*. New York: Russell Sage Foundation, 1930.

————. *Social Diagnosis*. New York: Russell Sage Foundation, 1917.

————. *What Is Social Casework*. New York: Russell Sage Foundation, 1922.

ROBINSON, VIRGINIA. *A Changing Psychology in Social Case Work*. Chapel Hill, N.C.: University of North Carolina Press, 1930.

ROGERS, CARL R. "A Theory of Therapy, Personality, and Interpersonal Relationships, as Developed in the Client-Centered Framework." In *Psychology: A Study of A Science*, edited by S. Koch. Vol. 3. New York: McGraw–Hill, 1959.

ROSALDO, MICHELLE Z. *Knowledge and Passion: Ilongot Notions of Self and Social Life*. Cambridge: Cambridge University Press, 1980.

ROSS, HEATHER L., and SAWHILL, ISABEL V. *Time of Transition: The Growth of Families Headed by Women*. Urban Institute, 1975.

RUESCH, JERGEN, and BATESON, GREGORY. *Communication: The Social Matrix of Psychiatry*. New York: W. W. Norton & Co., 1951.

RUEVENI, URI. *Networking Families in Crisis*. New York: Human Sciences Press, 1979.

RUSSELL, CANDYCE. "Circumplex Model of Family Systems: III.: Empirical Evaluation with Families." *Family Process* 18 (Mar. 1979):29–45.

SARRI, ROSEMARY, and GALINSKY, MAEDA J. "A Conceptual Framework for Group Development." In *Individual Change Through Small Groups*, edited by Paul Glasser, Rosemary Sarri, and Robert Vinter. New York: Free Press, 1974.

SATIR, VIRGINIA. *Conjoint Family Therapy*. Rev. ed. Palo Alto, Calif.: Science and Behavior Books, 1967.

SCANZONI, JOHN. *The Black Family in Modern Society*. Boston: Allyn and Bacon, 1971.

SCHERZ, FRANCES. "What Is Family Centered Casework?" *Social Casework* 34, no. 8 (Oct. 1954):343–348.

SCHORR, ALVIN L. *Filial Responsibility in the Modern American Family*. Washington, D.C.: Social Security Administration, Department of Health, Education and Welfare, 1960.

―――. "Views of Family Policy." *Journal of Marriage and the Family* 41 (Aug. 1979):465–467.

SCHWARTZ, WILLIAM. "Private Troubles and Public Issues: One Social Work Job or Two?" *Social Welfare Forum*. New York: Columbia University Press, 1969.

―――. "The Social Worker in the Group." In *Social Welfare Forum 1961* New York: Columbia University Press, 1961, pp. 146–177.

SCHWARTZMAN, JOHN. "Normality from a Cross-Cultural Perspective." In *Normal Family Processes*, edited by Froma Walsh. New York: Guilford Press, 1982, pp. 383–424.

SEABURY, BRETT. "Arrangement of Physical Space in Social Work Settings." *Social Work* 16 (Oct. 1971):43–49.

SEELBACH, WAYNE C., and SAUER, WILLIAM. "Filial Responsibility Expectations and Morale Among Aged Persons." *The Gerontologist* 17 (1977):492–499.

SELVINI-PALAZZOLI, MARA. "Comments on Dell's Paper." *Family Process* 20 (Mar. 1981):44–45.

SELVINI-PALAZZOLI, MARA, ET AL. "Family Rituals: A Powerful Tool in Family Therapy." *Family Process* 16 (Dec. 1977):445–453.

―――. "Hypothesizing—Circularity—Neutrality: Three Guidelines for the Conductor of the Session." *Family Process* 19 (Mar. 1980):3–12.

―――. *Paradox and Counter Paradox*. Eng. Translation. New York: Jason Aronson, 1978 (Italian editors, Milan: Feltrinelli Editore, 1975).

―――. "The Problem of the Referring Person." *Journal of Marital and Family Therapy* 6 (Jan. 1980):3–9.

―――. "A Ritualized Prescription in Family Therapy: Odd Days and Even Days." *Journal of Marriage and Family Counselling* 4 (1978):3–9.

―――. "The Treatment of Children Through Brief Therapy of Their Parents." *Family Process* 13 (Dec. 1974):429–442.

SETLEIS, LLOYD. "An Inquiry into the Moral Basis of the Family." *Social Casework* 59, no. 4 (Apr. 1978):203–210.

SHANAS, ETHEL. *Family Relationships of Older People*. New York: Health Information Foundation Research Series, no. 20, 1961.

―――. "Older People and Their Families: The New Pioneers." *Journal of Marriage and the Family* (Feb. 1980):9–15.

―――. "Social Myth as Hypothesis: The Case of the Family Relations of Old People," *The Gerontologist* 19 (1979):3–9.

SHANAS, ETHEL, and STREIB, GORDON, eds. *Social Structure and the Family: Generational Relations*. Englewood Cliffs, N.J.: Prentice–Hall, Inc. 1965.

SHERMAN, SANFORD. "Family Therapy as a Unifying Force in Social Work." In *Expanding Theory and Practice in Family Therapy*, edited by Nathan Ackerman, Frances Beatman, and Sanford Sherman. New York: Family Services Association of America, 1967, pp. 20–28.

SHYNE, ANN, and SCHROEDER, A. *National Study of Social Services to Children and Their Families*. Washington: National Center for Child Advocacy, United States Children's Bureau, 1978.

SILVERMAN, ALIDA G., and BRAHCE, CARL I. "As Parents Grow Older: An Intervention Model." *Journal of Gerontological Social Work* 2 (Fall 1979):77–85.

SIMON, RICHARD. "Behind the One Way Mirror, An Interview with Jay Haley." *The Family Therapy Networker* 6 (Sept./Oct. 1982):18–25; 28–29; 58–59.

SKOLNICK, ARLENE. *The Intimate Environment: Exploring Marriage and the Family*. Boston: Little, Brown and Company, 1973.

SOUTHARD, E. E. "The Individual Versus the Family as Unit of Interest in Social Work." In *Proceedings*, National Conference on Social Welfare, 1919.

———. "The Kingdom of Evil: Advantages of an Orderly Approach in Social Case Analysis." In *Proceedings*, National Conference of Social Work, 1918.

SPARK, GERALDINE. "Grandparents and Intergenerational Family Therapy." *Family Process* 13 (June 1979):225–238.

SPECK, R. V., and ATTNEAVE, C. *Family Networks*. New York: Vintage Books, 1973.

SPEER, D. C. "Family Systems: Morphostasis and Morphogenesis, or 'Is Homeostasis Enough?' " *Family Process* 9 (1970):259–278.

SPIEGEL, JOHN P. "The Resolution of Role Conflict within the Family." In *The Patient and the Mental Hospital*, edited by Milton Greenblatt, Daniel J. Levinson, and Richard H. Williams. New York: Free Press of Glencoe, Illinois, 1957.

———. *Transactions: The Interplay Between Individual, Family and Society*. New York: Science House, 1971.

STACK, CAROL B. *All Our Kin: Strategies for Survival in a Black Community*. New York: Harper & Row, 1974.

STAPLES, ROBERT. "The Black American Family." In *Ethnic Families in America: Patterns and Variations*, edited by C. H. Mindel and R. W. Habenstein. New York: Elsevier North Holland, 1976.

STEIN, HERMAN. "The Concept of the Social Environment in Social Work Practice." *Smith College Studies in Social Work* 30 (June 1960):187–210.

STEIN, HERMAN, and CLOWARD, RICHARD. *Social Perspectives on Behavior*. New York: Free Press, 1958.

STEIN, IRMA. *Systems Theory, Science, and Social Work*. Metuchen, N.J.: Scarecrow Press, 1974.

STEIN, THEODORE J. *Social Work Practice in Child Welfare*. Englewood Cliffs, N.J.: Prentice–Hall, Inc., 1981.

STEINMETZ, S., and STRAUS, M. *Violence in the Family*. New York: Dodd, Mead, 1975.

STEVENSON, GEORGE S., and SMITH, GEDDES. *Child Guidance Clinics: A Quarter Century of Development*. New York: Oxford University Press, 1934.

STREAN, HERBERT. "Role Theory, Role Models, and Casework: Review of the Literature and Practice Applications." *Social Work* 12 (Apr. 1967):77–88.

SUNLEY, ROBERT. "New Dimensions in Reaching-Out Casework." *Social Work* 13 (Apr. 1968):64–74.

SUSSMAN, M. "Relationships of Adult Children with their Parents in the United States." In *Social Structure and the Family*, edited by E. Shanas and G. Streib. Englewoods Cliffs, N.J.: Prentice–Hall, Inc., 1965, pp. 62–92.

SUSSMAN, MARVIN B. "Family, Bureaucracy, and the Elderly Individual: An Organizational Linkage Perspective." In *Family, Bureaucracy, and the Elderly*, edited by E. Shanas and M. B. Sussman. Durham, N.C.: Duke University Press, 1977, pp. 2–20.

————. "The Family Life of Old People." In *Handbook of Aging and the Social Sciences*, edited by R. Binstock and E. Shanas, New York: Van Nostrand Reinhold, 1976.

————. "The Family Today: Is It an Endangered Species?" *Children Today* 7 (Mar.–Apr. 1978):32–37, 45.

————. "The Isolated Nuclear Family: Fact or Fiction." *Social Problems* 6 (1959):333–340.

SUTHERLAND, JOHN W. *A General Systems Philosophy for the Social and Behavioral Sciences*. New York: Braziller, 1973.

SWENSON, CAROL R. "Social Networks, Mutual Aid, and the Life Model of Practice." In *Social Work Practice: People and Environments*, edited by Carel B. Germain. New York: Columbia University Press, 1979, pp. 213–38.

————. "Using Natural Helping Networks to Promote Competence." In *Promoting Competence in Clients*, edited by A. Maluccio. New York: Free Press, 1981, pp. 125–151.

TERKELSON, KENNETH G. "Toward a Theory of the Family Life Cycle." In *The Family Life Cycle: A Framework for Family Therapy*, edited by Elizabeth A. Carter and Monica McGoldrick. New York: Gardner Press, 1980, pp. 21–52.

THERNSTROM, STEPHAN; ORLOV, ANN; and HANDLIN, OSCAR, eds. *Harvard Encyclopedia of American Ethnic Groups*. Cambridge, Mass.: Harvard University Press, 1980.

TILLICH, PAUL. "The Philosophy of Social Work." *Social Service Review* 36 (Mar. 1962):13–16.

TOWNSEND, PETER. "The Structure of the Family." In *Old People in Three Industrial Societies*, edited by E. Shanas et al. New York: Atherton Press, 1968:132–74.

TURNER, VICTOR W. *The Ritual Process: Structure and Anti-Structure*. Chicago: Aldine, 1969.

U.S. BUREAU OF THE CENSUS. *Marital Status and Living Arrangements*, March 1980. Current Population Reports, Series P-20, NV. 365. Washington: U.S. Government Printing Office, 1981.

U.S. DEPARTMENT OF HEALTH AND HUMAN SERVICES. "The Status of Children, Youth, and Families 1979." Washington, 1980.

U.S. GENERAL ACCOUNTING OFFICE. *The Well Being of Older People in Cleveland, Ohio*. Washington, 1977.

UNITED STATES NATIONAL CENTER FOR HEALTH STATISTICS. "Final Natality Statistics, 1978." March 1978.

UNIVERSITY OF MICHIGAN SURVEY RESEARCH CENTER. *Five Thousand American Families*. Ann Arbor, 1974.

VINTER, ROBERT D., and SARRI, ROSEMARY. "Malperformance in the Public Schools: A Group Work Approach." *Social Work* 10 (Jan. 1965):3–13.

VOGEL, EZRA, and BELL, NORMAN. "The Emotionally Disturbed Child as the Family Scapegoat." In *A Modern Introduction to the Family*. edited by N. Bell and E. Vogel. New York: Free Press, 1960.

WALLERSTEIN, JUDITH S., and KELLY, JOAN B. "Children and Divorce: A Review." *Social Work* 24 (Nov. 1979):468–475.

WALZ, T.; WILLENBRING, G.; and DEMOLL, L. "Environmental Design." *Social Work* 19 (Jan. 1974):38–46.

WATTS, J., and SKIDMORE, F. *Household Structure: Necessary Changes in Categorization and Data Collection*. Prepared for Census Bureau Conference Issues in Federal Statistical Needs Relating to Women, Bethesda, Md.: date unknown.

WATZLAWICK, PAUL. *How Real Is Real?* New York: Random House, 1976.

WATZLAWICK, PAUL; WEAKLAND, JOHN; and FISCH, RICHARD. *Change: Principles of Problem Formation and Problem Resolution*. New York: Norton, 1974.

WATZLAWICK, PAUL; BEAVIN, JANET; and JACKSON, DON. *Pragmatics of Human Communication*. New York: Norton, 1967.

WEEKS, G. A., and L'ABATE. L., "A Bibliography of Paradoxical Methods in Psychotherapy of Family Systems." *Family Process* 17 (Mar. 1978):95–98.

WEISS, VIOLA W., and MONROE, RUSSELL R. "A Framework for Understanding Family Dynamics," Part I and Part II. *Social Casework* 40 (Jan./Feb. 1959):3–9.

WELLS, RICHARD A., and DEZEN. A. E. "The Results of Family Therapy Revisited: The Nonbehavioral Methods." *Family Process* 17 (1978):251–274.

WERTHEIM, ELEANOR S. "Family Unit Therapy. The Science and Typology of Family Systems." *Family Process* 12 (Dec. 1973):361–376.

————. "The Science and Typology of Family Systems II. Further Theoretical and Practical Considerations." *Family Process* 14 (Sept. 1975):285–309.

WHITE, ROBERT W. "Motivation Reconsidered: The Concept of Competence." *Psychological Review* 66 (Sept. 1959):297–333.

————. "Strategies of Adaptation." In *Human Adaptation*, edited by Rudolf H. Moos. Lexington, Mass.: Heath, 1976, pp. 17–32.

WHITE HOUSE CONFERENCE ON FAMILIES. *A Summary: Listening to America's Families*. Washington: November 1980.

WIENER, NORBERT. *Cybernetics*. New York: Wiley, 1948.

————. *The Human Use of Human Beings*. New York: Doubleday, Anchor Books, 1954.

WILENSKY, HAROLD L. *The Welfare State and Equality*. Berkeley: University of California Press, 1975.

WILENSKY, HAROLD L., and LEBEAUX, CHARLES N. Paperback ed. *Industrial Society and Social Welfare*. New York: Free Press, 1965.

WOLIN, S. J., ET AL. "Disrupted Family Rituals: A Factor in the Intergenerational Transmission of Alcoholism." *Journal of Studies on Alcohol* (1980):199–214.

————. "Family Rituals and the Recurrence of Alcoholism Over Generations." *American Journal of Psychiatry* 136 (1979):589–93.

WYNNE, LYMAN C., ET AL. "Pseudo-Mutuality in the Family Relations of Schizophrenics." *Psychiatry* 21 (May 1958):205–220. Reprinted in *A Modern Introduction to the Family*, edited by Norman W. Bell and Ezra F. Vogel. New York: The Free Press, 1960, pp. 573–594.

ZALD, MEYER. "Demographics, Politics, and the Future of the Welfare State." *Social Service Review* 51 (Mar. 1977): 110–124.

ZAPPOLO A. "Characteristics, Social Contacts, and Activities of Nursing Home Residents, United States, 1973–74 National Nursing Home Survey." *National Health Survey*. Dept of Health, Education, and Welfare, series 13, no. 27. Washington: U.S. Government Printing Office, 1977.

Author Index

Ackerman, N., 17, 18, 19, 91, 92, 143, 146, 388n.
Allen, J., 383n, 397n.
Anderson, A., 328, 392n.
Aponte, H., 383n., 388n.
Aptekar, H., 14–15, 388n.
Attneave, C., 201, 202, 385n., 388n.
Auerswald, E., 69, 71–72, 74, 114, 389n.

Bales, R., 90, 389n.
Ballesteros, D., 287, 389n.
Bandler, L., 292, 389n.
Bane, M., 38, 389n.
Barbaro, F., 49, 389n.
Barnes, J., 385n., 389n.
Bartlett, H., 5, 389n.
Bateson, G., 18, 19, 60, 71, 98, 99, 101–2, 103, 104, 331, 332, 382, 389n.
Beatman, F., 19, 388n.
Beavers, R., 386n.
Beavin, J., 72, 101–2, 406n.
Beck, D., 36, 389n.
Beels, C., 383n., 389n.
Bell, J., 18
Bell, N., 92, 93, 405–6n.
Benedict, R., 290, 389n.
Bergin, A., 381n.
Bermann, E., 302, 389n.

Bertalanffy, L. Von, 64, 65, 382n.
Biestek, F., 133, 389n.
Billingsley, A., 25, 390n.
Birdwhistell, R., 25, 390n.
Blenker, M., 366, 390n.
Boehm, W., 382n., 390n.
Boll, E., 106, 390n.
Bossard, J., 106, 390n.
Bostwick, G., 386n., 394n.
Boszormenyi-Nagy, I., 77, 80, 213, 384n., 390n.
Boulding, K., 64, 130, 390n.
Bowen, M., 16, 18, 19, 77–80, 83, 84–87, 91, 100, 114, 206, 212, 213, 231, 234–35, 255, 265, 266, 272, 278, 361, 365, 383n., 384n., 390n.
Boylin, N., 387n., 390n.
Bradbury, K., 47, 390n.
Brager, G., 386n., 390n.
Brahce, C., 371, 404n.
Briar, S., 6, 8, 390n.
Broderick, C., 18, 98–99, 100, 390n.
Brodey, W., 22, 69, 390n.
Brody, E., 358, 387n., 390n.
Bronfenbrenner, U., 24, 390n.
Buckley, W., 68, 96, 383n., 390n.
Burgess, E., 27, 51, 390n.
Butler, R., 355, 361–62, 391n.

409

Cannon, W., 65, 391n.
Caplow, T., 25, 218, 391n,
Carlson, J., 277, 391n.
Carter, E., 77, 176, 236, 265, 385n., 391n.
Cloward, R., 42, 45, 71, 382n., 391n.,
    401n., 404n.
Cohen, M., 383n., 393n.
Collins, A., 386n., 391n.
Colon, F., 265, 391n.
Compton, B., 8, 133, 391n.
Costin, L., 86, 391n.
Coyle, G., 21, 391n.

Degler, C., 24, 391n.
Dell, P., 328, 391n.
DeMoll, L., 383n., 406n.
Demos, J., 24, 391n.
Dezen, A., 381n., 406n.
Dobrof, R., 387n., 391n.
Donzelot, J., 86, 391n.
Duhl, B., 281, 392n.
Duhl, F., 79, 281, 383n., 391n., 394n.
Duncan, G., 47, 392n.
Durkheim, E., 71

Erickson, G., 92, 188, 388n.
Erickson, M., 313
Erikson, E., 70–71, 360, 363, 392n.
Erikson, K., 386n., 392n.

Fagan, R., 69, 394n.
Falicov, C., 287, 392n.
Fanshel, D., 50, 392n.
Farber, B., 277, 392n.
Feldman, H., 30, 392n.
Ferber, A., 383n., 389n.
Ferreira, A., 99, 100, 392n.
Fisch, R., 53, 331, 406n.
Fischer, J., 382n., 392n.
Fisher, L., 328, 392n.
Fishman, H., 144, 145–46, 399n.
Fogarty, T., 77
Forster, E., 97
Framo, J., 212, 213, 254, 392n.
Franklin, P., 124, 392n.
Friedman, E., 249, 387n., 392n.
Furstenberg, F., 36, 392n.

Galaway, B., 8, 133, 391n.
Garfield, S., 381n., 394n.
Germain, C., 4, 60, 69, 70, 112–13, 117,
    393n.
Gershenson, J., 383n., 393n.
Giele, J., 28, 47, 53–54, 57, 393n.
Gil, D., 85–86, 393n.
Gitterman, A., 147, 385n., 393n.
Glasser, R., 387n., 395n.
Glazer, N., 44, 393n.
Goffman, E., 106, 393n.

Goldberg, G., 386n., 399n.
Goldscheider, C., 286, 393n.
Goldstein, H., 60, 393n.
Goldstein, S., 286, 393n.
Gomberg, R., 18, 19, 394n.
Goode, W., 25, 394n.
Goodman, L., 362, 387n., 396n.
Gordon, S., 387n., 390n.
Gordon, W., 5, 70, 382n, 394n.
Gray, W., 383n., 394n.
Grinker, R., 122, 382n., 394n.
Grinnell, R., 386n., 394n.
Gross-Andrew, S., 387n., 394n.
Grosser, C., 386n., 394n.
Grosser, G., 80, 400n.
Guerin, P., 18, 77, 152, 383n., 394n.
Gurman, A., 76, 381, 394n.

Habenstein, R., 286, 399n.
Haley, J., 18, 90, 98, 103, 124, 144, 148,
    297, 313, 315, 328, 382n., 389n., 394n.
Hall, A., 69, 394n.
Hardman, D., 382n., 383n., 395n.
Hare-Mustin, R., 328, 395n.
Harris, L., 37, 38, 395n.
Hartman, A., 71, 158, 383n., 385n., 386n.,
    395n.
Havighurst, R., 387n., 395n.
Hearn, G., 60, 382n., 395n.
Hill, Reuben, 55, 397n.
Hill, Robert, 25, 288, 357, 397n.
Hoffman, L., 74, 84, 86, 87, 164, 298, 326,
    328, 333, 382n., 395n.
Hoffman, W., 42, 396n.
Hogan, T., 92, 396n.
Hollis, F., 15, 396n.
Holloway, S., 386n., 390n., 396n.
Huang, L., 287, 396n.

Ingersoll, B., 362, 387n., 396n.

Jackson, D., 18, 19, 60, 66, 71, 72, 94, 101,
    102, 103, 300, 389n., 396n., 406n.
Janchill, Sister M. P., 60, 396n.
Jarrett, M., 13–14, 396n.
Jenkins, S., 50, 286, 287, 288, 396n.
Jones, J., 328, 392n.
Jones, M., 36, 389n.
Josselyn, I., 17, 396n.

Kahn, A., 45, 382, 396n.
Kaminsky, M., 387n., 396n.
Kantor, D., 81–82, 93, 272, 281, 295,
    392n., 396n.
Karpel, M., 82, 273, 396n.
Karrer, B., 287, 392n.
Kelly, J., 82, 406n.
Keniston, K., 32, 33, 35, 36, 48, 396n.

Kenworthy, M., 15–16, 397n.
Kerr, M., 79, 396n.
Kiev, A., 158, 396n.
Kingston, M., 286, 396n.
Klugman, J., 85, 397n.
Kniskern, D., 381n., 394n.
Kuhn, T., 3, 215, 397n.
Kyte, N., 386n., 394n.

L'Abate, L., 328, 406n.
Ladner, J., 288, 397n.
Laing, R., 265, 397n.
Laird, J., 382n., 383n., 395n., 397n.
Lasch, C., 25, 397n.
Lassey, M., 277, 391n.
Lassey, W., 277, 391n.
Laszlo, E., 59, 397n.
Lazerwitz, B., 277, 392n., 397n.
Lebeaux, C., 382, 406n.
Le Bow, M., 304, 397n.
Lebowitz, B., 387n., 397n.
Lee, P., 14–16, 397n.
Lehr, W., 81–82, 93, 272, 295, 396n.
Leichter, H., 18, 71, 397n.
Leik, R., 55, 397n.
Leslie, G., 81, 397n.
Levy, C., 382n., 397n.
Lewis, M., 387n., 391n.
Lewis, O., 122, 171, 397n., 398n.
Liberman, R., 304, 398n.
Lidz, T., 71, 90, 398n.
Lippett, R., 60, 398n.
Litwak, E., 37, 387n., 391n.
Locke, H., 27, 390n.
Long, L., 74, 164, 395n.
Lowry, R., 26, 398n.
Lubove, R., 20, 397n.
Lutz, W., 59–60, 398n.
Lynd, H., 25, 398n.
Lynd, R., 25, 398n.

McAdoo, H., 25, 38, 398n.
McBroom, E., 292, 398n.
McGoldrick, M., 176, 391n. (See also Orfanidis)
Maluccio, A., 70, 133, 136, 386n.
Mannino, F., 385n., 398n.
Marmor, T., 42, 396n., 398n.
Maslow, A., 71, 398n.
Merriam, S., 361, 398n.
Merton, R., 71, 382n., 398n.
Meyer, C., 4, 17, 60, 122, 382n., 399n.
Meyer, J., 136, 399n.
Middleman, R., 386n., 399n.
Miller, D., 356, 366, 399n.
Miller, H., 131, 382n., 383n., 399n.
Miller, J., 65–66, 67, 68, 96, 399n.
Minahan, A., 5, 60, 131, 384n., 401n.
Mindel, C., 286, 392n., 399n.

Minuchin, S., 71, 82, 83–87, 88, 89, 90, 91, 144, 145–46, 271, 283, 301, 310, 384n., 385n., 399n.
Mitchell, C., 18–19
Mitchell, W., 71, 397n.
Monroe, R., 17, 406n.
Montalvo, B., 312–13, 383n., 385n., 399n.
Moore, M., 16, 399n.
Moore, S., 106, 399n.
Morgan, J., 47, 392n., 399n.
Moroney, R., 28, 37, 46–47, 51, 355, 357–358, 399n.
Moynihan, D., 43–44, 48, 400n.
Myerhoff, B., 106, 362, 399n., 400n.

Napier, A., 118, 400n.
Ndeti, K., 157, 400n.
Nehrke, M., 387n., 390n., 400n.
Newman, S., 355, 400n.
Nixon, R., 42, 51

Ohlin, L., 71, 391n.
Olson, D., 82, 83–87, 271, 381n.
Orfanidis, M., 263, 265, 384n., 391n. (*see also* McGoldrick)

Palazzoli, M., 90–91, 97, 98, 117, 141–42, 146, 147, 148, 150, 205, 239, 307, 318, 327, 328, 329, 330, 331, 403n.
Pancoast, D., 386n., 391n.
Papp, P., 128, 142, 281, 282, 319, 328, 331, 333, 334, 385n., 387n., 400n.
Parsons, T., 90, 382n., 400n.
Paul, N., 77, 80, 213, 400n., 401n.
Peck, R., 360, 401n.
Perlman, H., 59, 91, 133, 401n.
Phillips, J., 71, 401n.
Piaget, J., 71
Pike, V., 51, 401n.
Pincus, A., 5, 60, 131, 384n, 401n.
Pinsof, W., 381n., 401n.
Piven, F., 42, 45, 391n., 401n.
Polansky, N., 292, 401n.
Pollack, O., 33, 382n., 401n.
Prosky, P., 124, 392n.
Puner, M., 355, 356, 401n.

Quezada, A., 288, 401n.

Rabkin, R., 331
Radin, N., 383n., 401n.
Rainwater, L., 43, 401n.
Ramey, J., 38, 401n.
Rappoport, R., 401n.
Reagan, R., 53, 54
Red Horse, J., 401n.
Reid, W., 402n.
Rein, M., 42, 43, 56, 402n.
Reiss, D., 105, 215, 319, 402n.

Reynolds, B., 5, 7, 14, 45, 121–22, 381–
     82n., 402n.
Rice, D., 394n.
Rice, R., 27, 34, 35, 39, 49, 402n.
Richmond, M., 5, 12–13, 28, 29, 402n.
Ritterman, M., 383n.
Rizzo, N., 383n., 394n.
Robinson, V., 14, 402n.
Ross, H., 47, 402n.
Ruesch, J., 60, 402n.
Rueveni, U., 201, 202, 402n.
Russell, C., 82, 83, 173, 400n., 402n.

Sarri, R., 383n., 402n., 405n.
Satir, V., 18, 19, 61, 143–44, 146, 152,
     304, 387n., 402n.
Sauber, M., 50, 396n.
Sauer, W., 357, 403n.
Sawhill, I., 47, 402n.
Scanzoni, J., 288, 403n.
Scherz, F., 16, 403n.
Schorr, A., 45, 49, 357, 403n.
Schroeder, A., 48, 403n.
Schwartz, W., 6, 136, 403n.
Schwartzman, J., 76–77, 403n.
Seabury, B., 136, 383n., 403n.
Seelbach, W., 357, 403n.
Selvini-Palazzoli (*see* Palazzoli)
Shanas, E., 359, 387n., 403n.
Shapiro, V., 386n.
Sherman, S., 18, 19, 20, 388n., 403n.
Shinn, E., 50, 392n.
Shore, M., 385n., 398n.
Shyne, A., 48, 403–4n.
Silverman, A., 362, 371, 396n., 404n.
Simon, R., 382n.
Skidmore, F., 28, 406n.
Skolnick, A., 30, 285, 404n.
Sobey, F., 386n.
Southard, E., 13, 404n.
Spark, G., 77, 80, 213, 384, 390n., 404n.
Speck, R., 201, 202, 404n.
Speer, D., 94, 96, 404n.
Spiegel, J., 29, 99, 382n., 404n.
Sprenkle, D., 82, 83, 173, 400n., 404n.
Stachowiak, J., 304
Stack, C., 25, 38, 288, 385n., 404n.
Staples, R., 288, 404n.
Stein, H., 382n., 404n.
Stein, I., 60–61, 404n.

Stein, T., 386n., 404n.
Steinmetz, S., 80, 404n.
Straus, M., 80, 404n.
Strean, H., 382n., 404n.
Streib, G., 387n., 403n.
Sunley, R., 122, 404n.
Sussman, M., 24, 37, 39, 355, 359–60,
     387n., 404n., 405n.
Sutherland, J., 383n., 405n.
Swenson, C., 386n., 405n.

Taschman, H., 304n.
Thernstrom, S., 385n., 405n.
Thomas, E., 304
Thomas, M., 27, 51, 390n.
Tillich, P., 382n., 405n.
Townsend, P., 353, 405n.
Tucker, J., 48
Turner, V., 97, 405n.
Timms, N., 136, 399n.

Vinter, R., 383n., 405n.
Vogel, E., 92, 93, 405–6n.

Wallerstein, J., 82, 406n.
Walters, M., 386n.
Walz, T., 383n., 406n.
Watson, J., 60, 398n.
Watts, J., 28, 406n.
Watzlawick, P., 53, 61, 71, 72, 101–2, 331,
     406n.
Weakland, J., 53, 103, 331, 389n., 406n.
Weeks, G., 328, 406n.
Weiss, V., 17, 406n.
Wells, R., 381n., 406n.
Wertheim, E., 96, 98, 100, 406n.
Westley, B., 60, 398n.
Whitaker, C., 118, 124, 146, 400n.
White, R., 70, 406n.
Whitehead, A., 62
Wiener, N., 60, 67, 406n.
Wilensky, H., 78, 97, 111, 382n., 406n.
Willenbring, G., 383n., 406n.
Wynne, L., 19, 83–87, 406n.

Yancey, W., 43, 401n.

Zald, M., 407n.
Zappolo, A., 356, 407n.
Zimmer, A., 387n., 394n.

Subject Index

Abortion, 36
Ackerman Brief Therapy Project, 117, 129
Adaptation, 66–69
    family, 295–97
    and rituals, 322–24
Address, forms of, 143–44
Affect, 214
Agency relations, 208–10
Aging, the
    and (their) children, 365–70
    cultural views of, 356–57
    and environment, 359–60
    and family, 36–37
    and family history, 360–62
    family visiting, 355–56
    individual approach, 119
    in nursing homes, 355–56
    variation, 356–57
Alliances, strengthening, 317
American Indian families, 51
Analogic communication, 102–3, 303
Assessment
    of the eco-map, 164
    of family, 269–70
    of family communication, 302–4
    of family cultural norms, 288–89
    of family history, 16–17
    of family roles, 284–94

    of intergenerational family, 215–27
    of power in families, 300–301
    producing change, 232–33
Assignments
    techniques for giving, 313–16
    typical, 316–19
    use for change, 312–19
Authority, 131

Birth control, 35–36, 47
Black families, 38, 42–43, 288–89
Boston Psychopathic Hospital, 13
Boundaries
    family, 270–71, 295–97
    family and change, 295–97
    spouse subsystem, 275
Boundary
    change, 198
    concept of, 63, 65
    family's external, 81–83, 168–69
    family–environment, 168–69, 179, 180

Caring and caring for, 273–74
Carnegie Council on Children, 32
Case definition, 118–19
Case management, 118–19, 333–34
Case manager, 189
Cases, sharing, 209–10

Casework, history of, 12
Ceremonies, family, 298–99
Change, 212–14
  family, 93–100
  "meta," 197
  planning of, 232–37
  principles in intergenerational work,
    233–37
  through rituals, 323–25
Change target, identification of, 187
Changing rituals, 324–25
Charity Organization Society, 13
Child Abuse and Prevention Act, 104
Child guidance movement, 15–16
Child placement, 7
Child welfare, 50–52
  adoption, 51
  family reunification, 51
  Indian children, 51
  policy, 50–52
  and rituals, 324
Childbirth, 35–36
Chinese–American Families, 286–87
Civil liberties, 49
Client's life space, 121–22
Coach, role of, 255–57
Coalition of Family Organizations, 53, 55
Cohesion, family, 84, 320
Collegial support, 119–20
Communication
  altering content of, 248–49
  analogic, 102–3, 303
  digital, 102–3, 303
  family, 100–104, 302–4
  principles of, 101
  teaching of, 304
Communication process
  complementary, 104
  digital and analogic, 102–3
  double bind, 103–4
  invalidation, 104
  paradox, 104
  symmetrical, 104
Competence, 291–92
Complementarity, 104
  of role, 291
Comprehensive Child Care Plan, 51
Conference on Family Diagnosis, 17
Confidentiality, 141–42
Congruence of expectations, 136–38
Consensus, in families, 98
Construction of reality, 198–99
  family, 104–7
Consultation and supervision, 119–20
Contacts, initial, 111
Contracting, 133–42
  in conjoint interviews, 140
Counterparadox, 327–31
  definition, 329

Counterparadoxical stance, 330
Crisis, 66
Cultural diversity, 90
Cultural norms, 275–77
  roles, 286–89
Cultural rules, 298–99
Cultural transitions, 287
Cut offs, 86, 251–52, 226, 227, 366
Cybernetic process, 233–34, 303–4
Cybernetics, 18, 67, 303

Dead, connecting with the, 249–52
Detriangulation, 241–44, 317
Differentiation, 78–79, 85–86, 212–14,
    274–75, 280
Directives, techniques for giving, 313–16
Discrimination, 55, 321
Disengagement, 84, 272–73
Divorce, 35, 47
  contracting in, 135
  emotional, 272
  rituals, 323
  value issues, 43
Double bind, 103
  societal, 164
  therapeutic, 327

Eco-map, 9
  assessing inner family system, 169–70
  as assessment tool, 158–64
  cognitive mastery, 190–91
  in engagement and planning, 190–91
  instructions for drawing, 159–64
  uses and applications, 184–86
  visual impact, 185
Ecological assessment
  deprived family, 171–76
  overburdened family, 176–79
  socially isolated family, 180–84
  worker, agency, and service network,
    170–71
Ecological principles for practice, 72–74
  change principle, 72–73
  defining program and need, 72
  equifinality, 73
  "least intervention" idea, 74
  life experience as model for change, 74
Ecological systems perspective, 11, 60
Ecologically-oriented practitioner, 112–13
Ecology, metaphor for practice, 6, 9, 69–72
Elderly population
  caregiving, 36–37
  contact with children, 36–37
Emotional system, family, 214
Enactment, 148, 310–12
Engaging families, 143–46
Enmeshment, 83, 272–73
Entitlement, 188
Entropy, 64–65

Epigenesis, 296
Epistemology, 9
   Western thought, 62
Exaggerating problematic interaction, 319
Experience and change, 310–25
Extended families, 37–38

Family
   adaptation, 95–96
   and aging, 354–70
   alternate forms, 25
   assessment as a system, 269–304
   assessment of communication, 302–3
   black, 288–89
   caretaking, 46–47
   changing composition, 36–39
   changing functions, 32–33
   changing roles of women, 33–34
   Chinese–American, 286–87
   cohesion, 84
   colonial times, 24
   coordinating services to aging, 359–60
   culture, 77
   current views of, 23–25
   cut offs, 226–27
   defiance-based, 331
   definition of, 31
   deprived, 171–75
   differentiation, 85–86
   disengagement, 84
   emotional system, 217
   engaging, 143–46
   enmeshment, 83
   forces for change, 93–100
   forces for stability, 93–100
   hierarchy, 90–91
   homeostasis, 94–98
   and individualism, 24–25
   isolated, 183–84, 203–5
   issues in defining, 25–31, 42
   Jewish, 277
   membership, 82, 271
   Mexican–American, 287–88
   misconception and stereotypes, 25
   morphogenesis, 96
   morphostasis, 96
   needs, 164–65
   norms, 275
   open, 179
   overburdened, 176–79
   paradox, 327
   power, 90–91
   relationship with the state, 46–48, 55–56
   of remarriage, 89
   resource for aging, 355, 357–58
   rituals, 105–7, 319–25
   roles, 90–93
   and schizophrenia, 66
   single parent, 39

   structure, 85–93
   survival of, 38–39
   as unit of attention, 4
   variation of forms, 29
   women's movement, 24
Family allowances, 45
Family assessment, 16–17
Family Assistance Plan, 42–43
Family boundaries, 81–83
Family breakdown, 24
Family-centered practice
   agency support, 118–19
   definition, 4–9
   definitional issues, 20–21
   domain, 8
   general systems theory and group
     work, 11, 21
   generalist model, 11
   and methods, 21
   as a model, 4–5, 9–10
   rehabilitation, 7
   specialization, 10–11
Family-centered practitioner
   as explorer, 7
   intervention, 7–8
   roles, 5, 7
Family change, 295–97
Family choreography, 281
Family communication, 100–104
   consensus, 98
   governance, 99–100
   punctuation, 101–2
Family culture, 67–68
Family day care, 7
Family definitions
   delineating family boundaries, 26–27
   family of commitment, 30–31
   functional approach, 28
   by household, 27–28
   implications for practice, 29
Family diagnosis, 17–18
Family–environment boundary
Family–environment relationship
   assessment of, 166–68
   inner family system assessment, 169–70
   target and resource for change, 187–
     209
Family game, 90
Family Impact Seminars, 45
Family interviewing, 142–54
Family hierarchy, 90–91
Family mapping, 283–84
Family migration, 221–22
Family network therapy, 201–5
Family of origin
   assessment, 215–27
   contact with, 237–41
Family of origin work
   with aging, 361–65

Family of origin work (*cont.*):
    case illustration, 257–65
    summary, 266–68
    worker's own family, 265–66
Family organization, 88–93
Family paradigm, 105
Family policy
    current and future trends, 54–56
    definitions, 44–46
    developmental and preventive views,
        45–46
    dilemmas in, 52–53
    family impact definition, 44–45
    goals, 46
    health and mental health, 52
    individual focus, 12–14
    individualism vs. familism, 50–52
    influence in family, 54
    national family policy debate, 48–50
    parameters, 41–46
    poverty, 45
    redefinition of the family, 52–53
    rehabilitative views, 45–46
    relationship with economic and political
        policy, 42–43
    role of practitioner, 56–57
    "safety net" philosophy, 46, 55
    tax credits, 55
    typology of content areas, 53–54
Family Policy Advisory Board, 53
Family projection process, 79, 86
Family Protection Act, 49–50, 53, 55
Family reunification, 51
Family roles, 223–24, 284–94
    informal, 92–93
Family rule system, 94, 96, 297–302
    changing rules, 97
    meta rules, 97
Family scapegoat, 92–93
Family sculpture, 281–83
Family Service Agencies, 11, 14–15
Family Service Association of America, 15
Family and society
    birth control, fertility, and childbirth,
        35–36
    changing relationship, 32–33
    extended–nuclear debate, 37–38
    family as mediator, 31
    marriage, divorce, and remarriage, 35
Family sociology, 18
Family system, change, 305–25
Family themes, 225–26
Family theory, 75–108
Family therapy movement, history of,
    18–19
Family traditions, conflicting, 321–22
Family's construction of reality, 104–107
Feedback systems, 303–4
Fertility, 35–36

Filial responsibility, 355
Fusion, 78–79, 85–86, 274–75, 365–66

Gender roles, 277, 286–87
Gender subsystem, 275
General systems theory, 9, 18, 22, 59–69
    contribution to social work theory, 63–64
    crisis, 66
    definition of system, 62–63
    entropy, 64–65
    as epistemological platform, 61–64
    frames of reference, 63
    homeostasis by "moving steady state,"
        65–66
    information exchange, 65, 67
    isomorphisms, 63
    living systems, 64–69
    metaphors and analogies, 64
    power, 68
    processes of adaptation, 66–69
    in psychiatry, 60–61
    in social work, 59–60
    visual portrayal, 64
Generalist–specialist issue, 10–11
    methods, 10
Genogram
    in child welfare, 230
    defined, 215
    differential use, 227–28
    instructions for drawing, 215–17
    management issues, 228–29
    use of in health care, 230, 371
    use of with aging, 360–63
    use with groups, 228–29
Georgetown Family Center, 265
Georgetown Family Symposia, 265
Getting started, 111–32
Goals of family work with aging, 366–67
Gossip in presence, 148–49
Grandchildren, 365–67
Greek chorus, 328, 334
Group, family of origin, 228–29
Group work and the family, 11, 21

Health care and the family, 370–72
Health patterns, 223
Historical perspective, 333
History, family, 152–53
History-taking, 227–28
Holocaust, children of survivors, 251
Homemaker and home health aide, 7
Homeostasis (or "moving steady state"),
    65–66
Household
    changing American, 38–39
    as definition of family, 38–39
Hypothesizing, 147–48, 299–300
Hypothetical questions, 151–52

"I-position," 274, 280, 350, 365, 367
Iatrogenic effects, 333–34
Illness
  impact on family, 370–71
  as solution, 371–72
Indian Child Welfare Act, 51
Individualism, 77
  vs. familism, 114
Initial contact, 111–12, 121–22, 124
Intake, telephone, 126–27
Intergenerational households, 355
Intergenerational perspective, 76–80,
  212–14 (*see also* Family of origin)
Intergenerational relations, views of,
  357–58
Intergenerational time, 153
Interviewing
  beginnings, 148
  families, 142–54
  families of origin, 252–54
  gossip in presence, 148–49
  questions, 150–52
  ranking questions, 150–51
  tracking sequences, 149
Invalidation, 104
Invisible loyalties, 80
Isolation of aging, 359–60
Isomorphisms, 63

Jewish families, 277
Jewish Family Service, 18–19
Joining, 144–45
Juneteenth Day, 320

Kinship systems, 288

Learning and change, 306–10
Leaving home rituals, 323–24
Letter writing, 239–40
Life review, 360–62
  and family, 360–62
  living history, 362
Lifestyle, family, 314–15
Loss, 249–52
  on genogram, 224
  unresolved, 80
Loving and caring, 78–88, 273–74

Manpower policy, 48
Mapping families, 283–84
Marital assessment, 274–75
Marital conflict, 86
Marital couples and genogram use, 228–29
Meals on Wheels, 7
Meaning systems, family, 104–7
Medicaid, 47
Mental health agencies, 123
Mental hygiene movement, 12
Mental Research Institute, 97, 101

Meta communication, 101
Meta rules, 97, 300–302
Metaphors, 194
  use of, 308–309
Mexican–American families, 257–58
Middletown, 25
Migration, family, 221–22
Milan Family Therapy Group, 117, 141,
  299–300, 308, 327, 384
Milford Conference, 10
Minority families, 27
Modeling, 197
Moral Majority, 44
Morphogenesis, 96
Morphostasis, 96
Mother, role of, 199–200
Motivation of clients, 121–22, 314
Moynihan Report, 42–43
Multigenerational transmission process, 79

Names, significance, 217–19
Naming patterns, 217–19
Nathan Ackerman Family Institute, 117,
  124, 239, 252
National Association of Social Workers, 6
National Conference of Charities and
  Corrections, 12–14, 16
National Institute of Mental Health, 19
National Research Council, 33–35, 48
Neptune effect, 206
Network therapy, 201–5
  applications, 204–5
New Right, 44, 49, 55
New York School of Social Work, 14
Nonverbal communication, 302
Nonvoluntary clients, 131
Norms, family, 275
Novel solutions, 331–32
Nuclear families, 37–38

Occupations, 222–23
Office arrangements, 116–17
Outreach, 122

Palo Alto Group, 331–32
Paradigm, family, 105
Paradox
  criticisms of, 328
  definition, 328
  family, 327
  and social work values, 130
  therapeutic, 327–30
Parental child, 276–77
Parental subsystem, 88
Parsimony, principle of, 333–34
Persistence
  family, 326–27
  going with the, 128
Person-to-person relationship, 234–35

Philadelphia Child Guidance Clinic, 384, 387
Positive connotation, 146, 307–8
Poverty, 42, 45, 189
Power
    in families, 90–91, 98–100, 300–302
    governance by rule, 99–100
    zero-sum confrontations, 98
Prediction, 331
Preliminary agreement, 133–35
Prescribe the symptom, 332
Problem as solution, 308
Problem identification, 118–19
Projection process, family, 86
Protective service, initial contact, 134
Pseudomutuality, mutuality, and non-
    mutuality, 83
Psychiatry and casework, 13–14
Psychoanalysis, application to family life, 17
Psychoanalytic psychology, 12, 15–16
Punctuation, reframing, 307
Punctuation in communication, 101–2

Questions
    "before and after," 151
    hypothetical, 151–52
    ranking, 150–51

Racism, 43
Referring person, 205–206
Reframing, 307–308
Rehabilitation and the family, 371–72
Relationship in social work practice, 15
Relevance, 113
Remarriage, 35, 89
Reminiscence, 361–63
Replacement phenomenon, 220
Resistance, 125–26, 128–29
    family, 326–43
    family of origin, 236
Reversals as tasks, 318–19
Right to Life, 44
Rites of passage, 322–24
Ritualized assignments, 319–20
Rituals, 105–7, 319–25
    and change, 198, 319–25
    in child welfare, 324
    Christmas gift opening, 297–98
    cultural, 320–23
    family, 106–107, 298–99
    repressive, 324–25
Roles
    ambiguity, 290–91
    change, 244–47
    continuity, 290
    family, 90–92, 223–24, 284–94
    flexibility, 292, 294
    formal assessment of, 290–92

induction, 136–38
informal, 92–93
informal assessment of, 293–94
informal assignments, 292–94
reversals, 246–47
Rules, 300–302
    changing, 97
    family, 94, 96–98, 297–302
    family and symptoms, 299

Salience, 113
Schismogenesis, 104
Schismogenic escalation, example of, 373
Sculpture, family, 282
Secrets, 248–49
Self-determination, 131
Separateness and connectedness, 82–88, 271–75
    differentiation, 85–86
    disengagement, 84
    emotional cut-off, 78, 86
    enmeshment, 83
    family cohesion, 84
    fusion, 85–86
Service, accessibility to, 121
Shaman, 157–58
Sharing of self by worker, 145
Sibling position, 220–21
Sibling subsystem, 89
Simulations, 158
Single-parent families, 39, 43, 276–77
Skill development, 312
Smith College School for Social Work, 13
Social change, 20
Social construction of reality, 198–201
Social diagnosis, 12–13
Social networking, 192–94
Social policy
    and aging, 358–59
    definitions, 42
    parameters, 41–46
    relationship with economic and political
        policy, 42–43
    value context, 43–44
Social reform, 188
Social Security, 56
Social Services amendments, 51
Social stage of interviews, 144
Social systems theories, 59
Social work
    diversity, 5
    divisions in the profession, 19–20
    institutional vs. residual, 7
    mission, 6–8
    specialization, 10
    values, 8
Social work history
    a family focus, 11–22
    organization by specialization, 20–22

Social work practice
  defining, 4–10
  domain, 6
  prevention, 7
Social work practitioner, role of, 15–16
Social work relationship, 15 (*see also*
    Transference)
Social worker
  frame of reference, 228
  starting where worker is, 112
Space as resource for change, 195–98
Space requirements for family-centered
    practice, 116–17
Spouse subsystem, 88
Stability, family, 93–100
Strategic approach, 142
Structural change, 310–12
Subsystem, family, 275
Supervision requirements for family-
    centered practice, 119–21
Supportive environment for family-
    centered practice, 114–21
Surprise in family interventions, 141–42
Symmetry, 104
Systems (*see also* General systems theory)
  living, 64–69
  perspective, 59
  theory, 167

Tasks, 197, 312–19
  assignments, 312–19
  typical, 316–19
Teaching about families, 309–10
Team, 141
  consultation, 117
Teenage childbearing, 36
Temporary Foster Care Project, 185–86
Time
  ancient, 153–54
  dimensions, 152–54

requirements for family-centered
    practice, 117–19
  as resource for change, 194–98
Toxic issues, 225–26
Tracking sequences, 149–50
Transference, 15, 255
Transitions, family, 323
Triangles, 79–80, 91, 241–44, 278–80
  altering, 311–12
  perverse, 196
Triangulation, 68

Underritualized families, 298–90, 320
Unit of attention, 12, 113–14
  an ecological conception, 69–70
University of Michigan, 47
Unresolved losses, 80

Values, 14
  family-centered practice, 8–9
  self-determination, 8
  and social policy, 43–44
  social work practice, 8
Variation in aging, 356
Visiting aged relatives, 355–56
Visits to family of origin, 237–39

War on Poverty, 20
Welfare state, 47–48
White House Conference on Families, 44,
    49, 53
Women, role of, 199–201
Women's issues, 33–34
Worker, activity counts, 117–18
  frame of reference, 112–13
  own family of origin, 265–66
  role in intergenerational work, 255–56

Zero-sum confrontations, 98